Handmaids of the Lord

Cover image: St Olympia

Olympia was born in 361 AD into a wealthy and noble family. Her father was the senator Anicius Secundus and, through her mother, Alexandra, she was the granddaughter of the noted eparch Eulalios. After the death of her parents, Olympia inherited great wealth. She distributed this to the poor and needy, the orphaned and the widowed. She was also very generous with her donations to churches, monasteries, hospices, and shelters for the homeless. She was appointed as a deaconess by the holy Patriarch Nectarius (381–397) and provided great assistance to the hierarchs of Constantinople, including Amphilochius, the Bishop of Iconium, Onesimus of Pontum, Gregory of Nazianzus (the Theologian), Peter of Sebaste, Ephiphanius of Cyprus. She was great friends with all of these great holy Fathers of the Church. She was especially close to St John Chrysostom. He had high regard for Olympia and he showed her goodwill and spiritual love. When the hierarch was unjustly banished, Olympia and some other deaconesses (Pentadia, Proklia, and Salbina) were deeply upset. After the death of St John Chrysostom on 14 September 407, Olympia passed away in exile somewhere in Nicomedia on 25 July 408. Shortly before her death, Olympia gave instructions that she wanted her remains to be placed in a coffin and tossed into the sea, leaving her final resting place to Divine Providence.

Handmaids of the Lord:

Women Deacons
in the Catholic Church

Jane Coll

GRACEWING

First published in England in 2013
by
Gracewing
2 Southern Avenue
Leominster
Herefordshire HR6 0QF
United Kingdom
www.gracewing.co.uk

ISBN 978 085244 772 7

Nihil obstat: Deacon William T. Ditewig PhD, *Censor deputatus*
Imprimatur: ✠ Rt Rev Hugh Gilbert, OSB
 Bishop of Aberdeen
 17 September 2012

The *Nihil obstat* and *Imprimatur* are declarations that a book or pamphlet
is free from doctrinal or moral error. No implication is contained therein
that those who have granted the *Nihil obstat* or *Imprimatur* agree with the
contents, opinions or statements expressed.

Typeset by Gracewing

Cover design by Bernardita Peña Hurtado

*Dedicated to the memories of Rev Kenny MacLeod,
faithful minister of his own flock and any strays that he
found along the way, and of Margaret Coll, my
Pluscarden sister*

CONTENTS

ABBREVIATIONS

AAS	*Acta Apostolicae Sedis* (the Vatican gazette, which gives the original texts of official documents, usually in Latin).
AG	Second Vatican Council, Decree on the Church's Missionary Activity *Ad Gentes Divinitus*, 1965.
CCC	*Catechism of the Catholic Church*, 1994.
CIC	*Code of Canon Law*, 1983.
DCDA	International Theological Commission, *From the Diakonia of Christ to the Diakonia of the Apostles*, 2003.
DMLP	Congregation for the Clergy, Directory on the Ministry and Life of Priests, 1994.
DV	Second Vatican Council, Dogmatic Constitution on Divine Revelation *Dei Verbum*, 1965.
ECF	*Early Church Fathers* (tr. by Maxwell Staniforth), 1968.
ECW	*Selections from Early Christian Writers* (ed. and tr. by Henry Gwatkin), 1958.
EE	Pope John Paul II, Encyclical Letter on the Eucharist and the Church *Ecclesia de Eucharistia*, 2003.
EN	Pope Paul VI, Apostolic Exhortation Proclaiming the Gospel *Evangelii Nuntiandi*, 1975.

GS	Second Vatican Council, Pastoral Constitution on the Church in the Modern World *Gaudium et Spes*, 1965.
LG	Second Vatican Council, Dogmatic Constitution on the Church *Lumen Gentium*, 1964.
MD	Pope John Paul II, Apostolic Letter On the Dignity and Vocation of Women *Mulieris Dignitatem*, 1988.
ND	J. Neuner and J. Dupuis, *The Christian Faith: Doctrinal Documents of the Catholic Church.* London: HarperCollins, 1991.
NJB	New Jerusalem Bible.
NJBC	New Jerome Biblical Commentary.
OT	Old Testament.
PO	Second Vatican Council, Decree on the Ministry and Life of Priests *Presbyterorum Ordinis*, 1965.
RSV	Revised Standard Version.
SC	*Sources Chretiennes*. Paris: Cerf, 1942–.
ST	*St. Thomas Aquinas: The Summa Theologica* (Benziger Bros. Edition 1947) tr. Fathers of the English Dominican Province.
TDNT	Theological Dictionary of the New Testament.
VC II vol. I	A. Flannery, Vatican Council II: The Conciliar and Post Conciliar Documents vol. I. Dublin: Dominican Publications, 1975.

VC II vol. II   A. Flannery, Vatican Council II: More Post Conciliar Documents. Leominster: Fowler Wright Books Ltd, 1982.

The Scriptural quotations are from the New Jerusalem Bible. The translations for most of the modern Vatican documents are taken from the Vatican web site, as this is the official version. For those who prefer paper sources, they are also available from the Catholic Truth Society, publishers to the Holy See, although the wording may vary slightly.

ACKNOWLEDGEMENTS

T HIS WORK IS not so much my own composition as a 'collecting together' of the work of many other more able scholars. I wish to record my grateful thanks to them for providing me with such stimulating background material. Living in a remote part of the country, my biggest problem throughout this work was in accessing this material and I am indebted to the monks of Pluscarden Abbey for regularly providing me with a room, a pile of books and their support, friendship and prayers. I also benefited from the libraries of several local clergy and am grateful to them for taking the time to help me. In particular, the Free Church of Scotland minister, the late Rev Kenny MacLeod, provided material on the Presbyterian form of church governance, the sacraments and references to Calvin. He also introduced me to the work of Edmund Clowney, which gave me an important insight into the teachings of St Paul on women. The Episcopal priest, Rev Wendy Knott, pointed me in the direction of female (as opposed to feminist!) commentators on the Bible. Of course, the most important local clergyman was my own parish priest, Fr John Allen, who encouraged me throughout and guarded me against potential distractions.

Various friends have read through the manuscript at various stages and this work has greatly benefited from their constructive comments and encouragement.

My husband has not only uncomplainingly tolerated erratic domestic arrangements, but he has also been a valuable critic and I thank him and the extended family for their tolerance, even when they were not at all sure what it was that was keeping me so busy.

INTRODUCTION

THIS WORK HAS had a long gestation period. The initial impetus came from a series of short summaries of Catholic teaching on topical subjects produced by the Scottish Bishop's Conference some years ago. I felt that the summary on why the Church could not have women priests was inadequate.[1] While I had no problem with the teaching itself, I had serious reservations about the way in which it was being explained. Surely an organisation with the resources of the Catholic Church could do better! Perhaps some of those campaigning for women priests would have remained loyal to the Church if she had made a better job of explaining her teaching to them.

Then, while I was studying for a BA Divinity, some lecture notes and background reading stimulated an interest in the role of deaconesses in the early Church. I resolutely ignored this interest for two reasons; just keeping up with the course work was demanding enough, and I had a horror of being branded as a supporter of women priests. However I did choose the topic of ordination for the final essay. While doing background reading for this essay, I was intrigued by the phrase from *Lumen Gentium*[2] on bishops having the fullness of the sacrament of ordination and wondered where this left priests and deacons.

Having completed the degree and taken a rest, I decided to return to study and to that phrase in *Lumen Gentium*. I very quickly realised that I could not study the sacrament of ordination without including a discussion on the place of women. Those deaconesses of the early Church were looking over my shoulder!

As I researched the topic, I realised how easy it is to get lost in a sea of obscure arguments and I developed a certain sympathy for those Church leaders whom I criticise in my first paragraph! Yet the 'bottom line' is really not so very complicated. Many people today seem to forget that ordination is a sacrament. All sacraments have to be based on the words and actions of Jesus, so having the College of Bishops, the successors to the apostles, in charge of the Church is not simply one of several possible management structures, it is the structure that was instituted by Jesus Christ. In chapter five, I argue that several female followers of Jesus could be given the title of 'apostle', indeed St Thomas Aquinas calls Mary Magdalen 'The apostle to the apostles'. However I also show that Jesus deliberately ensured that only the twelve male apostles were present at the Last Supper and only they were given the authority to loose and bind. Jesus gives no hints that he was simply conforming to sociocultural norms, preventing him from giving women leadership roles because the culture of the day would not have tolerated this. This argument may well have some truth in it but Scripture does not tell us that this was Jesus' motive. The Last Supper was a private event and women could easily have been included. Indeed, women would normally be part of the traditional Passover meal, on which the Last Supper is based. It has been argued that women 'must have been present', but that is not what Scripture tells us. If they had been given the power to confect[3] the Eucharist, they could then have presided at the gatherings of the early Church, which were also held in private houses, often owned by women. This did not happen, despite women playing leading roles in setting up local churches. So an all-male priesthood was deliberately and freely established by Jesus Christ and practised by the early Church, both during the lives of the apostles and after. It has only been seriously challenged recently.

When the Anglican Communion debated the introduction of women priests, Pope Paul VI had to decide which of various arguments he would use in his response. Rather to everyone's surprise, he did not address any of the current arguments[4] but argued from Scripture, Tradition and the Magisterium—Christ had chosen only men, the Church had always imitated this and consistently taught that it was in accordance with his plan for his Church. Pope Paul's letter to the Archbishop of Canterbury, written in July 1975, was followed by a more detailed exposition the following year in *Inter Insigniores*. This did not end the debate and Pope John Paul II issued *Ordinatio Sacerdotalis* in 1994 which repeated the 'bottom line' that Jesus had freely chosen an all-male apostolate and the Church does not have the authority to change a practice which is rooted in the will of Christ. He ended this short document with the instruction to the whole Church that the debate was now closed.[5] Sadly, this did not happen.

While it is true that the Church is about love not laws, all human institutions, from the nuclear family to the United Nations, need a set of rules and regulations. Without this we have anarchy. The Church has to have a structure whereby it can declare with authority that certain teachings are true or false. The challenge to this structure by people who refuse to accept the binding nature of *Ordinatio Sacerdotalis* is causing great damage in the Church. It is also draining valuable resources in the form of academic personnel who would be more fruitfully employed in other areas. It is time for the debate to move in a more constructive direction!

I have three main aims in this work. The first aim is to understand the teaching that bishops have the fullness of the sacrament of ordination. This is a necessary foundation to understanding the sacrament of ordination and the relationship between bishop, priest and deacon. Only then can we understand the role of women within this sacrament. This understanding should lead us towards the second aim, which is to find an official office for women that is recognised by all, with its own liturgical rite in the *Pontificale Romanum*[6] and details of the duties pertaining to the office described in Canon Law. My hope is that this would go some way towards achieving my third aim of marginalising the debate on women priests, thus redirecting people's energies into more urgent concerns, such as bringing the gospel message to modern peoples and ending the scandal of division among the various Christian bodies.

The need for a more official role for women in the Church is self-evident. The current level of interest and debate would not exist if there was not a perceived need. Reasons for this need are various and include the changing role of women in all areas of life, the shortage of priests, the need for greater efforts at evangelisation and the need for both male and female voices to be heard within the Church. However it must be remembered that the female voice should not be shouting 'I demand the right to the sacrament of ordination' but should be whispering, and praying, 'How can I as an individual, and women as a group, contribute to the holiness of the Church?' —remember Elijah on Mount Horeb! (1 K 19:13).

The history of women's activity in the Church shows that they are physically, intellectually and emotionally capable of fulfilling the roles of bishop, priest and deacon. So the debate seems to centre on the sacrament of ordination that the male holders of these positions receive when they are given these offices within the Church. There are two possible approaches. We can either find an answer to the question 'Can women be ordained, and, if so, to what office?' or by-pass the debate and create a role that meets the pastoral need but leaves open the question of its sacramental character.

A look at the modern Church shows that step two has already been tried. There are numerous examples of women in leadership roles within the Church, whether it be in the Vatican Congregations, universities and colleges, advisory bodies or at parish level as catechists or even effectively running parishes as lay pastoral assistants. However, no matter how much influence and power women are given, the debate does not go away. If anything, it has intensified. There are now many women theologians who can present highly articulate arguments for women's ordination. Women running parishes argue that they are doing everything that a deacon does but without the official recognition, not to mention the grace of the sacrament! This situation is damaging to the Church as it causes disharmony among the very people who are trying to build it up, a process that will only succeed if it is founded on brotherly and sisterly love. So we have to accept that the approach of by-passing the debate will not work. We have to try to answer the question of whether or not women can be ordained, either to one of the existing offices or to a new office that would meet the needs of the modern Church.

Working Out a Solution

For a solution to be acceptable to all parties it must be in line with the teachings of Scripture, Tradition and the Magisterium. While a development of doctrine is allowable, contradiction of an existing doctrine is not. It is also important to accept that theological argument on its own will not bring a solution. There are many examples of eminent theologians using the same body of evidence to arrive at totally different answers. Sometimes this is because they had already decided on the answer before examining the evidence but it can also be that there is no one right answer or that the time is not right for the correct answer to be recognised and acted on. I believe that the time is now right for moving the debate forward.

I begin by looking at various reasons why the Church might want to reintroduce deaconesses. This is not a step to be taken lightly. In a recent conversation with a parish priest, he painted a very black picture of the possible consequences of this step: elderly parish priests would retire in protest; male deacons would protest/retire/not come forward in the first place; male and female deacons would be constantly arguing and vying for position; the female deacons would try to change everything; it would be impossible to come to decisions about anything. While none of these predictions are inevitable, there is no doubt that it would be a momentous step. I suggest that, rather than dwell on the potential problems, a more positive approach is to look at the various aspects of parish life that might be improved were female deacons to be part of Church life. I do this in the next chapter.

The reintroduction of deaconesses can only happen if it is compatible with the constant practice and teaching of the Church. All Church practice and teaching must in turn be compatible with the message of Scripture. So I will begin with the evidence of Scripture on four key areas: the foundation of the Church, the example of Our Lady, Jesus' teaching on women and St Paul's teaching on women.

The churches of the Reformation tried to base their faith on Scripture alone[7] but very quickly found that this did not work as the bible has 'hard places' that need explaining. The success of the Geneva Bible of 1560 was largely due to its copious notes. To the Catholic reader, these notes are clearly biased towards a Presbyterian theology. Indeed, even some Protestant readers found this bias unacceptable and we owe the existence of the King James Bible to King James VI and I feeling that the notes of the Geneva Bible were too egalitarian. The Catholic Church has always had Tradition and the Magisterium as counter-checks for any new theory or work of Scriptural exegesis.[8] These two terms need some explaining as they are often misunderstood, both within and outside the Church. So I will give a general explanation of each before applying them to the issue under discussion. Under the heading of Tradition, we will be looking at the constant practice of the Church with regard to bishops, priests and deacons, the beliefs about Our Lady and the role of women throughout history. Under the heading of the Magisterium, we will be looking at the formal teachings of the Church, as expressed in council documents, statements, liturgical rites and canon law. We will also look in more detail at the meaning of ordination as a sacrament of the Church. Then we will look at the formal teaching of the Church on Our Lady and on women in general.

The role of the theologian and his or her relationship to the Magisterium is also of relevance.

Having examined all the evidence, I will then gather together those facts that meet my criteria of being beyond reasonable doubt and being consonant with Scripture, Tradition and the Magisterium. I will show that, while the Church cannot ordain women as priests, she could ordain women as deacons.

Readers who support the idea of women priests will note that I have avoided the standard literature on the subject. They will, with justification, argue that I have presented an unbalanced argument, which could never conclude in favour of women priests. My defence is that I specifically set out to examine only that material which was in agreement with the Magisterium of the Church. I have quoted from two women writing in support of women priests (Ruth Edwards and Rosemary Nixon). However it is obvious from the context that they are not arguing from within the Roman Catholic Tradition and that I do not support their views.

It was clear from the beginning that structuring this study around the headings of Scripture, Tradition and the Magisterium was not the simplest arrangement. However I have persisted with it for several reasons: it is essential to demonstrate that my findings are acceptable under all of these headings; it is an approach that allows me to cover all the areas that I wanted to cover in a reasonably logical manner and it is an approach that does not seem to have been used by other writers in this area. Should you, the reader, find yourself getting lost among all the various sections, I suggest that you refer back to the contents page to remind yourself of where you are. I hope that this does not happen too often!

While the plan is to examine our topic under the separate headings of Scripture, Tradition and the Magisterium, the dividing line between them may not always be obvious as they are so interdependent. I will almost inevitably end up quoting Scripture under the heading of both Tradition and the Magisterium and blending the constant practice of the Church with its constant teaching. Before getting too annoyed with this lack of accuracy, I ask you to remember the words of the Vatican II document on revelation, *Dei Verbum*:

> Sacred Tradition and Sacred Scripture form one sacred deposit of the word of God, committed to the Church ... This teaching office is not above the word of God, but serves it, teaching only what has been handed on ... It is clear, therefore, that Sacred Tradition, Sacred Scripture and the teaching authority of the Church, in accord with God's most wise design, are so linked and joined together that one cannot stand without the others.[9]

Through this work, I have referred to both 'deaconesses' and 'women deacons'. It is a matter of personal preference which of these to use. I have tended to prefer 'deaconesses' to emphasise the link with the early Church.

Notes

[1] See Appendix I for a copy of the statement.

[2] LG §21 and §26 (1964).

[3] The technical term for the priest's power, through the prayers of consecration during Mass, to effect the transubstantiation of the bread and wine into the body and blood of Jesus Christ.

[4] The 'iconic' argument (that the priest is an icon of Christ and therefore has to be male); the 'faulty anthropology' argument (that Church leaders have a faulty understanding of feminine behaviour and intellect—see chapter ten 'Tradition: Women' for details) and the sociocultural one, explained above.

[5] In response to a formal request for clarification of the status of this teaching, the Congregation for the Doctrine of the Faith issued a statement in 1994 declaring the teaching infallible. (See S. Butler, *The Catholic Priesthood and Women: A Guide to the Teaching of the Church*. (Hillenbrand Books, Chicago, 2007), p. 15.)

[6] The official Church manual containing all the standard liturgies for administering the sacraments.

[7] A. McGrath, *Reformation Thought* (Oxford: Blackwell Publishing Ltd, 1999[3]), p. 61.

'The phrases *"sola scriptura"* and "by faith alone", express the basic Reformation belief that no source other than Scripture need be consulted in matters of Christian faith and practice.' See also chapter seven 'Some General Notes' and notes 7 and 8.

8   Study of the biblical texts, using all available literary disciplines, in order to better understand their meaning.

9   DV §10.

1 WHY ROCK THE BOAT?

IN THE FOLLOWING chapters we will be examining many sources to show that the ordination of deaconesses could be reintroduced without contradicting Scripture, Tradition or the Magisterium. We first need to discuss in detail why the Church might want to take this step. Despite the arguments put forward here, such a move would inevitably upset some people as being contrary to the Church that they felt familiar with and would be seen by others as opening the door to women priests. So there would need to be powerful reasons for taking this step. My personal list of reasons contains five points. As mentioned in the introduction, I am concerned about the damage being done by the 'women priests' movement. We need to reduce the time and effort being wasted on this debate and turn people's attention to other pressing matters. Linked to this is the need for more teaching from a feminine perspective, giving a better balance to theological debates and improving the quality of magisterial documents, thus hopefully improving their 'acceptance rate'. The Church also needs to be seen to be practising what it preaches about men and women being 'equal but different', the phrase that sums up the teaching of Pope John Paul II on the relationship between men and women (see the section on Edith Stein and John Paul II). My fourth reason for arguing for change is that having an official role for women would encourage a wider variety of women with a genuine desire to serve the Church to come forward. Lastly and perhaps less importantly, but still desirable, it would improve the public image of the Church and strengthen her teaching authority.

Are any or all of these reasons sufficient to justify taking such an important step? The answer will depend on the reader's own inclinations. Those in support of the idea will agree that female deacons would help in these areas and more. Those against the idea will argue that these suggested outcomes are not guaranteed and the arguments supporting them are pure speculation. When an academic figure within the Church read this work, he did not find anything in it that was directly against Church teaching yet he did not accept the conclusion that the Church could ordain women as deacons. His main criticism was that I had not shown why deaconesses were necessary in order for the Church to progress in her two tasks of spreading the gospel and growing in holiness. All the baptised have a share in this task. He announced firmly that, if individual women want to make a more formal commitment to the Church, they can become nuns.

When pondering on the academic's comments, I decided that the argument about women becoming nuns was not valid as it does not meet the criteria of creating a Church where men and women are 'equal but different', as the last few popes have insisted is the case. The male equivalent of nuns are monks, not deacons. Men can make a formal commitment to the Church and be ordained as deacons while remaining active in their families and communities. Indeed, this involvement in everyday secular life is often quoted as one of their strengths. There is no comparable role for women. It can be argued that there is also no role for women comparable to bishops and priests and that therefore the 'equal but different' rule does not apply to the hierarchy of the Church. I would reply that bishops and priests represent Christ the Head of the Church. Everyone else, including deacons, are members of the body of Christ, where they are equally made in God's image, loved by Him and have a duty to serve His Church as best they can according to their situation and abilities. For some men, this includes becoming deacons and it would be to the advantage of the Church if this option was also open to women, otherwise there is a lack of balance:

> It therefore remains for us to meditate more deeply on the nature of the real equality of the baptised which is one of the great affirmations of Christianity: equality is in no way identity, for the Church is a differentiated body, in which each individual has his or her role. The roles are distinct, and must not be confused; they do not favour the superiority of some vis-à-vis the others, nor do they provide an excuse for jealousy; the only better gift, which can and must be desired, is love (1 Cor 12-13).[1]

It also occurred to me that my thought processes and the academic's response give a good example of a typically feminine and masculine approach to the same problem.[2] The academic is thinking of the Church as an institution with a specific job to do and is looking for efficient ways of achieving its aims. Innovation and change can only be justified if they progress the aims of the institution. I am thinking of people within the Church and am looking for ways in which they can contribute to the best of their abilities. I am looking for a system that will achieve, or at least promote, balance, fairness, peace and harmony. Both approaches are commendable. We both have a deep loyalty to the Church and a desire to serve it as best we can, we just have different approaches, based on our different natures. I suggest that the Church needs both these approaches in any problem-solving activity, or indeed any searching for the way ahead, if she is to arrive at a balanced solution. In response to the recent child abuse scandals, an Italian woman theologian has suggested that, if women had been involved in the decision-making processes at parish and diocesan level, many of the cases would have been handled quite differently.[3] There would have been more emphasis on the needs of the victims, and indeed of the perpetrators, and less on the need to protect the Church as an institution.

This example can be used to demonstrate that having women in official roles within the parish and diocese can indeed help the Church's mission. In order to spread the gospel, the Church must have a certain respect and be seen as an example of love of neighbour. To be more precise, the individual priests must be seen as examples of Christ-like love of others. A letter to all parishes from Pope Benedict XVI marking the forty-seventh World Day of Prayer for Vocations talked of the Old Testament prophets enduring rejection and persecution because of their witness to the divine message.[4] Such rejection and persecution, even today, can result in renewal and strengthening within the Church. However, if the rejection is the result of sinful behaviour on the part of the Church representatives, then it has the opposite effect. No one is going to accept the gospel message from an organisation that they regard as corrupt, inept and misguided. Better handling of the various child abuse cases would have helped the Church to 'weather the storm' without quite so much damage. She will survive and may well emerge stronger, but would it not have been so much better for both the institution and the individuals involved if the incidents had been better handled in the first place? So having women in the hierarchy could help the Church to spread the gospel.

This example can also be used to demonstrate that an official role for women in the Church could help it to grow in holiness. The Church can only grow in holiness if the individuals that make up the Church do so. This will only happen if their leaders set an example. As Pope Benedict pointed out,

> God's free and gracious initiative encounters and challenges the human responsibility of all those who accept his invitation to become, through their own witness, the instruments of his divine call. This occurs in the Church even today: the Lord makes use of the witness of priests who are faithful to their mission in order to awaken new priestly and religious vocations for the service of the People of God.[5]

Priests have the duty to act as models that others will want to copy. Pope Benedict identifies three key characteristics that he regards as essential for effective priestly witness: friendship with Christ, complete gift of self to God and a life of love of others. A public image of priests and bishops as potential paedophiles or protectors of them, no matter how inaccurate, is not a positive model! It is for individual priests to present a positive image of the priesthood as a life corresponding to Pope Benedict's description. Not everyone who feels called to serve the Church can achieve this and discernment is required by both the individual and those responsible for his selection and training. Selection panels consisting of both males and females might be better at identifying those men who might pose a risk to others, those who are sincere but on the wrong 'career path' and those who do have the necessary qualities. Indeed there is some uncorroborated evidence to suggest that the introduction of the practice of including nuns and female lecturers on selection panels has contributed to the reduction in abuse cases in recent years. So having women in the hierarchy could help the Church to grow in holiness.

While the topic of child abuse is emotive and deserves the highest priority in anyone's 'problems to be solved' list, there are other topical problems that I feel would also benefit from the ministry of female deacons. I will mention five of them.[6]

The first area of concern is the position of lay people who find themselves running parishes. There are many parishes in Britain, and the rest of Europe, that are effectively being run by lay people, both men and women. In other parts of the world, lay people are responsible for huge areas and expect a priest to visit only once or twice a year. These lay people have various titles and levels of training. I only have a detailed knowledge of one lay pastoral assistant, working in the North of Scotland. When finding out about her role, it occurred to me that she was in a very difficult position. She was 'neither fish nor fowl', as the old saying goes. She had made a solemn promise to serve the parish under the authority of the parish priest, yet much of her time had been spent running the parish in the absence of a parish priest. She was seen as the Church's representative by other organisations but was technically a lay person. She did everything that a deacon would have done but without the benefit of the sacrament of ordination. She did not seem to have any network of support. Without a standard pattern or role model to conform to, neither she nor the parishioners had any way of measuring her performance or deciding what was or was not appropriate for her to do. Without a parish priest, she had no one to act in obedience to, to report to, or even to receive support from. Her academic qualifications may have been the equivalent of those of a priest or of a deacon – but they may not. With this pattern being repeated across the country, we have the potential for confusion, chaos and a loss of a sense of the universal Church. Bringing all of these leaders under the umbrella of the order of the diaconate would provide some degree of standardisation, at least within each country. It would provide a set of rules understood by all parties. It would clarify the relationship between the deacon/ess, the parish priest, the bishop and the community of whom the deacon/ess is the servant. Perhaps most importantly, it would allow the parish leader to benefit from the grace of the sacrament of diaconal ordination.

When Vatican II was discussing the reintroduction of the permanent diaconate they recognised that many people were already exercising the ministry in an unofficial capacity. The documents *Lumen Gentium* and *Ad Gentes* laid down the basis of the permanent diaconate, whose ministry includes 'preaching the word of God as catechists or presiding over scattered Christian communities in the name of the pastor and the bishop, or practicing charity in social or relief work.'[7] As women are now also performing these tasks, it would be of great assistance to them if they could receive the grace of the sacrament of ordination in order to be more effective in their ministry.

Our next scenario is that of contact with Moslem women, whether with the aim of spreading the gospel or of simply improving mutual understanding and friendship. Even in modern secular countries such as Britain, this can present a problem for an all-male priesthood and diaconate. There seems to be a tendency for Moslem women to be more radical in their practice of their faith than were their parents. Perhaps this is a way of trying to retain their cultural identity. It can also apply to British converts to Islam, anxious to demonstrate their sincerity and their willingness to adopt the customs of their new faith. Whatever the motivation, it results in a growing group of women, even in this country, who are cut off from the normal avenues of social contact with Christian men. The situation in countries that are officially Moslem is considerably more difficult. It is this very situation that faced the early Church, when the solution was to ordain suitable women as deaconesses with the specific remit of ministering to women in their own homes. We could perhaps learn a lesson from history and reintroduce this role for women. This possibility has been recognised in the Church for some years: 'Women will be especially capable of making contact with non-Christians through other women and through families. In some cultures they alone are capable of doing this work.'[8] Thus, the women concerned would be helping to spread the gospel. They would also be examples of living a life of holiness. Pope Benedict said that 'The very life of men and women religious proclaims the love of Christ whenever they follow him in complete fidelity to the Gospel and joyfully make their own its criteria for judgement and conduct.'[9] The letter referred to those in the religious life, but the same principle would apply to deacons or deaconesses. This life of holiness would inspire others to follow their example.

The third area is outreach to children from non-religious backgrounds. This is a rapidly expanding group. For some children, their families think of themselves as Christian but they do not have any formal religious practices. Others are growing up in an atmosphere that is specifically anti-religion. The adults in regular contact with these children will be predominantly women. While all Christian women in contact with these children have a duty to both set a good example and teach as much as they can, this task would be particularly appropriate for female deacons. Remembering the Jesuit motto that the core values of the adult are in place by the time he or she is seven, this is a particularly important task.

The fourth area concerns the anti-abortion movement and, at the other end of life, the struggle against euthanasia and assisted suicide. Men can feel just as strongly on these issues as women and are just as active in the various campaign groups. However, especially in the area of abortion, the 'pro-choice' campaigners can portray men as ignorant of the issues involved and simply trying to control women. Women with an official position within the Church could be more effective in getting across the message that human life is sacrosanct from conception to natural death.

The fifth area to be looked at is that of ecumenical co-operation at parish level. The proportion of female ministers in the other Christian denominations is growing. A superficial problem sometimes raised is 'What do we call the fraternals, when several of its members are actually female?' This question can be a cover for a more deep-seated anxiety over the way in which clergy with overlapping parish boundaries relate to each other. The possible scenarios are too numerous to list. In each of them, simply being aware of the potential danger can make both parties reluctant to develop a close working relationship or to provide emotional support for each other. It is not inconceivable that an area could have an all-female ministerial team with the Catholic priest as the only male, leaving him in a rather difficult position. A deaconess would be seen as, if not actually an equal, at least an official representative of the Church. She could act as a non-threatening link between the Catholic priest and other ministers and their communities. This would also give her the opportunity to promote a better understanding of Catholic teaching and encourage the expression of love of neighbour, thus helping the mission of the Church.

In response to my academic critic's comments, I have looked at six topical situations where the presence of deaconesses in a parish would in fact contribute positively to the Church's mission to spread the gospel and grow in holiness. This has been something of a diversion, as spreading the gospel and growing in holiness were not on my original list of five reasons why change was needed but were added by my male critic. My original list was identified using my feminine approach. What result would we get if we examined this list using my academic critic's masculine approach? Is it possible to show that they would help the Church in her two-fold mission? Let us take them individually and find out.

- To reduce the time and effort being wasted on the 'women priests' debate.

This was discussed in the introduction. I had already identified a greater ability to spread the gospel message as a possible result of reducing the time spent on debating the role of women in the Church. The growth in holiness could come about as a result of this redirection of energies towards the gospel message. Women who are currently campaigning for an official role would be able to actually practice that role. Perhaps some of those who have left the Church because of a lack of progress in this area would come back. These women would be available to help the Church in her mission whether or not they became deaconesses. Those who did become deaconesses would be active in both teaching the gospel and giving an example of living a holy life.

- To have more balanced debate and better teaching documents.

This is discussed below with reference to the phrase 'equal but different'.

- To be truly 'equal but different'.

The phrase 'equal but different' is used as a summary of the message of Pope John Paul II in his work on the Theology of the Body. In this work, he is principally focusing on the relationship between men and women in marriage. However the general principle applies in all situations – men and women are equally loved by God and made in His image but were deliberately made as male and female, with all the differences that that implies. I mention it here in the context of the need for Vatican documents to be more comprehensible to the average reader. Such writings are designed to help our understanding of both Scripture and Church teaching and therefore help in spreading the gospel message.

Other references to being equal but different are in part IV, 'The Analogy of Faith', where I collect together my various arguments and come to a conclusion. I argue that, were deaconesses to be introduced, they would need to be on an equal footing with male deacons in order to prevent friction. I discuss getting the balance between deacons and deaconesses right. There would be opportunities for practising humility and tolerance, indeed for growing in holiness. I suggest that having a body of senior men and women advising the pope would both improve the image of the Church and strengthen the 'equal but different' argument. Improving the Church's image would perhaps help her to communicate with the wider world, thus facilitating the spreading of the gospel.

- To encourage women with a genuine desire to serve the Church to come forward.

This is discussed in the context of the psychological effect of being an official representative of the Church rather than simply a lay volunteer.[10] It is suggested that, if women had an official role, the type of women coming forward might be different. The knowledge that people were looking to them as representatives of the Church and examples of holiness might influence their behaviour and indeed help them to become holy. If the Church's official representatives grow in holiness, then the Church as an institution grows in holiness.

- To improve the public image of the Church and strengthen her teaching authority.

This has been mentioned above.

So there we have it: examining my feminine list of reasons for having deaconesses under specific headings identified by a masculine mind shows that they do in fact meet these masculine criteria for contributing to the Church's mission. If my reasoning is correct, deaconesses would help the mission of the Church both in the five general areas listed at the beginning of this chapter and in the six specific areas that are controversial topics of the moment. Other areas, both general and specific, could be added. Using both feminine and masculine thought processes has produced a more wide-ranging discussion, without altering my original conclusion. However no argument in this area is ever going to carry the weight of scientific accuracy. People are influenced by their own backgrounds, and instinctive feelings are as powerful as any academic argument. Change can cause doubt and division and must not be undertaken lightly.

The 'fall back' argument of people who just instinctively do not like the idea of deaconesses is that women can do all of these suggested tasks without necessarily becoming deacons. The same argument can be made for men, as deacons do not actually do anything that lay men and women cannot do. However the point is not so much what they do as who they are. As we repeated just a few paragraphs above, there is a great difference between being an official representative of the Church and being an active parishioner. The College of Bishops reintroduced permanent male deacons. I am arguing that, in order to be 'equal but different' they now need to reintroduce deaconesses. In the meantime, we can best help the Church by remembering the final words of *Lumen Gentium*:

> The entire body of the faithful pours forth instant supplications to the Mother of God and Mother of men, that she who aided the beginnings of the Church by her prayers, may now, exalted as she is above all the angels and saints, intercede before her Son in the fellowship of all the saints.[11]

Notes

[1] Pope John Paul II, Declaration on the Admission of Women to the Priesthood *Inter Insigniores* §6 (1976).
[2] See the section on theologians in chapter twelve 'Magisterium: Some General Notes' for a discussion of masculine and feminine ways of thinking. Examples of the effects of the modern feminist movement on secular life, with

discussions on male and female ways of thinking and acting, can be found in C. Kelly (ed.), *Feminism v Mankind* (Scarborough, Ontario: Canisius Books, 1990).

3 Her comments were published in an Italian newspaper and reported in *The Catholic Herald*. Unfortunately, I did not keep the details. Similar comments by Jon Snow, news presenter and commentator, were reported in the same paper on 29 October 2010.

4 Pope Benedict XVI, *Message of the Holy Father for the 47th World Day of Prayer for Vocations* (25 April 2010).

5 *Ibid.*, 3.

6 For a more detailed list, see Appendix IV and the summary of Phyllis Zagano's book *Holy Saturday*.

7 AG §16. See also the joint booklet by the Congregation for the Clergy and the Congregation for Catholic Education, *Permanent Diaconate*. (London: CTS, 2006) which gives a detailed description of the formation, ministry and life of the permanent deacon.

8 The Pastoral Commission of the SCEP, The Role of Women in Evangelization (1976) in VC II vol. II, p. 324, §5.

9 Pope Benedict XVI, *Message of the Holy Father for the 47th World Day of Prayer for Vocations* (25 April 2010), 8.

10 See chapter twenty-three 'Applying our Diagnostic Tools'.

11 LG § 69.

PART ONE

Scripture

2 INTERPRETING SCRIPTURE

A S THE ECCLESIAL communities of the Reformation fairly quickly realised, there is far more to Scriptural studies than simply reading the bible. The Scriptures were written in a mixture of Aramaic, Greek and Hebrew, which was first translated into Latin and then into the vernacular languages, which, being living things, change and develop. The translators were not always using the best possible sources. Indeed, scholars are still working on dating and transcribing ancient parchments, new examples of which are still being found. So the written words of the bible are not fixed formulae but are open to changing interpretation as our knowledge grows. These written words were originally based on verbal teachings and traditions. German scholars of the seventeenth century identified four separate authors of the Old Testament, each recording the oral and written history of Israel in their own style and with their own emphasis.[1] The New Testament teaching was first passed on from Jesus to the apostles verbally; there is only one example of Jesus writing, and that is in sand. When the teachings were written down, we were told that they did not contain everything that Jesus taught (Jn 21:25). Again, each author gave his own style and emphasis to his account.[2]

Scripture is the self-revelation of God to man, but how can we be sure of the message that it contains? Theologians have to look at several areas: what works are inspired and therefore genuine revelation? Are the translations accurate? How important is the historical/cultural background? What literary tools are acceptable? What is the relationship between faith and reason? We cannot look at all of these areas here. However it is important to look at some of them in order to understand the Church's decision-making processes and why she feels that she has the authority to make decisions that are binding on the whole Church.

Revelation

In the Old Testament, God revealed himself through the Law and the Prophets. This revelation, always incomplete, was concerned with His choice of the Israelites as the Chosen People and the behaviour that He expected of them. In the New Testament, Jesus is both the revealer of the Father (St Paul and the Synoptics) and the revealed (St John) and is the fullness of redemption. He came not to replace the Law, but to complete it:

> This plan of revelation is realised by deeds and words having an inner unity… By this revelation then, the deepest truth about God and the salvation of man shines out for our sake in Christ, who is both the mediator and the fullness of all revelation.[3]

The apostles were given the task of transmitting this revelation to the world (Mk 16:16), a task which they passed on to their successors.

> But in order to keep the Gospel forever whole and alive within the Church, the apostles left bishops as their successors, 'handing over' to them 'the authority to teach in their own place'. This sacred Tradition, therefore, and Sacred Scriptures of both the Old and New Testaments are like a mirror in which the pilgrim Church on earth looks at God.[4]

The Church teaches that public revelation ended with the apostles. It is therefore important that Church teaching is based only on works that are true to apostolic teachings. One of the tasks of the early Church was to identify those works which were genuinely of apostolic origin and could therefore be used for the liturgy and for teaching—what we now refer to as the canon of Scripture.

The Canon of Scripture

The word 'canon' derives from the Greek *kanon*, meaning rule or yardstick, and indicates that writings accepted as canonical meet agreed criteria on what can be regarded as authentic Sacred Scripture.

Jesus made it clear in both words and actions that the Jewish body of Sacred Scripture was to be retained: 'Do not imagine that

I have come to abolish the Law or the Prophets. I have come not
to abolish but to complete them' (Mt 5:17–18).

The early Christians adopted the Alexandrian Old Testament
canon, the Septuagint, as opposed to the Hebrew one, mainly
because it was written in Greek, the language of most of the new
Church.[5] New Testament writings were not at first regarded as
sacred: 'The expectation of a return of Christ in the near future at
first ruled out any notion of a new canon of Scripture corresponding to the new covenant.'[6] Ironically, St Jerome, despite being the
translator of the Bible into Latin, insisted that the Hebrew Bible
was the only canonical one. There was a lively correspondence
between Jerome and Augustine on the subject, with Jerome
defending his decision to base his translation of the Old Testament
on the original Hebrew and Aramaic and Augustine arguing that
the Greek Septuagint was authoritative for the Christian Church.[7]
Eventually the status of the New Testament writings had to be
clarified. The heresies of Marcion in the middle of the second
Century gave impetus to this.[8] The process of formalising the canon
seems to have been complete by the fifth century, although it was
not formally defined until the Council of Trent:

> The Council has thought it proper to insert in this decree a
> list of the sacred books, so that no doubt may remain as to
> which books are recognised by the Council.
>
> They are the following:
>
> Old Testament: the five books of Moses, i.e. Genesis, Exodus,
> Leviticus, Numbers, Deuteronomy, Joshua, Judges, Ruth,
> four books of kings, two of chronicles, the first book of Ezra,
> the second book of Ezra called the book of Nehemiah, Tobit,
> Judith, Esther, Job, the book of Psalms of David containing
> 150 psalms, Proverbs, Ecclesiastes, the Song of Songs,
> Wisdom, Ecclesiasticus, Isaiah, Jeremiah with Baruch,
> Ezekiel, Daniel, the twelve minor prophets i.e. Hosea, Joel,
> Amos, Obadiah, Jonah, Micah, Nahum, Habakkuk, Zepha-
> niah, Haggai, Zechariah and Malachi; two books of
> Maccabees, i.e. the first and the second.
>
> New Testament: The four Gospels according to Matthew,
> Mark, Luke and John; the Acts of the apostles written by
> Luke the Evangelist; fourteen epistles of the apostle Paul,

i.e. to the Romans, two to the Corinthians, to the Galatians, Ephesians, Philippians, Colossians, two to the Thessalonians, two to Timothy, to Titus, Philemon, and the Hebrews; two epistles of the apostle Peter, three of the apostle John, one of the apostle James, one of the apostle Jude, and the Revelation of the apostle John.

If anyone does not accept all these books in their entirety, with all their parts, as they are being read in the Catholic Church and are contained in the ancient Latin Vulgate edition, as sacred and canonical, and knowingly and deliberately rejects the aforesaid Traditions *anathema sit.*[9]

There were many works that were not included in the canon and even now people will put forward arguments for including works such as The Shepherd of Hermas. These are a set of writings describing the visions of the author, who is unknown but may have been the brother of Clement of Rome, the fourth pope. They were well known in the early Church and were often included in the liturgy. They did not make it into the canon of Scripture as there was no clear apostolic connection. One of the key factors in deciding the canonicity of a document was its link with the apostles.

Apostolic origin, real or putative, was very important, particularly for acceptance. The canonicity of Rev and Hebrews was debated precisely because it was doubted whether they were written by John and Paul respectively. Today we understand that such apostolic origin is to be taken in the very broad sense of 'authorship'.[10]

The main difference between Catholic and Protestant theologians on the subject of canonicity is the group of Old Testament writings known as 'deutero-canonical' or 'apocryphal'. These were not included in the Hebrew Bible but were included in the Greek and Latin versions. They are: I and II Maccabees, Tobit, Judith, Ecclesiasticus/Ben Sira, Wisdom of Solomon, Baruch and some parts of Daniel.

They were included in the list accepted as canonical at the Council of Trent. However

An examination of the sixteenth-century debates over the matter suggests that the only theological issue of any real importance which was linked to this question was whether or not it was proper to pray for the dead. The (apocryphal) Books of the Maccabees encourage this practice, which Protestant theologians were not inclined to accept.[11]

Having decided which writings are inspired by the Holy Spirit, theologians then have to explain how this inspiration works.

How inspiration works

If canonicity deals with the question of which books have divinely given authority for the theologian, then inspiration concerns the problem of how this authority is actually mediated or present in the books that the canon includes.[12]

There has been debate over the centuries as to how this inspiration worked. Were the writers in a trance and acting as scribes for a hidden voice? Did they actually hear a voice and write down what it said? The Jews of the Old Testament had three theories as to the mechanism of inspiration of the Torah. Either there was a form of telepathy between God's mind and that of Moses or God actually wrote the text or God dictated the text to Moses. There was an acceptance that even the lesser books of the Old Testament were written under the influence of the Holy Spirit. The New Testament writers also accepted the inspired nature of the Old Testament: 'All scripture is inspired by God' (2 Tm 3:16) and 'For no prophecy ever came from human initiative. When people spoke for God it was the Holy Spirit that moved them' (2 P 1:21). In the early Church there was an acceptance that the New Testament was also inspired. The earliest theory as to the mechanics of this was suggested by Athenagoras in the second Century. He thought that the authors wrote in a state of hypnosis. This really did not fit the facts, as Origen a century later pointed out. However it was not until the sixteenth Century that a more developed theory emerged. This was based on St Thomas's idea of God as the principle efficient cause and the writer as the instrumental efficient cause. In this theory, the prophet could acquire knowledge in one of three ways: by his natural senses, by having ideas infused into his mind and by ideas formed with divine aid. The important part was the next step when the prophet turned these thoughts into words. It is here that inspiration occurs. Later Thomists developed this theory to include the theory of verbal dictation, where the human author is no more than a recording scribe.[13] Any differences in literary style are explained as God accommodating himself to the styles of particular people and ages. Both the hypnotic and the dictation theories, if correct, would severely limit theological study. We could not increase our knowledge of the Bible by studying its history or literary styles or by applying our knowledge of the human mind. Every word would have to be accepted as inerrant.

Two other theories were specifically denied by Vatican I. The theory of 'subsequent approbation' suggested that, when the Church judged a book to be inspired, the infallibility of the Church meant that that book then became an expression of divine truth. The second theory is that of 'negative assistance', whereby the author wrote without any divine assistance unless he was about to commit an error. Vatican I insisted that divine works have God as their author.

Modern theorists tend to appeal to the analogy of faith and look to other aspects of Church life for help. Some common ground has developed in the idea of the dual influence of God working through his creation, human and material, and God directly influencing minds so as to cause the author to respond to his environment in the desired way. There is still debate on just how this influence occurs. There is also some consideration of the influence of communities and societies as a way of explaining those books of the bible that clearly had several authors. Can we speak of an inspired community?

Historical-Critical analysis

Until comparatively recently, Catholic theologians were not encouraged to use standard literary criticism techniques on Scripture. This changed with Pope Pius XII's encyclical *Divino Afflante Spiritu* in 1943. Catholic theologians were now free to join the growing band of scholars examining Scripture from many angles: 'The 20th century was marked by the development of new methods—form criticism, Tradition history, rhetorical criticism, canonical criticism and several others, including the light cast on the Old

Testament in its ancient Near Eastern context by archaeology.'[14] What theologians are never free to do is to treat non-canonical works as of equal weight to inspired Scripture. We have a specific body of literature, commonly referred to as 'the Bible' or 'Holy Scripture'. All Church teaching must be able to show that it has its roots in the bible and any developments of doctrine must conform to the teachings of Scripture. Other writings may be of benefit for private study or academic research but they cannot be used as the sole basis for official Church teaching.

Church Teaching

The very notion of 'official Church teaching' was challenged by the reformers of the sixteenth century, as indeed it had been by their predecessors, particularly Wycliffe (1324-1384). The Church replied at the Council of Trent, where the 'Decree on Sacred Books and on Traditions to be Received' (1546) stated that revelation was contained in both Scripture and Tradition. External traditions could be altered according to the customs of a place or the needs of a particular time. Traditions of faith had been handed down from the apostles and could not be changed. It was for the Church to determine the meaning of Scripture. Individuals must not

> Twist Holy Scripture in matters of faith and morals that pertain to the edifice of Christian doctrine, according to his own mind, contrary to the meaning that holy mother the Church has held and holds—since it belongs to her to judge the true meaning and interpretation of Holy Scripture.[15]

The next development was to clarify the position of the pope and the relationship between faith and reason. Vatican Council I was called by Pope Pius IX in response to the political and religious upheaval of the time. The Papacy had lost control of all its lands except Rome, with a resultant loss of influence. The Church was losing its temporal power throughout Europe and philosophers and scientists were presenting the Church with problems to which she had not worked out coherent answers. The Council sat from December 1869 to September 1870. The start of the Franco-Prussian war meant the end of the council and it only produced two constitutions, *Dei Filius*, on the faith of the Church, and *Pastor Aeternus*, defining papal infallibility.

Pastor Aeternus was the more controversial document at the time.[16] It has proved to be a stumbling block to ecumenism, perhaps because of a lack of understanding of its teaching and despite its being used rarely: 'According to most theologians, the popes of the last hundred years have uttered only one sentence of infallible teaching — the definition of the dogma of the assumption of the Blessed Virgin by Pope Pius XII in 1950'.[17] More importantly at the time, it confirmed the primacy of the pope and the centralisation of the Church on Rome. This was necessary in order for the Church to have the teaching authority that it needed. There had to be a clear understanding of the Church's role in defining doctrine and an acceptance of her power to declare a theory as acceptable or not. Yet the other denominations objected, and still do, to the Church's taking to herself the right to decide what was and was not authentic interpretation of Scripture: 'And a further chasm had opened not only between Roman Catholics and Protestants, but also between the Roman and Orthodox Churches.'[18]

For the purposes of this work, *Dei Filius* was in many ways a more important document. Produced in response to the many heresies of the day, it gave a clear statement of the Church's teaching on reason, faith and revelation. However all Church documents must be read in the light of their historical setting. We must be aware that they were written for a specific purpose and are not meant to contain all the Church's teaching on that topic.

> Each document pursues a very precise and quite limited purpose ... Each document is the result of an historical context, from which it draws its perspective, from which it borrows its special tone. Frequently directed against a very definite error, it implies, even in its exposition of Catholic doctrine, a proper and individual tone of emphasis which must be grasped. In no way does it claim to exhaust the doctrine living in the heart of the Church.[19]

So we need to remember that *Dei Filius* was written specifically to answer the main errors of the day, of which rationalism probably gave the greatest concern to the Church:

The constitution *Dei Filius*, voted for on 24 April 1870 was
the outcome of the discussions on the relationship between
reason and faith. Faced with the errors of rationalism,
pantheism, and fideism, the council defined the existence of
a personal God who could be attained by reason, while at
the same time affirming the necessity of revelation. There
could be no conflict between reason and faith.[20]

These teachings of Vatican I built on the existing teaching of the
Church. From the Book of Wisdom (Ws 13:1), through St Paul (Rm
1:19–20) to Thomas Aquinas (1,2,2) the message is always that man
can arrive at some knowledge of God through reason alone.
However there is also the understanding that human reason is
limited and that we depend on faith and revelation for a deeper
knowledge of God. St Anselm (1033–1109) gives a brief, if rather
circular, explanation of the link between faith and reason in his
work *Proslogion*, also titled *Faith Seeking Understanding*: 'I do not
seek to understand so that I may believe, but I believe so that I may
understand; and what is more, I believe that unless I do believe I
shall not understand.'[21] We can see the same meaning in the
teaching of Vatican I: 'Though the assent of faith is by no means a
blind impulse of the mind, still no man can "assent to the Gospel
message", as is necessary to obtain salvation, "without the illumination and inspiration of the Holy Spirit"'.[22] A more modern and
ecumenical note is struck by Avery Dulles: 'These religions
(Judaism, Christianity, Islam) profess to derive their fundamental
vision not from mere human speculation, which would be tentative
and uncertain, but from God's own testimony—that is to say from
a historically given revelation.'[23]

The Council of Trent (1545-63) had tackled the 'by faith alone'
question. It reaffirmed the need for Tradition and authoritative
Church teaching on Scripture in order to prevent errors of interpretation:

> The Council clearly perceives that this truth and rule are
> contained in the written books and unwritten Traditions
> which have come down to us, having been received by the
> apostles from the mouth of Christ himself or from the
> apostles by the dictation of the Holy Spirit, and have been
> transmitted as it were from hand to hand.[24]

Some 25 years before he called the First Vatican Council, Pope Pius IX issued an encyclical *Qui Pluribus*, with its attached *Syllabus Errorum* listing eighty errors, explaining Church teaching on faith and reason:

> For, though faith is above reason, there can never be found a real contradiction or disagreement between them, as both of them originate from the same source of immutable and eternal truth, from the good and great God and both so help each other that right reason demonstrates, safeguards and defends the truth of faith, whereas faith frees reason from all errors and through the knowledge of divine things enlightens, strengthens, and perfects it.[25]

The basic principles stated in *Qui Pluribus* are repeated in the Vatican I document *Dei Filius*, whose main purpose was to confirm past teachings and to present them in a modern way and with the full authority of the Council. Faith and revelation are two sides of the same coin: we need faith in God in order to accept the revealed truths of Scripture and the Traditional teachings of the Church. These revealed truths are also accessible to human reason and Vatican I insists that reason is an essential tool for deepening our understanding of God.

> However, though faith is above reason, there can never be a real discrepancy between faith and reason, since the same God who reveals mysteries and infuses faith has bestowed the light of reason on the human mind, and God cannot deny himself, nor can truth ever contradict truth ... Not only can there be no conflict between faith and reason, they also support each other since right reason demonstrates the foundations of faith and, illuminated by its light, pursues the science of divine things, while faith frees and protects reason from errors and provides it with manifold insights.[26]

The crises that caused the Councils of Trent and Vatican I were those of errors in theology. By the second half of the twentieth Century, the main problem was not which belief people supported but that they did not believe at all. At least in Western Europe and North America, Church leaders, both ordained and lay, were clamouring for reforms within the Church in order to bring it more into tune with modern life. Vatican II tried to do this. The dogmatic constitution, *Dei Verbum*, extended the teaching of Trent and Vatican I on the relationship between Scripture, Tradition and the Magisterium by looking in more detail at their interconnectedness and at the idea of the Scriptures as inspired literature which, nevertheless, needs interpretation.

> But, since Holy Scripture must be read and interpreted in the sacred spirit in which it was written, no less serious attention must be given to the content and unity of the whole of Scripture if the meaning of the sacred texts is to be correctly worked out. The living Tradition of the whole Church must be taken into account along with the harmony which exists between elements of the faith.[27]

Vatican II occurred in very different circumstances from Vatican I in that it was not a time of particular difficulty in the Church. So the main purpose of the Council was quite different:

> The Council was … above all to strive calmly to show the strength and beauty of the doctrine of the faith … Our duty is to dedicate ourselves with an earnest will and without fear to that work which our era demands of us, thus pursuing the path which the Church has followed for 20 centuries.[28]

Chapter One of *Dei Verbum* starts with a reminder that it is working within a long Tradition of the Church:

> Therefore, following in the footsteps of the Council of Trent, and of the First Vatican Council, this present Council wishes to set forth authentic doctrine on divine revelation and how it is handed on, so that by hearing the message of salvation the whole world may believe, by believing it may hope, and by hoping it may love.[29]

It then tells us that we can learn about God and our salvation through Christ 'the mediator and sum total of Revelation'. God has spoken to us through Abraham, Moses and the prophets. Finally, he sent his Son, who completed divine revelation with the message that we can gain eternal life. With the help of the Holy Spirit, man has faith in these revelations, which he can also grasp through human reason.

So Vatican II makes it clear that its teaching is the teaching of Trent and Vatican I, which it quotes several times even in this short first chapter. However it has its own character: 'It is enlightening to compare two similar sentences from Vatican I and Vatican II on the very fact of revelation. We immediately note that the *Theocentric* character of Vatican I has been replaced by the *Christocentric* character of Vatican II.'[30]

Since Vatican II, there has been continuing controversy over the status of its teachings. Despite the efforts just discussed, some argue that it represents a rupture with the constant teaching of the Church. This approach has gained the title of 'the hermeneutic of discontinuity'. Groups on both the far right and far left use this reasoning to argue for changes as diverse as returning to the Tridentine Mass and allowing women priests. Those defending the orthodoxy of Vatican II argue for 'the hermeneutic of continuity'. Cardinal Ratzinger, now Pope Benedict XVI, has been a consistent supporter of the hermeneutic of continuity. In a book-length interview in August 1984, he made his position very clear:

> This schematism of a *before* and *after* in the history of the Church, wholly unjustified by the documents of Vatican II, which do nothing but reaffirm the continuity of Catholicism, must be decidedly opposed. There is no 'pre-' or 'post-' conciliar Church: there is but one, unique Church that walks the path towards the Lord ... There are no leaps in this history, there are no fractures, and there is no break in continuity.[31]

More recently, he took the opportunity of the fortieth anniversary of the end of Vatican II to repeat this message: 'The Church, both before and after the council, was and is the same Church, one, holy, catholic and apostolic, journeying on through time.'[32]

Summary

The above discussion may have seemed rather irrelevant to our stated aims. However it is important to understand Church teaching on Scripture. Only then can we understand why the Church places so much emphasis on the continuity of its teaching. Scripture itself does not change, therefore its message does not change. The only thing that can change is the way in which that message is presented.

We have seen that the Canon of Scripture was carefully selected, with the help of the Holy Spirit, as those teachings that had direct links with the apostles. Their purpose is to reveal God's plan for our salvation. In order to reveal this we need both faith and reason. Theologians have an obligation to explain the meaning of Scripture but always within the authority of the Magisterium. The teaching of the Church on the balance between faith and reason and their use in interpreting Scripture can be traced from the beginnings of the Church through the two Vatican councils and into the most modern summary of Church teachings, the *Catechism of the Catholic Church*.[33] One important lesson for those people today who are campaigning for change is that the Church tends to react to calls for change with statements reiterating the established teaching. The classic example of this was the Council of Trent. Instead of doing the expected and reforming the Church to bring it more into line with modern thinking, the council reaffirmed the constant teachings. This reaction and its effects should give pause for thought to those demanding similar reforms today: 'But this funeral of Christianity, as Chesterton once wrote, was interrupted by the least expected incident of all—the corpse came to life.'[34]

Notes

[1]   See l. Boadt, *Reading the Old Testament: An Introduction* (New York: Paulist Press, 1984), p. 89.

[2]   For a discussion of this, see G. Stanton (ed.), *The Gospels and Jesus* (Oxford: OUP, 1989), or R. Brown, *An Introduction to the New Testament* (New York: Doubleday, 1997).

[3]   DV § 2 (1965).

[4]   *Ibid.* § 7.

[5]   A large Jewish community had existed in Alexandria for centuries and numbered about a million at the time of Jesus. Because they had become Greek speaking, they translated their sacred books into Greek.

[6]   Paul Neuenzeit, 'Canon of Scripture', in K. Rahner, *Encyclopaedia of Theology* (London: Burns and Oates, 1975), p. 172.

[7]   See M. Vessey, 'Jerome' in A. Fitzgerald, (ed.) *Augustine Through the Ages: An Encyclopedia* (Cambridge: Eerdmans, 1999), p. 461. This debate was to resurface at the time of the Reformation.

[8]   See Appendix VI for an explanation of Marcionism.

9   The General Council of Trent fourth session. 'Decree on Sacred Books and on Traditions to be Received' in ND, §211–213.

10 'Canonicity' in NJBC, p. 1044, §51.

11 A. McGrath, *Christian Theology: An Introduction* 3ʳᵈ ed. (Oxford: Blackwell Publishing Ltd., 2001), p. 160.

12 A. Nichols, *The Shape of Catholic Theology* (Collegeville, The Liturgical Press, 1991), p. 111.

13 See R. Brown in the NJBC, p. 1156 §44.

14 A. Suelzer and J. Kselman, 'Modern Old Testament Criticism' In NJBC p. 1129, §79.

15 The General Council of Trent Fourth Session. 'Decree on Sacred Books and on Traditions to be Received' (1546), in ND, p. 79, §215.

16 For a standard treatment of the history of the Council, see P. Hughes, *The Church in Crisis: A History of the General Councils, 325-1870* (London: Burns and Oates, 1960), pp. 294-324, where he discusses the various fears expressed by bishops opposed to defining the doctrine.

17 F. Fiorenza and J. Galvin, *Systematic Theology vol. I* (Minneapolis: Fortress Press, 1991), p. 125. In fact, most theologians would also include the declaration of 1854 on the Immaculate Conception.

18 B. Till, *The Churches Search for Unity* (Harmondsworth: Penguin Books, 1972), p. 183. The author was an Anglican priest with wide experience of ecumenical movements. Judging by my various conversations with ministers from other denominations, this statement is still valid. Indeed, the Vatican today recognises a similar resistance to its desire to speak the truth. The following quote comes from a doctrinal note of the Congregation for the Doctrine of the Faith, *Aspects of Evangelisation* §3 (Dec 2007): 'Often it is maintained that any attempt to convince others on religious matters is a limitation of their freedom. From this perspective, it would only be legitimate to present one's own ideas and to invite people to act according to their consciences, without aiming at their conversion to Christ.'

19 R. Latourelle, *Theology of Revelation* (Cork: Mercier Press Ltd., 1968), p. 303.

20 J. Comby and D. Mc Culloch, *How to Read Church History* vol. 2 (London: SCM Press, 1989), p. 137.

21 B. Ward (tr.), *The Prayers and Meditations of St Anselm: With the Proslogion* (Harmondsworth: Penguin Books, 1973), p. 244.

22 First Vatican General Council, Third Session, Dogmatic Constitution *Dei Filius* (1870), in ND §120.

23 A. Dulles, *Models of Revelation* (Dublin: Gill and MacMillan, 1976), p. 3.

24 The General Council of Trent, Fourth Session. Decree on Sacred Books and on Traditions to be Received (1546), in ND §210.

25 Pius IX encyclical letter *Qui Pluribus* (1846), in ND §107.

26 First Vatican General Council, Third Session, Dogmatic Constitution *Dei Filius* (1870), in ND §133-135.

27 DV §12.

28 CCC, p. 2.

29 DV §1.

30 Latourelle, *Theology of Revelation*, p. 487.

31 J. Ratzinger and V. Messori, *The Ratzinger Report* (San Francisco: Ignatius Press, 1993), p. 35.

32 Pope Benedict XVI 'Christmas Address to the Roman Curia', in *L'Osservatore Romano*, (4 January 2006), p. 5, col.1.

33 See especially §26-67.

34 Hughes, *The Church in Crisis*, p. 294.

3 THE CHURCH AS GUARDIAN OF THE TRUTH

T HERE ARE MANY aspects to the study of the Church as an institution: for example, the Church as community, the body of Christ, the creation of the Holy Spirit, the people of God. Here we are concerned with its role as guardian of the truth.[1] In order to teach and uphold the truth, the Church has to have been founded in Scripture and given the ability, guided by the Holy Spirit, to discern truth from error.

The Church is usually taken to have its beginning with the confirmation of the apostles at Pentecost, although the Last Supper is also important here, as recognised in *Ecclesia de Eucharistia*: 'By the gift of the Holy Spirit at Pentecost the Church was born—yet a decisive moment in her taking shape was certainly the institution of the Eucharist in the upper room.'[2] In addition to Pentecost and the Last Supper, the resurrection, Paul's mission to the gentiles and the fall of Jerusalem in AD 70 have also been proposed as possible birth dates. It could even be argued that the Church has her roots in the Old Testament and the original 'chosen people'. One's preferred birth date will depend on one's view of what the Church is.

In ordinary language 'the church' can mean the building used for Sunday worship or the denomination to which it belongs or the world-wide Christian community.[3] In theological language it can mean all of these and more. The most definitive teaching on the Church in the Roman Catholic Tradition is the document *Lumen Gentium* (LG) from the Second Vatican Council. It avoided any one definition. It aimed to 'unfold more fully to the faithful of the Church and to the whole world its own inner nature and universal mission.'[4]

Lumen Gentium talks of the various images of the Church—the sheepfold, the field, God's building, Jerusalem above, the bride of Christ, a body of whom Christ is the head, a community of faith, hope and charity.[5] The earliest formal attempt to define the Church was at the Council of Constantinople of AD 381. (The Council of Nicaea of AD 325 had concentrated on the beliefs of the Church.) Their definition is still used: 'Practically all Christians, however divided in other respects, are united in professing their faith in "one, holy, catholic and apostolic Church"'.[6]

The various Christian denominations who share the Nicene creed represent a bewildering variety of beliefs and often have very little in common other than this creed. While we must respect others' beliefs, the mutually exclusive nature of some of these beliefs means that they cannot all be true. We believe that the Roman Catholic Church has been given the tools to discern true teaching, principally the Magisterium:

> In order to preserve the Church in the purity of the faith handed on by the apostles, Christ who is the Truth willed to confer on her a share in his own infallibility ... It is the Magisterium's task to preserve God's people from deviations and defections and to guarantee them the objective possibility of professing the true faith without error.[7]

We will be discussing the teachings of the Magisterium in more detail later.

The Church in the Gospels

Jesus does not give a clear blueprint for the Church which he came to found, instead he preaches the 'Kingdom of God/heaven' and prepares a small group of followers to continue this preaching. Indeed, the Greek word *ecclésia* (which the Septuagint used to translate the Hebrew *qahal*, assembly summoned by God) was used only twice in the Gospels, both in Matthew. 'So now I say to you, you are Peter, and on this rock I will build my community and the gates of the underworld can never overpower it. I will give you the keys of the kingdom of Heaven: whatever you bind on earth will be bound in heaven; whatever you loose on earth shall be loosed in heaven' (Mt 16:18) and 'If he refuses to listen to them, report it to the community; and if he refuses to listen to the community, treat him like a gentile and a tax-collector.' (Mt 18:17). As Matthew lays great stress on the Kingdom of Heaven, scholars have concluded that he was deliberately making the connection between the Kingdom and the Church.[8]

> We share the opinion of various exegetes who have pointed out that Matthew is particularly attentive to the continuity between, on the one side, Jesus' proclaiming the kingdom of heaven and, on the other, its accomplishment in the Christian community, i.e. the Church.[9]

Matthew 16:18 has the added significance of being the 'Petrine text' on which the claims to supremacy of the bishop of Rome are based.[10] This doctrine has had its greatest challenges in the rift between the Eastern and Western Churches, finalised by the rejection of the findings of the Council of Florence (1439-1445) by the Eastern Church and the Reformation movement in the sixteenth century. In reply, the Church of Rome reaffirmed its claim to supremacy at the first Vatican council in 1870. The dogmatic constitution *Pastor Aeternus* taught that

> Therefore, if anyone says that it is not according to the institution of Christ our Lord Himself, that is, by divine law, that St Peter should have perpetual successors in the primacy over the whole Church; or if anyone says that the Roman Pontiff is not the successor of St Peter in the same primacy, anathema sit.[11]

Modern popes continue to claim supreme authority, although their language does not seem so strong:

> Among all the churches and Ecclesial Communities, the Catholic Church is conscious that she has preserved the ministry of the successor of the apostle Peter, the Bishop of Rome, whom God established as her 'perpetual and visible principle and foundation of unity'.[12]

The key factor in this debate is the teaching that it was Jesus who chose Peter as the head of the Church. Peter's own character and behaviour were not such as to cause him to be recognised as the natural leader of the group of apostles — we hear that the apostles argued over who should take the place of honour (Mk 9:35). While he acted as spokesman for the group on several occasions (especially on the road to Caesarea Philippi – 'You are the Christ, the son of the living God' (Mt 16:16) and 'Lord to whom shall we go? You have the message of eternal life' (Jn 6:68), he also denied Jesus three times. Biblical scholars support the authenticity of Matthew 6:18–19, based on its Semitic idioms[13] and the novelty of its message; a promise that had no roots in Jewish tradition and for which there was therefore no motive to invent it.[14] The name change is significant and far more than a 'nickname'.

> Since the Hebrew mind equates the name with the reality named, to impose a new name on a person means somehow to bring to being a new personality. The new being consti- tuted by the character is not meant solely to raise the person to a level ontologically higher. Since it is intended for the sake of a mission that needs to be carried out, it is dynamic by its very nature.[15]

So Simon becomes Peter, the rock on which the Church is built. Despite his personal failings, he has been chosen as the head steward of the kingdom of God. The gifts needed to perform this task will be given to him at Pentecost. In the meantime, Jesus warns him that he will be tempted and prove weak but that he will have the task of strengthening the other apostles: 'Simon, Simon! Look, Satan has got his wish to sift you all like wheat, but I have prayed for you, Simon, that your faith may not fail; and once you have recovered, you in turn must strengthen your brothers' (Lk 22:31–32).[16]

We hear that Peter did indeed recover and exercise his leader- ship even before Pentecost. The first recorded action of the apostles after the ascension is that they spent their time in prayer together. The second is that Peter announced that they would have to replace Judas and decided how to do this. This is important as it is Peter's first act as head of the Church but it also has significance in that it gives us some insight into the role of the apostles in the early Church. Peter's instructions give us the first definition of an apostle; Judas must be replaced by a man who has been an eye-witness of Jesus' public life from his baptism by John to his ascension. He must be a witness to his resurrection. He must be capable of understanding the significance of these events in order to serve with the other apostles in their task of spreading the kingdom and guarding the authenticity of its teaching. There were clearly many men who could have been appointed to replace Judas. Considering the world-wide task of the apostles, it might have been more practical to appoint many of them. Why did Peter feel that he had to appoint one and only one? Peter himself quotes Psalms 69 and 109 (Ac 1:20)[17] as reasons for leaving Judas's affairs to others and replacing him so that the twelve will be complete: 'The will of God is at stake. Peter knows that Jesus had intended to establish a new Israel through the mediation of the twelve. Because Pentecost is coming, the group should not lack any members.'[18]

It is significant that, when James, son of Zebedee, is executed in AD 44 (Ac 12:2), no substitute is appointed. By this time, the apostles have already delegated sufficient of their powers to others to allow the Church to continue growing without them. These successors of the apostles continue to this day in the task of serving the truth of the resurrection. Of course, not all scholars see the link between Jesus' teaching, the early Church and the modern Church in this way: 'It is natural that those who accompanied Jesus played a part in the later Church. But of that group of disciples as a school for Church leaders there was certainly never any thought.'[19] We will discuss the arguments for the bishops of the Church as successors of the apostles in chapter fourteen. Here we must continue to look at the development of the Church as described in Scripture.

The Church in Acts and Paul

The word 'church' had appeared only twice in the gospels. In Acts it is used twenty-three times. The church in Jerusalem is soon joined by several other churches, who are independent but recognise the authority of Jerusalem. A hierarchy quickly develops, with the twelve apostles joined by 'seven men of good reputation' (Ac 6:3)[20] then *episcopoi* and presbyters. While the roles of the various office bearers is not always clear, there is a traceable link through history.

Paul uses the word 'church' sixty-five times. What is new in the writing of Paul is the development of a theology of the church—it is the body of Christ and he is its head (Ep 1:22–23; Col 1:18). Christ is to the Church what a husband is to his wife.[21]

That either the early or the modern Church is a true reflection of the wishes of Jesus is debated. Nowhere in Scripture does Jesus give any indications of how he wanted the Church to develop. This can be understood if we accept that Jesus' first priority was to call the Jews to repentance and only after their rejection of him and his followers does the need arise to have a separate organisation: 'It is clear from the Acts of the Apostles that, when the Christian community began, it was hoping for the whole of Israel to follow the crucified and risen Messiah, now at God's right hand (Ac 2:39).'[22] Jesus' conferring of authority on Peter (Mt 16:19) and on the other apostles (Matthew 18:18) allowed the early Church to adapt itself to its post-Jewish situation. However it still had the same aim as had Jesus himself—to proclaim the Kingdom. The very last sentence in Acts describes Paul during his two years under house arrest in Rome: 'He welcomed all who came to visit him, proclaiming the kingdom of God and teaching the truth about the Lord Jesus Christ with complete fearlessness and without any hindrance from anyone'(Ac 28:31).

Summary

Jesus came to proclaim the kingdom of God and set up the Church to achieve this. The Church is hierarchical by nature and the pope, the successor of Peter, has supreme authority. The apostles passed their authority on to their successors. The roles of bishop, priest and deacon gradually evolved. Within the Roman Catholic Church, this evolution has as its starting point and model the priesthood of Christ, as described in Scripture. The notion of the priesthood of the laity, also based on Scripture, became an important issue at the time of the Reformation and has become popular in the post-Vatican II Church. We need to look at these two concepts in more detail.

The Priesthood of Christ

The priesthood is one of the most obvious differences between the pre- and post-Reformation churches. Although Calvin himself accepted the role of Christ as priest,[23] the theology of the priesthood belongs mainly within those churches that have retained the offices of bishop, priest and deacon. The following discussion is based mainly on the work of Jean Galot and his study of the difference between the ordained priesthood and the priesthood of the laity. While Galot is not universally acclaimed,[24] he is respected as both an academic and a loyal servant of the Church. His teachings on the priesthood will not lead us to contradict those of the Magisterium, which would defeat our aim of presenting findings compatible with Scripture, Tradition and the Magisterium. He has also studied the place of women's ministry in the Church but I have not been able to find them in English translation.[25]

Galot begins his study of the priesthood by examining the criteria for defining the nature of the priesthood. Rather in the style of the *Summa*, he first looks at criteria that he then discards. Sociological models, looking at the qualities needed in a priestly leader in order to meet the needs of his community, are inadequate as they are not sufficiently grounded in the life and teachings of Jesus Christ. Comparative religious studies are of only limited value. They can give us a general picture of the development of a priestly class but the pagan notion of priesthood falls so far short of the Christian that this picture tells us nothing of the richness of the salvific and mediatory role of the Christian priest. Even Old Testament studies are of value only in that they allow us to identify what is new in the Christian priesthood:

> The mystery of the incarnation has exceeded by far the doctrinal framework of Jewish religion and the messianic expectation. A transformation of worship is implied. The act of redemption brings about a change also in the conditions surrounding the offering of sacrifice.[26]

Galot states that only in Christ himself can we find an adequate definition of the priesthood because Christ both instituted the priesthood and was the perfect model of it. Arguments against this include that Christ founded a priesthood of the faithful but not an authoritarian, ministerial priesthood; that communities must be free to follow the impulses of the Holy Spirit; that priests cannot represent Christ as representation applies only to suffering and service, so hierarchy, prestige and power must be excluded. In reply, he argues that it is arbitrary to regard Christ as the prototype of the priesthood of the faithful only. As discussed elsewhere,[27]

Christ chose the group of twelve apostles for a specific mission, distinct from that of the rest of his followers. Just as he has authority and power from his father, so will they. However it is of a very different quality from earthly authority. Scripture tells us that 'You call me Master and Lord, and rightly, so I am. If I, then, the Lord and Master, have washed your feet, you must wash each other's feet. I have given you an example so that you may copy what I have done to you' (Jn 13:14–15). Also 'For the Son of Man himself came not to be served but to serve, and to give his life as a ransom for many' (Mk 10:45) and this is the example that the apostles must follow. The same sentence in Matthew reads 'just as the Son of Man came not to be served but to serve, and to give his life as a ransom for many' (Mt 20:28). Mark's 'for' gives the sentence an explanatory purpose; Matthew's 'just as' gives it an exemplary one. So apostolic, and therefore priestly, authority and power certainly exist but they exist in order to serve, Christ having given both teaching and example of authority and power as service. To argue that theologians need more freedom to allow for the workings of the Holy Spirit or to adapt the priesthood to modern conditions is to miss the point that both the priesthood and the Church were instituted by Jesus Christ and led by the Holy Spirit, who cannot work apart from Christ. Any proposed changes in practice or understanding must remain within the boundaries set by Scripture. As Jesus was called 'priest' only in the Letter to the Hebrews, never used the word of himself and did not explicitly lay down a priestly structure for the Church, we need to work out carefully what these boundaries are.[28]

There are two main reasons given for Jesus not referring to himself as a priest; he did not want to be limited by historical linguistic usage and his priesthood was of a different order from the Jewish priesthood of the day.[29] A new order was being set up and it needed a new understanding of leadership, authority and power, expressed in new ways 'New wine into fresh skins' (Mk 2:22). Jesus' priesthood was new in that it was not hereditary, it was based on unconditional love rather than man-made rituals and laws (hence the parable of the good Samaritan), it was to be respected as an institution (hence the instruction to the cured leper to show himself to the priest), it was focused on his person, not on a building (hence the statement that here was something greater than the temple).

This new priesthood can be described as having two aspects, the sacred and the ministerial.

> In the first place ... the priest possesses a sacredness imma-
> nent in his own person, for he sustains a privileged relation
> to the godhead: through his mediation God's action and
> presence are disclosed. In the second place, the priest may
> be described as the 'minister': he carries out ritual and cultic
> functions or other religious functions.[30]

Jesus' sacred priesthood is ontological in that it is expressed in his human nature; he was consecrated and sent into the world by the Father (Jn 10:36). His holiness is absolute because his whole human nature is also divine. Yet he was consecrated in order to take an active part in the world, not to withdraw from it. As the centre of the new religion, Jesus Christ's humanity means that this new religion depends on inter-personal relationships, involving all of humanity in an active co-operation with the Holy Spirit and is based on love, not fear.

Jesus' ministerial priesthood is expressed in the image of the good shepherd (Jn 10:11). Jesus feels sorry for the crowds who are like sheep without a shepherd and teaches them (Mk 6:34). Reminiscent of the prophet Ezekiel (chapter 34), he wants to gather all the lost sheep into one sheepfold, to nourish them and care for them. Jesus cares for his sheep even to the point of sacrificing his life for them because he has come, not to be served but to serve and to give his life as a ransom for many (Mk 10:45). It is this service to mankind that makes his priesthood ministerial. The salvific effect of Jesus sacrifice is made available to all generations through two events, the Eucharistic meal and the forgiveness of sins: 'It is in the Eucharistic meal that the shepherd is to impart life and carry out his mission' and 'the life-giving mission of the shepherd is carried out also through the remission of sins. Jesus grants the remission of sins with authority and proves the efficacy of this remission by healing the body'.[31]

At his trial, Jesus tells Pilate that 'It is you who say that I am a king. I was born for this, I came into the world for this, to bear witness to the truth; and all who are on the side of truth listen to my voice' (Jn 18:37). In this one sentence, we have Jesus describing himself as king, prophet and shepherd/priest. The image of the good Shepherd helps us to understand Jesus as priest, sacrificing himself, and as prophet, teaching the crowds, the work of the prophets. The sheep listen to him because they recognise his voice (Jn 10:4) and other sheep will also listen, but only after he has given up his life for them. The roles of shepherd and king are at the opposite ends of the social spectrum in any society. Jesus combines them through his emphasis on love and service. His prophetic, evangelical mission will only be successful through his self-giving on the cross. His kingship gives him the power to lead, but as a shepherd leads his sheep, not through fear or force. There are no examples of Jesus using his power to harm or punish anyone. Even Judas is not excluded from the group and is not reprimanded when he betrays Jesus.

The Letter to the Hebrews is the only Scriptural document to speak explicitly of Jesus as a priest. It takes as its starting point Jesus' statement at his trial, when he answers the high priest by quoting Psalm 110, thereby claiming to be 'a priest forever of the order of Melchizedek' (Ps 110 v.4). Like Melchizedek, Jesus is a king without a human father, who owed his priesthood to his own nature, not to being a member of a priestly tribe. In addition, Jesus' priesthood is perfect and eternal. 'It follows, then, that his power to save those who come to God through him is absolute, since he lives for ever to intercede for them' (Heb 7:25). Hebrews presents Jesus' priesthood as eternal but also human (Heb 5:1) as the priest has to be able to empathise with people in their ignorance and weakness. Because of the need for this humanity, Jesus was not a priest before the incarnation, however he continues to be a priest in heaven. Indeed, his priesthood only reached completion when he entered heaven. He continues the priestly function of mediation by asking the Father to apply the fruits of his one sacrifice to mankind. Jesus is 'the mediator of a new covenant' (Heb 12:24) won for us by the shedding of his blood.

The Letter to the Hebrews stresses the royal aspect of Jesus' priesthood by linking it with the king-priest Melchizedek. However it also acknowledges Jesus as shepherd and prophet. Jesus' prophetic role is confirmed in the very first sentence of the letter: 'At many moments in the past and by many means, God spoke to our ancestors through the prophets; but in our time, the final days, he has spoken to us in the person of his Son' (Heb 1:1–2). At the end of the letter we read that he is 'the great Shepherd of the sheep, by the blood that sealed an eternal covenant' (Heb 13:21).

> The title 'great shepherd' attests that the author did not intend to confine himself rigorously to a ritual framework in his description of Christ's mediation … The mention of Moses and Joshua suggests that the priestly mediation of Jesus is at the same time the mediation of the head and leader of the people.[32]

Finally, the Letter to the Hebrews suggests that 'Because Christ possessed the omnipotence of God's own Word, he was able to accomplish what Jewish sacrifice could not secure, namely, the remission of sins'.[33]

Summary

The priesthood instituted by Christ is more than that shared by all the faithful, it is passed on to the apostles as a specific function for a specific group of men. It is also quite distinct from the Jewish priesthood. This new priesthood is both sacred and ministerial. The sacred nature of the priesthood is expressed through four main characteristics; its centre is Jesus Christ; it is universal; it is dynamic and it is based on love, not fear. The ministerial nature is expressed through the image of the shepherd whose mission includes sacrifice, service and the priestly functions of prophet, cult and kingship. The Letter to the Hebrews confirms the *tri munera* of Christ as priest, prophet and king.

We mentioned at the beginning of this section that Calvin accepted the idea of Jesus Christ as a priest and much of what Galot says about the priesthood of Christ would have been acceptable to Calvin. Where the pre- and post- Reformation churches differ is on the teaching on the apostles as heirs to the priesthood of Christ. We need to look at this in more detail.

The Apostles as Successors of Christ

The Letter to the Hebrews uses the term 'priest' only for Christ. However it also refers to leaders of the community, both past (Heb 13:7) and present (Heb 13:17). These leaders preached and were to be obeyed. They were distinct from the rest of the community; 'Greetings to all your leaders and to all God's holy people' (Heb 13:24). While the Letter emphasises the one priesthood of Christ, it is compatible with the doctrine of these leaders participating in this one priesthood.

> The principle that the priesthood of Christ is unique excludes the value of any other priesthood constituted independently of it, but not of a priesthood that takes its origins from Christ's own priesthood, and prolongs it, or makes it manifest, in the life of Christians here below.[34]

The gospels make it clear that Jesus chose the twelve apostles from a much larger group of his followers (Lk 6:13) and that this choice was his alone. He did not ask for volunteers or make a shortlist of those with the desired characteristics. 'He now went up onto the mountain and summoned those he wanted. So they came to him and he appointed twelve' (Mk 3:13) and 'You did not choose me, no, I chose you' (Jn 15:16). The only reason that Jesus gives us for choosing twelve apostles is that they are to judge the twelve tribes of Israel (Mt 19:28). However there are many examples of them being treated as a privileged group who receive extra instruction, are given the power to forgive sins (Jn 20:20–22), to celebrate the Eucharist (Lk 22:19), and to evangelise the world (Mt 28:18–20), baptising in the name of the Trinity and passing on all the teachings that Jesus had given them. A particularly significant episode is the sending of the twelve to 'proclaim the kingdom of God and to heal' (Lk 9:2) and of the seventy-two (Lk 10:1–16).[35] This has been interpreted as Jesus passing on his own priesthood, which included leadership, the proclamation of the Word and the performance of sacramental acts[36] and teaching them that the exercise of power is in reality a service.[37]

We have already seen that there is a hierarchy within this group and that Peter was chosen as its leader and the rock on which the Church was to be built. Those who deny that the apostles inherited the priesthood of Christ, will also deny the role of Peter as the first leader of the Church.

> The interpretation which maintains that only Peter's faith, not Peter himself, was established as the foundation of the Church does not correctly reflect the intention expressed by Jesus. It is the man who now carries the name of Cephas; it is Peter as a person who constitutes the foundation stone of the Church, not merely his faith, nor the contents of it.[38]

We can understand this better if we remember that 'It is generally known that the Hebrew mind sees a great significance in names: to give a man a new name is to bestow a new reality upon him, to fashion or refashion his personality anew'.[39]

So Jesus' action of changing Simon's name to Peter could be said to cause an ontological change in him. It is significant that, immediately after this name change, Peter is given supreme authority 'I will give you the keys of the kingdom of Heaven: whatever you bind on earth will be bound in heaven, whatever you loose on earth will be loosed in heaven' (Mt 16:19). The Scriptural passages of relevance to the primacy of Peter are too numerous to quote and can be found in any theological diction-ary.[40] The position of Peter is a necessary part of his role as leader of the Church. Again, the Scriptural references to Peter's mission are too numerous to quote individually.[41]

We have seen that several events are significant in the process of Jesus conferring his priestly powers on the twelve. If only one event could be chosen as the central one, most people would choose the Last Supper, when Jesus instructed the apostles to 'do this in memory of me'. From this developed the Eucharist, the centre of our liturgical life. However, it was not until after Pentecost that the apostles exercised their priestly powers. Galot sees in the events of Pentecost the origins of priestly ordination. The apostles had been chosen and given their mission during Jesus' own ministry, culmi-nating at the Last Supper. He asks the Father to consecrate them (Jn 17:17) and he imposes hands on them and blesses them as his last act before ascending to the Father (Lk 24:50). At Pentecost, they receive the Holy Spirit and immediately begin to exercise their ministry of spreading the good news, led by Peter.

After Pentecost we hear surprisingly little about the apostles. They remain in Jerusalem as a group, concentrating on preaching (Ac 2:14–46; 3:12–16; 4:2) and bearing witness to the power of God (Ac 2:14–21; 3:1–11; 4:5–31). They are regarded as in charge of the universal Church, with Peter at their head (Ac 10:48; 15:7–12). Even Paul accepts their authority. While James, who was not one of the original twelve but became one of the group, is in charge of the church in Jerusalem, we are not told of the others having any specific ministry outside Jerusalem.

From Acts and the letters and epistles, we hear of the development of the early Church. The evidence for any one form of governance is unclear, hence the various practices found in modern Christian denominations, all claiming to be the authentic interpretation of Scripture. The title of 'apostle' is reserved to the twelve by Luke in Acts, yet he uses it for Paul and Barnabas when they were preaching in Iconium (Ac 14:4,14). Earlier, he had described them as prophets and teachers (Ac 13:1). Why the change? 'One day while they were offering worship to the Lord and keeping a fast, the Holy Spirit said, "I want Barnabas and Saul set apart for the work to which I have called them." So it was that after fasting and prayer they laid their hands on them and sent them off' (Ac 13:2–3). Saul and Barnabas travel to Cyprus and preach there. From this point on, Saul is called Paul. The change from a Semitic to a gentile name denotes his new mission as the apostle to the gentiles (Barnabas had also had a name change, being originally 'Joseph' (Ac 4:36)). This was the second time that Saul had had hands laid on him. We hear that Ananias had laid hands on him and said 'Brother Saul, I have been sent by the Lord Jesus, who appeared to you on your way here, so that you may recover your sight and be filled with the Holy Spirit' (Ac 9:17).

Paul himself uses the title 'apostle' in a much wider sense than Luke, including those who had any leadership roles in the community. Paul's main concern was for the building up of the community; positions of authority were a necessary part of this process in order to have a mechanism for common tasks, decision making and discipline (1 Co 16:1–4 and Rm 15:26). His letters give us some idea of the structures in place in his churches. 1 Thessalonians 5:12 tells us that the community had several leaders who were to be treated with consideration, respect and affection. 1 Corinthians 6:1–11 tells the community that they must settle any disputes among themselves and not take their complaints to pagan courts. Indeed, it is better to suffer injustice than to take someone to court. 1 Corinthians 9:14 says that 'the Lord gave the instruction that those who preach the gospel should get their lives from the gospel.' While Paul himself prefers not to receive payment from the communities to which he brings the gospel, he defends the right of others to expect material support from these communities. Galatians 6:6 says that 'When someone is under instruction in doctrine, he should give his teacher a share in all his possessions.' In the Letter to the Philippians, Paul addresses the letter to the people and their leaders. He uses the Greek words *episkopoi* and *diakonoi*. *Diakonoi* is translated as 'deacons' or 'helpers' without controversy. The word 'episkopoi' is variously translated as 'bishops',[42] 'overseers',[43] 'elders',[44] 'presiding elders'[45] or 'church leaders'.[46] In 1 Corinthians and Ephesians 4:11–12, Paul tells us that teaching and leadership are gifts of the Spirit, to be used in the service of the Church.

Acts tells us that the early Church appointed seven helpers for the apostles, so that they could 'devote ourselves to prayer and to the service of the word' (Ac 6:4). Whether these seven were ordained as presbyters or as deacons will be debated in the section on the Magisterium. Here, all we need to know is that the apostles delegated some of their duties to others. This process was continued by Paul and the others who founded churches, with the consent of the apostles (Ac 14:23). There were also presbyters in Jerusalem, indeed Peter calls himself a presbyter (1 P 5:1). These leaders have teaching (Ac 8:35), cultic (Ac 8:38) and shepherding (Ac 20:28–29) functions.

The letters to Timothy and Titus give us the 'final word' on the structure of the early Church before we have to move on to non-Scriptural sources. They mention three different office bearers: bishop, presbyter/elder and deacon. 1 Timothy 3 and Titus 1:7–9 give lists of the characteristics to be looked for in both bishop and deacon. The presbyters form a group or council with the authority to appoint leaders by the laying on of hands (1 Tm 4:14).[47] Later, he mentions presbyters who are to be honoured and over whom

Timothy seems to have authority 'Never accept any accusation brought against an elder unless it is supported by two or three witnesses' (1 Tm 5:19). He also describes an order of widows in chapter 5:3–16. These seem to be more than simply women left without family to support them as they must be over 60 and of good character and can then be enrolled. Women are also mentioned in the passage about the qualifications for deacons (1 Tm 3:8–13) but it is not clear whether they were the wives of deacons, female deacons or women with a role in the Church similar to that of deacons.[48]

The pastoral letters, while mentioning bishops, presbyters and deacons, do not make it clear how these positions relate to each other. Timothy has clearly been given the role of leader, with specific instructions to preserve sound doctrine (1 Tm 1:3–4) and to rebuke sinners (1 Tm 5:20). As the role of bishop includes overall supervision, it seems that Timothy was a bishop. He has authority over the presbyters (1 Tm 5:19) but was appointed by them (1 Tm 4:14), possibly with a more senior figure present (2 Tm 1:6). The presbyters have a share in authority but also preach and teach (1 Tm 5:17). The qualities needed in deacons are listed but there is no mention of what they do.

It is clear that, by the time of the pastoral letters, the structure of the Church is established and is not a matter of controversy; what is important is the character of the person fulfilling the function. The lack of detail on the structure has, however, caused problems for the post-Reformation churches, where there is division and disagreement over what is the most 'Scripturally sound' form of administration. The following quote is lengthy but suggests a reasonable compromise and summary:

> (The early communities were governed by elders/presbyters, continuing the practice of the Old Testament). These *episkopoi* (presiding elders) who are not yet 'bishops' ... seem in some passages, Tt 1:5, 7; Ac 20:17, 28 to be identical with the elders. The Greek word *episkopos*, taken over from the gentile world, ... indicated the duty of an officer, while *presbyteros* indicated the status or dignity of the same officer. The *episkopoi* in the college of presbyters may have taken turns to carry out their official duties cf. 1 Tm 5:17. It is quite certain that Christian *presbyteroi* or *episkopoi* were not merely concerned with the

practical side of organising things: they had to teach, 1:9; 1
Tm 3:2; 5:17, and govern, Tt 1:7; 1 Tm 3:5. They were
appointed by the apostles, Ac 14:23 or their representatives,
Tt 1:5, by the imposition of hands 1Tm 5:22 … their powers
derived from God, Ac 20:28 and were charismatic, 1 Co 12:28
… These heads of the local community who developed into
our priests (*presbyteroi*) and bishops (*episkopoi*) were helped
by *diakonoi* (deacons).[49]

Of course, this summary would not be universally accepted. While
some post-Reformation churches retained a hierarchical structure
similar to that of the Catholic Church, some tried to eliminate this
altogether. It is worth remembering that

The Pastorals have always provided grist for the mills of
later churchmen who wish to prove that their own favoured
form of church government … represents the oldest and
divinely sanctioned form. Few scholars approve of such
exploitation of the Pastorals, partly because of the gaps in
our knowledge; no one is sure whether bishops and elders
were identical or different, though the prevailing view is
that they were identical.[50]

Summary

Having exhausted the Scriptural sources of information on the
apostles as successors of Christ, what conclusions can we come to?
We have found that the apostles were selected by Jesus to form a
group, with Peter at their head, to whom he passed on a share in
his mediatory powers as priest, prophet and king. The apostles
were the guardians of true teaching and the source of authority in
the early Church. They passed this authority on to other leaders
as the Church grew. We can identify elements of the sacrament of
ordination in the rituals surrounding this conferral of power—the
laying on of hands is regularly, though not always, mentioned. For
Peter and Paul at least, there is the suggestion of ontological
change, symbolised by a name change that is related to their new
role. While the hierarchical structure of the early Church is not
clear, each community had leaders who were, if they so wished,
supported financially by that community. By the time of the

pastoral epistles, the Church has bishops/elders, presbyters and deacons, although their precise functions are not clear.

The priesthood of the apostles is derived from the priesthood of Christ. We said earlier that the concept of the priesthood of Christ was also linked to the concept of the priesthood of the laity. It is now time to examine this in some detail.

The Priesthood of the Laity

As with the priesthood of Christ, we can see a prefiguring of the idea of a common priesthood of the faithful in the Old Testament. There are several references to a general priesthood, not limited to the tribe of Levi. The following are typical examples:

- Exodus 19:6 'For me you shall be a kingdom of priests, a holy nation',
- Deuteronomy 7:6 'For you are a people consecrated to the Lord your God; of all the peoples on earth, you have been chosen by the Lord your God to be his own people',
- Leviticus 11:45 'Yes, it is I, the Lord your God, who brought you out of the land of Egypt to be your God: you must therefore be holy, because I am holy',
- Leviticus 19:2 'Be holy, for I, the Lord your God, am holy',
- Isaiah 61:6 'but you will be called "priests of the Lord" and be addressed as "ministers of our God"',
- Jeremiah 2:3 'Israel was sacred to the Lord; the first fruits of his harvest'.

The notion of a priestly people does not detract from the duties assigned to the tribe of Levi, who are still responsible for the cultic rituals. Just what was meant by the phrase is debated. One theory on its meaning is that, as priests were generally the only people in a community who could read and write, God was saying that he wanted the Israelites to be a literate people. They did seem to give more emphasis to teaching the basics of reading and writing to the children, or at least the boys, than was the norm in the surrounding peoples. This was to allow them to study the Torah. However a more plausible explanation is that 'Semantically parallel to "holy nation", it probably means sacred among the nations, as priests are among the people.'[51] Whatever the Old Testament meaning of the phrase, Jewish priests of the tribe of Levi became exclusively associated with sacrifice in the temple—they were not involved in prophetic or kingly duties and no one else could perform their duties. They therefore became redundant when the temple was destroyed in AD 70: '(They) had as a body no continuing function, though individual priests could become scribes or teachers of the law. Thereafter, however, Jewish religious leaders would be rabbis, not priests.'[52] The early Christian communities avoided the word 'priest' to avoid confusion with the Jewish priests. After the destruction of the temple, this was not a problem.

The Old Testament notion of the cultic priest and the priesthood of the people prepared the way for the teachings of the New Testament. We do not need to delve into the meaning of the Old Testament priesthood of the people, as it is replaced by a completely new order in the New Testament. By offering his own body on the cross, Jesus Christ becomes both priest and sacrificial victim. This replacement of the old sacrificial order with the new is one of the main themes of the Letter to the Hebrews. The old priests could only purify people from physical defilement and had to repeat their sacrifices over and over again because they were only using animal blood. 'He has no need to offer sacrifices every day, as the high priests do, first for their own sins and only then for those of the people; this he did this once and for all by offering himself.' (Heb 7:27) and 'As it is, he has made his appearance once for all, at the end of the last age, to do away with sin by sacrificing himself' (Heb 9:26).

Just as the priesthood of the apostles and their successors is derived from that of Christ, so is the priesthood of all the people. Jesus himself makes it clear that his followers must share in his priestly sacrifice by taking up their own crosses (Mt 16:24) and proclaiming the good news, even if it leads to persecution and death (Mt 10:17–20).[53]

The epistles of Paul, Hebrews, James and Peter, as well as Revelation, are all relevant to the discussion of the universal priesthood. Paul does not teach specifically about the priesthood. However he uses many priestly metaphors. 1 Corinthians 3:16–17 refers to the people as the temple of God, the dwelling of the Holy Spirit and therefore sacred and 1 Corinthians 6:19–20 refers to the body as 'the temple of the Holy Spirit'. 2 Corinthians 1:21–22 tells us that we are anointed, marked with his seal and carry the Holy Spirit in our hearts. Ephesians 1:13 and 4:30 repeat that the Holy Spirit has marked us with his seal (usually assumed to refer to baptism). So the message from these epistles is that 'Baptism gives rise to a state of belonging to God, a consecration: the Christian is a sanctuary in which the Holy Spirit dwells. From this primary consecration there emerges a way of life that gives glory to God.'[54]

The Letter to the Philippians has a double message; not only is faith true worship and therefore a sacrifice, so is charity: 'Since faith is itself a sacrifice, everything in the life of a Christian takes on a priestly quality. Even the gesture of the Philippians (is sacrificial). Henceforth, charity constitutes the true worship, just as faith does.'[55] This message is reinforced in James. The most relevant quote from 1 Peter is verse 2:5, referring back to both Exodus 19:6 and Isaiah 43:20–21:

> By sharing the life of the risen Lord, Christians become with him a household formed by the Holy Spirit … Christians, viewed corporately as a body of priests (cf. 2:9), present their lives of faith and love to God as a sacrifice (cf. Rom 12:1; Eph 5:2; Phil 4:18).[56]

Finally, Galot identifies three passages in Revelation, all referring back to Exodus 19:6, as relevant to the theme of the priesthood of the laity; Rev 1:6; 5:10 and 20:6.

> We have here both a participation in the priesthood of Christ and a consecration to Christ … What stands out most of all is the royal quality of this priesthood … Here, then, 'priest' refers to the way of life made available to mankind by the Redeemer: the participation in his holiness and in his glorious life as the Risen One. No ministry is involved. Nothing suggests priestly function.[57]

We can see that the New Testament vision of a universal priesthood applies to all the baptised, both as a community and through the faith and good deeds of the individual:

> Thus the whole Church, and in it each individual Christian incorporated into it by baptism and confirmation, is the historically visible and tangible representation of the priest-

hood of Christ. Hence it can, by invoking the unique sacrifice of Christ, have direct access to God, share in his holiness and surrender itself as a sacrifice to the divine dispensation.[58]

The priesthood of Christ and the priesthood of the laity are both represented in the incident described in the gospel of John where Jesus has a conversation with the Samaritan woman (Jn 4:1–42). The episode is rich in allusions to the patriarchs and the symbolism of water in the Old Testament. We learn that true worship does not need a physical focus such as a mountain or a temple, but only belief in Jesus as the Messiah. So the ways of the Old Testament have been replaced. The Levitical priesthood, which depended on the temple, is now obsolete, as is all worship of, and at, physical shrines or holy wells. Salvation is available to Jew and gentile alike and we are all called to be apostles; even sinful women can spread the good news and bring people to Jesus. He is the source of 'living water', the Holy Spirit; and the Father seeks those who worship 'in spirit and truth'.

Some people use the story of the Samaritan woman, with its example of Jesus choosing a woman as an apostle, as an argument for giving women a share in the apostolic ministry of the priesthood. This is to ignore the difference between the priesthood of the apostles and the priesthood of the laity. We need to make this difference clear.

The two priesthoods

Both the universal priesthood of all the baptised and the ministerial priesthood have as their source the priesthood of Christ and therefore have features in common. The laity have the duty to put their faith into action by taking part in communal liturgical worship, by passing on the good news to the pagans and by good deeds. The ministers do not discard these duties when they take on new ones. The duties specific to their ministry can be seen as these same actions, but in a specialised form. So the minister does not just take part in the liturgy but plays a leading and essential role in liturgical worship; preaching and teaching are not activities to be practised whenever a suitable opportunity arises but are central elements of his ministry; he devotes his whole life to the service of others. However it would be a mistake to view the minister as simply a member of the laity who has taken on a leadership role within the community.[59]

The Vatican II document, *Lumen Gentium* gives a clear summary of what the common and ministerial priesthoods have in common and how they differ:

> Though they differ from one another in essence and not only in degree, the common priesthood of the faithful and the ministerial or hierarchical priesthood are nonetheless interrelated ... The ministerial priest, by the sacred power he enjoys, teaches and rules the priestly people; acting in the person of Christ, he makes present the eucharistic sacrifice, and offers it to God in the name of all the people. But the faithful, in virtue of their royal priesthood, join in the offering of the Eucharist. They likewise exercise that priesthood in receiving the sacraments, in prayer and thanksgiving, in the witness of a holy life, and by self-denial and active charity.[60]

Jesus called the twelve and treated them as a distinct group with a distinct mission; they are to be the shepherds of God's people. At the same time, Jesus teaches that we are all being called to be part of the kingdom. So the two forms of ministry are being established at the same time. There is no historical development of one from the other. The apostolic ministry is a full-time job and St Paul reminds the Church that they have a duty to provide for the physical needs of their leaders. Those who devote themselves to this work to the exclusion of family life will receive their reward in Heaven (Mt 19:29).

Summary

While the Old Testament prepares us for the idea of the priesthood of the laity, the New Testament priesthood is of a quite different order. It is clear from the teachings of Jesus himself and the writings of Paul, Peter, James and the author of Revelation that baptism confers a form of priesthood by giving us a share in the priesthood of Christ. Our faith in Jesus Christ is to be expressed in worship of God and good deeds; our very lives are a sacrifice. However there is a clear difference between the priesthood of Christ as it was handed on to the apostles and as it was handed on to the whole Church. The apostolic priesthood is one of service through leadership and preaching, necessitating dedication of one's whole life to the task. The priesthood of the laity, on the other hand, involves living a life of faith and charity within the every-day settings of work and family life.

Having examined the teachings of Scripture on the Church, we need to move on to the second of the four specific steps listed in the introduction, the example of Our Lady.

Notes

1   For other aspects of the theology of the Church, see chapter eight on Tradition and the Church and chapters thirteen and fourteen on the liturgy and sacraments.

2   Pope John Paul II, Encyclical Letter *Ecclesia de Eucharistia* §5 (1995).

3   It is worth noting here that there is a convention regarding the use of 'C' or 'c' for 'church'. The general rule is to refer to the universal Church but particular churches. Protestant churches, lacking Apostolic Succession are, strictly speaking, ecclesial communities. So the correct form is 'church'.

4   Second Vatican Council, Dogmatic Constitution on the Church *Lumen Gentium* § 69 (1964).

5   LG §6-8.

6   F. Sullivan, *The Church We Believe In* (Dublin: Gill and MacMillan Ltd, 1988), p. 3.

7   CCC §889-890.

8   According to the *New Jerusalem Bible*, the whole gospel is structured round this theme; see p. 1606 and 4:17f.

9   P. Schmidt, *How to Read the Gospels: Historicity and Truth in the Gospels and Acts* (Slough: St Pauls, 1993), p. 148.

10   Pope Stephen (254–257) was the first pope to invoke this text as the source of his authority.

11   The First Vatican General Council, Third Session. Dogmatic Constitution *Dei Filius* (1870), in J. Neuner and J. Dupuis, *The Christian Faith: Doctrinal Documents of the Catholic Church*, 5th ed. (London: HarperCollins, 1992), p. 245, §824.

12   John Paul II, encyclical letter, *Ut Unum Sint* §88 (1995).

13   For example, a Jewish audience would recognise the link between the promise made to Peter and the replacement of Shebna with Eliakim as master of the royal palace, by the will of God (Is 22:15-23).

14   See J. Galot, *Theology of the Priesthood*, (San Francisco: Ignatius Press, 1985), p. 78.

15   *Ibid.*, p. 202.

16   'You' is plural in verse 31 but singular in verse 32.

17   Ps 69:25 'Reduce his encampment to ruin and leave his tent unoccupied'. Ps
     109:8 'let someone else take over his office'.
18   Galot, *Theology of the Priesthood*, p. 155.
19   E. Schweizer, *Church Order in the New Testament* (London: SCM Press Ltd.,
     1961), p. 28.
20   See part III on the Magisterium for a discussion on whether or not this was
     the institution of the order of deacons.
21   See J. McKenzie, *Dictionary of the Bible* (London: Geoffrey Chapman, 1965),
     p. 35 for more examples.
22   J. Redford, lecture, 'The Synoptic Gospels' at Maryvale Institute, Birmingham,
     September 2004.
23   J. Calvin, *Commentaries on the Epistle of Paul the Apostle to The Hebrews*,
     translated by J. Owen (Grand Rapids: Baker Book House, 2007), p. 106, where
     he is commenting on Heb 4:14 and states 'For we have said that the Son of
     God sustained a two-fold character when he was sent to us, even that of a
     teacher and of a priest.'
24   K. Osborne accuses Galot of misinterpreting LG in his *Theology of the
     Priesthood*, p. 118: 'Galot interprets the New Testament passages by reading
     into them his own preconceived ideas. His interpretation is not exegesis but
     eisegesis.' See K. Osborne, *The Permanent Diaconate* (New York: Paulist Press,
     2007), p. 28, f. 27.
25   J. Galot, *La donna e i ministeri nella chiesa* (Assisi: Cittadella editrice, 1973),
     discussed in G. Macy, *The Hidden History of Women's Ordination: Female Clergy
     in the Medieval West* (Oxford: OUP, 2008), p. 13, where Macy says that 'Galot
     took the position that the ancient deaconesses of the Eastern Church were in
     fact sacramentally ordained', p. 13. (As Galot was recommended to me by a
     priest who does not support the idea of women deacons, I cannot be accused
     of simply selecting sources that suit my argument!)
26   Galot, *Theology of the Priesthood*, p. 23.
27   See also chapter eight 'The Church: Apostolic Succession'.
28   See also chapter eight 'Tradition: The Church' and chapter fourteen 'The
     Magisterium: Ordination'.
29   Jesus did use titles for Himself that tell us who He was and what His mission
     was. 'I am the Good Shepherd' is perhaps the best known and 'Son of man'
     the least understood. The Gospel of John has seven 'I am-' sayings confirming
     his divinity and his post- resurrection ability to meet all our needs.
30   Galot, *Theology of the Priesthood*, p. 38.
31   *Ibid.*, p. 47.
32   *Ibid.*, p. 60.
33   *Ibid.*, p. 62.
34   *Ibid.*, p. 66.
35   The number twelve symbolises the twelve tribes of Israel and the seventy-two
     the traditional number of gentile nations — see footnote to the chapter heading
     for Lk 10 in the *New Jerusalem Bible*.
36   Galot, *Theology of the Priesthood*, p. 77.

37 F. Amiot and P. Grelot, 'Authority' in Leon-Dufour (ed.), *Dictionary of Biblical Theology* 2nd ed. (London: Burns and Oates, 1988), p. 38.

38 Galot, *Theology of the Priesthood*, p. 79.

39 *Ibid.*, p. 73.

40 Leon Dufour lists Jn 1:35–42; Mt 4:18–22; Mt 10:2; Mt 17:1; Mk 1:29; Mt 16:16; Jn 6:68; Mk 16:7; Jn 20:1–10; Lk 24:34; 1 Co 15:5; Ac 10–15; Ga 2; Ga 1:18; Ga 2:11–14.

41 Leon Dufour lists them as Mt 16:13–23; Lk 22:31 and Ac 1:13; 1:15; 5:1–11; 2:14–36; 2:37–41; 10:1–11,18; 9:32; 3:1–10; 9:36–42; 11:1–18; 15:1–35; Ga 1:18–2:14; Ga 1:18; Mt 16:18; Jn 21; Jn 10:1–28; 10:16, 11:52, 10:28; 1 P 2:4.

42 Revised Standard Version, confraternity text, the authorised version, as used in the Scott Family Bible.

43 Used in the New International Version with a note 'traditionally "bishops"'.

44 Lamsa's translation of the Peshitta Aramaic version.

45 *Jerusalem Bible* and NJB. The footnote to the JB says 'The word "episcopos" ("overseer", "supervisor" or "shepherd") had not yet acquired the same meaning as "bishop" cf. Tt 1:5f.' The footnote to the NJB repeats this information but only offers 'overseer' as an alternative translation.

46 *Good News Bible.*

47 2 Tm 1:6 suggests that it was the author of the letter who laid hands on Timothy—perhaps he was present with the elders or was one of them.

48 See notes 52 and 64 of chapter five for a discussion on this.

49 Footnote to Tt 1:5 in the NJB.

50 J. Zeisler, *Pauline Christianity* (Oxford: OUP, 1990), p. 136.

51 NJBC comments on Ex 19:6.

52 T. D. Alexander, B. S. Rosner (ed), 'Priests', in *New Dictionary of Biblical Theology,* (a presbyterian/evangelical publication), pp. 696–701.

53 For other Scriptural references, see Appendix II, section A.

54 Galot, *Theology of the Priesthood*, p. 109.

55 *Ibid.*, pp. 110–111.

56 NJBC comments on 1 P 2:5, p. 905.

57 *Ibid.*, p. 105.

58 E. Niermann 'Priest' in K. Rahner (ed), *Encyclopaedia of Theology* (London: Burns and Oates, 1975), pp. 1281–1285.

59 For further discussion on this topic, see part III on the Magisterium, especially the Reformation, Luther and the Council of Trent.

60 LG §10.2.

4 OUR LADY

THERE IS AN impressive and ever-growing body of literature on who and what Mary was and how this is applicable to our lives today. Much of this is devotional in nature, designed to lead us to Jesus through a greater love for his mother. Here, we are interested in the 'bare bones' of what Scripture tells us of Mary.[1] Any extrapolation from the text can only be in the light of what we know of the aims and objectives of the writers. (It seems safe to assume that what the writers said about Mary was part of their overall aim.) So an understanding of why the Scriptures were written can give us some insights into what they say about Mary.

There are several Old Testament passages that are claimed to be referring to Mary

> The following division has been suggested: texts applicable to Mary only by accommodation, Judges 15:9, Proverbs 8, Sirah 24; texts of debatable relevance, Jeremiah 31:22, Psalm 45, the Song of Songs; texts certainly relevant, Genesis 3:15, Isaiah 7:14, Micah 5:2 … Vatican II also pointed to the strong moral link between the Old Testament concept of the 'Poor of the Lord', the *anawim*, and Mary (LG §55).[2]

The 'certainly relevant' texts are 'I shall put enmity between you and the woman, and between your offspring and hers; it will bruise your head and you will strike its heel' (Gn 3:15); 'The Lord will give you a sign in any case: it is this: the young woman is with child and will give birth to a son whom she will call Immanuel' (Is 7:14); 'But you, (Bethlehem) Ephrathah, the least of the clans of Judah, from you will come for me a future ruler of Israel, whose origins go back to the distant past, to the days of old' (Mi 5:2). These texts tell us little about Mary—she will be the enemy of the devil, will become the mother of Jesus while still young (some translations give 'virgin' instead of 'young woman') and will be from the tribe of David, based in Bethlehem.

St Paul only mentions Mary once, and then does not even use her name: 'But when the time had fully come, God sent his Son,

born of a woman, born a subject of the law, to redeem the subjects
of the law, so that we might receive adoption as sons' (Ga 4:4–5).
The overall purpose of the letter is to warn the Galatian church not
to be deceived by those who were arguing that Paul did not have
authority to teach and that it was necessary to observe at least some
Jewish practices. Section 4:1–11 of the letter argues that Christians
are children of Abraham, not by performing deeds of the law, but
by faith. Just as orphans are dependent on guardians until they
reach maturity, so the descendants of Abraham needed the law
until they were redeemed by Christ. The phrase 'born of a woman'
is included to emphasise that Jesus, having a Jewish mother, was
a descendant of Abraham and subject to the law. Belief in Jesus
makes us adopted sons of God through the power of the Holy
Spirit.[3] The phrase 'born of a woman' is used in other writings to
emphasise the frailty of human nature (Jb 14:1) and the unworthi-
ness of man (Jb 15:14, 25:4). Therefore, regarding Mary, this phrase
tells us only that she was a Jewish mother who brought her son up
within the law.

The gospel of Mark is the shortest and almost certainly the
oldest of the synoptic gospels.[4] It is thought to have been written
by the Mark who was a companion of Peter in Rome. Because of
its emphasis on the suffering and death of Jesus, it is thought to
have been written to warn the Christians of Rome that persecution
was coming and was part of being a follower of Jesus. Mark tells
us nothing about the nativity or early life of Jesus, starting his
narrative with Jesus being baptised by John. Mark uses a technique
of 'framing' ideas by repeating a motif before and after the main
point and it is as part of this that he mentions Mary, 'And when
his friends heard it, they went out to seize him, for they said "He
is out of his mind"' (Mk 3:21). There follows the accusation by the
Pharisees that Jesus casts out devils by the power of Satan and
Jesus' reply that a house divided against itself cannot stand. He is
working by the power of the Holy Spirit, not Satan. We then return
to Jesus' family, 'Now his mother and his brothers arrived and,
standing outside, sent in a message asking for him. A crowd was
sitting round him at the time the message was passed to him,
"Look, your mother and brothers and sisters are outside asking
for you". He replied "Who are my mother and my brothers?" And

looking at those sitting in a circle round him, he said "Here are my mother and my brothers. Anyone who does the will of God, that person is my brother and sister and mother"' (Mk 3:31–35). The overall theme of Mark's gospel is the coming of the kingdom of God. So the message of this section is that anyone who wants to be considered as part of Jesus' family and have a share in his house/kingdom needs to do the will of God. A message to the Pharisees is that family connections are not enough, being Jewish is not enough, being Jewish and keeping the laws is not enough. These things are not even essential; all that is needed is to do the will of God—as Mary did.

We cannot be sure whether or not Mary was part of the first group of relatives or joined them later. Perhaps they called on her to come with them in the hope that she would influence Jesus to 'come quietly'. Perhaps she came with them to make sure that they did not use physical force and did not prevent Jesus from continuing his mission. We have no way of knowing.

The only other mention of Mary in the gospel of Mark is 'This is the carpenter, surely, the son of Mary, the brother of James and Joset and Jude and Simon? His sisters, too, are they not here with us?' (Mk 6:3). Some people have read this to mean that Jesus had brothers and sisters in the normal way of family life. They believe that Mary and Joseph had led a normal married life and Mary's virginity only applied until after Jesus' birth. Others point out that both the Aramaic and Greek words for brothers and sisters includes cousins, aunts and uncles. There is no way of deciding between these two possibilities purely on the textual evidence. It has also been pointed out that referring to Jesus as 'son of Mary' departs from the usual practice of naming the father, not the mother. The most popular theory is that Joseph was dead by this point but it has also been suggested that Mark was stressing Jesus' divine origin or that it is an accusation of illegitimacy.[5]

Mark's gospel tells us that Mary still lived in or near Nazareth (3:21–35 and 6:1–6 occur in Nazareth) and takes an interest of some kind in his welfare. We need to turn to the other evangelists to find out more.

Matthew seems to have been writing his gospel for a mainly Jewish-Christian community as he stresses the links with the Old

Testament and the ways in which Jesus fulfils the prophecies about the coming of the Messiah. Matthew starts his gospel with a genealogy. This will be discussed in more detail below in the section on women in the New Testament. Here we only need to note that, in the gospel of Matthew, the angel appears, not to Mary, but to Joseph, who has to make his own 'fiat'. Matthew emphasises the message of his genealogy by calling Joseph 'son of David' (Mt 1:20).

He then tells the nativity story from the viewpoint of Joseph. However he does make clear that Jesus is conceived by the power of the Holy Spirit 'She was found to be with child through the Holy Spirit' (Mt 1:18) and that the birth confirms the prophecy that 'Look! The virgin is with child and will give birth to a son whom they will call Emmanuel' (Mt 1:23). He does not tell us any more about Mary. Other than the various speculations about the significance of the genealogy, all we can glean from Matthew is confirmation that Mary was a virgin at least until after Jesus' birth.[6]

The gospel of Luke is the main source of information on Mary. Here, Mary is at the centre of the nativity story. This is told in parallel with the nativity story of John the Baptist and in a style reminiscent of the Old Testament miracle births. We are first introduced to Mary by the angel Gabriel:

> In the sixth month the angel Gabriel was sent by God to a town in Galilee called Nazareth, to a virgin betrothed to a man named Joseph, of the House of David; and the virgin's name was Mary. He went in and said to her, 'rejoice, you who enjoy God's favour! The Lord is with you!' She was deeply disturbed by these words, and asked herself what this greeting could mean, but the angel said to her 'Mary, do not be afraid; you have won God's favour. Look! You are to conceive in your womb and bear a son, and you must name him Jesus.' ... Mary said to the angel 'But how can this come about, since I have no knowledge of man?' The angel answered ... And Mary said 'You see before you the Lord's servant, let it happen to me as you have said' (Lk 1:26–38).

The first sentence is more Christological than Mariological in that it confirms that Jesus was born of a virgin into the house of David, so he is of divine origin and fulfils the Old Testament prophecies.

We then move on to learn something of Mary herself; she is full of grace and the Lord is with her.[7] Mary is more concerned with the meaning of the greeting than the presence of an angel, but thinks before speaking. When the angel continues with his message, she replies with a simple, practical, reasonable, question.[8] Her response to the angel's message is the key point in the narrative:

> She commits herself to the ways of God in a consummate act of faith (v.38). Luke has shown us a further moment in the early Church's growing understanding of the person and the role of Mary: she is a woman who was called to be the virgin mother of Jesus. Her acceptance of that consummate vocation makes her—in Luke's story line—the first person to risk everything for the sake of Jesus Christ: the first of all believers.[9]

Mary goes with haste to her cousin Elizabeth, who greets her with the phrase 'Blessed are you among women ...' Mary replies with the *Magnificat*. Luke does not specify that Mary stayed until the birth and circumcision of John, as he always finishes one story before beginning the next, but this would have been the normal pattern and fits with the information that Elizabeth was six months pregnant at the time of the annunciation and that Mary stayed with Elizabeth for three months. Luke then gives us the nativity story 'And everyone who heard it was astonished at what the shepherds said to them. As for Mary, she treasured all these things and pondered them in her heart' (Lk 2:18–19). Luke tells us that Jesus was circumcised according to the Law. While at the temple, they met Simeon who prayed over the child in words that the parents did not understand 'As the child's father and mother were wondering at the things that were being said about him, Simeon blessed them' (Lk 2:33). Simeon warned Mary 'and a sword will pierce your soul too' (Lk 2:35). Then Anna came and praised God and told everyone about the child. For the next twelve years, Mary, Joseph and Jesus live in Nazareth and go up to Jerusalem every year to celebrate the Passover. Then we have the story of Jesus staying behind in the temple, to the distress and bewilderment of his parents. When Joseph and Mary find Jesus, it is Mary who speaks, but she gives Joseph his place as Jesus' legal father 'your father and I'. Again, they do not understand what is being said:

'But they did not understand what he meant' (Lk 2:50). Luke ends the story of Jesus' childhood by telling us 'His mother stored up all these things in her heart' (Lk 2:51).

We next hear of Mary in the incident quoted in Mark 3:31–35. Luke makes it clearer than Mark that Jesus is not rejecting his natural family but emphasising that anyone who hears the word of God and does it is part of his family, Mary being the first New Testament example of this. A similar message is contained in the passage where a woman in the crowd cries out 'Blessed is the womb that bore you and the breasts that fed you' and Jesus replies 'More blessed still are those who hear the word of God and keep it!' (Lk 11: 27–28).

Luke's final mention of Mary is in Acts 'With one heart all these joined constantly in prayer, together with some women, including Mary the mother of Jesus, and with his brothers' (Ac 1:14).

Luke is writing for a gentile readership who are not familiar with Palestine or Jewish customs. Acts in particular may have been written with the wives of influential political figures in mind. So Luke stresses the compassion of Jesus and his sympathy towards women. He also stresses that, while Jesus is the promised Messiah, this does not mean that the end of the world is imminent. Jesus stands at the centre of time, not the end. It is now the age of the Church, whose task it is to spread the good news to the ends of the earth. Bearing these motives in mind, what does Luke's gospel add to our knowledge of Mary? He tells us several times that she did not fully understand who Jesus was but pondered on the events of his birth and childhood. Her blessedness is due to her obedience to the will of God, even when she is not sure what is going on and where it might lead her. However it is not a blind obedience as she thinks about these strange events and continues to ponder on them as Jesus grows up. She obeys the rules of the Old Testament regarding Jesus' circumcision and the keeping of the Passover. She stays with the apostles in the upper room after the ascension. So we can say that Mary is a contemplative who obeys the will of God as soon as it is made known to her and works out the whys and wherefores afterwards; she is law-abiding, a loyal wife and devoted mother but also a founder-member of the Church.

We have already mentioned that Luke likes to end one story before beginning another. He also likes to begin and end in the same geographical place. The gospel begins and ends in Jerusalem. Acts begins in Jerusalem but ends in Rome because Rome is the new Jerusalem. Jesus is conceived in Nazareth and ends his childhood there. Do these techniques help us to learn more about Mary? We first hear of Mary at the annunciation when she agrees to become the mother of Jesus and her last appearance is just before Pentecost, the birth of the Church. Some authors suggest that Luke is thus presenting Mary as the mother of the Church.[10] Whether or not she can be described as the mother of the Church from the gospel of Luke alone is probably debatable.[11]

Mary is the only person to appear in the infancy narratives, the public ministry of Jesus and the early Church. This can be seen as a journey of faith, with Simeon warning her that her journey will not be easy. Several writers link his prophecy 'And a sword will pierce your soul too' (Lk 2:35) with the sword of discrimination of Ezekiel 14:17 and conclude that 'Mary, too, the model believer, will have to decide for or against God's revelation in Jesus; family ties do not create faith.'[12]

A simpler explanation, and one that fits with Luke's writing style, is that he is linking the beginning and end of Jesus' life and reminding us that Mary's life will not be an easy one; doing the will of God is more likely to lead to pain and suffering than otherwise and being chosen by God is not linked to worldly success. This was a message that the early Church needed to learn. Both these explanations can be combined:

> Luke inserts this parenthesis into the prophecy of Simeon to instruct his readers that Mary's *fiat* did not lift her out of the necessary puzzlement, anxiety and pain which often arises from the radical nature of the Christian vocation. Despite her remarkable initiation into the Christian mystery, she still had to proceed through the rest of her life, 'treasuring in her heart' the mysteries revealed to her.[13]

So we can add to our knowledge of Mary that she provided the early Church with a model of perseverance in faith despite personal sufferings.

There remains the gospel of John as a Scriptural source of information on Mary. The style is quite different from that of the synoptics and much of the content is unique to this gospel. The overall message is clear, and indeed, is stated at the end of the gospel 'These are recorded so that you may believe that Jesus is the Christ, the Son of God and that believing this you may have life through his name' (Jn 20:31). However modern scholars also believe that John was writing for a Jewish-Christian community, newly evicted from the synagogues. He was telling them that Jesus really was the Messiah and they must remain loyal to him. John uses several formal writing techniques to reinforce his message; symbolism, inclusions, parallelism and even chiastic parallelism.[14] These were all familiar to readers of the Old Testament. Nothing in the construction of the gospel is left to chance and these techniques have to be taken into account when reading the gospel. The first thing to note in John's material on Mary is that he does not call her by her name but refers to her as 'woman' or 'the mother of Jesus'. The word 'woman' is used at the wedding feast of Cana (Jn 2:4) and at the crucifixion (Jn 19:26). The same word is used in the final discourse where Jesus compares the distress turning to joy of the apostles after his death with the distress turning to joy of a woman in childbirth (Jn 6:21). All three of these incidents also include the theme of 'the hour'. Just as a pregnant woman cannot either avoid or choose the time of her suffering, so Jesus must face his hour of suffering, but also triumph, at the appointed time. This will be a time of joy at the birth of the Church.

The symbolism of the wedding feast of Cana is too rich to go into in detail here and not all suggestions are universally accepted. John uses both titles for Mary—'mother of Jesus' and 'woman'. Jesus tells her that his hour has not yet come and she tells the servants to do whatever he tells them. He then performs his first miracle, or 'sign' as they are called in John. The use of the word 'woman' links Mary to Eve, the 'woman' of Genesis 3:1–20 who is tempted by the devil and becomes the mother of all men. Just as Eve ignored the word of God and brought sin into the world, so Mary brings the Word into the world and tells the servants to listen to him. Thus, she initiates 'the hour' of Jesus, which will end on the cross with him addressing her as 'woman' for the second time as he redeems mankind from the sin that Eve introduced. Yet the story also tells us that, during Jesus' public ministry, Mary is important only as a disciple, not as family. The phrase 'what is this to me and to you' is used to distance himself from his domestic family.

> Thus the fourth gospel agrees with the other three that Mary had no role in the ministry as Jesus' physical mother. The Jesus who asked his disciples not to give any priority to family (Mark 10:29–30; Matthew 10:37; Luke 14:26) was not himself going to give priority to family.[15]

The primary purpose of this sign is to show the disciples that Jesus is the fulfilment of the Old Testament promises, often expressed in wedding imagery, of a radical renewal of the covenant which will be accompanied by an abundance of wine (for example, Amos 9:13–14). The incident is important because of its outcome; it 'revealed his glory; and his disciples believed in him' (Jn 2:11).

There are several messages to be read into John's description of Mary and the beloved disciple at the foot of the cross: they represent all the children of God, gathered together by the Son of Man 'lifted up' from the earth (see Jn 3:13–14; 8:28; 11:51–52; 12:32–33); Mary is referred to as 'mother' five times in the section 19:25–27, emphasising her new role vis-à vis the beloved disciple. She is now the mother of the Church.[16] Mary and the beloved disciple stand together at the foot of the cross as examples of perfect discipleship.

A further message from the miracle at Cana is the other miracle at Cana — the healing of the official's son (Jn 4:46–54). John emphasises that both miracles result from examples of perfect faith by constructing both stories along the same pattern. Yet it is the woman who is the first person to have faith in Jesus and to communicate this faith to others 'do whatever he tells you' (Jn 2:5). So what does John add to our understanding of Mary? She is the new Eve, the mother of the Church, the perfect example of faith and of discipleship.

Despite, or perhaps because of, the lack of Scriptural evidence, the figure of Mary has inspired devotion only second to that given to her son. She has been used as an example of every womanly quality desired by the society of the day.[17] Currently, she is seen as a model for women in developing countries who are fighting for both the physical necessities of life and personal and national autonomy.

> The poor have rediscovered her solidarity with them as a village woman, a poor woman of the people, a member of a people oppressed by an occupying force, a refugee woman fleeing with her newborn child from the wrath of a murderous ruler, a bereaved mother of a victim of unjust execution.[18]

This attitude to Mary is not the prerogative of modern feminists or liberation theologians but expresses established devotion to Our Lady. When Pope Pius XII announced the Marian year of 1953–1954, he said that we must pray to the Mother of God for various special groups, including the oppressed, exiles and refugees, the homeless and the prisoner.[19] A year later, when he marked the end of the Year by establishing the feast of Mary, Queen of Heaven, he encourages those persecuted for their faith to pray to her and all to pray to her as the Queen of peace.[20] Mary is also important to feminist theologians;

> Mary is a real woman, surrounded by other women. She is also 'woman', daughter of Zion, the feminine other who rectifies and thereby completes the image of God reflected in humanity. The God of patriarchy becomes the God who mothers all creation when the daughters of Zion become co-equal with the sons.[21]

Such feminist theology is not necessarily vehemently anti-Church, more part of the everlasting struggle to overcome the effects of original sin, 'Your desire shall be for your husband and he shall rule over you.'

> While I think many feminist theologians fail to acknowledge the extent to which Christianity has challenged and overcome some of the more extreme aspects of patriarchy ... it is also true that the Catholic Church still clings to a vision of femininity and masculinity ... that makes it a deeply patriarchal institution. This is despite the fact that in the image of Mary as the archetype of the Mother Church and in the feminine identity given to the Church, there is also a powerful matriarchal element in Catholicism.[22]

Summary

The Old Testament tells us that Mary will be the enemy of the devil, will become the mother of Jesus while still young and will be from the tribe of David.

What do the gospels and Acts together tell us about Mary? Paul tells us that she was a Jewish mother who brought her son up within the law. Mark tells us that Mary still lived in or near Nazareth and takes an interest of some kind in his welfare. Other than the various speculations about the significance of the genealogy, all we can glean from Matthew is confirmation that Mary was a virgin at least until after Jesus' birth. Luke gives us more details: Mary is a contemplative who obeys the will of God as soon as it is made known to her, pondering on it later; she is law-abiding, a loyal wife and devoted mother but also a founder-member of the Church. Luke may be describing Mary as the mother of the Church. John is much clearer on this—she is the new Eve, the mother of the Church, the perfect example of faith and of discipleship.

Modern exegetes, especially women, see Mary as a model for those who suffer poverty and oppression. Her exalted status reminds us that man and woman were created as helpmates, equally loved by God, equally created in his image and equally deserving of respect.

Having examined Scriptural teaching on Mary, we now need to move to the third key area of our plan, the teaching of Scripture on women in general.

Notes

1   See also chapters nine and sixteen on Our Lady and the summaries in part IV.
2   M. O'Carroll, 'Mary in the Bible' in *Theotokos: A Theological Encyclopedia of the Blessed Virgin Mary* (Eugene: Wipf and Stock Publishers, 1982), p. 82.
3   J. Fitzmyer, 'The Letter to the Galatians' in NJBC article 47:25–26.
4   As stated in R Brown, *An Introduction to the New Testament* (New York: Doubleday, 1997), p. 115.
5   See F. Moloney, *Mary; Woman and Mother* (Collegeville: The Liturgical Press, 1989), p. 7 footnotes 9 and 10.
6   S. Loone, 'The Forgotten Annunciation' in *The Pastoral Review* vol. 5 issue 6, pp. 40–44.

7   The phrase 'you who enjoy God's favour' is also translated as 'full of grace' (RSV, with a footnote giving 'O favoured one' as an alternative).

8   There has been some speculation that her reply suggests a vow of perpetual virginity but this is denied by both Moloney (p. 21 f. 18) and the New Jerusalem Bible (p. 1687 f. u).

9   Moloney, *Mary: Woman and Mother* p. 23.

10   *Ibid.*, p. 29.

11   At Vatican II there was great debate over how to present Church teaching on Mary. Eventually, a chapter on her was added to the statement on the Church, *Lumen Gentium*, emphasising her position as mother of the Church, although the document did not use this title. Paul VI gave Mary this title in his concluding address to the 3rd session of Vatican II. See the chapter on Our Lady in part III for more details.

12   NJBC, p. 684 (43:34).

13   Moloney *Mary: Woman and Mother*, p. 27.

14   Chiastic (or inverted) parallelism is a technique of repeating ideas, words or phrases in reverse order, usually represented as A, B, C, B^1, A^1, with the letter representing the key word or idea of the line or section. The central line or section gives us the principal meaning of the passage. It is a common technique in the Old Testament (see Isaiah 55:8) and can extend over many verses. The main proponent of the extensive use of chiastic parallelism in John is Peter Ellis in *The Genius of John: A Composition Critical Commentary on the 4th Gospel* (Collegeville: The Liturgical Press, 1984).

15   R. Brown, *The Community of the Beloved Disciple* (New York: Paulist Press, 1979), p. 195.

16   For details, see Moloney, *Mary: Woman and Mother*, pp. 41–50.

17   See M. Warner, *Alone of all Her Sex* (London: Picador, 1985).

18   E. Johnson, 'Saints and Mary' in F. Fiorenza and J. Galvin, *Systematic Theology*, *vol. 2* (Minneapolis: Fortress Press, 1991), p. 163.

19   Pope Pius XII, encyclical letter, *Fulgens Corona* §39 (1953).

20   Pope Pius XII, encyclical letter, *Ad Caeli Reginam* §50 (1954).

21   T. Beatty, *Rediscovering Mary: Insights from the Gospels* (Liguori: Triumph Books, 1995), p. 119.

22   *Ibid.*, p. 13.

5 WOMEN

In the Old Testament

T HE MOST SIGNIFICANT sayings on women are contained in the first few chapters of the Old Testament. In Genesis 1:27 we are told that God created man and woman in his own image. In Genesis 2:18–24 we are told that woman was made as a helper for man so that he should not be alone and that a man and his wife become one flesh. These two versions of the creation of mankind give us two ways of looking at our relationships with God and with each other.

> Genesis 1 clearly refers to there being an order in creation, the writer of Genesis 2 seems less interested in order and more interested in completeness. Both order and completeness are ways of speaking of perfection. Whereas in Genesis 1 mankind completes and perfects creation, in Genesis 2 man and woman complete and perfect each other.[1]

This perfection is understood by looking at our relationship with nature, with each other and with God. In order to participate in the story of creation, we have to understand and work within our human natures, expressed as both man and woman.

> Genesis 2 is concerned with the relatedness of things one to another. Being related to God, the earth (*adamah*), the garden, the animals and to other human beings is of the very essence of being human … Genesis 1 has a particular interest in the 'divisions' of creation. These divisions promote life and mankind is divided into 'male and female' in order that together, in a whole host of ways, they may participate in the creative activity of God.[2]

In Genesis 3:16 we are told that woman's subjection to man is the result of original sin and not part of God's original plan. The significance of these verses has been explored in depth in John Paul II's series of lectures *The Theology of the Body*, which we will look at in chapter eight.

The other Old Testament references to women are as varied as is human nature and tend to reflect their historical/cultural background. Abigail, wife of Nabal, saves her husband's men from being slaughtered by David, saves David from committing an atrocity and is presented as being wiser than either of them (1 S 25:1–44).[3] Judith and Esther are heroines who saved the whole tribe of Israel. A good wife is a gift from God (Pr 18:22). However women are the cause of man's downfall, from the time of Adam to the present day (Si 25:24) and the male Jew daily thanks God that he was not born a gentile, a woman or an ignoramus.

The Old Testament legal system seems to have given women some protection but on average treats them as second-class citizens. However women were given respect at a domestic level. Sons are instructed to respect their mothers as much as their fathers (Ex 20:12; Lv 19:3; Dt 5:16; 21:18). Women's song and dance were essential parts of festive celebrations (Ex 15:20; Jg 11:34; 1 S 18:6; Ps 68:25; Si 3:11) and cultic festivals (Dt 12:12; Jg 13:20, 23; 1 S 1:1–4; 2 S 6:19). Women were professional mourners at funerals (2 Ch 35:25; Jr 9:16–20).

One interesting group of Old Testament women are the prophetesses—Miriam (Ex 15:20), Deborah (Jg 4), Huldah (2 K 22:14–20; 2 Ch 34:22–28), Noadiah (Ne 6:14) and the wife of Isaiah (Is 8:3).[4] Remembering that Old Testament prophets were not the equivalent of modern fortune-tellers but the messengers of God, bringing his teachings, messages and warnings to the people, these women performed the same task as male prophets. However there was a significant difference:

> Apart from Miriam's ministry in song and the song of Deborah and Barak, women prophets in the Old Testament ministered privately to individuals rather than publicly to large groups ... (They were distinct from priests and kings.) Thus the Old Testament also foreshadows both the New Testament's encouragement of women to prophecy in churches (Acts 21:9; 1 Cor 11:5) and its prohibition of their teaching or governing the whole Church (1 Tm 2:11–15; 3:2; 1 Co 14:33–35).[5]

A similar idea is expressed by Cardinal Ratzinger when discussing the role of women such as Judith and Esther: 'It is significant that the woman always figures in Israel's thought and belief, not as a priestess, but as prophetess and judge-saviour. What is specifically hers, the place assigned to her, emerges from this.'[6]

In the New Testament

Information on the lives of women in first century Palestine is scarce. In keeping with the norms of the day, women's contribution was so taken for granted that it was not considered worth mentioning. We need to remember that, just because a story does not mention the presence of women, it does not mean that they were not there. Of the four versions of the miracle of the multiplication of the loaves, only Matthew's account mentions that there were women and children there and he only does so to add to the dramatic effect of their being five thousand men there; the women and children were not included in the count.

Women play their most important roles at the beginning and end of the gospel accounts. Mark has least to say, starting his gospel with the adult Jesus being baptised. However he does name three of a group of women who had followed Jesus from Galilee and witnessed the crucifixion. Two of them also saw where he was buried and three saw the empty tomb and took a message from the angel to the apostles. One was the first witness of the risen Jesus.

Luke seems to have a more positive attitude to women than Matthew or Mark. His account of the nativity story is from the viewpoint of Mary and he gives us some details of the group of women who travelled with Jesus and the apostles 'With him went the twelve, as well as certain women who had been cured of evil spirits and ailments: Mary, surnamed Magdalene, from whom seven demons had gone out, Joanna the wife of Herod's steward Chuza, Susanna, and many others who provided for them out of their own resources' (Lk 8:2–3).

Luke is the only gospel to include the story of Jesus calling at the home of Martha and Mary, with Martha rushing about preparing a meal and Mary sitting at Jesus's feet listening to him. Jesus tells Martha that Mary's choice (to listen to the word of God) is the one essential in life. Both women are disciples in that they are followers of Jesus. They can be thought of as representing both the active and the contemplative ways of living the gospel message. We learn a bit more about them in the gospel of John (Jn 11:1–44), who tells us that they are the sisters of Lazarus. In the story of the raising of Lazarus from the dead, discussed below, we see that Martha is still rushing about and Mary is still sitting down. When Mary does go to meet Jesus, she throws herself at his feet, which she later anoints with nard. John also tells us that Jesus loved both sisters. He treats them as individuals, not merely the sisters of Lazarus, whom Luke does not even name. He praises Mary for her choices but it is to Martha that he reveals himself as the resurrection and the life. It is Martha who demonstrates a theological understanding and faith equal to that of Peter. So Jesus values both the active and the contemplative life styles and both Luke and John use women to demonstrate this.

Luke is the only evangelist to record the women of Jerusalem weeping for Jesus as he went to be crucified, in contrast to the male crowd shouting 'Crucify him! Crucify him!'. Luke may have included these details to appeal to the Roman matrons who may have been the intended readership of his gospel. His account of the women's involvement in the burial and resurrection is very similar to Mark's version.

As with all aspects of the gospel of John, his message regarding women is complex. In the interests of simplicity, I will concentrate on the three most detailed episodes; the Samaritan woman at the well, the conversation with Martha at Lazarus's tomb and the role of Mary Magdalen on Easter Sunday. Having said that, none of these episodes are simple in themselves and I will be giving a summary of the most relevant points only!

Jesus's conversation with the Samaritan woman is the longest conversation in the gospel. This is remarkable on several counts; Jewish men did not converse with women in public, regarded all women as potential occasions of sin and therefore to be avoided and regarded Samaritan women as permanently unclean. Jesus not only engaged the woman in conversation but treated her as an intelligent person, deserving of his time and worthy to be the first to whom he directly reveals that he is the Messiah (Jn 4:26). She becomes an apostle by bringing word of him to her village. 'Many

Samaritans of that town believed in him on the strength of the woman's words of testimony' (Jn 4:39).[7]

The story of the raising of Lazarus, Jesus's last sign, has links with the first sign, the wedding feast at Cana. In both, women draw Jesus's attention to a problem without actually asking him for help. Mary implies faith in him by telling the servants to do whatever he tells them; Martha also has faith as she says that her brother would not have died if Jesus had been there and that God would grant whatever Jesus asked of him. Yet, like Mary, she does not specifically ask him for a miracle. The following conversation with Martha is significant because it contains one of Jesus's 'I am' statements 'I am the resurrection'. As with the Samaritan woman, Jesus chooses to reveal a fundamental truth about himself and his mission to a woman and she expresses belief in his teaching. There is a parallel between Martha's expression of faith and that of Peter in John 6:69. Martha says 'I believe that you are the Christ, the Son of God, the one who was to come into this world' (Jn 11:27). Peter says 'You have the message of eternal life, and we believe; we have come to know that you are the Holy One of God' (Jn 6:68). It is significant that a woman, who cannot be taught the Torah or given any formal education, gives a confession of faith that is just as theologically accurate as that of the first leader of the Church. Jesus then provides her with proof of his claim by raising Lazarus from the dead. John carefully tells us that it is the fourth day since Lazarus's death. The Jews believed that the soul stayed in or near the body for three days after death so, by the fourth day, there could be no claims that he had simply recovered from a coma of some sort.

The role of Mary Magdalen as the first person to see the risen Lord and to receive instructions from him to tell the disciples that he is risen (in effect, to be an apostle), is discussed below. Here it is worth mentioning that John links this incident with the parable of the Good Shepherd:

> John compares the disciples of Jesus to sheep who know their shepherd's voice when he calls them by name (10:3–5). This description is fulfilled in the appearance of the risen Jesus to Mary Magdalene as she recognises him when he calls her by her name 'Mary' (20:16) … It is clear that John

has no hesitation in placing a woman in the same category
of relationship to Jesus as the Twelve who are included in
the 'his own' in 13:1.[8]

So the gospel of John has some strong messages about the role of
women. They are important in their own right and he does not
refer to them simply as someone else's mother, wife or daughter.
They are worthy of being taught the gospel message, which they
understand just as readily as any man. They can act as valid
witnesses and apostles by spreading the good news. They were
loved by Jesus and regarded as his friends. By mixing and
conversing with women, Jesus is demonstrating that they are not
to be kept in social isolation in order to save men from sinning; it
is up to the men to control their emotions.

   A final point to note is that John involves women in the major
turning points of Jesus's life. The transition from village carpenter
to miracle worker occurs after the prompt from Mary 'They have
no wine' (Jn 2:3). The first revelation of his role as the Messiah is
to the Samaritan woman. The first revelation that he is the source
of eternal life is to Martha (Jn 11:25). This incident also ends his
period as a teacher and miracle worker. He can no longer appear
in public as the Pharisees have decided to have both him and
Lazarus killed (Jn 11:53–54). Mary, presented by John as the sister
of Martha, anoints him in preparation for his death and burial and
thus gives Judas a reason to betray Jesus; Jesus's approval of this
extravagance is the 'last straw' for the apostle whom John portrays
as a thief and already in thrall with the devil (Jn 12:1–8). Women
remain at the foot of the cross and witness his death. A woman
was the first to see the empty tomb and to see the risen Lord.

   Despite John's insistence on the importance of women in the
gospel story, he does not mention them at the Last Supper. We
have left the gospel of Matthew to the end of this section as it has
some unique verses in the genealogy that are important for our
discussion.

Women in Matthew

The New Testament gospels of Matthew and Luke give genealogies
of Jesus. Starting a biography or history with a genealogy was quite
common in Jewish literature as it demonstrated the purity of line

of the subject. This was particularly important for the descendants of Aaron and of David. Before men could be recognised as priests, they had to show that they were descended from Aaron and their wives had to have a purely Jewish ancestry going back at least five generations. Ezra 2:61 gives an example of sons of priests returning from exile and being barred from the priesthood because their genealogies could not be found in the public records. The descendants of David had significance as the source of the promised Messiah.

There is general agreement that Matthew started his gospel with a genealogy in order to show that Jesus was descended from David and was the fulfilment of the Old Testament prophecies about the coming of the Messiah.[9] Other reasons have been suggested. Danielou points out that the phrase 'the book of the genealogy of … ' is echoed in only two places in the Old Testament, Genesis 2:4 and Genesis 5:1 and concludes 'Clearly Matthew is establishing a parallel between the creation of Adam and the incarnation of the Word'.[10] There is also general agreement that Matthew has adapted the material available to him for his own purposes. The genealogy is deliberately divided into three groups of fourteen names each. This might have been a device to make it easier to memorise as there are fourteen names from Abraham to David and the other groups are adjusted to match.[11] It may also be based on the numerical value of 'David' using the system of gamatria.[12] An appealing explanation is given by Graffy —

> The number of generations, three times fourteen, or six times seven, is deliberate. Apocalyptic speculation had asserted that the final age would be the seventh age. Matthew deliberately places the time of Jesus after six groups of seven generations. It is the time of fulfilment.[13]

The three groups have been variously classified as patriarchs, prophets and priests,[14] patriarchs, kings and unknowns[15] and the three stages of Jewish history: up to David shows man as born for greatness; up to the exile shows man loosing greatness and up to Jesus shows him regaining it.[16]

The gospel of Matthew is generally considered not to be sympathetic to women. However Matthew includes some interesting unique material on women. His genealogy names five women:

Tamar, a Canaanite or Aramean, who, through an act of deceit, bore the twins Perez and Zerah by her father-in-law Judah; Rahab, a Canaanite prostitute; Ruth, who was the Moabite wife of Boaz; Bathsheba, who committed adultery with king David while married to Uriah the Hittite and Mary 'of whom Jesus was born'.

Luke places his genealogy after the infancy narrative and baptism of Jesus and before his public ministry. It has several differences to Matthew's list and does not include any women. As women would not normally be included in genealogical lists, Matthew must have had a reason for naming these five. Mary is identified as the mother of Jesus but in such a way that the narrative does not state that Joseph was the father. Matthew perhaps felt that he had to name her as she is the only human parent of Jesus.[17] However, the genealogy is traced down to Joseph rather than Mary because Jewish law only recognised inheritance through the father.

Another aspect of Jewish marriage laws that is important for understanding the genealogies is that of Levirate law marriages. This law applied to marriages where the husband died childless; his brother had a duty to marry the widow and raise children in his name. Here the first son of the marriage was regarded as the legal son of his mother's previous husband and inherited this man's property. So Tamar's first son was the heir of both Onan and of Er as both had died childless. There is an indication of inheritance disputes here, as the narrative tells us that the first-born twin, Perez, had in fact been preceded by the hand of his twin, Zerah, who had been marked as the first by the midwife. We are perhaps being reminded of Cain and Abel, Jacob and Esau. Whether the message is about inheritance disputes or the will of God superseding man-made rules is difficult to say. We know that Perez was recognised as the heir as he is named as an ancestor of Boaz. Despite being the legal heir of Judah's sons, not Judah himself, the verse reads 'may your family be like the family of Perez, whom Tamar bore to Judah' (Rt 4:12). Ruth's first son was the legal heir of Chilion, as he had died childless. Yet, both the books of Ruth and of Matthew name Boaz as the father, 'Salmon fathered Boaz, Boaz fathered Obed, Obed fathered Jesse and Jesse fathered David' (Rt 4:22) and 'Salmon fathered Boaz, whose mother was Rahab, Boaz fathered Obed, whose mother was Ruth, Obed fathered Jesse; and Jesse fathered King David' (Mt 1:5–6). The book of Ruth also tells us that Ruth's firstborn was adopted and raised by Ruth's first mother-in-law, Naomi. Perhaps, while the Levirate law was honoured in practical matters such as inheriting property, genealogies recorded the actual blood links? Another problem is that, on purely historical grounds, Salmon could not have been the father of Boaz. It is possible that Matthew is simply copying the information from Ruth ignorant of, or simply ignoring, its inaccuracies as it suits his purposes. Matthew's genealogy is also an abbreviation of that in 1 Chronicles 2:9–16 but Chronicles uses 'Salma' rather than 'Salmon' as the father of Boaz. Could they be different people, with Chronicles being the correct version? Chronicles also lists Boaz as the father of Obed. Several of the genealogies in Chronicles name women, but as wives and sisters, not as heirs or ancestors. The purpose in naming them seems to be to clarify the line of ancestry of the males. So there is doubt about the source of the genealogy in Ruth:

> This second genealogy cannot be the work of the author of Ruth. Contrary to the whole point of the story, Boaz is named as the father of Obed, Elimelech's name disappears, and Ruth's piety no longer has the same meaning; the law of the levirate and the filial piety implicit in this is lost to view. But a different, universalist theme emerges: the foreigner, Ruth, is the ancestress of David, and hence of Christ, as the gospel was later to emphasise.[18]

The purpose would have been to emphasise the line from Perez to David. The overall purpose of the book of Ruth is to praise the virtue of *hesed,* (fidelity, especially covenant fidelity). This covenant extends to those gentiles who are willing, as Ruth was, to accept the God of the Jews. Rabbinic literature often celebrated Ruth as the true proselyte and interpreted her life as prefiguring Messianic events.[19] A link can be made between Ruth's words to Boaz 'Spread the skirt of your cloak over your servant for you have the right of redemption over me' (Rt 3:9) and those of the angel Gabriel at the annunciation 'The Holy Spirit will come upon you and the power of the Most High will cover you with its shadow' (Lk 1:35).[20]

Several reasons have been put forward for the presence of the first four female names in Matthew's genealogy. Some are more persuasive than others and none are totally convincing. In most cases, they say more about their proposer than about the women involved.

Jerome suggested that, as they were all sinners, they demonstrated that God can save his people from their sins.[21] However several of the male names were also known sinners, so the female names were not necessary. Ruth is not portrayed as a sinner and, in Jewish tradition, Tamar is not recognised as one (Gn 38:26). Even Rahab is hailed as a heroine in both Jewish and Christian tradition (Jos 2:1–21; 6:17, 22–25 Heb 11:31; Jm 2:25). A similar theory is that, as they all entered irregular marital unions, they are preparing us for Mary's irregular pregnancy by reminding us that we should not criticise what God has chosen to bless. This puts Mary in some rather dubious company and seems insulting to her. Also, Ruth's marriage to Boaz was not regarded as irregular, indeed it was held up as an example of fidelity to the Law. Rahab's pre-marital life was irregular but we know nothing of the marriage itself.

Some feel that the inclusion of these women gives Jesus a more inclusive and realistic human ancestry. The women represent the various problems present in all human history, so Jesus is truly human. Luther popularised the idea that, as gentiles and foreigners, they represent the bringing of salvation to the gentiles, a message that Matthew reinforces with the story of the magi.[22] These suggestions are unconvincing as the men of the genealogy had their fair share of problems and did not need women to introduce more, they were not all known gentiles and the Jews regarded Rahab and Ruth as converts to Judaism.

Then there are more factual, historical suggestions, such as that they all play an important role at major turning points in the history of Israel, however this is really only true of Rahab and Bathsheba.[23] A more elaborate argument is that they all have an extraordinary, personal role in the history of the Davidic dynasty. Genesis 49:10 says that the Messiah will come from the line of Judah, and Tamar prevents the tribe from becoming extinct; Rahab, who declared her faith in the Lord (Jos 2:9–10) secured the entry into the promised land; Ruth married the one ordained for her by

Law; Bathsheba ensured that the prophecy of Nathan (2 S 7:8–16) came true by interceding with David on Solomon's behalf. While this theory sounds convincing at first reading, it does not stand up to close examination. In fact Judah had another son who could have continued the line; Rahab acted for all Israel, not just the tribe of Judah; Boaz could have married someone else without affecting the Davidic dynasty; 2 Samuel 7:8–16 refers to a son of David but it is not clear that this also had to be a son of Bathsheba.[24]

We now move on to the more modern, psychological readings of the list. It is suggested that they are examples of women showing initiative and courage when called by God to preserve the God-willed line of his Messiah. As only Mary is aware that she is being so called, this seems unduly complimentary to the others.[25] Again, the theory that they all prefigure Mary's role as intercessor is unconvincing as the women themselves were unaware of this role. They did however act as intercessors, in that their actions saved those around them; Tamar saves Judah from the consequences of his refusal to allow her to have children; Rahab saves her family and kin; Ruth saves Naomi; Bathsheba turns David from being the most powerful king to being the most religious one. So perhaps there is some truth in this theory.

A feminist reading of the genealogy suggests that they all represent those things that men fear in women: Tamar causes death and practises deceit and incest; Rahab practises treason and deceit; Ruth loves another woman and practises incest and deceit; Bathsheba represents the dread of menstrual blood and of draining the man's power, she was an occasion of grave sin for David.[26] Jesus's relationships with women redeem them from this list of faults and fears. However the psychology behind this argument is not universally accepted and the descriptions of the women's motives can only be speculative. It could hold the key to the answer if we look on it as, not redeeming women from these faults, but teaching the apostles that, despite these faults, women are just as loved by God as men. Jesus's treatment of women who were bleeding (Mt 9:20–22) or were adulterers (Jn 8:3–11) gives support to this.

The theory that comes closest to the one that I will describe below is to be found in a commentary on Matthew by a woman theologian:

> The genealogy is best interpreted as examples of 'higher righteousness' ... (those who had the power to act but did not) are taught the lesson of higher righteousness by Tamar, Rahab, Uriah and Ruth ... Additionally, the genealogy highlights women who were initially removed from traditional domestic arrangements; unmarried, separated from their spouse, widowed, or prostitutes. Although the genealogy ultimately associates all the women with men, it also indicates that marriage is not (contrast 1 Timothy) the prerequisite for righteous action or salvation.[27]

While these suggestions are not mutually exclusive and several may be part of the answer, none are entirely convincing.

It may be possible to work out Matthew's reasoning for his genealogy by looking at how he constructs the rest of the gospel. The main theological emphases are Christology, ecclesiology and escatology.[28] The gospel is carefully constructed around five 'great discourses', possibly a reflection of the five books of the Pentateuch. Matthew frequently refers back to the Old Testament and presents Jesus as the new Moses—he has not come to replace the Law but to complete it. He has greater authority than Moses and can adapt the Law 'You have heard how it was said ... But I say this to you' (Mt 5:21–22). He is consistently critical of Jews who do not believe in Jesus and is sympathetic to gentiles. There is general agreement that Matthew was a Jewish Christian writing for a prosperous community, possibly Antioch, around the time of the Christians being expelled from the synagogues. So a major concern is to reassure this community that Jesus is the promised Messiah and his Church is the legitimate heir to the Old Testament promises. Another major concern is to demonstrate that Jesus came to save all who have faith in him, gentiles as well as Jews.

Matthew tells the nativity story from the point of view of Joseph. He breaks it up into five sections, each with an Old Testament quotation. He portrays Joseph as someone who obeys the Law as it has been handed down to him but with thoughtfulness and compassion for the sinner, not in a rigidly legalistic way. His behaviour throughout the events of Jesus's incarnation and birth is blameless. He treats Mary with consideration even when he assumes that she must have sinned. He listens to the word of God and acts upon it without stopping to count the personal cost.

> The hero of Matthew's infancy story is Joseph, a very sensitive Jewish observer of the Law … In Joseph, the evangelist was portraying what he thought a Jew (a true pious believer) should be and probably what he himself was.[29]

In general, Matthew gives a very masculine view of events. The following four scenes show a pattern of Matthew giving shorter versions of the events than either Mark or Luke, suggesting a lack of interest in the events as stories about individual women.

8:14–15 — Jesus heals Peter's mother in law, who then rose and served him,

9:18–26 — a ruler asks Jesus to come to his house and restore his daughter to life,

9:20–22 — a woman who had had a haemorrhage for twelve years is cured by touching the fringe of Jesus's garment as he goes to raise the ruler's daughter from the dead,

26:6–13 — while at the house of Simon the leper in Bethany, a woman comes in and anoints Jesus with expensive ointment. Jesus praises her for preparing him for burial. (This incident is mentioned in all four gospels. Matthew gives the shortest version.) However there is also material unique to Matthew. The Canaanite woman whose daughter is possessed by a demon (Mt 15:21–28) receives slightly more detailed treatment than in Mark, who describes the woman as a Syro-Phoenician (Mk 7:24–30). Bauckham links this incident in Matthew with Rahab, the Caananite ancestor of Jesus:

> Like Rahab she takes the initiative and asks boldly for the kindness she so desperately needs (Josh 2:12–13). Like Rahab she receives the mercy for which she had asked (Josh 6:22–25). Finally, and very importantly, like Rahab, because of her faith, she is a first exception to a rule about Canaanites.[30]

By beginning this story with the woman calling Jesus 'Son of David', Matthew is making a link with his genealogy and reminding the reader that God also shows mercy to gentiles, paving the way for the new Church's mission to all those willing to put their faith in Jesus. (Mark describes the woman as Greek, does not use the phrase 'Son of David' and does not commend her for her faith.)

Another incident unique to Matthew is found in verse 27:19, where we are told that Pilate's wife sent him a message asking him to have nothing to do with 'that righteous man'. This shows a gentile in a good light and emphasises the hatred of the leading Jews towards Jesus.

All four gospels tell us that a group of women followed Jesus from Galilee to Jerusalem and were present at the crucifixion. Mark tells us that 'Mary of Magdala and Mary the mother of Joset took note of where he was laid' (Mk 15: 47) and they went to the tomb as soon as the Sabbath was over. Here they found the empty tomb and were instructed by an angel to tell the apostles to go to Galilee, where Jesus would meet them. 'And the women came out and ran away from the tomb because they were frightened out of their wits; and they said nothing to anyone, for they were afraid' (Mk 16:8).[31] Matthew tells us that Mary of Magdala and the other Mary (presumably the mother of James and Joseph mentioned a few verses previously) were sitting opposite the sepulchre while Joseph of Arimathaea attended to the body of Jesus and rolled the stone over the entrance. They later came back and were met by an angel who told them to go and tell the disciples that Jesus has risen, which they did, meeting Jesus on the way. Luke suggests that many women followed Joseph of Arimathaea to the tomb and returned on the first day of the week. They all saw an angel and reported back to the apostles. John does not mention any women witnessing the burial of Jesus but does say that the tomb was near to the place of crucifixion. He only names one woman, Mary Magdalen, as visiting the tomb on the first day of the week but quotes her as speaking to Peter in the plural 'We do not know where they have put him' (Jn 20:2). While Peter and the other disciple are the first to enter the tomb, it is only Mary who sees the angels and the risen Jesus. Jesus gives her a message for the apostles.

The synoptic versions of the burial and resurrection all stress that the women took careful note of where Jesus was buried, presumably in order to be sure of finding it again when they returned with the spices. Thus, the women were the only ones who could tell the apostles where the tomb was. Matthew and John have the women as the first to see the risen Jesus. All four have the angel/s and/or Jesus giving the women a message to take to the disciples. There are many possible conclusions to be drawn from these few events.[32] Perhaps the most significant for our purposes is that these women met the definition of 'apostle':

> According to Acts 1:2f and 1:21, three things characterise the apostle a) the apostle must have been a disciple of Jesus b) only a reliable witness of the ministry, passion and resurrection of Jesus can be an apostle ... c) but the decisive criterion for apostleship is the fact of having been sent by Christ to proclaim the gospel (Acts 1:8; 10:42).[33]

While it could be debated whether or not the women were disciples, it could also be debated whether or not the apostles met the second criteria, as only the women followed Jesus along the Via Dolorosa and only John was at the foot of the cross. To deny the title of 'apostle' to the twelve would be illogical; if they do not fit the definition, it needs to be reworded. However rewording definitions in order to include women risks the accusation of 'fiddling the evidence', so do they really fit the definition of disciples? The simplest definition is 'A person who freely puts himself in the school of a teacher and shares his views is a disciple.'[34] The dictionary goes on to list the characteristics of Jesus's disciples as being called by Jesus and by the Father; having a personal attachment to Jesus and being willing to share his cross. The 'women of the resurrection' included many who had been cured of various illnesses, who supported Jesus and the apostles from their own resources and who had been followers of Jesus throughout his ministry in Galilee. We know that they were witnesses to both his miracles and his teaching as the angel at the empty tomb tells them to 'Remember what he told you when he was still in Galilee ... And they remembered his words' (Lk 24:6–8). They shared his cross as best they could by devoting their lives to the welfare of himself and his followers, by refusing to desert him and by attempting to give his body the traditional embalming. They obeyed the instructions to tell the apostles of his resurrection even though they must have realised that they would not be believed. They would seem to meet all the criteria necessary for the title of a disciple. They thus meet the three criteria of apostleship listed above. Mary Magdalen has been recognised as having a limited apostolic role ever since St Thomas Aquinas gave her the title of 'apostle to the apostles' but Bauckham suggests that a whole group of women deserve this title:

> Using the word 'apostolic' in this Pauline sense (1 Cor 9:1), the women were apostolic eyewitness guarantors of the traditions about Jesus, and the Gospel stories about their visit to the tomb and encounters with the risen Jesus are the textual form eventually given to the witness that they must have given orally during the early decades of Christian life and mission.[35]

We can now conclude that Matthew, despite his general lack of interest in the activities of women, accepted their apostolic role in the few days after the crucifixion. He is not so much anti-women as too focused on the messages that he is trying to convey to allow space for superfluous detail. So he has not named the women in the genealogy simply to add interest or to make some general point or even to remind us of the sinfulness of women in general. They are there to convey messages relevant to the main concerns of Matthew's gospel.

It seems beyond dispute that the main function of the genealogy is to demonstrate that Jesus is descended from the greatest man of faith, Abraham, and from David, as the Old Testament prophecies demand. It is not necessary to mention the first four women in the genealogy in order to achieve this. So why are they there? Is there a link with Matthew's liking for the number five? Perhaps he is using them to emphasise the need for faith? Do they highlight his themes of Christology, ecclesiology and escatology? I would suggest that, when investigating this, we need to remember Matthew's habit of telling stories from the male viewpoint. Is the important thing about these women actually their male partners?

Tamar (linked with Judah, the fourth male name) Rahab (linked with Salmon, the tenth male name) and Ruth (linked with Boaz, the eleventh male name) are named in the first section and the wife of Uriah is named with David, who both ends the first section and begins the second. So the only link with the number five seems to be that there are five women in total, including Mary. There is certainly a link with the need for faith as all five women displayed faith in God's ability to look after them (see below). There is no obvious link with the three great themes or the five discourses.

Perhaps Matthew wanted to mention Ruth because she was portrayed in Rabbinic literature as prefiguring the Messiah. Having included her, he wanted to make the number up to five. Mary is an obvious choice and the others are included because of their links with Ruth (widows, gentiles, irregular marriages). This argument does not seem very convincing, as the connections between Ruth on the one hand and Tamar, Bathsheba and Rahab on the other do not seem sufficiently strong to be a primary motive for including them. If Ruth was the starting point because of her messianic links, we would expect the other names to be drawn from those women who are said to prefigure Mary, such as Hannah. This leaves the male characters in the stories.

Raymond Brown suggests that 'Davidic parallelism is strong in the genealogy and the last days of Jesus's life.'[36] Perhaps a look at the events of Jesus's last days will show parallels with either the women or the men involved in these four stories.

Matthew 21:1–11 describes Jesus's triumphal entry into Jerusalem, with the crowd hailing him as the son of David. This cry is continued by groups of children in the temple the following day. Over the next few days, Jesus teaches in the temple and answers various accusations from the Pharisees and the Sadducees. The barren fig tree is used by Jesus as an opportunity to tell his apostles that faith can move mountains and 'And if you have faith, everything you ask for in prayer, you will receive' (Mt 21:22). Having just been reminded by children of Jesus's Davidic ancestry, does the barrenness and death of the fig tree and the reference to faith remind us of Tamar (whose name means 'palm tree')? The discussion on the resurrection of the dead with the Sadducees (Mt 22:23–33) certainly does, as it is both based on the same Mosaic law that Judah broke by refusing to allow Tamar to marry his last son and involves a woman who marries several brothers. Perhaps Tamar's refusal to give up, strengthened by her faith in God's justice, is an example for us to follow. Also, Tamar was supported by God because she was motivated by a desire to fulfil the Law, as we should be. Judah, who had earlier agreed to murder, then sell, his brother is at fault in refusing to put his son at risk but keeps his promise of payment to the roadside prostitute, admits his fault and makes amends. Later, he plays an honourable role in his dealings with Joseph in Egypt (Gn 44:18–34). Does his name remind us of Judas, who sold information that put the Son of God's life at risk, tried to return his payment and gave in to despair? Perhaps Matthew's reason for including Tamar is not so much to remind us of her story but to draw attention to the behaviour of Judah and provide a positive parallel to Judas's negative behaviour. This would fit with Matthew's overall lack of interest in the activities of women and his frequent comparisons with the Old Testament. It is almost a happy coincidence that Tamar was highly regarded by the Jews because of her heroic efforts to keep the levirate marriage laws, was a Canaanite and demonstrated faith in God's ability to help her.[37]

Rahab is recognised by future generations as a woman of faith in the God of Israel (Heb 11:31, Jm 2:25) and what she asked for, protection for herself and her family, she received. Bauckham may be correct, and Rahab is linked to the Canaanite woman of 15:21–28 but she was also a recognisable symbol in Matthew's community of both having faith and putting it into effect by good deeds. Could Matthew be using this to draw our attention to the men of the story? Joshua and the two spies do keep their promise to Rahab and save, not only her immediate family but 'all who belonged to her' (Jos 6:23). As with Boaz, they are rewarded for upholding the Law generously. Other than the quote in the story of the fig tree, it is difficult to make a more concrete connection than that. However, bearing in mind Rahab's fame and that she was listed as the mother of Boaz, this may be enough reason for her inclusion. A possible connection with Judas is that they were both traitors—Rahab to her fellow citizens and Judas to Jesus. Because Rahab's behaviour was based on faith in the power of the Israeli God, it had positive outcomes. Because Judas's behaviour was based on greed and selfishness, it had negative outcomes. Rahab also has a connection with Mary; when the Israeli spies are escaping, they warn her not to betray them and she replies 'Let it be as you say' (Jos 2:21), the same phrase that Mary uses to the angel Gabriel at the Annunciation. As the Annunciation story is in Luke, not Matthew, this might be a coincidence, but Matthew almost certainly was familiar with Luke, so there is a possible connection.

Ruth, whose name means 'companion', like Tamar, benefits from the Law regarding a man's duty to his family. Through this, and her faith in the advice of her mother-in-law, they both gain the security that they have been seeking. Boaz acts throughout in a generous and honourable way. Having decided to marry Ruth, he risks losing her by offering her first to the other male relative who had a prior claim under the Law. However he links the offer to the ownership of a field and the combined deal is not attractive to the other relative. Boaz was a wealthy man and could have taken Ruth as either wife or concubine. He could also have offered to do a deal with his relative by sharing out Naomi's inheritance with the field to the relative and Ruth to Boaz. He resisted both these temptations and, by honouring the Law, gained both Ruth and the field. The elders bless the acquisition of Ruth and the field by Boaz with the words 'And through the children Yahweh will give you by this young woman, may your family be like the family of Perez, whom Tamar bore to Judah' (Ruth 4:12). There are no obvious links between the story of Ruth and the passion and death of Jesus. It would be stretching the point to link Naomi's field with that bought by the elders with Judas' thirty pieces of silver or with the 'plot of land called Gethsemane' (Mt 26:36), unless the link is the Judah/Judas parallelism, for which the above quote is relevant. Boaz achieved what he wanted by scrupulously following the Law, Judas by treachery. Boaz prospered and became the great-grand-father of David, Judas killed himself.

Bathsheba is performing the ritual cleansing after her monthly periods when we first meet her. She appeals to David for help when she discovers that she is pregnant and her appeal is answered. Despite David's treatment of both her and her husband, she is looked after and David becomes a reformed person.[38] However his triple sin (adultery, trying to pass the child off as Uriah's, murder) has cost the lives of both Uriah and the child. Bathsheba is not identified by name in the genealogy but as the mother of Solomon and widow of Uriah. It is easy to see why being the mother of Solomon is worth mentioning, but why is being Uriah's widow important? Uriah had to be killed by David because he refused to break the code on ritual purity during battle by having sex with Bathsheba. He also refused to enjoy his home comforts while the rest of his unit slept in the open. Uriah is seen to be a good soldier, leading by example and obeying both ritual and military codes. David on the other hand, corrupted by wealth and power, has sent his army into battle while he himself stayed behind to enjoy the safety and luxury of his palace. Judas also began as a zealous Israelite and was not questioned as one of the elite followers of Jesus, indeed he was given the responsibility of managing the group funds. Like David, he became corrupted. He began to steal from the funds and one sin led to another. Unlike David, he gave in to despair.

There is, literally in some cases, a red thread running through the stories of these women. Tamar bore twins and, during labour, the midwife tied a red thread round the hand of the twin, Zerah, who should have been the firstborn but was pushed out of the way by Perez.[39] Rahab identified her house by a red cord given to her by the two spies (Jos 2:18), reminding us of the blood of the Passover lamb smeared on the lintels of the Israelites, saving them from death (Ex 12:7). Bathsheba has just finished menstruating when David first sees her and her husband is killed in battle at David's command. According to Matthew, the soldiers put a scarlet cloak round Jesus when mocking him as 'king of the Jews' (Mt 27:29).[40] The colour red is not mentioned anywhere in the book of Ruth, although the story begins with the death of three men and it is these deaths that move the story in the necessary direction.

Looking at the women of the genealogy from the point of view of their male partners makes it difficult to examine any parallelism with the women already discussed who were present at the death, burial and resurrection of Jesus. Any connections are at a more subtle level than simply one group of women having things in common with another group of women. Looking at the stories of these women in their own right, they remind us that, if we have faith in God and obey the Law, everything we ask for we will receive. There may be parallelism with the barren fig tree. The story of Tamar has parallelisms with the debate on the resurrection with the Sadducees. The four women have several points of contact other than simply being ancestors of Jesus. We have already mentioned their faith. Tamar, Ruth and Rahab are gentiles and Bathsheba was married to a gentile. Tamar and Bathsheba cause repentance and reform in the male of the story. Tamar and Ruth depend on the levirate laws to secure their place in society. Bathsheba and Rahab are caught up in wars and both take active steps to ensure the safety of their immediate family (Bathsheba ensures that Solomon is anointed as king). Tamar, Ruth and Bathsheba are all widowed. Tamar and Rahab have both played the part of prostitutes. Ruth is not a prostitute but does take the initiative and offer herself to Boaz. Tamar, Rahab and Ruth are all praised in New Testament literature.

It is also possible to find links between the men of these stories and Jesus's last few days. The clearest link is in the Tamar story where Judah, whose name is the same as Judas, can be seen as a positive parallel to Judas's negative behaviour. Indeed, it is possible that, having chosen Tamar for this reason, Matthew added the other three as much because of their links with each other as for any parallelism with Judas. Perhaps, wanting to include Tamar and having to include Mary, he simply chose the most relevant other names to make up the number five. His choice was influenced by both the women's links with each other, their strong faith and a certain parallelism between their male partners and Judas. Jesus's warning to the chief priests and elders that 'tax collectors and prostitutes are making their way into the kingdom of God before you' (Mt 21:31) may also have influenced the choice as the genealogy reminds the listeners that indeed prostitutes can be favoured by God if they have faith, so Jesus is not simply using empty rhetoric.

The parallelism between these men and Judas is speculative but can be made, at least tentatively. Joshua used Rahab's treachery to achieve his goal, just as Jesus did not stop Judas from betraying him even though Matthew makes it clear that Jesus was aware of his plans. Joshua won through being honourable. He continued to win as long as he obeyed God but lost when God's rules were broken. Boaz resisted temptation and kept the Law, receiving the blessing of the elders; David became corrupt but repented and trusted in God's forgiveness. In each of these cases, the people were in a similar situation to Judas but reacted in a positive way, with the result that they prospered. The need to have faith in adversity, one of Matthew's main messages, is thus emphasised in the first few verses of his gospel. For Matthew's community of Jewish Christians, steeped in the Old Testament, the mere mention of the women's names would have been enough to allow them to bring to mind the moral behind the stories of both the women themselves and the men involved with them. Giving the male names would not have carried so specific a message as they played a far more varied role than did the women. Matthew's portrayal of Joseph in the infancy narrative gives a role model of the perfect Jewish male for the readers to aspire to.

Summary

We have seen that Tamar enabled Judah to keep the levirate law despite his own reluctance. Boaz too was in no hurry to fulfil his obligations to Ruth until she reminded him of them. David may have continued in his corrupt lifestyle if Bathsheba had not expected him to take responsibility for her pregnancy. Rahab provided practical help for the escaping spies. So the message from Matthew's genealogy is speculative but could be that the role of women is to be examples of faith; of keeping the law and being 'helpmates' to the men in their lives, encouraging them to do the right thing. This notion of 'helpmate', as in Genesis, does not include any suggestion of inferiority. The four women of the genealogy were determined, innovative, independent. They sometimes used forceful and bold methods of helping the men to do the right thing. Judah even admits that Tamar had behaved in a more honourable way than he had. There is no hint of them being passive or self-effacing. They are not walking three steps behind their lords and masters with downcast eyes but standing behind those to whom they have a responsibility in order to push them in the right direction.

Back to the main debate

Jesus's own attitude to women has been used as an argument both for and against giving women greater leadership roles in the Church. He lived in a society where women had almost no place in religious rituals, were not taught the Torah and were excluded from the main chamber of the synagogue. They were regarded as incapable of acting as witnesses and could not inherit property, although they could own it if they had been gifted it by their fathers or husbands; hence Luke 8:2–3 can say that a group of women provided for Jesus and the apostles 'out of their own resources'. They were not meant to engage in conversation with men, even including their husbands.[41] Jesus ignored all of these conventions by conversing with, and even teaching, the Samaritan woman at the well (Jn 4:1–39):

> It is the longest recorded private conversation in the gospels. Jesus declares openly for the first time, and that to a woman, that he was the Messiah. When she asked him in what place God should be worshiped, Jesus did not tell her not to bother about liturgical questions and to leave that to men; on the contrary, he gave her a full and satisfying answer.[42]

Jesus told Martha that Mary had chosen the better part by attending to him rather than domestic tasks (did the phrase 'sitting at his feet' signify his acceptance of Mary as a disciple/pupil, as it would have done if the author had been describing a male and a rabbi?); he treated Martha and Mary as friends and it was to Martha that he first revealed that he was the resurrection (Jn 11:25); he defended a prostitute (Lk 7:36–50) and an adulteress; he worked miracles on and for women (Lk 7:11–15); he used stories of women in everyday situations as parables (Mt 13:33, Lk 15:8–10, Lk 18:1–8); he defended the stability of marriage. This was more revolutionary than it sounds to us today. In those times Shammai law allowed a man to divorce his wife only for sins against chastity but Hillel law allowed a man to divorce his wife for minor domestic failings, or even if he found someone else more attractive. Women had no right to divorce their husbands. As he approached the end of his ministry, Jesus foretold that the actions of the woman at Bethany who anointed him with nard would be remembered wherever the gospel was preached (Mt 26:13).[43] Pope Benedict XVI, in a Wednesday address interprets this as Jesus wanting 'These witnesses of the Gospel ... to be known and their memory to remain alive in the Church.'[44] Jesus told Mary Magdalen to bear witness to the apostles of the empty tomb on Easter morning (Jn 20:17). St Thomas Aquinas, despite his Aristotelian view of women (see chapter ten), gave Mary Magdalen the title 'apostle of the apostles' because of this and said of her 'Just as a woman had announced to the first man the words of death, so also a woman was the first to announce to the apostles the words of life'.[45] A modern scholar, who also might not be expected to emphasise women playing a prominent role, concludes that 'In short, Jesus' attitude towards women was, in his time, "revolutionising", through him, woman is placed "side by side with man, having equal rights as a child of God"'.[46]

Despite this attitude to women, Jesus did not appoint any women to leadership roles, either during his lifetime or after the resurrection. Many arguments have been given for this, the most common being that the social/cultural attitudes of the day would not have allowed for this. Jesus did however redefine leadership:

> In sayings such as Luke 22:25–27, quoted above, and in his parabolic action of washing the disciples' feet (Jn 13:1–20), Jesus made the demeaning service of women and slaves to their social superiors characteristic and therefore also emblematic of the role of leaders in the new kind of social group he was fashioning among his followers. [47]

Those arguing for change say that, because Jesus was restricted in his choices by social/cultural attitudes, the Church is not bound to adhere to his example.[48] There have been several studies of the subject:

> In April 1976 the revamped PBC completed a two-year requested study of the Bible as to whether women could be ordained to the priestly ministry of the eucharist. The confidential results were illegally 'leaked' to the press (text and comments, see *Women Priests* (ed. L and A Swidler; NY 1977) 25–34, 338–46). Reportedly, PBC member scholars voted 17–0 that the New Testament does not settle the question in a clear way, once for all; 12–5 that neither Scripture nor Christ's plan alone excluded the possibility. The documentation behind the reasoning was not published.[49]

Despite this, the Church still teaches that she does not have the authority to ordain women as priests. The modern Church has given several reasons for refusing to change. The simplest summary is that we cannot tell what Jesus's motives were and therefore cannot judge whether or not his choice of men only was intended to be binding for all time. We do know that the apostles followed his example in this. We therefore have to accept this practice in a spirit of obedience, assuming that there was a good reason, which may be one of those already suggested or something still to be revealed.[50]

St Paul

The remaining works of the New Testament do not help us greatly as their comments on women are as contradictory as those of the Old Testament. St Paul has traditionally been seen as against women taking a public role in the Church (1Co 11:1–16; 1 Co 14:34–35), yet entrusts Phoebe with his important letter to the Romans (Rm 16:1), describing her as a deaconess. The address by Pope Benedict XVI, quoted in chapter one and below, comments on this passage: 'Although at that time the title (*diakonos*) still did not have a specific ministerial value of a hierarchical character, it expresses a genuine exercise of responsibility on the part of this woman in favour of that Christian community'. [51]

In Paul's first letter to Timothy, he lists the qualities needed in elders and deacons. Verse 11 refers to women. This is often taken to refer to the wives of deacons but the original Greek lends itself most readily to the sense of the women as deaconesses.[52] He seems to regard women praying and prophesying as a regular occurrence, acceptable as long as their heads are covered (1 Co 11:5). He encourages women converts to convert their pagan husbands (1 Co 7:16) and uses the homes of women as local centres.[53] He describes Euodia and Syntyche as having struggled hard for the gospel with him (Ph 4:2–3). 2 Timothy 1:5 is usually assumed to mean that Timothy was educated in the faith by his grandmother and mother, whom Paul praises. Even before his conversion Paul seems to have recognised that Christian women played an active part in Church life, as he included them in his persecutions 'Saul then began doing great harm to the church; he went from house to house arresting both men and women and sending them to prison' (Ac 8:3). Despite these examples of a positive attitude to women, Paul also forbids women to teach or have authority over a man (1 Tm 2:11–13; Tt 1:5–9). There have been many attempts to explain Paul's teaching. Before looking at some of them, it is helpful to remind ourselves of the most relevant texts. These can be found in Appendix II, section B.

While we tend to think of the debate over the role of women in the Church as belonging to the last fifty years or so, it can be traced back much further. The early Quaker women were an amazingly heroic group who fought and suffered for the rights of women to speak in public long before the words 'suffragette' or 'feminist' had been invented. Possibly the earliest written theological work from a feminist viewpoint was written by Margaret Fox, wife of George Fox, founder of the Quaker movement. She wrote a paper on the right of women to speak in public in 1666. Commenting on 1 Corinthians 14:34–35, she argued that St Paul was ordering both men and women to be silent if there was malice, disorder or confusion in the assembly. (The previous verses set out the way of running an assembly.) If people are speaking in tongues, they must do so in an orderly way, with an interpreter: 'If there is no interpreter, then let each of them be quiet in the assembly and speak only internally and to God' (1 Co 14:28). So both men and women are under the Law of obedience and must not speak unless they can meet the conditions for an orderly assembly as laid down in chapter 14:26–34. Similarly 1 Timothy 2:11 is addressed to women purely in relation to their husbands, not to the rest of the Church. His other comments apply only to those women who had been immodest in their dress. This general line of interpretation is supported in an address at the Wednesday General Audience given by Pope Benedict XVI:

> The apostle admits as something normal that women can 'prophecy' in the Christian community (1 Cor 11:5), that is, pronounce herself openly under the influence of the Holy Spirit, on the condition that it is for the edification of the community and in a dignified manner. Therefore, the famous exhortation 'the women should keep silence in the churches' must be relativised (1 Cor 14:34).[54]

When Pope Paul VI declared Teresa of Avila and Catherine of Siena to be Doctors of the Church in 1970, he had to explain how women could be classed as teachers despite Paul's teaching. He distinguished between teachers within the official hierarchy of the Church and the duty of all the baptised to actively participate in the priesthood of all the faithful. The title of 'Doctor of the Church' does not entail hierarchical functions of teaching and can therefore be given to women. Also, through baptism, women have a share in the priesthood of all the faithful and 'This enables and obliges her to "profess before men the faith received from God through the Church" (*Lumen Gentium* chapter 2, no 11)'.[55]

A modern variation on the theme comes from Morna Hooker.[56] Her arguments are dense but can be summarised as follows. In general, if a woman dishonours her head, she dishonours her husband and God. Her head, uncovered, is the glory of her husband (and a distraction to other men?). Normally, covering her head in public symbolises that she is acting under the authority of her husband. However, when praying, the woman should be giving glory to God and the angels, not to her husband. So the symbolism involved in women in Church wearing veils is related but different to the normal practise. Women now take an active part in prayer and prophecy, for which they need authority and power from God; by covering the glory of man, woman can reflect the glory of God with 'authority'/ 'a veil'

> Far from being a symbol of the woman's subjection to man, therefore, her head-covering is what Paul calls it—authority: in prayer and prophecy she, like the man, is under the authority of God. Although the differences of creation remain, and are reflected in the differences of dress, it is nevertheless true that in relation to God 'there is neither male nor female; for you are all one in Christ Jesus'.[57]

Hooker's argument, then, is that women with uncovered heads are giving glory to their husbands, with covered heads are giving glory to God and acting under His authority. There is also a suggestion that 1 Corinthians 14:34–35 is an interpolation as it appears at the end of the chapter as verses 39 and 40 in some of the ancient manuscripts.[58]

Yet another argument appears in NJBC, based on 1 Corinthians 11:1–16: Paul is arguing that men and women are made differently by God and should express this difference in their appearance. The Corinthians seem to have taken a previous teaching of Paul on the equality of the sexes too literally and have abandoned the tradi-tional hairstyles. The result is that they cause confusion to visitors—male homosexuals of the period generally grew their hair long and dressed it in elaborate styles more fitting to women, lesbians copied the spartan style with short hair.[59]

> Paul takes it for granted that women play a leadership role in the community (v5). She enjoys this authority precisely as a woman, and so must stress her sex by her hairdo ... The basis of Paul's argument in vv 7–10 was the creation account, which Jews used to prove that woman was inferior to man ... Paul now flatly excludes such an interpretation. 'Woman is not otherwise than man.' In the Christian community woman is no whit inferior to man ... 'All things are from God:' the fact that woman is the source of man (contrast v3b) is also a manifestation of the divine intention and nullifies the Jewish interpretation of Gen 2:21–23.[60]

Whatever one's interpretation of these passages of Paul (and the similar ones in 1 Tm 2:11) it is useful to remember the advice of 2 Tm 2:14: 'Remind them of this, and charge them before the Lord to avoid disputing about words, which does no good, but only ruins the hearers'. Instead, we need to remember the 'analogy of faith' and look at the teachings of Paul as a whole. Each individual letter is addressed to a specific community, often in response to abuses and problems within that community. It is therefore dangerous to focus on any one section without comparing it with the rest of the works of Paul. Paul advises married couples to treat each other as equals, to love and respect each other. He reminds us that, before God, there is no male and female but all are equal. Combined with his acceptance of women as prophets, house leaders, messengers and helpers, his strictures on women's behaviour in Church can easily be dismissed as culturally defined. However this is a very dubious methodology, open to wishful thinking and even abuse.

One writer who has worked hard to present a non-polemical solution to Paul's attitude to women is Edmund Clowney:

> Paul, then, teaches both the headship of the man over the woman and the interdependence of the man and the woman. It would be a mistake to suppose that the second statement cancels the first. Rather, it qualifies the first by showing that the subordination is with respect to roles, not being.[61]

He points out that Paul is using the model of a family in his teachings on how the Church should be organised. Just as the father is the head of the household, so men are responsible for the churches. He differentiates between public, authoritative teaching and governance, which are reserved to men, and more private teaching and leadership, which can be exercised by women. He bases this approach on the creation account in Genesis. He concludes that women must not be in positions of authority over men because this disturbs the natural order:

> Eve's initiative reversed the relationship that she should have maintained with Adam. She decided to eat of the tree, and Adam followed her. When the Lord pronounced the curse against the woman, he reinstated a relationship that Eve had reversed in her sin.[62]

Clowney argues that Paul accepts that women can exercise ministry but not in a ruling function. Thus they can pray in public as this does not involve bringing God's authoritative word to the Church. As long as it is done in an orderly way, anyone can pray during the services. Similarly, anyone can prophecy as 'When a woman has the prophetic gift, she speaks the word of the Lord. Her authority is not her own but the direct authority of the Lord.'[63] He interprets 1 Timothy's comments on women and deacons as referring to women deacons, not the wives of deacons.[64] Paul refers to Phoebe as a deacon and describes her as a servant of the church of Chenchrea, using language that suggests that she holds a specific office in that church rather than that she is a general helper. He also commends her to the community in Rome in language that suggests that she has an official position in the Church:

> The charge Paul gives the Roman church concerning Phoebe does not merely commend a friend to their fellowship. He formally requests recognition for Phoebe, and full support for her activities ... If Paul had not called Phoebe a *diakonos* at all, the fact of his commending her for support by the Roman church in her work indicates that she is entitled to formal recognition in any case.[65]

For a writer who insists on the headship of men and the subordination of women, this argument for recognising Phoebe as exercising an official role in the Church might seem surprising. The key to Clowney's logic is his differentiation between ruling and serving, reminiscent of Bauckham's assertion, quoted in the previous section, that Jesus had redefined leadership as an act of service:

> We must not forget that the offices of bishop/elder and deacons are different, and that, in this letter (1 Tim) and elsewhere, rule is a distinguishable function for which gifts of the spirit are provided (1Tim 5:18; Rom 12:8; 1Cor 12:28).[66]

There is therefore no contradiction in his conclusion that women were, and can be again, ordained deacons in the Church. 'Paul asked the Roman church to recognise Phoebe, not only as a deacon of Cenchreae, but also as one authorised to discharge a mission in Rome. He charged the church to aid her in her ministry.'[67] One of the attractions of Clowney's argument that the key to understanding Paul's teaching on women is in separating activities involving exercising authority from those of service is that it allows us to look at the teachings of Paul as a whole. The seeming contradictions can be explained without having to resort to suggestions of interpolations, male prejudice or cultural conditioning. Even if 1 Corinthians 14:34–35 is an interpolation, a commonly held belief, it does not affect his basic argument. However, to accept Clowney's interpretation of Paul is to accept that, while women can be ordained as deacons, they cannot be ordained as elders/bishops or priests.[68] For some, this is unacceptable discrimination, illogical and a misinterpretation of Scripture. We will need to turn to Tradition and the Magisterium to find out whether or not his arguments are compatible with the rest of Church teaching.

Summary

Women were created by God as equal to men but different. Both are created in the image of God. Because of the sin of Eve, women have to constantly struggle to have this equality accepted by men. This struggle between good and evil can be seen in the laws of the Old Testament. Jesus demonstrated that the various taboos of the Old Testament no longer applied. There are many possible explanations of the teachings of Paul on the role of women, both at home and in Church. Of the examples that we have looked at, the one that seems to give the best 'fit' is that of Edmund Clowney. He argues that women can exercise an official diaconal ministry of service to the community, but not one that includes a ruling function.

Notes

1   R. Nixon, *The Priority of Perfection* (Edinburgh: Movement for Whole Ministry in the Scottish Episcopal Church, 1994), p. 7.

2   *Ibid.*, p. 10. See part III on the Magisterium for ideas on priesthood as relationship.

3   See also the discussion on Matthew's genealogy on the role of women vis-à-vis their male relatives.

4   Isaiah's wife's title of 'prophetess' may have been honorific, as we only know her as a mother. See S. Ackerman, 'Isaiah' in C. Newsom and S. Ringe, *The Women's Bible Commentary* (London: SPCK, 1992), p. 164.

5   'Prophecy' in the *New Dictionary of Biblical Theology*.

6   J. Ratzinger, *Daughter Zion: Meditations on the Church's Marian Belief* (San Francisco, Ignatius Press, 1977), p. 20.

7   See the section 'back to the main debate' for further comments on this episode.

8   R. Brown, *The Community of the Beloved Disciple* (New York: Paulist Press, 1979), p. 192.

9   For example, W. Barclay, *The Daily Study Bible vol. 1* (Edinburgh: St Andrew's Press, 1975), chapter 10.

10   J. Danielou, *The Infancy Narratives* (London: Burns and Oates Ltd., 1968), p. 12.

11   See Danielou *The Infancy Narratives*.

12   B. Viviano, 'The Gospel According to Matthew' in R. Brown, J. Fitzmyer, R. Murphy, *The New Jerome Biblical Commentary* (London: Geoffrey Chapman, 1990), 42:10, p. 635.

13   A. Graffy, *Trustworthy and True: The Gospels Beyond 2000* (Dublin: The Columba Press, 2001), p. 169. The number seven generally symbolises completion, for example, the seven days of creation.

14   Danielou, *The Infancy Narratives*.

15   A. Graffy, *Trustworthy and True*, p. 169.

16   Barclay, *The Daily Study Bible vol. 1*.

17   But Luke does not name Mary, instead saying 'Jesus ... being the son, so it was thought, of Joseph son of ... '(Lk 3:23).

18   *New Jerusalem Bible* footnote to Ruth 4:18–22.

19   See M. O'Carroll, *Theotokos: A Theological Encyclopedia of the Blessed Virgin Mary* (Eugene: Wipf and Stock Publishers, 1982), p. 31.

20   Several commentators link Boaz's skirt with the protective wings of the Lord

(See NJBC 35:19).

21 Similar arguments are put by R. Brown: 'it is the combination of the scandalous or irregular union and of divine intervention through the women that explains best Matthew's choice in the genealogy.' See *The Birth of the Messiah* (London: G. Chapman, 1977), p. 73.

22 See Brown *The Birth of the Messiah*, p. 72.

23 See F. Moloney *Mary: Woman and Mother* (Collegeville: The Liturgical Press, 1989), p. 11.

24 For details of this, and other arguments, see R. Laurentin, *The Truth of Christmas* (Massachusetts: St Bede's Publications, 1986), p. 340.

25 See Moloney, *Mary: Woman and Mother*, p. 11.

26 See A. Ulanov, *The Female Ancestors of Christ* (Enfield: Daimon Verlag, 1993).

27 A. Levine, 'Matthew' in C. Newsom and S. Ringe (ed.), *The Women's Bible Commentary* (London: SPCK, 1992), p. 253.

28 R. Brown, *An Introduction to the New Testament* (New York: Doubleday, 1997).

29 R. Brown, as quoted by R. Rolheiser in *The Catholic Herald* 11 December 2009.

30 R. Bauckham, *Gospel Women: Studies of the Named Women in the Gospels* (Edinburgh: T and T Clark, 2002).

31 The Revised Standard Version gives a footnote saying that some ancient manuscripts conclude Mark with the women reporting to Peter and the other apostles. The NJB concurs, with extra details of other possible endings. For a discussion on the women's reactions, see Bauckham, *Gospel Women*, p. 286.

32 For some of them and references to other sources, see Bauckham, *Gospel Women*, p. 257.

33 A. Javierre, 'Apostle' in K. Rahner, *Encyclopaedia of Theology* (London: Burns and Oates, 1975).

34 X. Leon Dufour, 'Disciple' in *Dictionary of Biblical Theology* 2nd ed. (London: Burns and Oates, 1988).

35 Bauckham, *Gospel Women*, p. 189.

36 Brown, *An Introduction to the New Testament*, p. 218.

37 Ulanov points out that the faith of all the women was not a blind, passive thing but gave them the courage to use their initiative and imagination (see *The Female Ancestors of Christ* p. 13). The early Christians needed a similar courage.

38 It can be argued that it is not Bathsheba who causes this reform but the prophet Nathan (see 2 S 12:1–15). However Nathan would not have needed to reproach David if Bathsheba had not first appealed to him and he had not tried to evade the consequences of his actions.

39 A reminder of the other Old Testament stories of the second son being favoured over the first?

40 This example is something of a red herring, as the soldiers used their red capes as the nearest they could find to the purple cape that a king would wear. Mk 15:17 says 'they dressed him up in purple'.

41 See M. Hauke, *Women in the Priesthood? A Systematic Analysis in the Light of the Order of Creation and Redemption* (San Francisco: Ignatius Press, 1988), p. 327.

42   J. Morris, *Against Nature and God: The History of Women with Clerical Ordination and the Jurisdiction of Bishops* (London: Mowbrays, 1973), p. 114.

43   The identity of this woman is unsure. Early Church tradition linked her with Mary Magdalen but the synoptics do not name her and John presents her as Mary the sister of Martha. R. Brown suggests that the gospel writers are conflating two separate incidents.

44   Pope Benedict XVI, Address at Wednesday audience (14 February 2007). Also in Position Paper no. 425, p. 163.

45   *Ibid.*, p. 165.

46   Hauke, *Women in the Priesthood?*, p. 329, quoting Oepke, p. 785.

47   Bauckham, *Gospel Women*, p. 164.

48   See Hauke, *Women in the Priesthood?* p. 334 for a brief summary of the most common arguments and his replies.

49   NJBC, 72:38.

50   See S. Butler, *The Catholic Priesthood and Women. A Guide to the Teaching of the Church* (Chicago: Hillenbrand Books, 2007).

51   Pope Benedict XVI, Address at Wednesday audience (14 February 2007). Also in Position Paper no. 425, p. 166.

52   The footnote to verse 11 in the NJB is 'This instruction is probably intended for deaconesses, see Rm 16:1, rather than for the wives of deacons.' The RSV adds a note 'i.e., deaconesses'.

53   In both Acts and the epistles of Paul, all assemblies of the early Church take place in the homes of women (see J. Morris, *Against Nature and God*, p. 1).

54   Pope Benedict XVI, Address at a General Audience *Women of the Early Church* (14 February 2007). Also in Position Paper no. 425, p. 165.

55   Pope Paul VI 'Teresa of Avila: Sublime Mission' in *L'Osservatore Romano*, 8 October 1970, p. 7, column 1.

56   M. Hooker, *From Adam to Christ: Essays on Paul* (Cambridge: CUP, 1990).

57   *Ibid.*, p. 120.

58   See Morris, *Against Nature and God*, p. 121 and NJBC commentary on 1 Co 49:64, p. 81. However see also the comments by Hauke, *Women in the Priesthood?* pp. 365–396, discussed in the section 'The Analogy of Faith: The Theological Argument'.

59   J. Murphy-O'Connor '1 and 2 Corinthians' in J. Dunn (ed.), *The Cambridge Companion to St Paul* (Cambridge: CUP, 2003), p. 80. This argument is also suggested in Ziesler, *Pauline Christianity* (Oxford: OUP, 1990), p. 121.

60   J. Murphy O'Connor, 'The First Letter to the Corinthians' in NJBC 49:54, p. 809.

61   E. Clowney, *The Church* (Leicester: Inter-Varsity Press, 1995), p. 218.

62   *Ibid.*, p. 219.

63   *Ibid.*, p. 230. This interpretation is supported by J. Behb 'prophecy' in G. Kittel *Theological Dictionary of the New Testament, vol. II* (Michigan: Eerdman's, 1964), p. 665 commenting on 1 Corinthians 12 and 14. 'The principle … means in fact the controlling of the wild torrent of spiritual outbursts in the channel of the clear and disciplined but no less genuine and profound operation of the Spirit through the Word.'

64 Partly on the grounds that there is no mention of the wives of bishops and that the requirements for the women are very similar to that for deacons. See also page 46 and notes 48 and 51.
65 Clowney, *The Church,* p. 232.
66 *Ibid.,* p. 234.
67 *Ibid.,* p. 235.
68 Clowney uses the word 'ordination' to mean 'a blessing that invokes the presence of the Spirit for the work to which the individual is set apart', p. 234.

6 CONCLUSIONS FROM SCRIPTURE

W E HAVE NOW had a brief look at what Scripture is and what it has to say on the structure of the Church and the role of women, especially Mary. We have seen that Scripture is the inspired word of God. It cannot be altered or added to, but does need interpretation and explanation. This is one of the primary duties of the bishops of the Church.

The Church was established by Jesus Christ in order to spread the message of the coming of the kingdom of God. He appointed the twelve apostles as its first teachers, with Peter as their leader. They were given the authority to 'bind and loose'. In order to bring their message to 'all nations', they had to pass on their authority to their successors. The first example of this was the electing of Matthias to replace Judas (Ac 1:15–26). Jesus Christ exercised the functions of priest, prophet and king. He passed these functions on, in different ways, to the apostles as the leaders of the Church and to all the baptised.

Mary is held up as the perfect example of woman and mother. However the most that we can say from Scripture is that Mary was a young Jewish girl who was 'full of grace'.[1] As the 'new Eve', she is the enemy of the devil. She was a contemplative and the perfect model of faith; she was law-abiding, a loyal wife and devoted mother but also a founder-member of the Church, indeed the mother of the Church.

Women, with some notable exceptions, play a minor role in Scripture. This can be traced back to their expulsion from the Garden of Eden and the punishment given to them, 'Your yearning will be for your husband, and he will dominate you'. From then on, the relationship between men and women is one of a constant struggle to resist this effect of sin, which leads to tyranny, oppression and an impoverished society, and to achieve equality, both in the home and in the wider society, leading to a harmonious co-existence that allows both sexes to maximise whatever gifts they have been given. Only when this harmony is achieved can we claim to have the sort of society that was God's original intent. The writings of St Paul give us a good example of this struggle. Many

writers looking for a greater role for women in the Church argue
as follows:

> St Paul himself teaches the equality of men and women,
> either in marriage or in the service of the Church. However
> his writings on the behaviour of women in church have been
> used to deny women an active role in the Church throughout
> its history. Modern scholarship has shown that these writ-
> ings can be interpreted in the light of their cultural setting.
> A modern reading of them shows that they were directed at
> communities where the behaviour of both men and women
> at Christian gatherings had become unruly and where there
> was considerable sexual license. Christians had a duty to set
> a good example, both at home and in public.

While these arguments may be valid, they can be overplayed and
involve at least some 'educated guesses'. A more conservative
approach is that women can be servants of the Church but not rulers.

So what messages can we identify so far? The first is that the
Church is bound by the words of Scripture. She can translate and
re-interpret them for every generation but she cannot add to, delete
or ignore any part of them. Any re-interpretation that depends
more on wishful thinking than good scholarship will not bear good
fruit. Next, we saw that the Church was established by Jesus (see
especially Mt 16:18–19) as a hierarchical structure whose function
was to spread the good news of the Kingdom of God. The apostles
were the founder members and had the authority to make whatever decisions were necessary for the good of the Church.

The place of women in this Church is not clear. Mark and Luke
show that Jesus treated women with respect and ignored the
conventions of the day regarding women. Matthew seems to be
suggesting that the role of women is to provide the conditions
necessary for their male relatives to do the will of God. John gives
a similar but stronger message: women play crucial roles at all the
key moments in Jesus's life, helping him to do the Father's will;
they are the recipients of key statements about his mission; they
are loved by him and have the right to lead lives of either active
or contemplative discipleship. However it is difficult to separate
out the will of God from the cultural influences. Genesis 2:21–24,
the example of Jesus and the writings of Paul show that equality

is something to be worked towards. We can look to Mary for ideas on just how this equality is to operate. She was part of Jesus's life at all its stages, gave absolute obedience to God and pondered on the word of God. Despite this, Mary was not given an apostolic role by Jesus. She was not sent out with the apostles, is not mentioned at the Last Supper and, while she was said to be in the upper room, is not mentioned as receiving the Holy Spirit at Pentecost. Was this a sign that women were not to play a leading part in the Church or merely an acknowledgement that the socio-cultural conditions of the time would not allow for this? The argument can go either way and Scripture alone will not solve it. This is where Tradition and the Magisterium need to be consulted.

Before moving on, I would like to introduce some ideas to be returned to later. Perhaps, because Mary was already full of grace, she did not need to receive the sacrament of ordination at the Last Supper or the sacrament of confirmation at Pentecost. Mary, as the only perfect human being, had no need of the sacraments. She had experienced the indwelling of God in a physical way by carrying Jesus in her womb and in a spiritual way all her life. Perhaps Jesus did not ask Mary to be an apostle, not because he did not want to give women leading roles in the Church, but because he had another job for her. Perhaps Jesus did give Mary a leading role in the Church as its mother. We have seen that the Gospel of Luke hints at this and the gospel of John makes it explicit. The Church has given her this title but perhaps it needs to be pondered on more than it has been. How does this affect her role as a model for all other women in the Church?

In order to answer this question, we need to turn to the Tradition of the Church and see what it tells us of the Church and the role of women within it.

Notes

[1]   The traditional greeting of the angel Gabriel, the more accurate translation is 'you who enjoy God's favour'. The New Jerusalem Bible says that this is shorthand for 'you who have been and remain filled with the divine favour'. See the footnote to Lk 1:28. The RSV uses 'full of grace' but gives 'O Favoured one' as an alternative. I have used 'full of grace' as it is the more familiar phrase.

PART TWO

Tradition

7 SOME GENERAL NOTES

T HE NOTION OF Tradition is one of the great stumbling blocks in ecumenical debate. As with all such issues, much of the problem lies in centuries of dust-covered misunderstanding and hostility. This is not surprising, as this is an area that is rather poorly understood even in Catholic circles.

Tradition can be defined as 'The transmission of the Gospel in and through the Church from Christ and the apostles.'[1] To begin to understand its role in the Church, we need to return to Scripture and remind ourselves of the instructions that Jesus gave to the Apostles. Matthew tells us 'Go, therefore, make disciples of all nations, baptise them in the name of the Father and of the Son and of the Holy Spirit, and teach them to observe all the commands I gave you. And look, I am with you always, yes, to the end of time' (Mt 28:19–20). Mark tells us 'And he said to them, "Go out to the whole world: proclaim the gospel to all creation" ... while they, going out, preached everywhere, the Lord working with them and confirmed the word by the signs that accompanied it' (Mk 16:15–20). Luke says 'He then opened their minds to understand the Scriptures ... And now I am sending upon you what the Father has promised. Stay in the city, then, until you are clothed with the power from on high' (Lk 24:45–49). John has a 'double ending'. In verse 20:30, we are told 'There were many other signs that Jesus worked in the sight of the disciples, but they are not recorded in this book. These are recorded so that you may believe that Jesus is the Christ, the Son of God, and that believing you may have life through his name.' In chapter 21 we have the story of Jesus telling Peter to look after his sheep and the comment about John, which is usually interpreted as a comment on him outliving the other apostles.[2] The gospel then ends with the same message as in 20:30. If we combine these passages, we find that Jesus told the apostles to wait in Jerusalem until they received the Holy Spirit, then to go out to the whole world preaching the good news. He would be with them and would confirm their teaching by signs. Nowhere does he tell them to write an account of his life and teachings, either theological or historical; their job is to teach. Indeed, we are told that it would be impossible to write down everything that Jesus said and did. The writings that we know as the Scriptures were written down bit by bit and gathered together by the early Church. In making up the canon of Scripture, as discussed earlier, they depended on Tradition and the influence of the Holy Spirit to guide their selection. The apostles fulfilled their task of handing on the good news in several ways:

> This commission was faithfully fulfilled, first by the apostles who, by their oral preaching, by example, and by observances handed on what they had received from the lips of Christ, from living with him, and from what he did, or what they learned through the prompting of the Holy Spirit.[3]

While the apostles, or their followers, did write the gospels and epistles, they preached more than they wrote, did not write down everything that they knew (Jn 20:30; 21:25; 1 Co 11:34; 1 Th 5:1–2; 2 Th 2:5, 15; 2 Jn 12) and tell us to observe the traditions that had been taught to them:

> St Paul gave this advice to the Thessalonians: 'So then, brethren, stand firm and hold to the traditions which you were taught by us, either by word of mouth or by letter' (2 Thess 2:15); he congratulated the Corinthians because they 'maintained the traditions even as I have delivered them to you.' (1 Co 11:2): just as without repeating them he reminded the Thessalonians of the instructions he had given them verbally (1 Th 4:1–2; 2 Thess 2:15); finally he told the Corinthians that he would settle a certain number of points at his next visit (1 Co 11:34).[4]

St Paul, as quoted above, used the plural 'traditions'. In order to avoid confusion, the Church developed the practise of using the word in the singular and with a capital first letter. Thus, Tradition meant the unchanging practise of the Church, based on the teachings of the apostles. Modern practise is to reduce the use of capitals to a minimum. This has resulted in some confusion over the meaning of the word 'Tradition', to the extent that the 1993 Catechism felt the need to clarify the use of the word in the singular as opposed to the plural, more everyday meaning.

> Tradition is to be distinguished from the various theological, disciplinary, liturgical or devotional traditions, born in the local churches over time. These are the particular forms, adapted to different places and times, in which the great Tradition is expressed. In the light of Tradition, these traditions can be retained, modified or even abandoned under the guidance of the Church's Magisterium.[5]

The general principle of having an unwritten Tradition is not unique to the early Church. The Old Testament worked on the same principle. The Jews had the Scriptures and Talmud of the Old Testament and the Mishna of the Common Era. Both Talmud and Mishna were binding rules of daily life. The Talmud in particular was regarded as the word of God, given to Moses verbally. Because Tradition preceded Scripture, does not make it superior to Scripture.

> Hence there exists a close connection and communication between sacred Tradition and Sacred Scripture. Both of them, flowing from the same divine wellspring, in a certain way merge into a unity and tend towards the same end … Therefore both sacred Tradition and Sacred Scripture are to be accepted and venerated with the same sense of loyalty and reverence.[6]

The relationship between Scripture and Tradition was debated at Vatican I, as it had been a major issue for the reformers. Luther's policy of '*sola scriptura*' had to be addressed.[7] Luther denied that the Church had any authority to interpret Scripture. In a reply to Erasmus, he berated him: 'Is it not enough to have submitted your judgement to Scripture? Do you submit it to the Church as well? — why, what can the Church settle that Scripture did not settle first?'[8] The Church was confident in her teaching that Scripture on its own was not capable of sustaining the life of the Church. There had to be a mechanism for applying the message of Scripture to each generation, for checking any innovative interpretations, for validating all the rich liturgical and spiritual practises of the Church. The existence of an unwritten Tradition, of which the Church was custodian, met these needs. While the theologians of the time were agreed on the existence of both Scripture and Tradition, they were divided on the issue of how they related to each other. Some insisted that all truths were contained in both Scripture and Tradition and others thought that some truths could be contained only in Scripture and others only in Tradition: 'The first draft submitted to the Fathers of the Council stated that the Gospel in question was found and handed down to us partly in the holy Scriptures and partly in unwritten Traditions: *partim ... partim*.'[9] The final draft replaced *'partim ... partim'* with *'et'*, thus leaving the debate open. Even today, there are reputable scholars in both camps. It must be noted that the teaching of the Council referred only to apostolic Tradition. There are also ecclesiastical traditions, some of which have a direct divine or apostolic link,[10] some of which are modifications of apostolic practise[11] and some of which are purely ecclesial.[12]

As mentioned in chapter three in the section on the apostles as successors of Christ, the apostles began their preaching mission only after receiving the Holy Spirit:

> The Spirit is promised and given to the apostles and, in them, to the Church, so that they may be witnesses to the ends of the earth and the end of time (Acts 1:8)... In all this the Holy Spirit is not acting personally in the sense that his work is new or different from Christ's; he realises and gives an inner depth to what was said and done once and for all by Christ, which is the Gospel (cf. John 14:26; 16:12–13).[13]

The continuing existence of a universal Church with a shared body of beliefs and practises is due to the work of the Holy Spirit: 'For where the Church is, there also is the Spirit of God; and where the Spirit of God is, there is the Church and every grace. And the Spirit is truth.'[14] It is this trust in the working of the Holy Spirit in the Church that gives her the ability to pass on the apostolic teaching with confidence and authority.

Summary

Tradition is the name given to all the unwritten teachings of the apostles. It is the mirror image of Scripture. Together they form the deposit of faith entrusted to the Church and provide checks and balances for each other. The Holy Spirit guides the Church in her task of taking the gospel to the ends of the earth. This includes interpreting Tradition for each generation.

Notes

1   Y. Congar, *The Meaning of Tradition* (San Francisco: Ignatius Press, 2004), p. 57.
2   P. Perkins, 'The Gospel According to John', in NJBC 61:243, p. 985.
3   DV §7 (1965).
4   Congar, *The Meaning of Tradition*, p. 34.
5   CCC, §83b.
6   DV §9.
7   One of the foundation stones of Reformation theology, the slogan *sola scriptura* expressed the belief that Scripture was the sole source of Christian theology. Only those teachings that could be directly linked to Scripture had any binding force. (See McGrath, *Christian Theology: An Introduction* 3rd ed. (Oxford: Blackwell Publishing Ltd., 2001), p. 69).
8   M. Luther, 'The Bondage of the Will' in J. Dillenberger, *Martin Luther: Selections from His Writings* (New York: Anchor Books, 1961), p. 170.
9   Congar, *The Meaning of Tradition*, p. 41.
10 For example, attendance at Sunday Mass.
11 For example, the sacraments, some liturgy.
12 For example, some liturgical practises.
13 Congar, *The Meaning of Tradition*, p. 52.
14 St Irenaeus of Lyons, *Adversus Haereses*, II, 24, 1 in SC 211, p. 474. Translated from the Latin by a monk of Pluscarden Abbey. The Latin reads 'Ubi enim Ecclesia, ibi et Spiritus Dei, et ubi Spiritus Dei, illic Ecclesia et omnis gratia: Spiritus autem Veritatis.'

8 THE CHURCH

WE HAVE JUST seen that the teachings of the apostles included unwritten Tradition that has been handed down through the generations. The Church itself is both guided by and guides this, through the Holy Spirit. While the Church can grow and adapt itself to many different situations, it must stay true to this Tradition. In order to see just what this entails, we need to take a brief look at how the Church developed through the centuries.

The Church in History

All institutions have identifiable stages of development and this includes the Church. The post-resurrection church's first stage can be defined as the 'sub-apostolic age' as it was the years when people still has personal memories of the apostles. Then there was the age of the martyrs when Christianity was persecuted by the Roman authorities. This ended with the emperor Constantine legalising Christianity in 313. Since then the Church has been, to a greater or lesser extent, involved in the problems of state. Some argue that it became corrupted at this point and has never recovered, others that it was an essential part of its expansion.

The years up to Constantine are sometimes referred to as the pre-Nicene Church.[1] One of the main features of this period was the growing sense of community between the local churches. We can see from the letters of St Paul and Acts that the early Church consisted of discrete groups, usually in the large cities:

> Still, each local church was seen as possessing all that was necessary for its functioning as a church. Once evangelized and equipped with supervisors and presiders, once the community had been initiated into the Christian Scriptures and had been taught about the mysteries of baptism and eucharist, such a church associated with a city or part of a city could manage on its own.[2]

Despite this autonomy, we can identify several customs designed to nourish links between the various churches. As early as *c.*140 AD, Justin the Apologist records that the eucharistic prayers included prayers for all Christians, wherever they may be. The earliest Church leaders from the time of Clement and Ignatius exchanged and circulated letters of encouragement and exhortation. There seems to have been a very early acceptance of the pre-eminent position of the bishop of Rome and Clement of Rome felt that he had a duty of leadership over the church of Corinth. Just a few years later, Ignatius of Antioch addresses the Church in Rome as 'The church holding chief place in the territories of the district of Rome'.[3] By the time of the 'Tome of Leo' in AD 449, the authority of the bishop of Rome was well established. By the time of the first general council in Nicaea in AD 325, the bishops had already cooperated in several regional councils and were in the habit of gathering to assist at the installation of a new bishop. This practice was made compulsory at the Council of Nicaea (canon 4).

Gradually the churches organised themselves into regions with one bishop in charge of each region. There was a certain hierarchy among these regions based on their apostolic links, geographical location and political influence. Rome had strong links with both Peter and Paul, was the political centre of the known world and was in a convenient geographical position. So it is not surprising that it was quickly recognised as the senior church:

> The church of Rome intervened to re-establish order in the trouble spot of Corinth (see 1 Clement); it exercised a broad pastoral care for those troubled about penitential practices (see the *Shepherd of Hermas*); a Roman bishop undertook initiatives in regard to certain Eastern churches to settle disputes about the date of Easter; Rome had available a list of episcopal succession and eventually drew ecclesiastical conclusions from that list; a member of the Roman church formulated in the Apostolic Tradition appropriate liturgical practices; Rome undertook special acts of charity, notably financial support for other churches.[4]

The earliest descriptions available to us of the emerging Church come from the writings of the group of people known as the 'Early Fathers' or the 'Apostolic Fathers'. These were Clement of Rome (died *c*.97 AD), Polycarp (died *c*.155 AD), Ignatius of Antioch (died *c*.110 AD) and Irenaeus of Lyons (*c*.130–200 AD).[5] There is also the document, the *Didache*, which may have been composed as early as the end of the first century.

It is generally accepted that Clement was the fourth bishop of Rome, after Peter, Linus and Anacletus. Other than being the author of *The First Epistle of Clement*, nothing else is known of him. The epistle was written to the church in Corinth after they had ejected their leaders and installed new ones more to their liking, probably about AD 96. Clement writes as one with authority to rebuke bad behaviour and teach the virtues of peace and harmony. How he acquired this authority is not clear:

> Why the Church of Rome felt called upon to involve itself in the affairs of the church of Corinth we do not know, but Clement's tone does not falter and his authority seems assured … Although Clement does not write like a pope exercising his extraordinary jurisdiction, maybe a step had already been taken in that direction.[6]

The Church in Corinth was a turbulent one from the beginning, as is evident from the letters of St Paul. By the time of Clement, the fourth bishop of Rome, things do not seem to have changed. His epistle was written to them about the year 96 in an attempt to bring some order and peace to the community. One of the main aims of the epistle is to clarify the role of the Church leaders and emphasise the need for the Church to accept their authority:

> For Clement, the Christian ministry is something established by Christ and handed down from the apostles, along with the Christian Gospel and Christian teaching (ch. 42). In this chapter the ministers are referred to as 'bishops' and 'deacons'; elsewhere, however, Clement calls them 'presbyters'. The Christian ministry clearly stands in an apostolic succession, but the position of the bishop within this ministry lacks the clarity it assumes in later Christian Tradition.[7]

Clement argues that the Church leaders deserve respect and obedience because their authority does not depend on their personal qualities but on their position as descendants of the apostles. They have been chosen as leaders of the community by the apostles themselves and therefore have inherited the same authority that was exercised by the apostles. In chapter forty-two of the epistle, Clement traces authority as coming from God, through Christ, to the apostles:

> So, therefore, when the apostles had been given their instructions, and all their doubts had been set at rest by the resurrection of our Lord Jesus Christ from the dead, they set out in the full assurance of the Holy Spirit to proclaim the coming of God's kingdom. And as they went through the territories and townships preaching, they appointed their first converts—after testing them by the Spirit—to be bishops and deacons for the believers of the future. (This was in no way an innovation, for bishops and deacons had already been spoken of in Scripture long before that; there is a text that says, *I will confirm their bishops in righteousness, and their deacons in faith.*)[8]

Clement goes on to remind the Corinthians that the practice of appointing leaders comes from Moses, who was given a sign from God that the House of Levi was to serve in the priesthood.[9] The apostles, under the same authority, not only appointed bishops and deacons, but also made provision for their successors: 'They proceeded to appoint the ministers I spoke of, and they went on to add an instruction that if these should fall asleep, other accredited persons should succeed them in their office.'[10] As such, the bishops and deacons must be treated with respect for as long as they discharge their duties honourably:

> It is shameful, my dear friends, shameful in the extreme, and quite unworthy of the Christian training you have had, that the loyal and ancient church of Corinth, because of one or two individuals, should now be reputed to be at odds with its clergy.[11]

St Ignatius was the third bishop of Antioch. He was taken from there to martyrdom in Rome, probably in AD 110. On his journey, he wrote seven letters to other churches which were preserved by Polycarp and became widely known. The letters are similar in content, speaking of the glories of martyrdom, the importance of obedience to the bishop as a means of unity within the Church and teachings against docetism. In the following example, Ignatius starts from the premise of the unity of the Eucharist and moves from that to the authority of the bishop:

> Make certain, therefore, that you all observe one common eucharist; for there is but one Body of our Lord Jesus Christ, and but one cup of union with his Blood, and one single altar of sacrifice—even as also there is but one bishop, with his clergy and my own fellow-servitors the deacons. This will ensure that all your doings are in full accord with the will of God.[12]

In this next example, Ignatius is making basically the same point but reverses the order. This time, he moves from the need to show obedience to the bishop and clergy to the authority of the bishop being the one necessary condition for a valid Eucharistic celebration:

> Abjure all factions, for they are the beginning of evils. Follow your bishop, every one of you, as obediently as Jesus Christ followed the Father. Obey your clergy too, as you would the Apostles; give your deacons the same reverence that you would to a command from God. Make sure that no step affecting the church is ever taken by anyone without the bishop's sanction. The sole eucharist you should consider valid is one that is celebrated by the bishop himself, or by some person authorised by him. Where the bishop is to be seen, there let all his people be; just as wherever Jesus Christ is present, we have the catholic church.[13]

St Irenaeus of Lyon was also concerned with fighting heresies and his main work is the multi-volume *Against Heresies*. He paid particular attention to the need for unity under the bishops, who had received their authority from the apostles. He placed great emphasis on the role of Tradition in maintaining the purity and continuity of apostolic teaching against false doctrines, especially gnosticism:

> In this order, and by this succession (the papacy), the ecclesiastical Tradition from the apostles, and the preaching of the truth, have come down to us. And this is most abundant proof that there is one and the same vivifying faith, which has been preserved in the Church from the apostles until now, and handed down in truth.[14]

The Council of Constantinople of AD 381 gives us the first formal, doctrinal mention of the Church: 'We believe in ... one Holy Catholic and apostolic Church.'[15] During these early centuries of the Church, theologians had to defend the Church against both persecution and heresies. Christians needed a clear summary of just what it was that united them and was worth dying for. This period is marked by writings on such topics as Christology, the Trinity and grace which remain normative today.

In addition to the teachings of the early fathers, quoted above, on the structure of the Church, with its bishop, priests and deacons, there was debate over the nature of the Church. Clement had reminded us that the purpose of these Church ministers was to proclaim the coming of the kingdom of God and we have already seen that this was a foundational theme of the synoptic gospels, especially Matthew. These two aspects of teaching on the Church came together in the writings of Augustine, mainly in his work *The City of God*. This city is present on earth: 'I promised that (given God's gracious help) I would first refute the enemies of the City of God, who honour their own gods above Christ, the founder of the City.'[16] This City that Christ founded is the Church: 'Now philosophers against whose attack we are defending the City of God, that is to say, God's Church, think that ...'[17] The City, and therefore the Church, consists of both good and bad but only God can judge which is which. In the meantime, the Church, because it is founded by Christ and has a hierarchical structure with Christ as its head, has authority to teach and govern. Since St Augustine, this identification has never been challenged and the Church consistently claims authority by virtue of this identity.

The Second Vatican Council produced two documents of relevance to our topic, *Lumen Gentium* and *Gaudium et Spes*. Both avoided any hard and fast definitions. The most relevant section of *Lumen Gentium* is §5: the Church was founded by Jesus when he preached the arrival of the kingdom. This kingdom has to grow and spread and it is the Church's mission to achieve this. *Gaudium et Spes* included a section on the role of the Church in the modern world (section IV). It variously described the Church as 'the universal sacrament of salvation' and 'founded by Christ in time'. It has 'a saving and an eschatological purpose which can be fully attained only in the future world'.[18] The Church has but one purpose: 'that God's kingdom may come, and that the salvation of the whole human race may come to pass.'[19]

Despite the many post-Vatican II documents, there is little to add to *Lumen Gentium* and *Gaudium et Spes*. *Evangelii Nuntiandi*, written in 1975, describes the Church as 'The messenger of the Good News of Jesus Christ' and 'The visible sign of the encounter with God which is the Church of Jesus Christ'.[20] The Church has inherited the task of evangelisation started by Jesus:

> There is thus a profound link between Christ, the Church and evangelisation ... we can hear people ... continually claiming to love Christ but without the Church, to listen to Christ but not the Church, to belong to Christ but outside the Church. The absurdity of this dichotomy is clearly evident in the phrase of the Gospel 'Anyone who rejects you, rejects me'.[21]

Christifideles Laici was written in 1988. It quotes Pope Pius XII as defining the Church in 1946 as 'the community of the faithful on earth under the leadership of the Pope, the head of all, and of the Bishops in communion with him. These are the Church ...'[22] The kingdom is only mentioned by quoting from *Lumen Gentium*. *Ut Unum Sint* on ecumenism, written in 1995, refers to the Church only in reference to her sister churches. It does endorse *Lumen Gentium's* statement on the existence of holiness and truth in other churches: 'many elements of sanctification and of truth are found outside of its visible structure. These elements, as gifts belonging to the Church of Christ, are forces impelling toward catholic unity.'[23] *Ecclesia de Eucharistia* was written in 2003. It describes the Church as 'The People of the New Covenant'[24] but also talks of 'our communion with the Church in Heaven'.[25] It quotes *Lumen Gentium* §3 'The Church, as the Kingdom of Christ already present in mystery'. Here, the use of 'kingdom of Christ' emphasises earthly things. Scripture has three phrases; the 'kingdom of God', 'the kingdom of Heaven' and 'the kingdom of Christ'. The first two are synonymous. They refer to God's kingly rule and can be taken as being in either the present or the future tense. The third refers to the post-resurrection Church and was used for the first time by Peter in his speech to the crowd at Pentecost.

The only remaining document of note is the Catechism of the Catholic Church published in 1994. It examines the Church in the context of the creed. It traces the beginnings of the Church back to Adam and Eve: 'The gathering together of the People of God began at the moment when sin destroyed the communion of men with God'.[26] Other than that, it relies heavily on *Lumen Gentium*. It does extend *Lumen Gentium's* treatment of the dictum of the medieval Church that 'Outside the Church there is no salvation' by suggesting that 'Reformulated positively, it means that all salvation comes from Christ the Head through the Church which is his body.'[27]

It is important to remember among all these definitions and official statements that each local parish church and its congregation is part of the universal Church and the universal Church is present in it whenever the faithful gather together. So each individual member of the Church has a share in its dual mission of spreading the gospel and growing in holiness.

Summary

While many possible meanings of the word 'church' are acknowledged, its normal usage in Church documents is to signify a community of believers. There is agreement that the Church has the mission of continuing Jesus's task of proclaiming the coming of the kingdom. As part of this mission, the apostles were given the authority to loose and to bind (Mt 18:18; Jn 20:23). Peter has a pre-eminent position among them (Mt 16:18; cf. Lk 22:32). When Jesus told the apostles to take the gospel to all nations and that he would be with them to the end of time (Mt 28:20), he gave them to understand that their authority was to be passed on to all future generations. (See also 2 Tm 1:6.) Thus, the Church claims that bishops in direct succession from the apostles have a share in their authority to rule the Church. In order to exercise this authority, each individual bishop must be in communion with the universal College of Bishops both 'vertically' through history and 'horizontally' through the synods, congregations and papacy of his time.

> Hence one is constituted a member of the Episcopal body in virtue of sacramental consecration and hierarchical communion with the head and members of the body ... The order of bishops, which succeeds to the college of the apostles

and gives this apostolic body continued existence, is also the
subject of supreme and full power over the universal Church,
provided we understand this body together with its head the
Roman Pontiff and never without this head.[28]

The Church is hierarchical in structure by the will of Christ and must
not be confused with secular hierarchies. She is not an educational
establishment charged with preserving and passing on the teachings
of Jesus; she is the kingdom of God, the body of Christ, the sacrament
of salvation. Hence the rules that apply to secular hierarchies do not
necessarily apply to the Church. No one, male or female, has a right
to any office in the Church or 'promotion' within any department.
Office holders are servants of God and therefore of the Church;
promotion brings greater duties, not more money and power.

The office-bearers in the Church receive their authority through
the sacrament of ordination. In order to get a clearer understanding
of the hierarchy of the Church, we need to look at how the offices
of bishop, priest and deacon developed and how they are linked
together by the sacrament of ordination.

The Sacrament of Ordination

The Catechism of the Catholic Church defines the sacrament of
ordination as follows:

Holy Orders is the sacrament through which the mission
entrusted by Christ to his apostles continues to be exercised
in the Church until the end of time: thus it is the sacrament
of apostolic ministry. It includes three degrees: episcopate,
presbyterate and diaconate.[29]

It is the development of these three degrees of bishop, priest and
deacon that interests us here. The history of this development is
not as straightforward as the above statement may suggest. To
understand how it became as it is today, we need to go back to its
roots in the Old Testament.

Old Testament background

The concept of having people set aside for specific cultic duties is
common to most cultures. Today in Western societies, an outside
observer would be forgiven for assuming that these duties

included playing football and acting in TV dramas. However we
do still have a group of people set aside as religious leaders. The
role of priests and ministers has a very long history as Christianity
traces its theology of the priesthood back to the priesthood of the
Old Testament.[30] At the time of the patriarchs, we hear of Abraham
and his descendants offering sacrifices at sacred altars (Gn 12:7;
22). The head of the family exercises priestly functions; the only
person given the title of priest is the mysterious Melchizedek
'Melchizedek king of Salem brought bread and wine; he was priest
of God most high' (Gn 14:18). Once the Israelites have escaped
from Egypt and begin to form themselves into a nation, a hierarchy
develops. Moses is the leader, favoured by God and recipient of
the Ten Commandments. Next is his brother Aaron and Aaron's
sons Nadab and Abihu. Then there is a group of seventy elders
(Ex 24).[31] Aaron and his sons are set aside for priestly duties, with
holy garments to wear 'to give dignity and magnificence' (Ex 28:2)
and elaborate ordination rites (Ex 29; Lv 8). Later, the whole tribe
of Levi is also set aside for priestly duties (Nb 1:47–51; 3:5–13).[32]
These are very much centred on the Ark of the Covenant and, later,
on the temple. It is the duty of the priest to make daily offerings
of animals and grain as atonement for individuals and for the
community (Lv 1). There are also sin and guilt offerings by
individuals, through the priest. Peace offerings were made by
individuals or families in thanksgiving or to fulfil a vow.[33] Priests
are holy and must not defile themselves with practices that are
allowed for others (for example, they must only marry virgins (Lv
21:13). They must not have any physical blemishes (Lv 21:21). In
addition to their temple duties, priests act as proclaimers and
interpreters of the Torah and have a juridical role. During the times
of the monarchy, the king also performed religious rites.

> In the monarchy, the king performs several priestly func-
> tions ... He offers sacrifice, from Saul (1 Samuel 13:9) and
> David (2 Samuel 6:13,17; 24:22–25) ... he blesses the people
> (2 Samuel 1:18; 1Kings 8:14). However ... he is rather a
> patron of the priesthood than a member of the sacred caste.[34]

Local synagogues developed after the destruction of the temple in
575 BC and probably date from the exile in Babylon. They were
used for community worship and for teaching by the rabbis but

not for the elaborate rituals associated with the Temple. The development of synagogue worship was important to the survival of Judaism, as it allowed both the survival of large Jewish communities in gentile centres such as Alexandria and the survival of Judaism after the destruction of the temple by the Romans in AD 70. Synagogues were not run by priests but by a group of elders and an *archisynagogus* ('ruler of the synagogue') (Lk 8:41; Ac 18:8). Services were conducted by members of the congregation or by guests, in each case by invitation of the *archisynagogus*. By the time of Jesus, the rabbis were as important as the priests, if not more so.

New Testament developments

The title of 'Rabbi' or 'Rabboni' is translated as 'lord' or 'teacher' and was used by students when addressing scribes, their teachers of the sacred texts. It conveyed a deep sense of respect. The title is given to Jesus in the synoptics:

> The use of the address to Jesus is significant; it shows that both his disciples and those outside his circle, uncertain of what precisely his character and his mission were, treated him as one of the only class of religious leader which they knew.[35]

While there is no evidence of Jesus ever having been a teacher in that formal sense, we do hear of him being asked to preach in the synagogue, for example, in his home town of Nazareth (Lk 4:16–21) and in Capernaum (Mk 1:21; Jn 6:59).

While the gospels do not give Jesus the title of 'priest' (this title is given to Jesus explicitly only in the Letter to the Hebrews), Jesus himself makes it clear that he has come to fulfil the two functions of the Old Testament priest; to offer sacrifice and to act as mediator of the word. He also combines the Old Testament roles of priest, prophet and king:

> Jesus reunites these various types of mediation in his person: as Son of God, he is the eternal Word who accompanies and surpasses the message of the prophets; as Son of Man, he assumes in himself all humanity and is its king with an authority and love unknown until his time; as unique mediator between God and his people, he is the perfect priest through whom men are sanctified.[36]

Just as the Old Testament portrayed the Israelites as a priestly people, so too did Jesus expect his followers to be a priestly people.[37] The idea of what we now refer to as 'the priesthood of the laity' was clearly understood by the apostles. Paul urges the Romans 'to offer your bodies as a living sacrifice, dedicated and acceptable to God, that is the kind of worship for you' (Rm 12:1). Similar sentiments are expressed in Hebrews 9:14 and 12:28. Peter is quite explicit 'But you are a chosen race, a kingdom of priests, a holy nation, a people to be a personal possession to sing the praises of God' (1 P 2:9). The Book of Revelation also describes the faithful as priests, 'He loves us and has washed away our sins with his blood and made us a kingdom of priests to serve his God and Father ...' (Rev 1:6) and 'because you were sacrificed, and with your blood you bought people for God of every race, language, people and nation and made them a line of kings and priests for God, to rule the world' (Rev 5:9–10) and the souls of the martyrs 'will be priests of God and of Christ, and reign with him for a thousand years' (Rev 20:6).

However it is equally clear that, within this priesthood of all believes, there was a group set aside as leaders of the Church.[38] Jesus appoints the apostles only after a night of prayer 'In those days he went onto the mountain to pray; and he spent the whole night in prayer to God. When day came, he summoned his disciples and picked out twelve of them; he called them apostles' (Lk 6:12–13). There are several examples of this group of twelve receiving extra instruction 'He then opened their minds to understand the Scriptures' (Lk 24:45). Matthew and Mark end their gospels with Jesus's farewell instructions to the apostles 'And he said to them "Go out to the whole world; proclaim the gospel to all creation"' (Mk 16:15). John ends with the instruction to Peter to 'feed my sheep' (Jn 21:17). Here, Jesus is handing his own mission as the good shepherd on to Peter. When they first met, Simon was a fisherman and there are several parallels between Luke 5:1–11 and John 2:1–19.[39] However the apostles were to be more than preachers of the good news. The synoptics tell us of the institution of the Eucharist at the last supper with the instruction to 'do this in remembrance of me' (Lk 22:19). The apostles were to continue Jesus's sacrificial role, making his saving act present to all generations. John makes it clear that this role is not one of authority and power in any secular meaning but one of service. Jesus washes the feet of the apostles and 'If I then, the Lord and Master, have washed your feet, you must wash each other's feet' (Jn 13:14). They were to baptise and heal the sick (Mk 16:16–17). In other words, the apostles inherited Jesus's priestly ministry of word and sacrament, the same two elements that had existed in the Old Testament priesthood.[40]

An important distinction between the Old Testament priesthood and the priesthood inherited by the apostles is expressed by Jesus in his use of the image of himself as a shepherd. There are several messages here: a shepherd loves his sheep and is willing to lay down his life for them; shepherds live lives of simplicity and hard work; shepherds are looked down on, even despised, by the rest of society. So the apostles are not to expect the prestige and honour that goes with secular power. Instead: 'He intends to stress the humility which ought to characterise authority in the Church, a humility which translates itself into service and sacrifice.'[41]

Apostolic succession

It is clear from Jesus's instructions to the apostles to take the gospel to all nations and all generations, that they would have to pass on their mission and authority to others. Jesus does not give them instructions on how to do this, instead giving them the authority to do whatever is necessary for the good of the Church 'whatever you bind on earth will be bound in Heaven; whatever you loose on earth shall be loosed in Heaven' (Mt 16:19). There are three examples of individuals being given authority by the apostles to share in their mission. The first is in the appointment of a replacement for Judas. This is done by a group of about one hundred and twenty brethren selecting two candidates. After prayer, lots are cast to decide between them and Matthias is enrolled.[42] The second is the appointment of the seven helpers, when the apostles asked the wider body of disciples to select seven suitable men to whom they could delegate some of their tasks.[43] The appointment ritual was simply prayer and the laying on of hands.[44] We can see that both these examples included a selection process involving a large group of Jesus's followers, with the actual commissioning performed by the apostles. The third example, that of Saul, is rather different as the commissioning did not directly involve the apostles but came directly from Jesus. 'The Lord replied "Go, for this man is my chosen instrument to bring my name before Gentiles and kings and before the people of Israel"' (Ac 9:15). So Saul becomes, not just a follower of Jesus, but a proclaimer of the gospel 'For several days he was with the disciples at Damascus. And in the synagogues immediately he proclaimed Jesus saying, "Jesus is the Son of God"' (Ac 9:20). Saul joined the apostles in Jerusalem and was sent by them, first to Tarsus (Ac 9:30) and later to Cyprus. It is while in Cyprus that he begins to be called Paul. Despite not having been one of the original twelve apostles and being careful to respect the authority of the apostles based in Jerusalem, Paul insisted that he was also an apostle 'From Paul, a servant of Jesus Christ, called to be an apostle, set apart for the service of the gospel' (Rm 1:1).

Paul uses the word 'apostle' slightly differently from Luke, who reserves it for the original twelve. Paul includes James and 'all the apostles' to whom the risen Lord appeared (1 Co 15:7). He also refers to many co-workers as apostles, such as Silvanus, Timothy and Barnabas. However he also recognises the special position of the twelve apostles and claims a share in their mission and authority because he also was personally chosen by Jesus and knew the living Jesus, even if only as the risen Lord:

> It is evident that each of the original twelve was chosen personally by Jesus; a condition was personal knowledge of the Incarnate Word ... The constitution of the college of the twelve to carry on and continue the work of Jesus is done by the risen Christ.[45]

This definition of an apostle inevitably means that the title dies with the death of the last of the original group. We have already seen in chapter three that the apostles had the authority to pass on their mission and authority to their successors. There are several examples of Paul authorising leaders for the various church communities that he set up. However he still retains responsibility for these communities.

> Concretely, the apostolic authority is exercised in connection with doctrine, ministry and jurisdiction. Often Paul appeals to his doctrinal authority, because he believes himself able to hurl an anathema upon anyone who would announce a gospel different from his (Ga 1:8). Paul knows himself capable of delegating his own powers to others, as when he ordains Timothy by imposing hands upon him (1 Tm 4:14; 2 Tm 1:6), a gesture which Timothy could perform in his turn (1 Tm 5:22). Finally this authority is exercised by a real jurisdiction over the churches which Paul has founded and which are entrusted to him.[46]

We know very little about the work of the other apostles and the mechanisms used for passing on their authority to their successors. The very early Church saw itself as part of Judaism and continued with normal Jewish practices. There was also an expectation of the imminent *parousia*, hence a feeling that there was no need to worry about passing on authority to the next generation if the end of the world was approaching. Preaching could be based on synagogue worship. The courtesy of inviting guests to speak was of great benefit to the apostles in their preaching. (There are several examples of Paul making use of the local synagogue to spread the good news.) In this they were copying the example of Jesus, who used his visit to the synagogue in Nazareth to tell his 'home crowd' that he was the Messiah that they had been waiting for. The early Christians continued to join in the synagogue worship until they were banned by the Council of Jamnia in AD 70. When they had to form their own patterns of worship, these were modelled on the synagogue pattern of prayer, psalms and Scripture reading, with the addition of the eucharistic meal:

> There in essence and substance is the ritual of the Mass. The early communities had elders to govern them like the synagogue, ministers (deacons) to assist in the services and management of the assembly; and the Christian overseer (*episkopos*, bishop) in his earliest form was probably closely related in office and functions to the *archisynagogus*.[47]

As the Church's claim to authority depends on her claim that the bishops are in direct continuity with the apostles, we need to look at the transition from the Church of the apostles to the apostolic

Church in some detail. There are two approaches to apostolic continuity, historical and eschatological.

Historical continuity stresses the linear passing on of authority and mission from one set of individuals to another. We have the sending on a mission of Christ by God, the apostles by Christ and the early leaders of the Church by the apostles. Using this model, the apostles are seen as individual people invested with specific powers to spread the good news to the ends of the earth. Their task is to set up local churches throughout the world and appoint leaders to whom they can pass on their Christ-given authority. These leaders must be able to trace their right to rule and teach back in an unbroken line to the twelve apostles.

The eschatological model looks on the apostles as a body, or college, of believers, 'the twelve'. They are not so much individual followers as the founding body of a kingdom that is already present and to whom all are called. Both of these models are based on the picture of the early Church, as presented in Acts. Paul is the perfect example of the apostle sent to travel throughout the known world to set up local churches with their own leaders. Yet he is also linked to the church of James in Jerusalem:

> With the disappearance of the twelve from the Jerusalem church (dispersion for mission?) the scheme 'apostles and presbyters' is replaced with that of 'James and the presbyters' (Acts 21:18). The significance of this scheme lies in the eschatological nature of the Jerusalem church as the centre of the earth, where all mission converges in its final consummation (Rom 15:19) ... this model is transferred to the eucharist and through that to the episcopacy after the fall of Jerusalem.[48]

The writings of the early Church Fathers, Clement of Rome and Ignatius of Antioch, show that both of these models of the Church were in use from the very beginnings. Clement's letter to the Corinthians is a reproach to them for evicting their bishops and replacing them with others more to their liking.[49] Clement gives the historical events of God commissioning Jesus, who in turn commissioned the apostles. The apostles then appointed bishops and deacons. He reminds them that the appointment of bishops and deacons goes back to the time of Moses and is mentioned in

Isaiah.[50]If a bishop has been appointed in the correct way and is performing his duties blamelessly, no one has the power to remove him. So Clement's message is that the offices of bishop and deacon are ordained by Christ, are part of the ongoing history of the Church and any disruption of this reflects badly, not just on the individuals, but on the whole Church. 'Your thoughtlessness has brought the name of the Lord into disrespect, to say nothing of imperilling your own souls.'[51] However, Clement also has a vision of the Church as present for all men of all ages; all that is needed is brotherly love: 'For we have only to survey the generations of the past to see that in every one of them the Lord has offered the chance of repentance to any who were willing to turn to Him.'[52] and 'Though every generation from Adam to the present day has passed from the earth, yet such of them as by God's grace were perfected in love have their place now in the courts of the godly.'[53] Thus, the present configuration of the Church is part of God's loving care for all of mankind and any leaders who have been appointed by God, through his representatives on earth, must be treated with the reverence due to Christ himself.

Ignatius of Antioch, writing sometime between AD 98 and AD 117, sent seven letters to various churches. They place great emphasis on the importance of obedience to the bishop as the representative of Jesus Christ: 'For we can have no life apart from Jesus Christ; and as He represents the mind of the Father, so our bishops, even those who are stationed in the remotest parts of the world, represent the mind of Jesus Christ.'[54] Ignatius includes priests and deacons as sharers in the authority given to bishops: 'Let the bishop preside in the place of God, and his clergy in place of the apostolic conclave, and let my special friends the deacons be entrusted with the service of Jesus Christ ...'[55] While Ignatius does not spell out the historical link between Jesus Christ, the apostles and the bishops as clearly as does Clement, he does allude to it:

> Be as submissive to the bishop and to one another as Jesus Christ was to His father, and as the Apostles were to Christ and the Father; so that there may be complete unity, in the flesh as well as in the spirit.[56]

He regularly refers to the clergy as a group of advisors for the bishop: 'The clergy as the Apostolic circle forming his council'[57] and 'the bishop's council of clergy'[58] but does not tell us exactly what their duties are. He praises deacons and gives us some idea of their role. They 'serve the mysteries of Jesus Christ ... are not mere dispensers of meat and drink, but servants of the church of God'.[59] Deacons can also preach:

> Philo, the deacon from Cilicia who has been so well spoken of, is at present giving me his help in preaching God's word. So too is Rheus Agathopous, one of the elect, who has followed after me from Syria, and abjured this earthly life.[60]

Ignatius's letter to Polycarp, bishop of Smyrna tells us how he views the position of bishop. He advises Polycarp to attend to both his temporal and spiritual duties; to strive for unity above all else; to seek out the troublesome ones; to use gentleness and wisdom; to stand firm against heresy; to care for the widow; to be aware of all that goes on; to hold regular services; to preach against sins, especially those of the flesh; to give consent to marriages.[61] Ignatius' insistence on the need for obedience to the clergy as to the bishop suggests that the clergy shared in this lengthy list of tasks and were not merely advisers to help solve difficult problems or to give advice on who to choose for specific missions. Indeed, in his letter to the Smyrnaeans, he alludes to the bishop's authority to delegate tasks. 'The sole Eucharist you should consider valid is one that is celebrated by the bishop himself, or by some person authorised by him.'[62]

Polycarp was bishop of Smyrna when Ignatius passed through on his way to Rome and had been a disciple of the apostle John. Soon after the visit of Ignatius, he writes to the Church at Philippi. He gives his letter the title 'From Polycarp and his clergy', thus acknowledging his position as head of the Church in Smyrna. He refers to 'clergy and deacons' but does not mention bishops. He describes the qualities that clergy and deacons should posses, as he does for widows and young men and women. He advised young men that 'Our duty, therefore, is to ... be as obedient to our clergy and deacons as we should be to God and Christ.'[63]

Despite the above passages, it has to be said that the structure of the early Church took some time to develop and several models existed simultaneously in different centres. Thus the various forms of Church structure that exist today can all claim to be based on that of the early Church.

> Even the Pastoral Epistles, which come closest to laying down guide-lines for the choice of ministers, are geared to a particular social and theological context, and we may doubt whether their seemingly twofold pattern of overseer/elders and deacons was intended as a model for all time. Churches practising episcopal, presbyteral, congregational, and charismatic forms of ministry can all claim to find precedents in the New Testament.[64]

Edwards points out the importance of servanthood in Jesus's teaching. 'The bulk of the evidence suggests that Jesus was not interested in founding a hierarchy, but rather something more akin to a family, whose members serve one another.'[65] She contrasts this with the hierarchical nature of the Roman Catholic Church. However, as with so many modern writers, she confuses ecclesial with secular authority and power. The Church hierarchy is designed to preserve order and to advance the teaching of the kingdom of God. Positions of greater authority within this hierarchy are not designed to confer personal gain on the recipients but to give them the power needed to serve the Church more efficiently, hence the pope's title of being 'the servant of the servants of God'. Edwards goes on to examine the references to authority in John 20:23; Matthew 16:19; Matthew 18:18, as coming from Isaiah 22:22, and John 13:20; Matthew 10:40; Mark 9:37; Luke 10:16. She concludes that 'The most plausible interpretation of this complex evidence is that Jesus intended those commissioned to symbolise the whole Church or community of believers ...'[66] This may seem plausible to someone brought up with the collegial rather than the historical model of apostolic succession. To others, it seems to be a case of deliberately avoiding the obvious interpretation that Jesus set up a hierarchy of leaders to ensure that his teaching was passed on from generation to generation. What Edwards and other writers ignore is that the developing patterns of both worship and leadership in the Church were subject to two powerful influences—the apostles, with their successors, and the Holy Spirit.

> And so the Church in her teaching, life and worship, perpetuates and hands on to all generations all that she herself is, all

that she believes. This Tradition which comes from the Apostles, develops in the Church with the help of the Holy Spirit.[67]

While the early Church can provide examples of several forms of
both worship and leadership, these quickly became standardised,
as we have seen in the writings of Clement and Ignatius. This
process of standardisation was only possible because of the
hierarchical structure in place from the beginning, giving certain
individuals the power to make binding decisions. The Church
believes that the decisions as to which practices to accept and
which to abandon were guided by the Holy Spirit. So the pattern
of bishop, priest and deacon, while not the only possible interpretation of Scripture, is the pattern desired by God. Such decisions
can only be made in a Church with a strong sense of its right and
duty to exert authority; in other words, a Church with a strong
Magisterium. However, this is getting slightly ahead of ourselves.
Before looking at the Magisterium of the Church, we must both
summarise what we have found so far and look at the remaining
topics under the heading of the Tradition of the Church.

Summary

The Church has always taught that public revelation ended with
the death of the last apostle. From this point, Tradition takes over
as the safeguard of authentic doctrine. Within this Tradition, the
position of those who have received the sacrament of ordination
is crucial to the right ordering of the Church. By this sacrament,
the apostles passed on their authority and mission to bishops,
priests and deacons. While the precise terminology and duties
associated with these positions took some time to develop, we have
seen that it was recognised and accepted as the standard pattern
by the time of Clement, Ignatius and Polycarp, that is from AD 96.
Apostolic succession was seen as historical, with authority being
passed on from the Father to Jesus to the apostles to those they
appointed and to their successors using a set ritual of selection,
prayer and the laying on of hands. It was also collegial as the
apostles had formed a body which was the foundation of the
Church and their successors continued to act as guardians of the
unity of teaching and practice. These two ways of looking at the
early Church were not alternatives but complementary and both

expressed essential truths. Only those churches which were in both historical and collegial communion with the churches of Jerusalem, and then Rome, could claim apostolic succession. This communion depended on following the teachings and practice of the apostles, as recorded in Scripture or remembered by those who had heard them. Where several practices could all claim to be compatible with the apostolic teaching and the example of the early Church, the true practice was that which, through the guidance of the Holy Spirit, became the norm for the early Church.

Reserved to men alone

The above investigation into the development of the roles of bishop, priest and deacon in the early Church has taken for granted that these roles were filled by men. In modern times, this practice has been challenged. Many of the post-Reformation churches now have female ministers. Some even use the words 'ordained' 'priest' and 'bishop' for female office-holders. Despite the example of the women named in Scripture and the abbesses of the Middle Ages the Roman Catholic Church has consistently maintained that this is not an option.[68] We will look at the arguments for and against in detail later.[69] The one fact that cannot be disputed is that Jesus was conceived as a male. He did not just become human, he became a male human. Was this purely because the laws of nature demanded that he be either male or female and it was more convenient to be male, or does it have a deeper significance? We need to look at two aspects of this question, God as male and female and humanity as male and female.

God as Male and Female

One of the best known modern theologians in the field of the nature of God is Hans Urs von Balthasar. The work of Balthasar is important for the debate on the relative roles of men and women in the Church, partly because of his work on the nature of the Trinity and partly because of his influence on John Paul II. Balthasar's work makes for difficult reading and cannot be assimilated by merely dipping into his more accessible essays. The following quotes are lengthy but are necessary in order to give a sufficient summary of his thought processes to meet our needs here. The first two explain why we can think of Christ as having both masculine and feminine aspects.

> Balthasar's carefully qualified treatment of the question of gender in God follows the processions of God. That is, the Father, as the begetting origin-without-origin, is primarily (supra-) masculine (*über-männlich*); the son, as begotten and thus receptive (*der Geschehenlassende*) is (supra-) feminine (*über-weiblich*); but then the Father and the son, as jointly spirating the Spirit, are again (supra) masculine; the spirit then is (supra) feminine; finally, the Father, who allows himself to be conditioned in return *in* his begetting and spirating, himself thereby has a (supra) feminine dimension.[70]

This second quote, from Balthasar himself, continues this theme but concentrates on the Son as a man, the second Adam:

> The Word of God appears in the world as a man, as the 'Last Adam'. This cannot be a matter of indifference. But it is astonishing on two counts. For if the Logos proceeds eternally from the eternal father, is he not at least quasi-feminine vis-à-vis the latter? And if he is the 'Second Adam', surely he is incomplete until God has formed the woman from his side? We can give a provisional answer to these two questions as follows: however the One who comes forth from the Father is designated, as a human being he must be a man if his mission is to represent the Origin, the Father in the world. And just as, according to the second account of creation, Eve is fashioned from Adam (that is, he carried her within him, potentially), so the feminine, designed to complement the man Christ, must come forth from within him, as his fullness (Eph. 1:23).[71]

The third quote, again from Balthasar himself, is saying that the Son's task is to reveal the Father.

> As God, however, the Son must be equal to the Father, even though he has come forth from the Father. And since the Father has expressed his whole love—which nothing can hold back—in the Son, the Son is the perfect image of the Father, apt to represent the Father's self-giving in his creation in every respect ... This is the only way in which we can understand what Jesus means when he says 'He who

has seen me has seen the Father' (John14:9) amplifying it thus 'The Father who dwells in me does his work' (14:10).[72]

Balthasar points out that Jesus also does his own filial works (Jn 10:37; Ga 2:20; Rev 1:8, 18; 21:6, 22:16). Balthasar's writing on the inter-relationship of the persons of the Trinity as having masculine and feminine aspects is based on the premise that masculinity is generative and giving, femininity is receptive and nurturing. While there is a clear logic to this, it is not a universally accepted foundation for studying gender differences, either divine or human.

> Balthasar takes it for granted that the kind of difference there is between the sexes is essentially that between first and second, agent and patient; ... trinitarian difference does not strictly allow of 'first ' and 'second' but assumes an eternal simultaneity ... But the point is that such discussions are short-circuited by the assimilation from the start of passive-active to female-male difference, in what some would read as a reductive fashion.[73]

Other writers are even more direct in their criticism of Balthasar's work. Tina Beattie claims that the relationship between Balthasar and his colleague Adrienne von Speyr was flawed in that Balthasar read into von Speyr's work what was in fact reflections of his own thoughts; he used her to express the feminine aspects of his personality that he could not otherwise acknowledge. Beattie claims that he had an unrealistic idea of women as passive, silent, submissive, which both 'Lacks scriptural justification and bears little relation to the actual experience of women and mothers through history.'[74] The CCC reminds us that all human language is inadequate when speaking of God.

> By calling God 'father', the language of faith indicates two main things: that God is the first origin of everything and transcends authority; and that he is at the same time good-ness and loving care for all his children. God's parental tenderness can also be expressed by the image of mother-hood, which emphasises God's immanence, the intimacy between Creator and creature ... He is neither man nor woman: he is God. He also transcends human fatherhood and motherhood, although he is their origin and standard: no one is father as God is father.[75]

Indeed, while the Old Testament God is very much a masculine God, there are examples of him being spoken of as having feminine qualities.[76] So the idea that we are made in the image of God precisely as male and female, and that therefore God must have male and female characteristics, is not new. It has however gained a prominence in recent years that it has never had before.

One of the simplest explanations that I have found for referring to God as father is 'God is called "Father" rather than "mother" because the relationship with him is ultimately one into which we are growing (the goal), not the relationship from which we have come.'[77]

Humanity was made in God's image but also as male and female. It is important to look at these two ways of being human in order to understand the significance of Jesus as male. There is a popular belief that Jesus's sex was simply a necessity of his time. He could not have practised as an itinerant preacher and leader if he had been female because of the social norms of the day. However it is also possible that there is something intrinsically masculine about this role in all ages and also that Jesus, as Son of God, could only say 'those who have seen me, have seen the Father' as a male. We need to think about the ways in which men and women differ in order to think about Jesus as male.[78] We will do this with the help of Catherine of Siena (1347–1380), Edith Stein (1891–1942) and John Paul II.

Catherine of Siena was created a Doctor of the Church in 1970. While this does not give her writings the status of infallible statements, it does give them a certain authority. Catherine saw our likeness to God as present in our souls; just as God has a Trinitarian nature, so our souls have three qualities. The power, wisdom and clemency of the Trinity are reflected in the memory, intellect and will of the human soul. Created by the love of God, the soul searches for love:

> You made us in your image and likeness so that, by the three powers which we possess in one soul, we reflect your trinity and unity. They not only create a resemblance, but also a unity. Thus by the memory we resemble and are united to the Father, to whom Power is attributed; by the intellect we resemble and are united to the Son, to whom Wisdom is

> attributed; and by the will we resemble and are united to
> the Holy Spirit, to whom Clemency is attributed and who is
> the love of the Father and the Son.[79]

Catherine is not concerned with the differences between men and women. We are all equally made in the image of God and loved by him. We are made in such a way that we have to express God's love for us in our search for others to love. By creating an unequal world, God has given us the opportunity to express our love of neighbour by practising charity and humility. Catherine is not interested in challenging the social rules of the day regarding men and women. However she refuses to follow them herself, dedicating her life to prayer and works of charity. She does not hesitate to admonish the men in her life, be they brother, city ruler or pope. She provides both spiritual guidance and practical help and advice to all. A person's social standing is not important, what matters is that they grow in love of God and obedience to his will. Catherine does not hesitate to point out the faults of the clergy at all levels. She is particularly blunt with the Italian cardinals who refused to accept the authority of Pope Urban VI, using sentences such as 'Now you have turned away like vile and miserable knights: your very shadow has frightened you.' and 'If I look back at your life, I do not find it so good and saintly that your conscience should make you avoid lying.'[80]

Like Catherine of Siena, Edith Stein is a Doctor of the Church. Both women led unusual lives but were very different in character and background. Edith Stein was unusual on several counts. She was a German philosopher who converted from Judaism to Roman Catholicism in her early twenties, became a Carmelite nun and died in Auschwitz with her sister Rosa, who had previously joined her in the convent.[81] She was declared a Doctor of the Church and patroness of Europe by Pope John Paul II, whose own philosophy of the theology of the body was very much based on her work.

Here, we are interested only in Edith Stein's writings on the role of women in society. She believed that it was possible to identify traits that were typically masculine and other traits that were typically feminine. So both men and women have three aspects to their identity; being human, being a unique individual and being either male or female. Her experience as a teacher convinced her that males and females thought and acted in different ways and therefore would benefit from different educational methods. However she felt strongly that all careers should be equally open to men and women as they would bring different talents to the job, thus enriching the work experience for all involved. She talks of two main criteria that differentiate men from women. In the first instance, men are seen as more objective as they will devote themselves to one trade or subject and accept the discipline needed to pursue it. Women are more personal and will happily involve their whole being in what they are doing, taking an interest in both their own personal benefit from the activity and that of others. In the second instance, men can, as a result of their submission to a discipline, experience a one-sided development. Women have a greater urge towards becoming complete human beings and helping those around them to become so too.[82] Because of these differences, some jobs are more suited to women than others, such as teaching, social work, care of the young, medicine and nursing. This is not to say that men cannot bring their own gifts to those jobs or that women cannot do anything else. The important thing is that they remain as masculine or feminine in whatever position they find themselves. Women should not have to pretend to be men or loose what is specifically female about their own identities:

> We women have become aware once again of our singularity. Many a woman who formerly denied it has perhaps become aware of it, painfully aware of it, if she has entered one of the traditionally masculine professions and sees herself forced into conditions of life and work alien to her nature. If her *nature* is strong enough, she has perhaps succeeded in converting the *masculine* profession into a *feminine* one. And this self-awareness could also develop the conviction that an intrinsic feminine value resides in the singularity.[83]

I am reminded of the discussions regarding the career of Britain's first woman Prime Minister, Margaret Thatcher. When she was elected, there was much talk of the changes that this would make in the lives of ordinary women in Britain. These changes did not take place and the commonly perceived reason is that Mrs Thatcher coped with the stresses of being in such a male-dominated environment by repressing her feminine traits and concentrating on her masculine ones. Edith Stein would have counselled her to take advice from male colleagues but to remain true to her own unique, feminine nature. She would also have advised her to turn to Our Lady as both a role-model and a source of support:

> Those women who wish to fulfil their feminine vocations in one of several ways will most surely succeed in their goals if they not only keep the ideal of the Virgo-Mater before their eyes and strive to form themselves to her guidance and place themselves completely under her care.[84]

Stein did in fact have advice specifically for those in political life. She suggests that legislation drafted by men alone can be too removed from the practicalities of daily life. It needs to be balanced by the feminine concern for the individual.

> In legislation, there is always danger that resolution 'at the official level' will be based on the elaboration of the possibly most perfect paragraphs without their consideration of actual circumstances and consequences in practical life. Feminine singularity resists this abstract proceeding … The authentic feminine longing to remedy human need (can be) victorious over the (stalemate) of party viewpoints. Just as in legislation, feminine singularity can also work beneficially in the application of the law in bureaucracy, provided it does not lead to abstract validation of the letter of the law but to the accomplishment of justice for humanity.[85]

For Stein, this difference between male and female went much deeper than simply personality traits. A reviewer of one of her lectures '*On the Ethos of Women's Professions*', says that

> Manifesting brilliant reflection, she inferred from a formu-lated truth of St Thomas, '*anima forma corporis*' (the soul is the formative principle of the body), that inasmuch as the feminine body is a feminine body, this feminine body must also correspond to a feminine soul just as the masculine body must correspond to a masculine soul.[86]

In view of Stein's insistence on the complementarity of men and women, the need for both influences in both work and home and the importance of women having access to all career choices, one would not be surprised to find her supporting the argument for women priests. In fact she does not do so. She recognises that women were ordained to the diaconate in the early Church but never to the priesthood. She suggests that their admission to the priesthood cannot be forbidden on dogmatic grounds but that Tradition has always spoken against it.

> But in my opinion, even more significant is the mysterious fact emphasised earlier—that Christ came to earth as the *Son* of Man. The first creature on earth fashioned in an unrivalled sense as God's image was therefore a man; that seems to indicate to me that He wished to institute only men as His official representatives on earth.[87]

This is not to say that Stein believed that women should play a purely passive or subsidiary role in society. She suggests that in fact women have an exalted place in the divine plan as Jesus calls women to imitate the union that He shared with his mother: 'They are to be emissaries of His love, proclaimers of His will to kings and popes, and forerunners of His kingdom in the hearts of men.'[88] Indeed, we are all called to the imitation of Christ, in whom masculine and feminine are united in harmony: 'That is why we see in holy men a womanly tenderness and a truly maternal solicitude for the souls entrusted to them while in holy women there is a manly boldness, proficiency and determination.'[89]

John Paul II owed much of his work on the complementarity of men and women to the work of Edith Stein. He was not the first pope to write on the complementarity of the sexes, as Pope Pius XII wrote the following in 1945:

> As children of God, man and woman have a dignity in which they are absolutely equal ... But man and woman cannot maintain or perfect this equal dignity of theirs unless they respect and make use of the distinctive qualities which nature has bestowed on each sex.[90]

However it is John Paul II who popularised this topic with a body of work generally referred to as his *Theology of the Body*. He spoke and wrote on this theme over a period of five years from September 1979 until November 1984. Taking 'Have you not read that the Creator from the beginning made them male and female' (Mt 19:4) as his starting point, the first set of talks explored the original unity of man and woman, as described in Genesis. There were three stages in our development; original solitude, original unity and original nakedness. Original solitude was experienced by man before the creation of Eve, he was alone as he was neither animal nor God but human. Even in this solitary state, man's body is part of what and who he is; to cultivate and care for the garden of Eden needs a physical body. However God recognises that man is incomplete on his own and provides a helpmate for him, so humanity moves from original solitude to original unity. This event produces the first expression of joy by man:

> Joy in the other human being, in the second 'self', dominates the words spoken by the man on seeing the woman. All this helps to establish the full meaning of original unity... We must take into account ... the fact that the first woman, 'made with the rib taken from man' is at once accepted as a fit helper for him.[91]

Adam recognises Eve as of the same flesh as himself because her humanity is made visible in her body. Her physical appearance makes her instantly recognisable as a fellow human being, totally different from all the other created beings.

It may be that the image of God is chiefly in our souls. But Genesis reveals much more than that. Pope John Paul II finds something entirely new. The *imago Dei* is also in our bodies; in the body that shows itself to be in the nature of a sacrament. As the Catechism puts it, 'God impressed his own form on the flesh'.[92]

John Paul II goes on to elaborate on the idea of the body as a sacrament. Echoing the catechism definition of a sacrament as an outward sign of an inward reality, he says that the body is a sacrament in that it is a visible sign of its invisible nature.

> Thus ... a primordial *sacrament* is constituted, understood as a sign that efficaciously transmits in the visible world the invisible mystery hidden in God from eternity. And this is the mystery of Truth and Love, the mystery of divine life, in which man really participates ... The sacrament, as a visible sign, is constituted with man, inasmuch as he is a 'body' through his 'visible' masculinity and femininity. The body, in fact, and only the body, is capable of making visible what is invisible: the spiritual and the divine. It has been

> created to transfer into the visible reality of the world the
> mystery hidden from eternity in God, and thus to be a sign
> of it.[93]

However this sacramentality is only complete when in union with
another. Only when man is both original solitude and original
unity is he in the image of God.

> We can then deduce that man becomes the 'image and
> likeness' of God not only through his own humanity, but
> also through the communion of persons which man and
> woman form right from the beginning ... Man becomes the
> image of God not so much in the moment of solitude as in
> the moment of communion.[94]

Jesus's words in Matthew 19:1–9 draw out the ethical dimensions
of this state. Paul's letter to the Ephesians draws out the sacramental implications.

We have to move on to the third stage, original nakedness.
Before original sin, man and woman were unconcerned about their
nakedness as the sins that can be occasioned by viewing the body
of another did not exist. However their one concern after they sin
is their nakedness. They are ashamed to show themselves to God
or to each other. God takes pity on them and provides them with
clothes, a surprisingly tender and maternal gesture. From now on
the natural balance between man and woman is lost.

> Eve's desire for relationship with her husband will be
> thwarted by him. He will dominate her. In fact Adam will
> take on the very image of the tyrant-ruler that the devil's lie
> made God out to be. She will experience keenly this diffi-
> culty in her interpersonal communion with her husband and
> her children ... God's creation of humanity as male *and*
> female has become the worldly opposition of male *or* female.
> They experience anew opposition in their shared body. They
> still sense and respond to the call to unity but experience it
> as ever threatened by instability.[95]

Much of the remainder of John Paul II's work on the theology of
the body concerns the relationship between spouses. He includes
a section on Joseph and talks of the complementarity of Joseph's
and Mary's reactions to their separate annunciations. While Mary
questioned the angel, Joseph simply did what the angel told him

to do. John Paul II continued to talk of the fatherhood of Joseph but I found myself wondering about the comparisons between Adam and Eve as a couple and Mary and Joseph as a couple. The Early Fathers made much of Mary as the new Eve and from St Paul onwards, Jesus has been portrayed as the new Adam. Joseph tends to be ignored. Yet Mary and Joseph were a couple and in many ways give us a mirror image of Adam and Eve. Where Adam and Eve got things wrong, they got them right and in doing so righted the wrong caused by original sin. (See Appendix II, c) for some thoughts on this.)

I will end this chapter with some thoughts from a recently-retired doctor. While he does not have any theological qualifications, he has much experience of human nature. I found it interesting that his summary of what it means to be male or female was remarkably similar to that of Edith Stein.

> We have the stereotype of male and female at each end of a spectrum. These stereotypes are used and spoken of as clearly defined, which they are not in reality. These may be altered and modified by the environment from birth onwards. Genetic factors provide the basic bricks and mortar, but have a limited effect in the subsequent stages.
>
> Within our culture, we 'expect' a female to be able to: make a nest (home); give birth to and rear a baby—during these truly creative activities they may experience extremes of pain and pleasure. They have an instinctive empathy. There is an inbuilt ability to think laterally. They easily multi-task, verbally and physically. From adolescence they are cyclical—which can be very marked, and may embody irrational behaviour and unpredictability. There is frequently intuitive lateral thinking.
>
> We 'expect' a male to be able to: be an adequate hunter/gatherer. Willing/able to procreate as required. Less of their activities are intuitive. They are able to focus and concentrate on one task well, but risk losing a sense of perspective, becoming obsessed in an irrational way. They have the potential to become very good listeners, and strongly empathic. These skills need training and practice. They are prescriptive about matters they know and understand. They tend to be more decisive and objective which

may lead to rigidity of thought. Compartmentalism is second nature, and they are inclined to be secretive. Lateral thinking needs to be taught.

Having given these as examples, one must realise that the truth is that we are each made up of an individual collection of God-given attributes.[96]

Summary

Catherine of Siena is mentioned as an example of a woman who gave a non-sexual description of how we are made in God's image. She exercised authority within the Church with a disregard for either her own sex or that of those whom she guided and rebuked.

The relationship between masculine and feminine in both God and man has been examined in recent times by three major philosophers; Hans Urs von Balthasar, Edith Stein and John Paul II. Balthasar's work on God as both masculine and feminine is not without its critics but it has opened up a new area of study and has given some important insights into the relationship between God and his Church. Edith Stein spoke of an intrinsic difference between men and women, in their bodies, intellects and souls. While she argues for the equal dignity of men and women and for the right of women to enter any profession, she does not support the argument for women priests. Her work greatly influenced John Paul II's 'Theology of the Body' which expanded on her work on the complementarity of men and women and on how they were made in the image of God specifically as men and women. It also seems to reflect common perceptions of what it means to be male and female.

The implications of the work of these three and the many theologians who have studied them may become clearer in the next chapter. For the moment, we must content ourselves with noting that Jesus's masculinity would seem to have a deeper significance that mere convenience.

Notes

[1]   The Council of Nicaea of AD 325 was a watershed event for the Church.
[2]   M. A. Fahey, 'The Church', in F. Fiorenza and J. Galvin, *Systematic Theology*

    vol. II (Minneapolis: Fortress Press, 1991), p. 25.

3   St Ignatius of Antioch, *Letter to the Romans* in ECW, p. 85.

4   Fahey, 'The Church', p. 29.

5   Sometimes included because he had known Polycarp and his writings stressed the importance of the apostolic succession; sometimes excluded because of his later date. The group also includes Barnabas and Diognetus.

6   A. Louth, ECW, p. 20. It is worth noting that Vatican I confirmed that the Pope's jurisdiction is always 'ordinary', so the quote should perhaps read 'Although Clement does not write like a Pope exercising his ordinary jurisdiction …'

7   *Ibid.*, p. 21.

8   Pope Clement I, *The First Epistle to the Corinthians*, in ECW, p. 40, §42. The footnote to this quote is interesting in that it gives us an insight into the difficulties of interpreting those early texts. The authors had learnt their Scripture by heart and would quote it from memory, often conflating several different passages to suit the occasion. The editor of this translation of the letter has added the following information for those readers who might take the trouble to check Clement's sources: 'The Septuagint version of Isaiah ix,17 is "I will give thy rulers in peace and thy overseers (or bishops) in righteousness." By introducing the deacons we may suppose that Clement intends to bring out what he considers to be the true meaning of the prophecy.' (p. 51, footnote 21.)

9   Clement describes the incident in Numbers chapter 17 when the Lord God ended unrest among the Israelites by causing Aaron's staff to sprout into flower and fruit overnight in the Tent of the Testimony as a sign that he and his family—the tribe of Levi—were authorised to carry out the duties of the priesthood.

10   Pope Clement I, *The First Epistle to the Corinthians* in ECW, p. 41, §44.

11   *Ibid.*, p. 42.

12   St Ignatius of Antioch, *Epistle to the Philadelphians* in ECW, p. 94, § 4.

13   St Ignatius of Antioch, *Epistle to the Smyrnaeans* in ECW, p 103, §8. This includes the first known use of the phrase 'the Catholic Church'.

14   A. Roberts and W. Rambaut W. (tr.), *The Works of Irenaeus*, vol. 1 p. 262, part of the series *Ante-Nicene Christian Library*. The Latin can be found in St Irenaeus, *Adversus Haereses*, Livre III, tome II, 3,3,3 in SC, vol. 211, p. 38. It reads 'Hac ordinatione et successione ea quae est ab apostolis in Ecclesia traditio et veritatis praeconatio pervenit usque ad nos. Et est plenissima haec ostensio, unam et eandem vivificatricem fidem esse quae in Ecclesia ab apostolis usque nunc sit conservata et tradita in veritate.'

15   The First General Council of Constantinople, *Symbol of Constantinople*, (381), as quoted in ND, p. 9. See also chapter eight 'Scripture: The Church'.

16   St Augustine, *Concerning The City of God Against the Pagans*, Book XVIII, translated by H. Bettenson (London: Penguin Books, 2003), chapter 1, p. 761.

17   *Ibid.*, Book XIII, chapter 16, p. 16.

18   GS §40.

19   *Ibid.* §45.
20   EN §2 and 28.
21   *Ibid.* §16, with a reference to Lk 10:16.
22   Pope John Paul II, Apostolic Exhortation *Christifideles Laici* §9 (1988).
23   LG § 8.2.
24   EE §1.1.
25   *Ibid.* §19.
26   CCC §761.
27   *Ibid.* §846.
28   LG §22.
29   CCC §1536.
30   However note the comments in chapter three 'Scripture: The Church; The Priesthood of Christ' on the fundamental difference between the Old Testament and New Testament priesthood.
31   Moses' sister, Miriam was a prophetess and leader of the women (Ex 15:20).
32   But see J. McKenzie, *Dictionary of the Bible* (London: Geoffrey Chapman, 1965), for a description of their complicated history.
33   See L. Boadt, *Reading the Old Testament: An Introduction* (New York: Paulist Press, 1984), p. 273 for further details.
34   A. George, 'Priesthood' in X. Leon-Dufour, *Dictionary of Biblical Theology* (London: Burns and Oates, 1988), p. 460.
35   J. McKenzie 'Rabbi' in *Dictionary of the Bible,* p. 718.
36   George, 'Priesthood' in Leon-Dufour, *Dictionary of Biblical Theology,* p. 463. See also chapter three 'Scripture: The Church; The Priesthood of Christ'.
37   See chapter three 'Scripture: The Church; The Priesthood of the Laity'.
38   See chapter three 'Scripture: The Church'.
39   See J. Galot, *Theology of the Priesthood* (San Francisco: Ignatius Press, 1985), p. 83.
40   See also chapter three 'Scripture: The Church'.
41   Galot, *Theology of the Priesthood,* p. 49.
42   See Ac 1:15–26.
43   See chapter fourteen 'Magisterium: ordination' and the debate over whether these helpers were deacons or priests.
44   See Ac 6:1–6.
45   J. McKenzie, 'Apostle' in *Dictionary of the Bible,* p. 47.
46   X. Leon-Dufour, 'Apostles' in *Dictionary of Biblical Theology,* p. 26.
47   J. McKenzie, 'Synagogue' in *Dictionary of the Bible,* p. 856.
48   J. Zizioulas, *Being as Communion* (New York: St Vladimir's Seminary Press, 1997), p. 175, f. 16.
49   Dated April AD 96.
50   Quoting Isaiah 9:17.
51   Pope Clement I, *The First Epistle to the Corinthians,* in *ECW,* p. 42, §47.
52   *Ibid.,* in *ECW,* p. 25, §7.

53 *Ibid.*, in *ECW*, p. 43, §50.
54 St Ignatius of Antioch, *Epistle to the Ephesians* in *ECW*, p. 62, §3. Similar quotes could be cited from any of the seven letters.
55 St Ignatius of Antioch, *Epistle to the Magnesians* in *ECW*, p. 72, §6.
56 *Ibid* in *ECW*, p. 74, §13.
57 St Ignatius of Antioch, *Epistle to the Trallians* in *ECW*, p. 79, §3.
58 St Ignatius of Antioch, *Epistle to the Philadelphians* in *ECW*, p. 95, §8.
59 St Ignatius of Antioch, *Epistle to the Trallian* in *ECW*, p. 79, §2.
60 St Ignatius of Antioch, *Epistle to the Philadelphians* in *ECW*, p. 96, §11.
61 St Ignatius of Antioch, *Epistle to Polycarp* in *ECW*, p. 109, §1–4.
62 St Ignatius of Antioch, *Epistle to the Smyrnaeans* in *ECW*, p. 103, §8.
63 St Polycarp, *Epistle to the Philippians* in *ECW*, p. 121, §5.
64 R. Edwards, *The Case for Women's Ministry* (London: SPCK, 1989), p. 81.
65 *Ibid.*, p. 77.
66 *Ibid.*, p. 78.
67 DV §8.
68 See chapter ten and the writing of Joan Morris, *Against Nature and God: The History of Women with Clerical Ordination and the Jurisdiction of Bishops* (London: Mowbrays, 1973).
69 See part four 'The Analogy of Faith'.
70 D. Schindler, 'Catholic Theology, Gender and the Future of Western Civilisation' in *Communio* vol. XX, no 2 (Summer 1993), pp. 200–239.
71 H. U. von Balthasar, 'Dramatis Personae: Person in Christ' in *Theo-Drama: Theological Dramatic Theory* vol. III (San Francisco: Ignatius Press, 1978), p. 283.
72 *Ibid.*, p. 518.
73 R. Williams, 'Balthasar and the Trinity', p. 46, in Oakes (ed.), *The Cambridge Companion to Hans Urs von Balthasar*, (Cambridge: CUP, 2004), pp. 37–50.
74 T. Beattie, 'A Man and Three Women—Hans, Adrienne, Mary and Luce' in *New Blackfriars* vol. 79, no. 924 (February 1998), pp. 97–105.
75 CCC §239.
76 MD §8 (1988) gives examples of Scripture referring to masculine and feminine aspects of God—Is 42:14; 46:3–4; 49:14–15; 66:13 Jr 3:4–19; Ho 11:1–4; Ps 131:2–3.
77 In a pamphlet by Father Gregory CSWG *Ministry of Men and Women in the Church*. N.pl., n.pub. [accessed at Pluscarden Abbey].
78 See also the summary of the work of M. Hauke in chapter twenty 'The Analogy of Faith: The Theological Argument'.
79 From her *Letters* (L129–II–235) translated by Sister Mary Jeremiah in 'The Theological Anthropology of Catherine of Siena' in *Communio* vol. XX no 2 (Summer 1993).
80 G. Cavallini, *Catherine of Siena* (London: Geoffrey Chapman, 1998), pp. 104–105.
81 The background to the death of Edith Stein and her sister, Rosa is of interest. This was the direct result of the pastoral letter of the Dutch Roman Catholic bishop of Utrecht, read in all parish churches of his diocese on 26 July 1942, protesting at the treatment of the Jews. This gives us an example of masculine

thinking—perfectly admirable in itself but with the emphasis on general principles, ignoring the possible consequences for individual people. Pius XII (with typically feminine thinking born of long experience) would have advised against the letter, knowing its likely outcome. (See W. Herbstrith, *Edith Stein: A Biography*, (San Francisco: Ignatius Press, 1985), p. 178).

[82] E. Stein, *Essays on Woman*, translated by F. Oben (Washington: ICS Publications, 1987), p. 255.

[83] *Ibid.*, p. 254.

[84] *Ibid.*, p. 241.

[85] *Ibid.*, pp. 263–4.

[86] *Ibid.*, p. 21.

[87] *Ibid.*, p. 84.

[88] *Ibid.*, p. 84.

[89] *Ibid.*, p. 84.

[90] Pope Pius XII, Address to Members of Various Catholic Women's Associations *Questa Grande Vostra Adunata* (21 October 1945).

[91] Pope John Paul II, *The Theology of the Body: Human Love in the Divine Plan* (Boston: Paulist Books, 1997), p. 45.

[92] J. Keenan, *In God's Image: John Paul II's 'Theology of the Body* (Pluscarden Abbey: Pentecost Lectures, 2006), p. 5. See also CCC §704.

[93] Pope John Paul II, 'The Theology of the Body' as quoted in D. Crawford, 'Natural Law and the Body' in *Communio* vol. XXXV no 3 (Fall, 2008), p. 332

[94] Pope John Paul II, *The Theology of the Body*, p. 46.

[95] J. Keenan, *In God's Image: John Paul II's 'Theology of the Body'*, p. 14.

[96] Sent by e-mail, hence the rather abrupt sentence structure.

9 OUR LADY

T HE PROMINENCE OF Marian worship in the life of the Church is out of all proportion to the number of references to her in Scripture.[1] This is partly due to a natural devotion to the mother of our Lord. It may also be partly a consequence of the reformers rejection of such devotions. After the Reformation, devotion to Our Lady was seen as an 'identifier' of ones religious affiliation and as a result it was exaggerated among Catholic communities and increasingly suppressed among Reformed communities.

The Council of Trent (1546) discussed the place of Mary while examining the subjects of original sin, justification and the use of holy images.[2] They avoided giving her the title 'The Immaculate Conception' but did pave the way for it by specifically excluding her from the teaching that all humans are damaged by original sin. They confirmed that Mary, by the grace of God, was free of personal sin. They instructed the faithful to venerate statues and paintings of Our Lady because they represented her person. More important than these specific teachings was their general statement on the relationship between Scripture and Tradition. Following considerable debate,[3] the council declared that

> The Council clearly perceives that this truth and rule are contained in the written books and unwritten Traditions which have come down to us, having been received by the apostles from the mouth of Christ himself or from the apostles by the dictation of the Holy Spirit, and have been transmitted as it were from hand to hand.[4]

The Second Vatican Council supported this approach and added to it by teaching that Tradition is a living, growing understanding of the Scriptures, nourished by reflection, study and preaching: 'For as the centuries succeed one another, the Church, constantly moves forward toward the fullness of divine truth until the words of God reach their complete fulfilment in her.'[5] Vatican II also stressed the importance of the Magisterium for solving theological debates: 'It is clear, therefore, that sacred Tradition, Sacred Scripture and the teaching authority of the Church, in accord with God's most wise design, are so linked and joined together that one cannot stand without the others.'[6] The Council applied this principle specifically to theologians preparing the schema on Our Lady: 'Following the study of Sacred Scripture, the Holy Fathers, the doctors and liturgy of the Church, and under the guidance of the Church's Magisterium, let them rightly illustrate the duties and privileges of the Blessed Virgin ...'[7]

We cannot here look at all of these areas of study. The final document on the Church, *Lumen Gentium*, which did study these areas in detail, devoted a chapter to Our Lady, which we will examine in chapter sixteen, which we have been rather pre-empting in the above paragraphs. The reason for this is to demonstrate that there is more to Tradition than simply the early history of the Church. Tradition did not become calcified with the end of the Apostolic age, or even of the Fathers. However, the teaching of those who lived in the earliest years of the Church is of particular interest. So a brief look at what the Early Fathers had to say about Our Lady will be of relevance.

Ignatius of Antioch (d. *c.*110 AD), wrote seven letters while on his way to Rome to be martyred. He was concerned to emphasise the true humanity of Jesus and was the first writer after the gospels to name Mary. He defended the belief in her virginity and her participation in the plan of salvation. He is the source of the popular theory of the birth of the Saviour being hidden from Satan through Mary's marriage to Joseph.

Irenaeus, bishop of Lyon (d. after 193), is best known for his multi-volume work *Against Heresies* in which he defends the Church against the challenges of Gnosticism. Much of Irenaeus's work on Mary concentrates on the Eve/Mary typology—what Eve bound by her unbelief, Mary unbound by her faith. He makes several links: disobedience/obedience; death/life; mortality/immortality. Irenaeus wrote of Mary as an advocate and cause of salvation for the human race. He expressed his thoughts on the divine motherhood of Mary in terms that would later be used in the *Theotokos* debate. He had no doubts about the virginal conception. The marriage with Joseph was to hide the identity of Jesus from the power of the Devil until He was ready to reveal Himself. There are hints of the later theology of the relationship between Mary and the Church in his comment on the Magnificat 'Mary cried out prophetically in the name of the Church'.[8]

Origen (c.185–254 AD) was one of the most influential theologians of the third century. He argued for the virginity of Mary on the grounds that this was a sign of the divinity of Jesus. He also seems to have anticipated Augustine's ideas on conjugal relations as being sinful and the means by which original sin is transmitted. Therefore he argues for the perpetual virginity of Mary. Origen took the common Eastern view that the 'brothers of the Lord' were children of Joseph by an earlier marriage. Mary's marriage to Joseph was necessary in order to protect both Mary's reputation and the identity of her son. Origen had an exalted view of Mary as the spiritual mother of all those who strove to understand the gospels. However he does not seem to have regarded Mary as totally free of sin. He interprets Simeon's prophecy about a sword piercing her heart as foretelling her doubt at the foot of the cross. He also says that, if she had not doubted, Jesus would not have died for her sins. Basil the Great (330–379) is one of the Doctors of the Church. Basil's teaching on Mary follows those of Origen—the perpetual virginity of Mary, the doubt at the cross, the prophetic nature of the Magnificat. He followed Alexander of Alexandria, patriarch of Alexandria at the time of the Council of Nicaea (325), in using the term *Theotokos*.

Gregory of Nyssa (*c.*335–394 AD) emphasised the virginity of Mary. He was the first to suggest that she had been dedicated to the temple by her parents and had taken a vow of virginity. The temple priests chose Joseph as a husband for her on the understanding that he would honour her vow. Gregory also writes on the Eve/Mary theme and hints at Mary as a sinless example for others to aspire to. He teaches that the 'brothers of the Lord' were sons of a previous marriage of Joseph. Gregory emphasises the joy of Mary; she received the news of her pregnancy with joy and gave birth to Jesus in joy in contrast to Eve's pain and sorrow.

Ambrose (339–397) wrote extensively on the perpetual virginity of Mary. He also confirmed her sinlessness. He used many Old Testament images for Mary, including from the Song of Songs.

Mary had exemplary faith that did not desert her at the cross. He was the first Latin Father to use the phrase *'Mater Dei'*, the Western equivalent of the Greek *'Theotokos'*. Mary had a share in overthrowing the power of the Devil. She is a type of the Church. She was the temple of God, not a God of the temple and therefore must not be adored.

Jerome (c.347–420 AD), is best known for translating the Scriptures into Latin. In reply to a popular debate of his time over the rival merits of marriage and virginity, Jerome supported the perpetual virginity of Mary. He argued that 'Just as we do not deny what is written, we reject what is not written' and 'The first-born is not one after whom others come but before whom there was none.'[9] In other words, there is no Scriptural evidence for Mary and Joseph consummating their marriage after the birth of Jesus and therefore this idea is not to be believed.

Augustine (354–430), bishop of Hippo, stressed the virginity of Mary before, during and after the birth of Jesus. He clarified Gregory of Nyssa's idea of a vow of virginity. He explained the virginity *in partu* by comparing it to the ability of the risen Christ to pass through closed doors. Augustine was the first to give a systematic treatment of the marriage of Mary and Joseph. He argued that their joint virginity strengthened the marriage bond. Their marriage had all the goods of any marriage; offspring, loyalty and sacrament in Jesus, fidelity and indissolubility. As it is conjugal love that makes a marriage, not conjugal intercourse, theirs was a true marriage. Augustine mentions the Eve/Mary typology but prefers to speak of Christ as spouse of the Church. He uses the role of women at the resurrection to restore their dignity. Augustine placed great emphasis on Mary's faith. This was more important than her motherhood. He also compared Mary to the Church; both are virginal yet fruitful.

Summary

Mariology has been a popular subject throughout the history of the Church and it is impossible to summarise here its development through the centuries. The above brief look at the teachings of the Early Fathers shows that the core beliefs of the Church regarding Mary can be traced back to its earliest writings which tell us that she was the mother of God, was a perpetual virgin and was sinless. They talk of her faith as an example for us to follow, her role as mother of the Church and as a type of the Church. We will bring this teaching up to date in chapter sixteen.[10]

Notes

1   See chapter four 'Scripture: Our Lady'.

2   The following comes from M. O'Carroll, *Theotokos: A Theological Encyclopaedia of the Blessed Virgin Mary* (Eugene: Wipf and Stock Publishers, 1982), unless otherwise stated.

3   The *'partim ... partim'* debate mentioned in chapter seven.

4   The General Council of Trent Fourth Session. *Decree on Sacred Books and on Traditions to be Received* (1546), in ND, p. 77, §210.

5   DV, §8.

6   DV, §10.

7   LG, § 67.

8   St Irenaeus of Lyons, *Adversus Haereses* III,10,1 2 as quoted in M. O'Carroll, *Theotokos*, p. 190.

9   Both quotes from 'Jerome' in M. O'Carroll, *Theotokos*, pp. 195–197.

10   As a bit of a sideline, you may like to think of comparing the first family with the Holy Family—see Appendix II, section C.

10 WOMEN

A s we approach the subject at the heart of this present work, it is important to remind ourselves of the definition of 'Tradition', as the word is used by the Church:

> The Tradition here in question comes from the apostles and hands on what they received from Jesus' teaching and example and what they learned from the Holy Spirit ... Tradition is to be distinguished from the various theological, disciplinary, liturgical or devotional traditions, born in the local churches over time.[1]

So traditions can be adapted, added to or abandoned according to the needs of the time and place but Tradition is unchanging and carries the same authority as Scripture. 'Sacred Tradition and Sacred Scripture form one sacred deposit of the word of God, committed to the Church.'[2] Thus the practice of reserving ordination to men only, if part of Church traditions, could be changed, but, if part of apostolic Tradition, could not. The Church teaches that there is more to Tradition than the written word of Scripture, which itself took some time to be written down and whose final form was guided by Tradition. Yet Tradition and Scripture cannot contradict each other. So we must look to the message of Scripture, the teachings and practice of the apostolic Church and the constant practice of the Church in order to decide whether or not the diaconal ordination of women would be against Tradition, and therefore impossible for the Church to adopt, or merely against tradition and therefore a practise that could be changed.

We have already seen that Scripture alone cannot be used to settle the debate over the role of women in the Church. This debate is a very modern one, at least as far as the priesthood is concerned, as the question of ordaining women to the priesthood was simply unthinkable in a world where women could not go on to higher education or hold any positions of authority in the community. The only exceptions were those women who exercised authority in the name of their husbands or sons or who became queens. Yet, if we go back in history, we find that women did hold important positions in the Church. There has been much detailed and scholarly work done in this field over the last fifty years. Every so often, a book appears that is described as the definitive, and last, work on the subject. Yet the debate continues and more 'definitive and last' books appear. Much of the debate centres on the historical evidence for, or against, women being ordained as deacons or priests in the early Church. Unfortunately, this evidence is not conclusive and respected theologians have studied it in detail and arrived at opposite conclusions. The classic example of this are the works of Martimort, who argued against women deacons, and Gryson, who argued for women deacons:

> Two of the most influential studies on the ordination of women as deaconesses were those of the French scholars Roger Gryson and Aime Georges Martimort. Both analysed at length the historical documents related to this office in the first centuries of Christianity... So thorough was the treatment of the subject by these two scholars that all later studies are either based on, or refer back to, these important contributions.[3]

Macy gives a brief but useful summary of the more influential modern authors in this field. The most cursory examination of just a few of the works that he refers to tells us that there were indeed deaconesses in the early Church, both East and West. There are examples of the rites used to confer this diaconate, which were referred to as ordination rites and were, in all but minor details, the same as the rites used for male deacons. All authors agree on this but disagree on the significance of these findings. Those in favour of reintroducing deaconesses argue that 'what the Church has done in the past, she can do again'. Those against argue that these ordinations were not 'true' ordinations but blessings for specific roles within the Church as they did not include the crucial tasks of serving in the sanctuary, especially assisting at the Eucharist and distributing communion.[4] At their best, the arguments on both sides can become very technical and can depend on differing interpretations and translations of Latin and Greek documents belonging to a bygone age. For several decades, these arguments seemed to be trapped in a maze of ever increasing circles, getting nowhere. At their worst, the arguments on both sides descend into prejudice and emotion without any sound historical or theological basis.

Of the various books that I have read, two struck me as being innovative and exciting. One was by Gary Macy, as quoted above.[5] The other was by Joan Morris. *Against Nature and God* gives a detailed history of the role of abbesses in Britain and Europe during the Middle Ages. She begins by reviewing the evidence in the early Church for women with the title 'episcopa'. Here her evidence is similar to that found in Macy, Madigan and Osiek and others. Where she comes into her own is in examining the lives of women living in community. She points out that these communities go back to apostolic times (Ac 9:36). The nature of these communities changed over the centuries. The early Church included communities of canonesses whose duties were similar to those of deaconesses and who usually lived close to the church or cathedral to which they were attached. One of their duties was to sing the Divine Office in the church, part of the official daily liturgy of the Church. Gradually, they either died out as society changed, or were deliberately forced to adopt the rules of the contemplative orders by order of the hierarchy. Morris suggests that this attitude was related to the increasing insistence on celibacy for priests; this would be easier if their female counterparts were out of sight!

> Perhaps it was due to the greater insistence on the celibacy of priests that it was thought desirable to have canonesses cloistered in the way usual in the purely contemplative orders, and that canonesses should no longer be required to function in parishes or cathedrals but only in their own private chapels or churches.[6]

Within the cloistered orders, Morris traces a considerable degree of juridical power exercised by the abbesses. These abbesses were, on the whole, from noble, even royal, families and expected to have the same authority as would a queen or empress. Indeed, they needed this authority in order to maintain their monasteries:

> The women's abbeys, in the same way as the men's abbeys, depended on the revenues of large territories. These included villages and towns, arable land and rural districts, which the abbesses were obliged to look after and to legislate

for by means of civil and ecclesial courts ... superiors of
religious orders were 'overseers' of their own districts, and
as such they had what was later termed 'quasi-episcopal'
prerogatives.[7]

The system seems to have been a successful one, with the abbesses
quite capable of exercising their authority to the benefit of their
communities. Indeed, their area of independence from the diocesan
bishops gradually increased.

> During the Middle Ages there was a big growth of monastic
> freedom. Not only abbots and abbesses and their communi-
> ties were exempt from the bishop's authority, but the secular
> clergy serving them and the laity within the village churches
> belonging to the monasteries were also included in the
> exemption.[8]

This inevitably created tensions between both abbots and abbesses
and the local bishops as the abbots and abbesses were under the
direct authority of the pope rather than the diocesan bishop. Morris
quotes several examples of abbesses having to appeal to the pope
to have their independence respected. These disputes do mean that
we have written evidence of the authority exercised by these
abbesses, with the blessing of the popes of the day. Thus we know
that they could be in charge of joint male and female monasteries,
be responsible for the selection and training of priests, licence
priests to practise in their areas and be in charge of the spiritual
development of the monks and nuns in their communities. That
they heard the confessions of their nuns, and in some cases the
priests under their authority, is documented but it could be argued
that this was at the level of spiritual direction. It is not at all clear
whether those concerned regarded it as a sacrament inclusive of
absolution. Morris concludes that they did. They also read the
gospel and preached.

Morris concludes from her studies that women who became
abbesses received the sacrament of ordination; received the
outward signs of their new roles—mitre, crosier, pallium according
to local custom; received the titles of 'episcopa', 'Sacerdota
Maxima', 'sacerdos', 'praeposita' and 'Custos' and exercised the
duties of a bishop.[9] They did not, however, act as priests in the
celebration of the Eucharist: 'Even if the ordination was the same

as that of men, as women they would have of their own accord withheld from touching the Eucharistic species.'[10] This was due to the belief held by both men and women from Old Testament times that women were somehow impure during their monthly periods, an example of the 'faulty anthropology'[11] so derided by modern feminists.[12]

Morris gives several reasons for the eventual demise of the quasi-episcopal abbess. She argues that Christianity had been a liberating force for women:

> There are proofs that early Christian law, such as the Code of Justinian, sought to bring about greater equality between the sexes. The lives of the empresses of the Byzantine Empire and of Margaret of Scotland testify to the acceptance of women as rulers, including of Church affairs.[13]

This attitude changed in response to several influences. The Renaissance, the Reformation and the Council of Trent were of major importance. The spirit of the Renaissance romanticised all things classical and encouraged a return to the values of ancient Greece,

> It was only after the twelfth century when there was a slow return to Greco-Roman culture, reaching its zenith during the Renaissance, that the services rendered by abbesses was looked upon as wrong ... The dislike of women having any right to rule shows that the whole idea of what it means to rule had become repaganized. Administration was no longer considered a service but a right of domination, a right to laud it over another, which was the pagan idea of government and not the Christian one of humble service.[14]

The changes brought about by the Reformation and its response from the Church, the Council of Trent, enabled the male leaders on both sides to formalise this reactionary attitude towards female leaders:

> By the sixteenth century the opinion of Aristotle vied with that of Christ. It was only at this time that monks began to think they could not be in obedience to a woman ... The Reformation returned to a Hebrew and Old Testament evaluation of women, which allowed her a position in the home but in subservience to her husband ... (in the Middle

Ages) the idea of the vow of obedience taken by clergy and monks, besides the nuns, to the abbess was considered a highly commendable act.[15]

By the time of the Catholic response to the Reformation, the Council of Trent, the Aristotelian view of women had become universal and influenced the actions of the Council. In an attempt to eliminate abuses (and protect male clergy from temptation?) the Council imposed strict enclosure on all female religious orders, ordered them to join with a male congregation, whose abbot would be superior to their abbess, and placed them under the authority of the local bishop in his role as delegate of the Holy See.[16] A few monasteries resisted these changes and the last, Las Huelgas in Spain, retained independence until 1874.

This history of quasi-episcopal abbesses can be traced back to apostolic times, when women were the first, apart from the apostles themselves, to provide administrative leadership and to form Christian communities. 'For it is a noteworthy fact that all assemblies of Christian communities mentioned in the Acts of the Apostles and in the Epistles of Saint Paul are said to be in the houses of women.'[17] Records of women leaders of large communities of religious date from the fourth century, beginning with Marthana, deaconess of a mixed community in Seleucia, Asia Minor. By the fifth century there are descriptions of the identical ordination rites of abbots and abbesses. While the arguments, mentioned above, over the significance of the use of words such as 'ordained' or 'overseer' apply here, Morris's book is significant more for the evidence of the juridical power exercised by these abbesses. Regardless of their canonical status, they certainly demonstrated an ability to exercise the functions of a bishop, and did so for many centuries in many countries. They make a nonsense of the opinions of so many Church leaders of the eleventh century onwards regarding the academic and organisational abilities of women.

Finally, Morris reminds us of a point already made in chapter five: 'The Book of Genesis explains the domination of men over women as the result of the Fall and of sin. There is therefore a need for man to act against this tendency and to take steps to correct it.'[18]

Gary Macy's preface to his work acknowledges the scholarship of Joan Morris (and that of Frank Gillmann and Ida Raming) as the foundation on which he built. He adds two important findings to those covered by Morris and the other writers in this field. While Morris mentions Aristotle briefly as part of the influence of the Renaissance, Macy goes into more detail on the effect on theology of the reintroduction of Aristotelian philosophy. He also, and this is probably the chief contribution of this book, goes into great detail on the development of the meaning of the word 'ordination'. Several feminist writers have complained of women being written out of the history of the Church. Macy shows that they were also defined out of their place as ordained members of the Church. These two findings are closely linked.

Macy concentrates on the changes that took place in the Church in the eleventh to thirteenth centuries. As so often, the Church was in need of reform. There was an unhealthy lack of division between religious and secular affairs, with clergy at all levels involved in practical and political matters. European feudal land laws meant that the Church was a powerful landowner and even local priests in effect owned valuable properties. At the same time, the secular landowners often had control over the appointment of the priests and bishops. This caused many problems, particularly where the priests were married with families to support. They often regarded the church property as their own, to be passed on to their children, including the post of local priest.

> A historical factor in the promotion of celibacy in the Middle Ages was the problem which had already exercised minds in the 5th and 6th centuries — the effort to prevent the alienation of Church property, which might otherwise pass into the possession of the priest's family.[19]

It is often said that the Church discipline of priestly celibacy began in the twelfth century. While this is inaccurate, it is true that the practise of a celibate priesthood took some time to develop. It is based on several Scriptural passages.

> The biblical foundations for celibacy are taken to be the saying of the Lord about not marrying ('becoming a eunuch') for the sake of the kingdom of heaven (Mt 19:10ff); also the saying about leaving one's wife for the sake of Jesus

and the gospel (Mk 10:29) or for the sake of the reign of God
(Lk 18:29); and also the saying which affirms that in the
resurrection there will be no marriage (Mt 22:30; Mk 12:25).[20]

There are also the teachings of Paul that it is better to be able to
devote oneself exclusively to the work of the Church (1Co 7:32)
and that one should remain in whatever state one was in at
conversion. While these precepts were directed at all the faithful,
they were particularly applicable to the leaders (1 Tm, Tt).
However marriage was the norm for the first two centuries of the
Church. By the time of the Council of Nicaea in AD 325 celibacy
was expected. Canon 3 of the council states

> This great synod absolutely forbids a bishop, presbyter,
> deacon or any of the clergy to keep a woman who has been
> brought in to live with him, with the exception of course of
> his mother or sister or aunt, or of any person who is above
> suspicion.[21]

Men who had been married before ordination continued to be so
but were expected to remain continent. Unmarried men and
widowers were expected to remain unmarried. These rules seem
to have been honoured more in the breach than the observance, at
least by secular clergy. However monastic orders were always
celibate and the celibate/virginal state was highly honoured and
held up as the ideal. So the Church continued to expect it, at least
from the bishops. Gradually, the pattern in the Eastern and
Western Church changed. The East allowed priests to marry but
chose bishops only from those who had remained celibate. The
West introduced stricter and stricter rules in order to maintain a
celibate priesthood. The reintroduction of Aristotelian philosophy
into Europe in the eleventh century gave Church leaders a powerful tool to use in their struggle to maintain a celibate priesthood.
Without a detailed knowledge of human biology, Aristotle had
concluded that a pregnant woman merely provided food and
shelter for the foetus, allowing the male sperm to develop into a
human baby. He decided that half of these babies being female
was simply an error in the developmental process causing the male
material to become corrupted in some way. Thus, women were
incomplete or deformed men and therefore inferior to the com-

plete, correctly formed variety.[22] The Church adopted this picture of women with enthusiasm, enlarging on it as the centuries passed. By the thirteenth century, Thomas Aquinas could state without risk of contradiction that 'Only as regards nature in the individual is the female something defective and accidental'.[23] He goes on to say that, as part of the species as a whole, woman is not malformed (*manqué*) but is directed to the work of procreation. However, this important function was not enough to save women from distain. They were defective in their ability to reason, were weak mentally, physically and spiritually, were the source of sin through Eve and gave forth pollution on a monthly basis. 'Women were in effect considered to be monsters. Unnatural in birth, incompetent in mind and disgusting in their bodily functions, they were clearly inferior to men.'[24] It was a simple matter for the Church leaders to argue that physical contact with such creatures was not compatible with celebrating the Eucharist and handling the consecrated host. Celibacy was the only choice for men who felt called to serve the Church as priests. Given this general attitude, it was easier for the Church to gain support for stricter rules on celibacy. In 1074 Pope Gregory VII ended the concession allowing men who were ordained after marriage to continue to cohabit with their wives. Then the Lateran Council of 1139 declared the marriage of priests to be invalid. This finally solved the problem of priestly families claiming Church property as any children were illegitimate and therefore had no legal claim to their father's estate. It also discouraged women from entering into relationships with priests as they knew that any children would be illegitimate, a serious drawback in all but the poorest communities.

The Aristotelian view of women affected them in several ways. Their presumed lack of reasoning ability meant that they could not be allowed into the new universities; they were incapable of being in command or presiding over any organisation or project and therefore could not be given any position of authority; they could tempt man into sin and must therefore not speak in public—a view backed with quotes from 1 Corinthians 10:7 and 1 Timothy 2:14. It quickly became unthinkable for women to have any place in the liturgy of the Church, so much so that the evidence that they had had such positions was discredited and disbelieved. The only source of education was within religious communities, and even here it depended on the good will of the local clergy.

Complementary to this view of women was the revised Canon Law, based on the *Decretum* of Gratian of 1140. Gratian had chosen to adopt an early version of Roman law that placed stress on the father as head of the family: 'Women were considered as children or servants in canon law, subject to the protection and the correction of males. No longer were women considered the intellectual equals of men. They were flighty, unreliable and hopelessly ignorant.'[25] These views of women were arrived at by choices made by the men in power. Neither Roman Law nor Aristotelian philosophy were mandatory. Scholars could, and did, accept or reject them in whole or in part as opinions varied. It suited the Church to accept them, as it facilitated the drive to reform the Church, particularly in the area of a celibate priesthood. Pope Gregory VII, described as 'a legal genius',[26] was responsible for the acceptance by the Church of Gratian's research into the ancient Roman legal system. It has to be added that

> This was not a simple, well planned and crude grab for power. The reformers believed that they were purifying the church ... They believed they were using the best and brightest legal sources available in Roman law. They believed that they were using the most astute philosophy and best science available to them in the texts of Aristotle. They believed that Scripture supported their position and that this is what God wanted and what God intended.[27]

Important as the reforms in philosophy and law were to the position of women, it is in the third area that Macy examines that the most long-lasting effects were felt. This is where he looks at the redefinition of the sacrament of ordination. There are several strands to the argument: definition and use of the word 'ordination'; purpose of ordination (is it to a specific function in a specific place or spiritual powers to be exercised anywhere) and narrowing of this purpose from service to a community to celebrating the Eucharist.

Macy argues that the use of the word itself has become narrower and more specific over the centuries. Today, the word is used for the liturgical ritual that confers episcopal, priestly or diaconal orders. Originally, the word meant a change of role or function and was used in both a religious and a secular setting. He comments on a series of studies of the sacrament of orders written in 1957. 'Gy argued that the term *ordo* originated with the political structure of the Roman Empire in which powerful societal groups were known as *ordines* (orders).'[28] But

> contrary to the opinion offered by Gy in 1957, Beneden (supporting the work of Yves Congar) demonstrated that Christians adopted the concept of *ordo* from everyday usage and not from Roman social structure. According to Beneden, *ordinatio* for the early Christian indicated the appointment and consecration of a person to a particular charge or function.[29]

Thus kings and queens, emperors and empresses, as well as people entering religious life, were referred to as being ordained. Even within the religious, it was used for roles that today would not be considered as part of the clergy:

> The Roman pontifical of the thirteenth century also spoke of the 'ordination' of doorkeepers, lectors, exorcists and acolytes ... the evidence was mounting that a different definition of what ordination entailed and who could be ordained was developed in the twelfth and thirteenth centuries.[30]

Macy quotes Gy in support of this claim. Even if Benedin's criticism of Gy is valid and the word was not adopted from Roman social use, its widespread application before the twelfth century seems beyond dispute:

> In the ancient vocabulary (*ordinare*) meant not only the ordination prayer but the whole process which this prayer terminates. At the same time *ordinatio* was also used, in the high middle ages, for kings, abbots and abbesses, and by Christian Roman law for civil servants.[31]

Macy quotes several theologians who identify the twelfth and thirteenth centuries as a time of great change in the way in which the word was used.[32] Some specifically pinpointed this change to the Lateran Councils of 1179 and 1215.[33] In the early Church, 'ordination' comprised both the process of the community selecting and of inaugurating a person for a specific role within that community. The Lateran Councils used the word for the liturgical rite of inauguration only. More importantly, they introduced the practise of ordinations with universal application rather than for specific communities. Schillebeeckx highlighted this change of emphasis from ordination to a specific function within a specific community to ordination as the cause of an ontological change,[34] empowering the recipient to perform certain functions at any time or place.

> Schillebeeckx's work confirmed the conclusion of earlier scholars that there was a fundamental and significant change in the understanding of what constituted Christian ministry in the twelfth and thirteenth centuries … It was the intro- duction of Roman law and hence a more legalistic approach to ministry that caused the change, a change that occurred at the conclusion of and partly as the result of the eleventh- century reform movement.[35]

This change in the understanding of ministry centres on the importance of the Mass to Catholic worship. During the eleventh and twelfth centuries there was theological debate over exactly what was necessary for transubstantiation to occur — the words of institution, the Lord's prayer and the sign of the cross were all proposed as essential. There was also debate over who could confect the sacrament;

> At the beginning of the twelfth century, for instance, scholars were not at all in agreement that a priest alone could effect the transformation of the bread and wine into the body and blood of Christ. At least three twelfth century scholars are known to have put forward the theory that the words of consecration themselves confect, regardless of who says them.[36]

Macy suggests that the statement of the Lateran Council IV in 1215 on the Mass 'And this sacrament no one can effect except the priest who has been duly ordained in accordance with the keys of the Church, which Jesus Christ himself gave to the Apostles and their successors'[37] was not so much reiterating an established belief of the Church as answering a theological debate of the day. By teaching that only an ordained priest could consecrate the elements, the Church confirmed the position of the priest as someone set aside for the purpose of celebrating the liturgy, and especially the Mass. Because ordination caused an ontological change, the ordained man was empowered to exercise his priestly function anywhere and for the rest of his life[38] as his powers were not dependent on the community that he served.[39] In the years following the Lateran Council, all liturgical functions came to be defined more and more by their relationship to the Eucharist.[40] The priest was the leader of the community because he was the unique mediator of God's grace through his ability to consecrate the elements during Mass. He quickly became the only person thought fit to lead any liturgical activity. 'In the older definition of ordination, one officiated at ceremonies because one had been chosen by the community to lead the community; in the later understanding, one led the community because one was empowered to perform the ceremonies.'[41]

Macy argues that, under the older definition of ordination, as used in the early Church, both men and women were ordained and women served as deaconesses.

> Women functioned in their several liturgical and adminis-
> trative roles not as laity, but as ordained ministers. They
> were not ordained, however, as ordination would come to
> be understood from the 12th century on, that is, as receiving
> a personal irrevocable power to serve at the altar. They were
> commissioned for particular roles in particular communi-
> ties … so were men … Both men and women understood
> themselves to be ordained in the same way, although to
> different *ordines*.[42]

This last point, that men and women regarded themselves as having received the same sacrament of ordination, is at the centre of Macy's argument. He quotes examples of liturgical rites that place ordained women in the same rank as ordained men, and above the lesser ranks such as acolyte or lector. This implies that these women were accepted by both the congregations and the hierarchy of the Church as part of the clergy.[43] He accepts that those examples of women acting as priests are rare and probably examples of malpractise that were quickly suppressed.[44] However the examples of women as ordained to the roles of deaconesses and abbesses are numerous. One document, quoted by both Martimort and Madigan & Osiek, is a letter written in 1017 by Pope Benedict VIII (1012–1024) to the bishop of Porto, which was confirmed by Pope John XIX (1024–1032) and Pope Leo IX (1049–1054): 'The bishops of Porto saw confirmed on three occasions the privileges of celebrating in the Trastevere area "*omnem ordinationem episcopalem, tam de presbyteris quam diaconibus vel diaconissis seu subdiaconibus, ecclesiis vel altaribus …*"'.[45] Madigan and Osiek provide a translation: 'In the same way, we concede and confirm to you and to your successors in perpetuity every episcopal ordination (ordinationem episcopalem), not only of presbyters but also of deacons or deaconesses (diaconissis) or subdeacons.'[46] Martimort explains away the inclusion of deaconesses with a choice of two possible explanations:

> For were not these deaconesses the wives of deacons, consecrated at the same time as their husbands? However, there was another decretal, also addressed to the bishop of Silva Candida … This time we find deaconesses mentioned alongside nuns, which corresponds much more closely to the image that the Mainz pontifical provided for us.[47]

These quotes are interesting for several reasons. They are an example of the same piece of historical evidence being used by scholars who then arrive at opposite conclusions as to their significance. If the letter from Pope Benedict VIII is taken literally, it shows that women were ordained by bishops in Rome to the position of deaconess during the eleventh century. They came after deacons but before sub-deacons in the hierarchy. What it does not show is what these deaconesses did. Martimort suggests that they were the wives of the deacons. This is a popular theory and does have a certain logic to it. On ordination, the priest, and certainly the bishop, would be expected to be celibate. This necessitates his wife also being celibate. It has been suggested that she would have an honoured place in the community and be seen as sharing in her husband's ministry. This could be acknowledged by giving her a blessing and the title of deaconess. The obvious counter-argument to this is that there is no supporting evidence and the document quoted does use the word 'ordination', as do many other documents. It could explain why deaconesses are not mentioned in later documents as the reformed Church did not have married priests and therefore did not need this honorary position for their wives. However it does not explain the existence of deaconesses in the early Church before celibacy was expected.

The most important lesson to learn from these quotes is that people will believe what they want to believe and interpret the evidence accordingly. Because Martimort equates 'ordination' with priesthood, cannot find evidence for women sharing in the liturgy of the altar and does not believe in women priests, he cannot accept that women were ordained in the past and has to explain away any evidence to the contrary. Macy points out that, because they did not serve at the altar, does not mean that they were not ordained. To say that women did not serve at the altar and therefore were not ordained is to apply a definition of the sacrament that did not exist until the 12th century. Applying the definition of ordination that was used at the time that these texts were written gives the conclusion that these women were just as ordained as their male colleagues.

Under the influence of Lateran Council IV, ordination was seen as specifically instituted for those who took part in the liturgy of the Mass, priests and deacons. As we have already seen, women could not serve at the altar. So this new meaning of ordination in effect defined them out of the sacrament. The combination of the Aristotelian view of women, the revised code of canon law based on the old version of Roman law and the new definition of ordination caused women to loose all standing in the Church. Not only was it unthinkable that they could become ordained in the future, it was also unthinkable that they might have been so in the past. Any texts suggesting otherwise were either mistranslations or misunderstood.

I suggested earlier that this change in the definition of ordination had a more profound effect on the place of women in the Church than either the Aristotelian view of women or the effect of the revised canon law. This is because the other two could be, and indeed have been, changed. As the place of women in society gradually improved, so it did in the Church. Today, women can, at least in theory, exercise their talents for the good of the Church in any sphere and at any level with the one exception of the ordained diaconate and priesthood. Many scholars argue that it is now time for this last barrier to be removed. Macy himself supports this position but does realise that the argument is more complicated than simply presenting the evidence for the existence of deaconesses in the early Church:

> It is quite possible that history alone cannot solve this impasse, unless some new and irrefutable evidence appears to support one or the other position … the theological argument must be made that the definition of the late Middle Ages is proscriptive for the present … Different popes supported the different understandings of ordination, and Scripture can be (and has been) read to support or deny ordination to women.[48]

Much of the discussion in this section might seem to be more suited to part III on the Magisterium. It has been included here because the role of Tradition in the Church holds the key to finding some way forward in this debate. Macy, in common with many authors in this field, fails to mention the role of Tradition. While Tradition can develop, it cannot change completely and the Church cannot make decisions that contradict positions that it took previously. So the crucial point in this debate is not so much the historical facts or even the most suitable definition of 'ordination' but whether or not the changes brought about by the Lateran Councils were part of the legitimate development of doctrine or were 'From the various theological, disciplinary, liturgical or devotional traditions, born in the local churches over time'.[49] If they were part of the former, they cannot be changed, although they could be developed. If they are part of the latter, they could be changed in the same way that many of the other restrictions on the role of women have been.

Summary

I have concentrated on the work of two scholars, both historians and theologians, who provide evidence for the existence of deaconesses and abbesses who were ordained with the approval of the Church. They both acknowledge that there is insufficient evidence for the existence of women priests. Morris concentrates on the evidence for abbesses who exercised quasi-episcopal powers. Macy concentrates on the changing definition of the word 'ordination'. Both Morris and Macy identify changes in the eleventh and twelfth centuries as responsible for the loss of status by women. These changes are principally the reintroduction of Aristotelian philosophy, the adoption of Roman law as a basis for canon law and an emphasis on ordination as conferring an ontological change empowering the recipient to celebrate the Eucharist. Each of these changes individually was detrimental to the position of women. The cumulative effect was devastating.

The historical evidence on its own cannot solve the question of whether or not the modern Church should reintroduce deaconesses or allow women priests. The debate has to be a theological one. It has to look at the Tradition of the Church and decide whether or not the changes of the eleventh and twelfth centuries were legitimate developments of that Tradition. In order to do this, it needs to use the third source of authoritative teaching in the Church, the Magisterium. Before turning to this source, let us summarise what we have learned from this look at Tradition.

Notes

1   CCC, §83.
2   DV, §10.
3   G. Macy, *The Hidden History of Women's Ordination: Female Clergy in the Medieval West* (Oxford: OUP, 2008).
4   For a detailed examination of this point from the Greek Orthodox Church, see K. FitzGerald *Women Deacons in the Orthodox Church: called to Holiness and Ministry* (Massachusetts: Holy Cross Orthodox Press, 1999), especially chapter 6. Basing her arguments on the work of Professor Theodorou, she concludes that the deaconesses of the early Church were ordained, not simply appointed or given a blessing. This view was endorsed by the Inter Orthodox Theological Consultation held on Rhodes in 1988, which called for the re-establishment of the order of female deacons.
5   For an introduction to the work of Gary Macy, see his extended essay in G. Macy, W. Ditewig and P. Zagano, *Women Deacons: Past, Present, Future* (New York: Paulist Press, 2011). I would however ask the reader to treat the forward to this book and the essay by Phyllis Zagano with some caution as they occasionally express views, at least implicitly, that are at variance with the spirit of the Magisterium, if not the actual letter.
6   J. Morris, *Against Nature and God: The History of Women with Clerical Ordination and the Jurisdiction of Bishops* (London: Mowbrays, 1973), p. 11. She says on page 15 that the move of canonesses from the precincts of the cathedrals to

more distant quarters occurred in the twelfth century.

7   *Ibid.*, p. 17.
8   *Ibid.*, p. 20.
9   Modern rites for the induction of abbesses still include the presentation of, for example, a crozier where local custom allows.
10   J. Morris, *Against Nature and God*, p. 138.
11   A faulty view of feminine nature, based on the writings of Aristotle, as explained below.
12   K. FitzGerald, *Women Deacons in the Orthodox Church*, quotes several Early Fathers, particularly John Chrysostom and St Gregory the Great (see esp. p. 66) as teaching that women were not to be considered impure because of their God-given natures. She accepts that this teaching seems to have been ignored by both men and women.
13   J. Morris, *Against Nature and God*, p. 100. It must be pointed out that Margaret of Scotland was not the ruler of the country – her husband, Malcolm Canmore, was. However Margaret both called and influenced Church councils in Scotland and was responsible for modernising Church governance and bringing it into line with the rest of Europe.
14   *Ibid.*, p. 56.
15   *Ibid.*, p. 101.
16   They would thus seem to be ignoring the message of Martha and Mary, active and contemplative, equally loved by Jesus. See p. 45.
17   J. Morris, *Against Nature and God*, p. 1.
18   *Ibid*, p. 158.
19   L.M. Weber 'Celibacy', in K. Rahner *Encyclopaedia of Theology* (London: Burns and Oates, 1975), p. 179.
20   *Ibid.*, p. 178.
21   N. Tanner, lecture 'The Early Church Councils' at Maryvale Institute, Birmingham, June 2004.
22   Aristotle, *Politics: The Athenian Constitution*, translated by J. Warrington (London: Heron Books by arrangement with J. M. Dent and Sons Ltd, 1959?). 'Towards his wife he is in the position of a statesman governing fellow citizens. The male is naturally more fitted to command than the female … (a ruler expects respect and signs of his status, even if only ruling for a term) and it is in this relation that the male stands to the female *at all times,* not merely for a term.' p. 23.
23   ST XIII, 1,Q.92 a1.1.
24   G. Macy, *The Hidden History of Women's Ordination*, p. 121.
25   *Ibid.*, p. 119.
26   P. Hughes, *The Church in Crisis: A History of the General Councils, 325–1870* (London: Burns and Oates, 1960), p. 175.
27   G. Macy, *The Hidden History of Women's Ordination*, p. 126.
28   *Ibid.,* p. 27, quoting from an article by Pierre-Marie Gy.
29   *Ibid.,* p. 29 Pierre van Beneden studied the use of the word ordo in the first three centuries.

30 *Ibid.,* p. 28, quoting from a study by René Metz.
31 P. Gy, 'Ancient Ordination Prayers' p. 80, in G. Macy, *The Hidden History of Women's Ordination,* p. 30.
32 This view is supported by Piet Fransen in K Rahner (ed.), *Encyclopedia of Theology,* in his article 'Orders and Ordination' pp. 1122–1148. While he does not agree with Gy's theory that the hierarchy of the Church was modelled on civil powers, he does agree that the words '*ordinatio*' and '*consecratio*' were given narrower meanings in the twelfth century.
33 For example, Schillebeeckx, 'Ministry' p. 52, in G. Macy, *The Hidden History of Women's Ordination,* p. 31.
34 For a discussion on ontological change, see chapter fourteen 'Magisterium: ordination'.
35 G. Macy, *The Hidden History of Women's Ordination,* p. 32.
36 *Ibid.,* p. 42. The three were John Beleth and, probably, Bernard and Thierry of Chartres.
37 As quoted in G. Macy, *The Hidden History of Women's Ordination,* p. 46.
38 There was debate over whether or not this ontological change persisted after death, with the majority opinion being that it did.
39 It is important to remember that the idea of ontological change has always existed – remember Simon becoming Peter, as discussed in chapter three. Also, Canon Law requires bishop, priest and deacon to be ordained to serve in a specific area. Their powers are valid elsewhere but illicit without the authority of the local bishop.
40 This can be clearly seen in the work of St Thomas Aquinas – see chapter fourteen 'Magisterium: Ordination; Deacons'.
41 G. Macy, *The Hidden History of Women's Ordination,* p. 42.
42 *Ibid.,* p. 129.
43 For a comprehensive collection of these texts in the Western Church, see Madigan and Osiek. Examples are also to be found in Martimort, who opposes any form of ordination for women. The debate is not so much about whether or not women were given the title of 'deaconess' as about the significance of this title and the status of the ritual used to confer this title on them.
44 G. Macy, *The Hidden History of Women's Ordination,* p. 131.
45 A. Martimort, *Deaconesses* (San Francisco: Ignatius Press, 1982), p. 214. Neither book clarifies whether or not the two subsequent letters included the phrase about deaconesses or were simply renewing the privilege of conducting ordinations in general in the Trastevere area.
46 K. Madigan and C. Osiek, *Ordained Women in the Early Church* (Baltimore: The John Hopkins University Press, 2005), p. 147.
47 A. Martimort, *Deaconesses,* pp. 214–5.
48 G. Macy, *The Hidden History of Women's Ordination,* p. 131.
49 CCC, §83, as quoted at the beginning of this section as part of the definition of Tradition.

11 CONCLUSIONS FROM TRADITION

RADITION AND SCRIPTURE together form the deposit of faith, entrusted to the Magisterium of the Church. The Church is the kingdom of God on earth. It has a hierarchical structure, established by Jesus Christ and passed on through the College of Bishops, with the pope at their head. The transmission of authority is effected by the sacrament of ordination and has both a historical and collegial element. Ordination to the priesthood is reserved for men only. The origins of the priesthood go back to the Old Testament but there are fundamental differences between the priesthood of the old covenant and of the new. Jesus Christ is the one high priest and his sacrifice of himself cannot be repeated. We all have a share in this priesthood but the bishops, as successors to the apostles, have the extra responsibility of making Jesus's saving act present to all generations.

Because Jesus appointed only men as apostles, with the power to confect the Eucharist and forgive sins, the Church teaches that it cannot go against the Scriptural evidence and ordain women as priests. There is much debate over this. A modern school of theology, popularised by John Paul II's work on the theology of the body, suggests that Jesus's masculinity was an essential part of his identity as he was the Son of God, not just the child of God. This has implications for the debate on women priests.

Church Tradition on Our Lady goes back to Ignatius of Antioch and has consistently taught that she was the mother of God, remained a virgin all her life, was free from sin, gives us an example of faith and is both the mother of and a type of the Church.

The role of women in the Church has varied considerably. There is no historical evidence for the existence of legitimate female priests but there is evidence for deaconesses, from Paul's companion Phoebe until some time in the eleventh century. Neither Scripture nor Tradition can end the argument over their status and whether or not they could legitimately be reintroduced into the Church. We now need to turn to the teachings of the Magisterium.

Part Three
THE MAGISTERIUM

12 SOME GENERAL NOTES

W E ENDED THE last chapter by concluding that the historical evidence on the role of women in the Church was not conclusive enough to end the debate on female deacons. For the Church to decide what was or was not a legitimate development of Tradition, it had to refer to the authoritative teaching of the Church, the Magisterium.

The place of the Magisterium was defined in the Vatican II document *Dei Verbum*:

> Sacred Tradition and Sacred Scripture form one sacred deposit of the word of God, committed to the Church ... But the task of authentically interpreting the word of God, whether written or handed on, has been entrusted exclusively to the living teaching office of the Church, whose authority is exercised in the name of Jesus Christ.[1]

It is one of the primary duties of the bishops of the Church to ensure that the message of Scripture is authentically represented to each generation. They are assisted in this task by the work of theologians, who may be either ordained or lay, men or women.

> By their preliminary research theologians help to mature the judgement of the Church. By their technical skill they assist the bishops in the precise expression of Catholic doctrine. And even after the Magisterium has spoken, theologians play an important role in the reception and interpretation of doctrinal declarations.[2]

It is perhaps worth noting the use of the words 'help' and 'assist' which remind us that the theologian can advise but only the College of Bishops has the authority to make definitive statements.

The theologians in their turn base their work on a process of study and logical reasoning, usually very much influenced by previous magisterial statements, not on what non-believers like to call 'blind faith'. Yet there is a close link between the theologian's reasoning and his or her faith:

It should nevertheless be kept in mind that Revelation remains charged with mystery. It is true that Jesus, with his entire life, revealed the countenance of the Father, for he came to teach the secret things of God. But our vision of the face of God is always fragmentary and impaired by the limits of our understanding. Faith alone makes it possible to penetrate the mystery in a way that allows us to understand it coherently.[3]

So it is clear that there is a close relationship between theologians and the Magisterium of the Church. While the teaching authority of the Church rests with the Magisterium, the teaching itself does not arise in a vacuum. Before studying what the Church teaches, we need to be clear about its authority to do so and the status of its pronouncements. We have already seen that the Church believes that it has the right and duty to define the content of revelation.[4] This includes those Scriptural passages that are used to justify this belief, thus setting up an unavoidably circular argument. Fortunately, there is an influence outside of this circle; the guarantee of the validity of Church teaching ultimately rests on the guidance of the Holy Spirit. The above quote from *Dei Verbum* continues 'In accord with a divine commission and with the help of the Holy Spirit, it draws from this one deposit of faith everything which it presents for belief as divinely revealed.'[5] To deny the teaching of the Church is to deny that it is guided by the Holy Spirit. However there is a gradation in both the degree of authority with which this teaching is given and in the obedience expected of the faithful.[6] Here the work of theologians is important. We look at the work of several specific theologians in the other sections.[7] It might be worth pausing and thinking about the work of theologians in general.

Theologians

It is significant that the list of specific theologians mentioned in the above note contains eight men and only four women. There are several possible reasons for this imbalance. Perhaps I simply made this choice, many more women could have been included. There is some truth in this. However, as I specifically limited myself to theologians who are loyal to the Magisterium, my choice of women was severely restricted. It was also restricted because, until recently, it was difficult for women to gain the necessary educational background. Some male theologians have suggested that men are more suited to the discipline of theology than women, supporting the final possible reason, that there is a historical bias against women theologians. At the end of the day, does it really matter? I think that it does.

The classic definition of theology is that of Anselm; 'Faith seeking understanding' Since we are all called to faith, and to trying to deepen this faith, then theology is surely worth studying regardless of whether or not is was written by a man or a woman. However I think that there are good reasons for trying to get a better balance between the male and the female theological voices. There are even scientific reasons!

> Neurologists tell us that the brains of men and women react in different ways to the same stimuli; thus if our theological knowledge is to be as all-embracing as possible, it is obviously necessary for all questions to be analysed and commented on by both men and women.[8]

We discussed in chapter two that the teaching authority of the Church is closely linked to the work of theologians. John Paul II, who did so much to highlight the need for a balance of male and female, began his encyclical on the relationship between faith and reason with the sentence 'Faith and reason are like two wings on which the human spirit rises to the contemplation of truth ...'[9] Without female theologians, the wing of reason is clipped and we will fly in circles and struggle to reach our goal.

We have discussed in chapter eight that there are recognisable differences in the ways in which men and women think and work. Edith Stein gave an example of a political situation where an overly masculine approach produced a document that was so logically watertight that it defeated its aims by being quite unworkable in practise and left no room for diplomacy or compromise.[10] It is not difficult to think of many similar pieces of legislation today, especially in the areas of anti-terrorism, health and safety, and child-protection. It is probably not a coincidence that these areas all relate to the males traditional role of defending his family. What is missing is the feminine lateral thinking which can foresee the unintended restrictions on civic liberties and the unnecessary intrusions into daily life. It is possible that some of the recent clashes between politicians and religious establishments could have been avoided if more women had been involved in the debate. There is certainly a need for well-informed lateral thinking in response to the current political suppression of all aspects of public religious expression.

Other situations also suffer from a lack of balance. A look at the list of ecclesiastical writers referred to in the Catechism of the Catholic Church reveals that, of the sixty-seven names, only seven are women. Of these seven, three have only one quote and the most-quoted, Thérèse of Lisieux, has six. By comparison, Augustine has ninety-two quotes. The other sources used by the Catechism of the Catholic Church are Sacred Scripture (all male); professions of faith (all male); ecumenical councils (all male — Vatican II had four official female observers but they could not contribute to the formal debate.); pontifical and ecclesiastical documents (all male, although some of the more modern ones might have consulted women before making the final draft); canon law (post-Vatican II documents may have some female input?); the liturgy (all male). This situation does not even pay lip-service to the principle of 'equal but different'. The feminine voice is reduced to the faintest whisper. The work itself is a model of exactitude and precision. It is an excellent reference book but with little appeal to the more general reader. It is a classic example of a work that has been written by a committee. In common with most magisterial documents, the content is most worthy but the writing style is formulaic to the point of being unintelligible to the average reader. No matter how important the subject matter or inspiring the message, if it cannot be understood by its target audience, then it has failed. This applies to much of the literature coming from the Vatican. A few women on the drafting committees would help!

There is also the question of the public perception of the teaching voice of the Church. At the moment, it is all too easy for people to dismiss teachings that they do not like as being the product of elderly, celibate, male recluses who are totally out of touch with modern life. Women in particular can claim with some justification that the senior dignitaries of the Church are too removed from the realities of their lives to be able to pass judgement on them. While women could also be elderly, celibate recluses, it is more likely that they would at least appreciate the need to be seen to consult a wider range of opinion. They would also, at least in theory, be more able to empathise with women living in the wider world.

A more nuanced definition of theology than that of Anselm is that of Aidan Nichols: 'The task of theology is the disciplined exploration of what is contained in revelation.'[11] As the Church is the guardian of revelation, there is a close relationship between theologians and the hierarchy of the Church. So a greater proportion of female theologians would help to give the whole Church a more balanced approach, would perhaps result in more 'user-friendly' teaching and would give it a better public image. This is important, as the Church cannot function as the source of revelation unless she is accepted as an authoritative teacher of this revelation.

Just to prove that I am not alone in feeling that the sex of the theologian matters, here are some quotes from various Dominican theologians. The first is by Wojciech Giertych, OP, a member of the Polish province of friars and a theology teacher in Rome.

> If, however, our community life ceases to be demanding (and this sometimes happens in our communities, particularly in male communities, where we easily drift into individualism), and if we fail to make the effort to study theology, we are then helpless, and our spiritual life and our vocation may then crash ... Both the male and the female mind have both intellect and reason. But the female mind is more intellectual, and the male mind is more rational.[12]

The second quote is from Liam Walsh, OP, who is a member of the Irish province of friars. He has taught theology in Rome and Fribourg, Switzerland. He is writing an 'open letter' to his sister, also a Dominican theologian: 'Theology is the human taking hold of the Word of God ... Today it needs to include very explicitly the voice of women.'[13]

Lastly, we have Petronille Kayiba from the Democratic Republic of the Congo, where she teaches theology. She is a member of the

Dominican Sisters of the Rosary and has served as Provincial for her order and as Justice and Peace Promoter for Africa:

> The Church throughout all countries and continents needs women theologians to speak about God in a new way, accessible to all and understandable by all.[14]

Authoritative teaching

While the work of theologians is important at all times in the Church, it becomes crucial at the high-points of the workings of the Magisterium, the general councils. The first of these was at Nicaea in AD 325, the findings of which are summarised later. The reader will find an appendix at the end of this work defining some of the more important heresies of the church and giving a very brief summary of the other councils in the history of the Church. This will give the reader an idea of the issues that the Church has had to address over the centuries and may demonstrate why it cannot contradict previous authoritative teachings and has to be careful about introducing new practises as it cannot simply 'move with the times'.

Authority within the Church was an important issue for the three most recent Ecumenical Councils, those of Trent, Vatican I and Vatican II. We do not need to examine all these councils in detail, as the last summarised the teachings of the other two. 'The doctrine proposed by the Magisterium about itself is to be found in its fullest and most authentic form in the third chapter of Vatican II's Dogmatic Constitution on the Church.'[15] So we will concentrate on the teachings of Vatican II, rather than trace their development through the centuries. The teachings relevant to Church authority centre on the infallibility of the pope and the role of bishops. Vatican I had defined papal infallibility but had had to close before examining the role of bishops. So Vatican II set out to complete this task. In the Dogmatic Constitution on the Church (*Lumen Gentium*), it confirmed the pope as the successor of Peter, with an infallible Magisterium (§18). The bishops are the successors of the apostles (§20). This is all familiar teaching. There were two points of teaching that demonstrated a progression in the theology of the role of bishops; the principle of collegiality and the statement that the bishop receives the fullness of the sacrament of ordination.

Collegiality

The principle of collegiality is explained in chapter III, §22 of *Lumen Gentium*. The apostles formed a single college with Peter at their head, so the pope and bishops together form a college. The evidence for this as the constant practice of the Church is the practice, dating from the time of the apostles, of calling councils to discuss weighty matters, of bishops from throughout the world maintaining union with each other and with the pope, of several bishops being called together to consecrate a bishop-elect: 'One is constituted a member of the Episcopal body in virtue of sacramental consecration and hierarchical communion with the head and members of the body.'[16] Thus, a bishop can only exercise his power validly if he is in communion both with his fellow bishops and with the pope.[17] At the time of the council, there was much discussion over the wording of this section of the document. Many bishops were worried that the idea of collegiality threatened the teaching on papal infallibility:

> Theologians looking for discontinuity in doctrinal development often write as though Vatican II's teaching on collegiality, correctly understood, had overturned the 'papal absolutism' imposed by Vatican I. (However) The section of *Lumen Gentium* that deals with collegiality was carefully composed so as to make it unmistakably clear that the pope's powers of teaching and jurisdiction, as defined by Vatican I, were in no way curtailed.[18]

Lumen Gentium quotes extensively from the early Fathers to demonstrate that, while the doctrine was new to Vatican II, the general principle had always existed and the early Church acted as a College of Bishops, even if it did not call itself such.[19]

Lumen Gentium also refers to the teachings of several popes in the nineteenth and twentieth centuries who confirmed that bishops, while primarily responsible for their own dioceses, had authority to teach the whole Church, as long as they remained in communion with their fellow bishops.

Thus, we come to a better understanding of the fullness of
the priesthood of bishops. What is involved is a fullness
which, in the exercise of power over the universal Church,
is collegial by its very nature and subject to the authority of
the pope.[20]

Lumen Gentium §25 spells out the obedience due to the teaching of
bishops. While the problem of dissent from official teaching is here
being addressed on a world-wide basis, we can hear echoes of the
same problems that caused Clement to write his letter to the church
of Corinth so many centuries before:

> In matters of faith and morals, the bishops speak in the name
> of Christ and the faithful are to accept their teaching and
> adhere to it with a religious assent ... Although the indi-
> vidual bishops do not enjoy the prerogative of infallibility,
> they nevertheless proclaim Christ's doctrine infallibly when-
> ever, even though dispersed through the world, but still
> maintaining the bond of communion among themselves and
> with the successor of Peter, and authentically teaching
> matters of faith and morals, they are in agreement on one
> position as definitively to be held.[21]

This section of *Lumen Gentium* also uses the teaching of Pius XII to
expand slightly in Vatican I's teaching on papal infallibility.

> *Lumen Gentium* §25 incorporates materials from Pius XII,
> who taught in *Humani Generis* (1950) that when the pope
> teaches authoritatively, even without appealing to his
> supreme authority as successor of Peter, he is to be rever-
> ently heard as speaking in the name of Christ. Vatican II
> teaches that in such cases the faithful should proffer 'a
> religious submission of will and mind'.[22]

So the bishops, as the successors of the apostles, have a share in
the teaching authority of the whole Church. Each bishop can only
exercise this authority when he is in communion with both the
pope and his fellow-bishops. Teachings which enjoy the support
of the whole College of Bishops are to be treated as infallible. (This
means that documents such as the Catechism of the Catholic
Church are to be treated as containing the definitive teaching of
the Church.)

The Fullness of the Sacrament

The second development of doctrine of *Lumen Gentium* is its statement that bishops have the fullness of the sacrament of ordination.

> Chapter 3, which deals with the hierarchy, contains the most important doctrinal pronouncements of the entire council. On two occasions, *Lumen Gentium* uses the solemn words 'This sacred Synod teaches ...' The first instance is in article 20, which affirms that bishops have by divine institution succeeded to the place of the apostles. The second instance is in article 21, which states that episcopal ordination confers the fullness of the sacrament of orders. The council here exercises its doctrinal authority to settle a question previously disputed among theologians in the West.[23]

The significance of the phrase 'This sacred Synod teaches' being applied to the statement on the status of episcopal ordination has received surprisingly little attention. *Lumen Gentium* only uses the phrase 'fullness of the sacrament' twice. The first instance is as follows:

> And the Sacred Council teaches that by Episcopal consecration the fullness of the sacrament of Orders is conferred, that fullness of power, namely, which both in the Church's liturgical practise and in the language of the Fathers of the Church is called the high priesthood, the supreme power of the sacred ministry.[24]

The second occurrence of the phrase could easily be overlooked, yet it states the key principle on which the relationship between the bishop and his priests and deacons rests:

> A bishop marked with the fullness of the sacrament of Orders, is 'the steward of the grace of the supreme priesthood'.[25]

We will look at this point in more detail in chapter fourteen on the sacrament of ordination. It is also touched on in chapter twenty three. However, before moving on, we need to look at a most important source of authoritative teaching, canon law.

Canon Law

Canon law is concerned with discipline and practice within the Church. We tend not to regard it as part of the infallible teaching of the Church as infallibility has to do with Church teaching on faith and morals, which cannot change, whereas teaching on disciplinary matters can change. However some parts of canon law are infallible as they are concerned with the universal Church's teaching on matters relating to faith and morals. Even those parts that are not infallible still give a clear, concise statement of Church belief and practise. Anyone claiming loyalty and obedience to the Church is bound to obey all of its teachings, fallible and infallible.

The following excerpts show the relationship of the priest and deacon to the bishop. The priest exercises the same sanctifying office as the bishop but under the bishop's authority, the deacon does not share this office but assists in the liturgy.

> **Can 834**
>
> §1 The Church carries out its office of sanctifying in a special way in the sacred liturgy, which is an exercise of the priestly office of Jesus Christ.

The hierarchical relationship of bishop, priest and deacon is spelt out in Can 835, which also mentions the laity, albeit at the end of the list!

> **Can 835**
>
> §1 The sanctifying office is exercised principally by Bishops, who are the high priests, the principle dispensers of the mystery of God and the moderators, promoters and guardians of the entire liturgical life in the churches entrusted to their care.
>
> §2 This office is also exercised by priests. They, too, share in the priesthood of Christ and, as his ministers under the authority of the Bishop, are consecrated to celebrate divine worship and to sanctify the people.
>
> §3 Deacons have a share in the celebration of divine worship in accordance with the provisions of law.
>
> §4 The other members of Christ's faithful have their own part in this sanctifying office, each in his or her own way

actively sharing in liturgical celebrations, particularly in the Eucharist.[26]

The Code of Canon Law also considers bishops, priests and deacons in its section on the sacrament of Orders. The 1983 edition begins this section with two general statements:

Can 1008

By divine institution some among Christ's faithful are, through the sacrament of order, marked with an indelible character and are thus constituted sacred ministers; thereby they are consecrated and deputed so that, each according to his own grade, they fulfil, in the person of Christ the Head, the offices of teaching, sanctifying and ruling, and so they nourish the people of God.

Can 1009

§1 The orders are the episcopate, the priesthood and the diaconate.

§2 They are conferred by the imposition of hands and the prayer of consecration which the liturgical books prescribe for each grade.

In October 2009, Pope Benedict XVI issued a Motu Proprio with slight amendments to these two canons in order to clarify the role of the deacon.[27] Can 1008 now reads

By divine institution, some of the Christian faithful are marked with an indelible character and constituted as sacred ministers by the sacrament of holy orders. They are thus consecrated and deputed so that, each according to his own grade, they may serve the People of God by a new and specific title.

Canon 1009 has a third paragraph added, which reads

§3 Those who are constituted in the order of the episcopate or the presbyterate receive the mission and capacity to act in the person of Christ the Head, whereas deacons are empowered to serve the People of God in the ministries of the liturgy, the word and charity.

The effect of these changes is to clarify one of the most significant differences between priests and deacons; the first acts *in persona Christi capitis*, the second does not.

Canon law also distinguishes between the priest and deacon, who both receive the sacrament of ordination, and the minor orders of lector and acolyte, who receive their ministries through a 'rite of admission'. Before moving from one ministry to another, the candidate must have spent a specific time exercising his existing ministry. This allows both the candidate and his bishop to assess his suitability for the new ministry. The relevant sections are summarised here: [28]

Can 1024

Only a baptised man can validly receive sacred ordination. (The canon uses the Latin word 'vir', so meaning specifically male as opposed to female, not simply human.)

Can 1031

§1 The priesthood may be conferred only upon those who have completed their twenty fifth year of age, and possess a sufficient maturity; moreover an interval of at least six months between the diaconate and the priesthood must have been observed.

Can 1033

Only one who has received the sacrament of sacred confirmation may lawfully be promoted to orders.

Can 1034

§1 An aspirant to the diaconate or to the priesthood is not to be ordained unless he has first, through the liturgical rite of admission, secured enrolment as a candidate.

Can 1035

§1 Before anyone may be promoted to the diaconate, whether permanent or transitory, he must have received the ministries of lector and acolyte and have exercised them for an appropriate time.

§2 Between the conferring of the ministry of acolyte and the diaconate there is to be an interval of at least six months.[29]

It is clear from these excerpts that the roads to the diaconate and to the priesthood must follow clearly signposted routes. While they have much in common, they arrive at different destinations. Only someone who has been approved at each stage can be validly ordained. The statement that only men can be ordained remains binding until such time as the bishops of the Church collectively decide to change it.

Summary

The Church has the duty to interpret Scripture and Tradition for each generation. While it is helped by the work of theologians, only the Magisterium of the Church can make definitive statements. Historically, theologians have been predominantly male, resulting in a lack of balance, and possibly even clarity, in the presentation of Church teachings. The authoritative teaching of the Church comes from the College of Bishops, so the principles of collegiality and of bishops having the fullness of the sacrament of ordination are central to the debate. An important source of magisterial teaching is the Code of Canon Law. Two sections are of particular relevance to us, that on the relationship between the bishop and his priests and deacons and that on the sacrament of orders. The recent amendment to canon law *Omnium in Mentem* gave a crucial clarification of the difference between priests and deacons.

Notes

[1]   DV, §10.
[2]   A. Dulles, *The Craft of Theology: from Symbol to System* (New York: Crossroads, 1995), p. 107.
[3]   Pope John Paul II, Encyclical letter *Fides et Ratio* §13 (1998). Other sources of teaching on the relationship between faith and reason are in *Dei Filius* (Vatican I), *Aeterni Patris* (1879), *Dei Verbum* (Vatican II), and *Veritatis Splendor* (1993).
[4]   See chapter eight on apostolic succession and Church teaching.
[5]   DV, §10.
[6]   Dulles summarises the teaching of the CDF document *Instruction on the Ecclesial Vocation of the Theologian*, published in 1990 as describing four different types of pronouncement – see chapter nineteen 'Analogy of Faith: Progression or Digression?'
[7]   See chapter eight 'Tradition: The Church; Reserved to Men Alone.' for comments on H. U. von Balthasar, Catherine of Siena, Edith Stein, Pope John Paul II, Joan

Morris and Gary Macy. See chapters nineteen and twenty 'Analogy of Faith' for comments on Ratzinger, Newman, Martimort, Hauke, Müller and Butler.

8   B. E. Beaumont, untitled letter, in M. Ormond (ed.), *Building Bridges: Dominicans Doing Theology Together* (Dublin: Dominican Publications, 2005), p. 28.

9   *Fides et Ratio*, first sentence.

10 See chapter eight 'Tradition: The Church; Reserved to Men Alone' for information on Edith Stein.

11 A. Nichols, *The Shape of Catholic Theology* (Collegeville: The Liturgical Press, 1991), p. 32.

12 G. Wojciech, 'The Importance of the Study of Theology in the Dominican Tradition' in M. Ormond (ed.), *Building Bridges: Dominicans Doing Theology Together*, p. 40.

13 L Walsh, untitled letter in M. Ormond (ed.), *Building Bridges: Dominicans Doing Theology Together*, p. 202.

14 P. Kayiba, untitled letter in Ormond (ed.), *Building Bridges: Dominicans Doing Theology Together*, p. 90.

15 K. Rahner, 'Magisterium' in the *Encyclopaedia of Theology* (London: Burns and Oates, 1975), p. 874. The author directs the reader particularly to LG § 24–25.

16 LG, § 22.

17 See also chapter fourteen.

18 A. Dulles, 'Nature, Mission, and Structure of the Church' in Lamb and Levering, *Vatican II Renewal Within Tradition* (Oxford: OUP, 2008), p. 33. The author draws the readers attention specifically to LG § 22–24.

19 For some historical details, see the section in chapter fourteen on bishops.

20 J. Galot, *Theology of the Priesthood* (San Francisco: Ignatius Press, 1985), p. 185.

21 LG, §25.

22 A. Dulles, 'Nature, Mission, and Structure of the Church' in Lamb & Levering, *Vatican II*, p. 34. The quote is from LG § 25.

23 *Ibid.*, p. 32.

24 LG, §21. The footnote to this quote is important, as it gives historical credence to the teaching: In *Trad. Apost.* 3, ed. Botte, SC, pp. 27–30, a 'primacy of the priesthood' is attributed to the bishop. Cf. Sacramentarium Leonianum, ed. C. Mohlberg, Sacramentarium Veronense, Rome, 1955, p. 119: 'to the ministry of the high priesthood ... Make the height of your mystery complete in your priests' ... The same point is made in *Liber Sacramentarium Romanae Ecclesiae*, Rome 1960 pp. 121–122: 'Assign them the episcopal throne, Lord, to rule your Church and all the people'. Cf PL 78, 224.

25 LG, §26 quoting the prayer of episcopal consecration in the Byzantine rite: *Euchologion to mega*, Rome, 1873, p. 139.

26 CIC 1983.

27 Motu Proprio *Omnium in Mentem* (26 October 2009). See also the section below, Magisterium: Ordination.

28 CIC 1983, Book IV *The Sanctifying Office of the Church* Part I *The Sacraments* chap. II *Those to be Ordained*.

29 CIC 1983.

13 LITURGY

I N THIS CHAPTER, we turn to the active, visible work of the Church.

> The word 'liturgy' originally meant a 'public work' or a 'service in the name of/on behalf of the people'. In Christian Tradition it means the participation of the People of God in 'the work of God'. Through the liturgy Christ, our redeemer and high priest, continues the work of our redemption in, with and through his Church.[1]

This work of God is principally exercised through the sacraments, which give us a summary of the faith of the Church: 'When the Church celebrates the sacraments, she confesses the faith received from the apostles—whence the ancient saying: *lex orandi, lex credendi* ... The law of prayer is the law of faith: the Church believes as she prays.'[2] So we can learn about the Church's beliefs about the sacrament of ordination by looking at the liturgical rites used when conferring this sacrament.

As human beings, we make sense of the world around us through our senses. Jesus Christ understood this and used visible, tangible signs of his power—miracles were accompanied by words, touch, sometimes a physical medium such as water or spittle. At the Last Supper, bread and wine became the body and blood that was to be sacrificed for us. At Pentecost, the Holy Spirit was seen and heard as tongues of fire and wind. So the Church has always celebrated the sacraments by means of rituals that appeal to our senses. These have traditionally been described under the headings of 'form'(the words used) and 'matter' (the physical objects or gestures used). While all sacraments are instituted by Jesus Christ, the form and matter used can be decided by the College of Bishops. For the sacrament of ordination, the rituals have changed considerably over time and from one local Church to another. In Scripture, we find that prayer and the laying on of hands are used:

> Hence from the beginning, in appointing collaborators, they
> (the apostles) used a liturgical rite consisting of prayer and
> the imposition of hands, signifying the gift of a special grace
> in view of the task to be fulfilled. A similar rite was used for
> the appointment of the first deacons (Acts 6:6), and of the
> presbyters in the course of the journeys of St Paul (Acts
> 14:28).[3]

The same source provides support for the teaching of *Lumen
Gentium* on bishops having the fullness of the sacrament of ordination:

> An attentive study of liturgical documents, beginning with
> those of the greatest antiquity, reveals that the Church has
> always considered this rite to be a sacrament which confers
> the fullness of the priesthood and bestows a grace enabling
> the bishop to carry out his own special duties.[4]

Despite this long history, the details of the rites used and the
importance given to each part of the rite has varied over the
centuries. 'Only in 1947 did Pope Pius XII rule that the laying on
of hands was the only 'matter' necessary for the ordination of a
priest for Roman Catholics.'[5]

We now have a definitive pattern of the minimum necessary to
ordain a bishop, priest or deacon: 'The orders are the episcopate,
the priesthood and the diaconate. They are conferred by the
imposition of hands and the prayer of consecration which the
liturgical books prescribe for each grade.'[6] The prayer of consecration is different for each order, reflecting their different roles.

The rites of ordination for deacons, priests and bishops can be
found in Appendix II, section D. We can see from them that the
deacons have the ministry of serving at the altar. They are to excel
in love, care of the sick and of the poor. Priests are co-workers with
the bishop, spreading the gospel and bringing people to Christ.
Bishops receive the same spirit that God the Father gave to his Son
and the Son passed on to the apostles, the founders of the Church.
They are to be shepherds of the people and high priests. They have
the power to forgive sins, to assign ministries and to loose bonds.
They have the same authority that God gave to the apostles.

We can see from this that deacons are in a different relationship
to the bishop from the priest. The priest is a co-worker with the

bishop, the deacon is a servant of both the bishop and the community. The bishop inherits apostolic authority. Both deacon and priest depend on the bishop for their authority to exercise their vocation. Because the fullness of the sacrament of ordination, as stated in *Lumen Gentium*, resides in the bishop, he can delegate some of his priestly duties to one group and some of his duties of service to another group without damaging the unity of the sacrament.

Notes

[1] CCC, §1069.

[2] CCC, §1124.

[3] J. Lecuyer, 'Bishop' in K. Rahner, *Encyclopaedia of Theology* (London: Burns and Oates, 1975), p. 148 but note previous comments on the interpretation of Acts 6:6 as being more likely to be the institution of presbyters than deacons.

[4] *Ibid.*, p. 148.

[5] G. Macy, *The Hidden History of Women's Ordination: Female Clergy in the Medieval West* (Oxford: OUP, 2008), p. 24.

[6] CIC, can 1009.

14 THE SACRAMENT OF ORDINATION

W E HAVE HERE two words that rest at the centre of this work, 'sacrament' and 'ordination'.

Sacrament

> The Greek word *mystērion* was translated into Latin by two terms: *mysterium* and *sacramentum*. In later usage the term *sacramentum* emphasizes the visible sign of the hidden reality of salvation which was indicated by the term *mysterium* ... The seven sacraments are the signs and instruments by which the Holy Spirit spreads the grace of Christ the head throughout the Church which is his body.[1]

In the early Church, the word was used in a wide variety of situations but particularly for the rites of baptism and the Eucharist. Augustine was the first theologian to discuss sacraments in detail. He developed his sacramental theology during his debates with the Manichees and the Donatists. His teaching, scattered through many letters and sermons, is more a work in progress than a polished thesis. It is nevertheless of great importance as it provided the basis on which the medieval theologians built a more consistent and concise sacramental theology. A fundamental principle was that sacraments were one with the word of Christ. Scholars have identified five reflections of Augustine that were used by later theologians as the basis for modern sacramental theology.[2] The first of these was used in the old Penny Catechism when it asked 'What is a sacrament?' and provided the answer 'A sacrament is an outward sign of inner grace'. Sacraments had to include visible, tangible signs of the inner reality that was their true meaning. Secondly, sacraments had to be true to this inner reality, in other words, the physical sign had to bear some relationship to the effect of the sacrament. As sacraments are one with Christ, the head of the Church, sacraments are part of the Church, the body of Christ. The fourth point was important in both

Augustine's debates with the Donatists and future debates in the Church, that sacraments are efficacious regardless of the state of grace of the minister. They are effective because they are the word of Christ, not because of the holiness of the minister or of some power inherent in the materials used. Lastly, Augustine stated that the sacraments of baptism, chrismation and ordination conferred a lasting character and need not be repeated. Thus, he taught that people who had been baptised by schismatic ministers or who had temporarily apostatised did not need to be re-baptised. Priests who had left the Church and wished to return did not need to be re-ordained. These teachings are still held as valid today.

Augustine regarded many things as *sacramentum*. In the centuries since Augustine, the Church gradually reduced the rites that were regarded as sacraments until there was general agreement on the list of seven that was eventually ratified at the Council of Trent. Two theologians stand out between Augustine and Trent, Peter Lombard and Thomas Aquinas. Peter Lombard argued conclusively for seven sacraments. He also stressed that sacraments actually achieved something in that they caused a change in the recipient. Aquinas is greatly influenced by Augustine and also accepts these teachings of Lombard. His teachings are detailed and comprehensive, yet also clear and logical. They form the basis for all Church teaching from his time onwards. Aquinas defines sacraments as signs that cause what they signify:

> Signs are given to men, to whom it is proper to discover the unknown by means of the known. Consequently a sacrament properly so called is that which is the sign of some sacred thing pertaining to man; so that properly speaking a sacrament, as considered by us now, is defined as being the 'sign of a holy thing so far as it makes men holy'.[3]

Sacraments remind us of the passion of Christ, allow us to receive the power flowing from Christ's sacrifice and foretell our future glory.

> A sacrament properly speaking is that which is ordained to signify our sanctification. In which three things may be considered; viz. the very cause of our sanctification, which is Christ's passion; the form of our sanctification, which is grace and the virtues; and the ultimate end of our sanctifi-

cation, which is eternal life. And all these are signified by the sacraments. Consequently a sacrament is a sign that is both a reminder of the past, i.e. the passion of Christ; and an indication of that which is effected in us by Christ's passion, i.e. grace; and a prognostic, that is, a foretelling of future glory.[4]

At the core of all Aquinas's teaching on the sacraments is his insistence on the effect of the incarnation. Only through the humanity of Jesus Christ can the passion take place and only through the passion can we be saved. Reflecting both Jesus's dual nature as God and man and our dual nature as human body and spiritual soul, sacraments consist of matter (the physical elements) and form (the words used). Of these, Aquinas felt that the form was the more important as it expressed the faith of the Church: 'Now in all things composed of matter and form, the determining principle is on the part of the form, which is as it were the end and terminus of the matter.'[5] Neither form nor matter on their own is sacramental, so the water of baptism is just water until it is used as part of the rite of baptism. Similarly, only those rituals instituted by the human Jesus Christ for our sanctification can be called sacraments:

> In the use of the sacraments two things may be considered, namely, the worship of God, and the sanctification of man: the former of which pertains to man as referred to God, and the latter pertains to God in reference to man. Now it is not for anyone to determine that which is in the power of another, but only that which is in his own power. Since, therefore, the sanctification of man is in the power of God Who sanctifies, it is not for man to decide what things should be used for his sanctification, but this should be determined by Divine institution. Therefore in the sacraments of the New Law, by which man is sanctified according to 1 Cor. 6:11, 'You are washed, you are sanctified,' we must use those things which are determined by Divine institution.[6]

In other words, it is not for us to decide what God might or might not accept as a sacrament. He has given us the life and death of his son, as recorded in Sacred Scripture, as a source of salvation. We do not need anything more. While the Church may alter the specific details of a ritual over time, its essentials must have been set by Christ. Only the Church can judge what are acceptable variations and what are not. Sacraments are valid only if the minister uses the correct form and matter and has the intention of doing what the Church intends:

> With regard to all the variations that may occur in the sacramental forms, two points seem to call for our attention. One is on the part of the person who says the words, and whose intention is essential to the sacrament, as will be explained further on (Q 3a:64.8). Wherefore if he intends by such addition or suppression to perform a rite other from that which is recognized by the Church, it seems that the sacrament is invalid: because he seems not to intend to do what the Church does.[7]

The above quote from St Thomas Aquinas refers to a following section of the same question, Q 3a:64.8. This includes the following:

> Consequently, others with better reason hold that the minister of a sacrament acts in the person of the whole Church, whose minister he is; while in the words uttered by him, the intention of the Church is expressed; and that this suffices for the validity of the sacrament, except the contrary be expressed on the part either of the minister or of the recipient of the sacrament.[8]

The leaders of the Reformation challenged the Church teaching on the sacraments, with Luther initially accepting only baptism, penance and the Eucharist as being derived from Scripture:

> The first thing for me to do is to deny that there are seven sacraments, and, for the present, to propound three: baptism, penance, and the Lord's Supper … If, however, I were to use the language of Scripture, I should say that there was only one sacrament, [cf. 1 Tim 3:16] but three sacramental signs.[9]

He later reduced the list to baptism and the Lord's Supper, on the grounds that they were the only two with clear Scriptural evidence of the two things needed for a sacrament, the Word of God and a physical sign.

The Church replied at the Council of Trent. Its teachings relied heavily on those of Aquinas and still form the basis of Church teaching on the sacraments. Despite attempts by traditionalists to present Vatican II as a departure from the settled teaching of the Church, there is in fact a strong link between Trent and Vatican II.

> Trent approached liturgical matters from a different angle because its purpose was different ... Trent needed to consider the individual parts of the sacramental system and analyse the specific nature of each sacrament, whereas *Sacrosanctum concilium* was able to 'return to a more synthetic view of the liturgy'. Those who drafted *Sacrosanctum Concilium* saw themselves as building on the teaching of Trent and deepening it.[10]

This point is expanded on by the author a few pages later in an attempt to answer the 'hermeneutic of discontinuity' critics that we mentioned earlier in the section on interpreting Scripture:

> While those who wrote the schema of *Sacrosanctum Concilium* derived the norms and specific changes decreed from its theology, they were also careful to note when those norms and decreed changes could also be found in earlier sources. For example, the crucial distinction in article 21 between divinely instituted elements in the liturgy, which may not be changed, and elements that may be modified had been made by Pius XII, and the acknowledgement of the usefulness of the vernacular in the liturgy is taken from a statement in *Mediator Dei*. The rationale for openness to adapting the liturgy to other cultures was drawn from Benedict XIV's *Summi Pontificatus*. The affirmation of the bishop as the centre of the liturgical life of the diocese is based on extensive citations from Ignatius of Antioch ... A careful reading of the entire schema and its notes reveals that a significant number of what are sometimes assumed to be *Sacrosanctum Concilium's* 'new' norms and reforms in fact point to the example of earlier precedents.[11]

The most comprehensive summary of the teachings of the Church today is to be found in the Catechism of the Catholic Church.[12] The section on 'The Sacramental Economy' includes 58 footnotes citing sources of its teaching. These come from Scripture (36), the early Fathers (4), Thomas Aquinas (3), Trent (6), other Church councils

(2) and Vatican II (16). As the Vatican II documents in turn are heavily dependent on Scripture, the early Fathers and previous councils, we can see that Church teaching on the sacraments, as presented in the Catechism of the Catholic Church, is still based very much on the inherited teaching of the Church.[13] As stated at the Council of Trent, the Church recognises seven sacraments: baptism, confirmation, reconciliation, Holy Communion, matrimony, ordination and anointing the sick. There are three features that they all share. Most importantly, they all have their roots in the words and actions of Jesus Christ. They are part of the official liturgy of the Church and therefore have specific rituals to be followed, the rituals include prayers of anamnesis (God's saving intervention in human history),[14] epiclesis (a prayer asking the Father to send the Holy Spirit to bring us into communion with Christ)[15] and a doxology (thanksgiving and praise)[16] which remind us that the sacrament is the work of the Holy Spirit. They have three elements; form, matter and intention. The three sacraments of baptism, confirmation and holy orders confer a permanent character and cannot be repeated.

The links between this summary, our previous summary of the teaching of Augustine and with Aquinas are clear. So the Catechism of the Catholic Church's definition of a sacrament would have been acceptable to Church leaders at any stage in the Church's development:

> The sacraments are efficacious signs of grace, instituted by Christ and entrusted to the Church, by which divine life is dispensed to us. The visible rites by which the sacraments are celebrated signify and make present the graces proper to each sacrament. They bear fruit in those who receive them with the proper dispositions.[17]

While remaining true to this definition, Church teaching and practice on the sacraments has changed and developed over the centuries. Within the sacrament of ordination, the main changes, other than the gradual development of the roles of bishop, priest and deacon, have been in the inclusion or otherwise of the 'minor orders'.[18] By the middle of the third century in Rome there were acolytes, exorcists, doorkeepers, readers and sub-deacons. At various times in the history of the Church, their inductions were seen as independent sacraments, or degrees or grades within the sacrament of ordination. Gradually, these roles disappeared as permanent functions and became stages in the training of seminarians. Then Vatican II reintroduced the order of the permanent deacon. The matter and form also expanded and contracted according to the needs of the time. Indeed, they were not fixed until as late as 1947:

> Pope Pius XII tried to put an end to centuries of debate by declaring that bishops who participated in the ordination of a bishop were themselves co-consecrators and not merely assistants to the presiding bishop (Apostolic Constitution *Episcopalis Consecrationis*, 1944) and that the essential 'matter' and 'form' of ordination in the Roman pontifical were the imposition of hands and the central petition of the original Roman ordination prayers (Apostolic Constitution *Sacramentum Ordinis*, 1947).[19]

Ordination

It is surprisingly difficult to find a precise definition of the word 'ordination'. As with so many theological words and phrases, we have to remember that the English word is a translation of Latin, Greek or Hebrew, or indeed of a word that has come from Hebrew through Greek, then Latin, to English. The Catechism of the Catholic Church comes closest;

> The word *ordo* in Roman antiquity designated an established civil body, especially a governing body ... Today the word 'ordination' is reserved for the sacramental act which integrates a man into the order of bishops, presbyters or deacons, and goes beyond a simple *election, designation, delegation* or *institution* by the community, for it confers a gift of the Holy Spirit that permits the exercise of a 'sacred power' (*sacra potestas*) which can come only from Christ himself through his Church. Ordination is also called *consecratio*, for it is a setting apart and an investiture by Christ himself for his Church.[20]

There are several important points to be drawn from this definition: the word now has a narrower meaning than in antiquity; ordination is a sacrament conferring the gift of 'sacred power' and ordination is also a consecration as it sets the person apart for service in and for the Church.

In the modern West, the word 'ordination' is used exclusively for the liturgical rites of institution of bishops, priests and deacons. However the broader meaning, as used in the early Church, can still be seen in the rites of baptism and confirmation.

> The theological significance of this (laying on of hands) lies in the fact that it reveals the nature of baptism and confirmation as being essentially an ordination, while it helps us understand better what ordination itself means ... the immediate and inevitable result of baptism and confirmation was that the newly baptised would take his particular place in the eucharistic assembly, i.e. that he would become a layman—a member of a particular 'ordo' in the eucharistic community.[21]

While the above quote is referring to the Eastern Orthodox practices, it is also relevant to the Latin Church, which also regards the laying on of hands as an essential part of the rite and the effect of the rite as conferring a specific place in society: 'The baptismal seal enables and commits Christians to serve God by a vital participation in the holy liturgy of the Church and to exercise their baptismal priesthood by the witness of holy lives and practical charity.'[22] Also, 'This character (of confirmation) perfects the common priesthood of the faithful, received in baptism, and "the confirmed person receives the power to profess faith in Christ publicly and as it were officially"'.[23]

Zizioulas, a theologian of the Greek Orthodox Church, describes the Church as a relational reality. Ordination (in which he includes the sacraments of baptism and confirmation as they place the recipient in a specific 'ordo' in the Church and include the laying on of hands) does not so much take place within an existing community as it is constitutive of the community because the community can only exist if it has members who have been ordained into it. This can be seen in a practical way in that deacons, priests and bishops must be ordained for service within a specific diocese or religious community and the ordination rite must take place within the sacrament of the Eucharist, a communal event.[24] So the ontological nature of the sacrament is inseparable from the relationship with a specific community: 'If ordination is approached in this way, ministry ceases to be understood in terms of what it gives to the ordained and becomes describable only in terms of the particular relationship into which it places the ordained.'[25]

By thinking of the minister as a relationship between his community and Christ, we answer the 'ontological' versus 'functional' debate. This was a debate that began, in its modern form, in the 1950s and continues today. It centres on the principle that the three sacraments of baptism, confirmation and ordination confer a permanent character on the recipient. Therefore the effect of the sacrament is permanent and the sacrament cannot be either cancelled or repeated. This doctrine was confirmed at the Council of Trent. However some modern theologians have argued that these teachings were not meant to be permanently binding.[26] A movement, led mainly by Schoonenberg and Schillebeeckx, argues for abandoning the theory of priestly ordination causing an ontological change in the recipient. By replacing the notion of ontological change with one of functional capacity (a capacity to exercise a specific function in the community), the priesthood would be opened up to new patterns of working—part-time ministry, married priests, election by the community, worker priests and so on. There would also be ecumenical advantages, as this new model of priesthood would correspond more closely to the ministerial model used by so many other churches. In reply, the Magisterium has reiterated the teachings of the Council of Trent.[27] Indeed, it is difficult to see how the supporters of change can reconcile their views with Scripture. We have already seen that the change of name for Peter and Paul implies ontological change. The ministry, instituted by Jesus for his apostles and continued in the early Church, as described in Acts, is radically different from that of the Jewish priesthood. Followers of Jesus, principally the twelve apostles but also the other disciples, including the group of women mentioned by Luke (Lk 8:2–3), have to renounce their previous lives. Jesus lists the extent of the sacrifice that he expects (Mt 10:29) and suggests that celibacy should also be included (Mt 19:12).

> In this enumeration, three basic renunciations are discernible: marriage and family, possessions, and secular occupation. These renunciations impinge upon the essential dimensions of man's life: man's relational being which, through marriage and family, inserts itself into a network of social relationships and contributes to the natural growth of society.[28]

The following quotes show that the principles of ontological change and relationality go together. To become a relationship between Christ and the community necessitates a change in one's own nature that is most fittingly described as ontological.[29] To return to the Eastern tradition:

> In the light of the *koinonia* of the Holy Spirit, ordination relates the ordained man so profoundly and so existentially to the community that in his new state after ordination he cannot be any longer, as a minister, conceived in himself.[30]

And: 'Because of the relational nature of ordination, no ordained person realises his *ordo* in himself but in the community.'[31] The Western tradition has also recognised this consequence of ordination:

> Thus the essence of ordination and its validity depend only on the fittingness of the candidate to represent Christ in the community and the unity of the community in Christ … This fidelity (1 Cor 4:1–2) requires of the priest a *kenosis*, an emptying of all merely personal hopes and projects, all vanity and ambition, as the classical writings on the spirituality of priesthood have constantly insisted.[32]

The official teaching of the Church supports this view, while stressing the relationship between the priest and Christ. This relationship, created at ordination, affects the very identity of the priest by uniting him with Christ:

> Through the sacramental ordination conferred by the imposition of hands and the consecratory prayers of the Bishop, 'a specific ontological bond which unites the priest to Christ, High Priest and Good Shepherd' is established. Thus the identity of the priest comes from the specific participation in the priesthood of Christ … The life and ministry of the priest are a continuation of the life and the action of the same

> Christ … From this, one perceives the essentially relational
> characteristic (John 17:11–21) of the priests identity.[33]

The definition of different functions within the community and
the rites used to commission the person into the function took some
time to develop, and indeed are still developing as the needs of
the Church evolve through time. However there are some features
that have remained constant throughout the history of the Church:
'The ceremony of laying on of hands we find, indeed, to be an
invariable accompaniment of ordination in Scripture.'[34]

As discussed in chapters three and eight, the early Church
included a variety of ministries and of ways in which they were
commissioned:

> Christian community leaders are variously designated
> 'leaders' (Heb 13:7), 'elders' (*presbyteroi*, 1 P 5:1; Jm 5:14; Ac
> 11:30 etc.) 'presidents' (Rm 12:8; 1 Th 5:12–13), 'teachers' (Ga
> 6:6), as well as the more clearly specified 'overseers (epis-
> copoi, Ac 20:17, 28; Ph. 1:1; Tt 1:5ff) and assistants (diakonoi,
> Ph 1:1; 1 Tm. 3:1ff). 1 Co 16:15–16 contains several phrases
> implying functions of leadership; on the other hand, there
> are some lists of ministries without any clear reference to
> such functions (1 Cor. 12:28; Eph 4:11).[35]

Hawkins goes on to look at the most commonly used title for those
in the service of the churches, minister, in greater detail:

> The term (minister) should be understood in the light of its
> basic meaning of 'service' … Some ministers are commis-
> sioned directly by Jesus or given gifts of ministry by the
> Spirit, some are appointed by other Christians, while for
> other ministries, there is no evidence about how they came
> into being at all.[36]

The following quote gives us an idea of the antiquity of the various
liturgical rites and the complexity of the Church hierarchy, even
in this early stage of its development:

> The '*Apostolic Tradition*' dated apr. AD 236 gives the earliest
> known description of rites, including the offices of bishop,
> presbyter, deacon, sub-deacon, lector, confessors, widows,
> consecrated virgins, readers and sub-deacons. Pope
> Cornelius, in a letter to bishop Fabius dated AD 252 lists

> seven ranks in the Church of Rome—priests, deacons, subdeacons, acolytes, exorcists, lectors and porters.[37]

Bishops are ordained by their fellow bishops; presbyters and deacons by one bishop. Widows and readers are appointed rather than ordained and virgins and sub-deacons are named rather than appointed. We get some idea of the differentiation between the three major orders:

> The second-century evidence suggests that it is the significance that the office of bishop has in relation to the universal Church which effectively distinguishes it from the presbyterate, whose functions still relate primarily to the local Christian community... the function of the diaconate is 'not ... for priesthood, but for the service of the bishop'.[38]

Through the various liturgical rites, we can trace the development of a hierarchy within the early Church.

> The collegiality of bishop and presbyters was replaced by a greater emphasis on the collegiality of bishops with one another, as they began to meet together more regularly to make corporate decisions. The status of the diaconate also changed ... by the third century, there are signs of a gap opening up between the diaconate and the other two orders ... 'minor orders were also making an appearance. The most ancient seem to have been the reader and sub-deacon, and these are the only ones to feature consistently in the later rites of the East, but at Rome by the middle of the third century there were also acolytes, exorcists and doorkeepers.[39]

Through the centuries, ordination rites have always included four elements: election (at least for a bishop), prayer, the imposition of hands and the imposition of a symbol of office. Ordination always took place during the Mass. The rituals varied within this structure and from time to time there was debate over, for example, whether the laying on of hands or the imposition of the sign of office was the essential matter of the sacrament. It was not until 1947 that these details of the external rites were finalised.[40]

> Priests are made in the likeness of Christ the Priest by the Sacrament of Orders, so that they may, in collaboration with their bishops, work for the building up and care of the

> Church which is the whole Body of Christ ... They have been
> consecrated by God in a new manner at their ordination and
> are made the living instruments of Christ the Eternal Priest.[41]

Summary

We have shown that the Church's understanding of what a
sacrament is has developed over the centuries. Yet the most
modern official definition, contained in the Catechism of the
Catholic Church, does not differ in any essentials from that of the
early Church. The word 'sacrament' describes a rite with specific
words and actions which are part of the official liturgy of the
Church. By this rite, the recipients receive the grace proper to that
sacrament, giving then the means to fulfil their role in the Church.
Priestly ordination is one of these sacraments. It confers the grace
needed for the man to act *'in persona Christi capitis'*. In a sense, he
is no longer an individual but a servant of Christ and of the Church,
just as Christ was a servant of the Father. The ontological and
relational aspects of the sacrament are closely linked.

The early Church recognised up to seven ranks within the
sacrament of ordination. These ranks were later divided into major
and minor orders. Later still, the minor orders were reduced to
non-sacramental positions. Today, the sacrament of ordination is
conferred on bishops, priests and deacons. That this is a formal
hierarchy was defined at the Council of Trent, in reply to the
teaching of the Reformers: 'If anyone says that in the Catholic
Church there is no hierarchy instituted by divine ordinance, which
consists of bishops, priests and ministers, anathema sit.'[42] We will
now look at this hierarchy in more detail.

Bishop

A dictionary article by H. W. Beyer gives an interesting insight into
the use of the word 'bishop' in the Old Testament.

> The true theological sense of 'bishop' is as the translation of
> 'visitation'. Again, this takes a twofold form. In the prophets
> the visitation is usually one of judgement and punishment
> ... In a much weaker sense, the term is used for 'scourging'
> in the sense of judicial discipline in Lv. 19:20. For the most
> part, however, 'bishop' is not executed by men. It is a destiny

which comes on earthly creatures with more than human
force ... No less notable from the standpoint of the history
of the term are the two passages where it has the sense of
'office' (Nu 4:16, Psalmus Ischarioticus 108:8).[43]

In the New Testament, Jesus refers to his final visit to Jerusalem
as a 'visitation' (Lk 19:44) in the sense also used in Isaiah 10:3:
'What will you do on the day of punishment, in the storm which
will come from afar?' and repeated in 1 Peter 2:12: 'Maintain good
conduct among the gentiles, so that in case they speak against you
as wrongdoers, they may see your good deeds and glorify God on
the day of visitation.' We can see from the quote from 1 Peter that
the word is being used in an eschatological sense: 'But the day of
visitation may also be understood eschatologically as the great day
of judgement when everything will be made manifest and the
heathen will have cause to praise God for Christians.'[44] The word
'overseer', which is used by the Septuagint to translate the sense
of 'visitation', is used only five times in the New Testament. In 1
Peter 2:25 it is not used directly but in the sense of a
guardian/inspector/overseer 'You had gone astray like sheep but
now you have returned to the shepherd and guardian of your
souls'.[45] In the other four examples, it is clearly referring to leaders
of the Church: 'This title arises only where there are settled local
congregations in which regular acts are performed.'[46] The first
example is in Acts 20:28, where again it is translated as 'guardian':
'Be on your guard for yourselves and all the flock of which the
Holy Spirit has made you the guardians, to feed the Church of God
which he bought with the blood of his own Son.'

> To be sure, Paul in Acts 20:28 is simply depicting the work
> and task of responsible men in the congregation. But he is
> already directing his words to a definite circle whose
> members may be called 'overseers' in distinction from
> others.[47]

In the NJB, Philippians 1:1 is translated as 'Paul and Timothy,
servants of Christ Jesus, to all God's holy people in Christ Jesus at
Philippi, together with their presiding elders and the deacons.'[48]
The RSV uses 'bishops' instead of 'presiding elders', with a
footnote saying that it can be translated as 'overseers'. Its use is
clearly for an office, not an activity or a specific group of individ-

uals. This usage is also clear in 1 Timothy 3:1: 'to want to be a presiding elder is to desire a noble task' which goes on to describe the qualities needed for the office. The fourth example is in Titus 1:5–7, which refers back to Acts 14:23: 'and appoint elders in every town, in the way that I told you … The presiding elder has to be irreproachable since he is God's representative' (Tt 1:5–7). Again, the RSV uses 'bishop' for 'presiding elder'.

The title 'elder' is used both as a title of office and to denote the age of the person in relation to others. In Christian writings it is always used in the sense of a college of elders. The overlap in meaning between bishop/elder/presbyter/overseer cannot be overcome to everyone's satisfaction. It would be useful to remember the Old Testament sense of an office concerning judgement and punishment—so the bishop is more than a teacher or preserver of Tradition; he has a disciplinary role which is in some way related to the role of Jesus on the Day of Judgement. After all, Jesus did tell the twelve that they would sit in judgement over the twelve tribes of Israel, so it is not surprising that their descendants should have a similar role.

We have seen that the bishops are the successors to the apostles. It took some time for the early Church to develop a standardised form of liturgy and governance. However the essentials of the sacrament of ordination can be identified in the lives of the apostles:

> The Holy Spirit is conferred as a result of Jesus' words and deeds … Jesus had described the mission and the power of the Twelve. In the priestly prayer, he had asked of the Father that they be consecrated: *'Consecrate them in the truth'* (John 17:17). Even the imposition of hands, which is part of the rite of ordination, appears in Jesus' final gesture. Before the ascension, he lifts up his hands over the apostles to bless them, after promising them the power from on high through the gift of the spirit (Lk 24:48–50).[49]

Even as early as Clement's letter to the Corinthians in AD 96, we can see that the bishop was the central figure of the local church and that the bishop of Rome had a pre-eminent position. At first the Church was tolerated as a sect of Judaism. Then it was persecuted as atheistic and a threat to the unity of the empire. Then the emperor Constantine was converted to Christianity and granted freedom of religious practice to all in the Edict of Milan of AD 313. Christianity was declared the state religion of the empire in AD 380. Some argue that this was the downfall of the Church and some Protestant churches reject all Church teachings from this point on. Certainly, the history of the Church from the time of Constantine is one of increasing control by secular powers. This gradually gave rise to corruption on a grand scale.

Eventually, under Gregory VII (1073–1085), reform came in the form of centralisation of all power in Rome. In order to achieve this reform, the pope had to adopt a monarchical style of leadership. Papal legates ranked above bishops, cardinals became very powerful and more and more decisions were referred to Rome instead of being decided by the local bishops, who lost much of their authority. The tendency to define the sacrament of ordination by its relationship to the Eucharist, discussed in chapter ten, also affected this: 'Since priests possess such powers no less than bishops do, practically all the Schoolmen ... denied the episcopate a separate sacramental dignity.'[50] Eventually, procedures became so cumbersome that the administration of the Church was in danger of grinding to a halt and new forms of corruption developed, leading to the complaints of the Reformers. The Council of Trent (1545–1563) introduced many reforms as well as clarifications on matters of theology. Two influential reforms were that bishops had to live in their diocese and the clergy were to be trained in seminaries. So the quality of priests and bishops improved but the pope was still the central figure and source of all teaching and authority. In response to the Reformers, who denied the sacramentality of the position of priest/minister, Trent confirmed that ordination was a sacrament, which conferred grace and a permanent character.[51] Thus the ordained were permanently distinct from the laity. Within the hierarchy of the Church, the bishop holds the principle position:

> Therefore the holy Council declares that, besides the other ecclesiastical grades, the bishops, who have succeeded the apostles, principally belong to this hierarchial Order and have been, as the same apostle says, 'established by the Holy Spirit to govern (*regere*) the Church of the Lord' (cff Acts 20:28 Vulg); that they are superior to priests, confer the

> sacrament of confirmation, ordain ministers of the Church,
> and can perform most of the other functions over which
> those of a lower Order have no power.[52]

The ordination does not need the consent of either the laity or the
civic powers for its validity.

By the time of Vatican I (1869–1870), the Church had lost its
lands in Italy and the Pope could only stay in the Vatican with the
support of the army of Napoleon III; atheists and agnostics were
using both scientific and philosophical terminology to argue for
the non-existence of God and the position of the pope had become
weakened by the political situation in Europe. The Council was
called in response to the theological questions raised by the new
sciences and philosophy. However the bishops took the opportunity to campaign for a definition of papal infallibility. The work of
the Council was ended by the outbreak of war between France and
Germany and only two constitutions were published.[53] This meant
that, while the infallibility of the pope had been defined, his
relationship to the bishops had not. From the time of the Council
of Trent, there had been debate over this:

> The Council of Trent clearly distinguished the episcopate
> from the priesthood (D 967) but without specifying how it
> related to the primacy, so that much discussion ensued as
> to whether bishops receive their jurisdiction directly from
> God or through the pope.[54]

The argument centred on the nature of the sacrament of ordination.
Did the consecration of a bishop confer a separate order from that
of ordination to the priesthood or a 'dignity within an order'
conferring his new temporal, juridical powers?[55]

> The superiority of bishops is abundantly attested in Tradi-
> tion, and we have seen above that the distinction between
> priests and bishops is of Apostolic origin. Most of the older
> scholastics were of the opinion that the episcopate is not a
> sacrament; this opinion finds able defenders even now (e.g.,
> Billot, 'De Sacramentis', II), though the majority of theolo-
> gians hold it is certain that a bishop's ordination is a
> sacrament.[56]

If episcopal consecration was part of the sacrament of ordination, then it conferred the grace and character particular to that sacrament and the powers that came with it came directly from God. If it was a non-sacramental ceremony to mark the conferring of new powers and responsibilities, then these powers and responsibilities came from the pope, who therefore had the power to define their extent, and even remove them.

> Canonists of the twelfth and thirteenth centuries began to make a distinction between the powers of 'order' and of 'jurisdiction'. The former was given at ordination and was permanent, but the latter could be delegated, withheld, restricted, or withdrawn by competent ecclesial authority.[57]

Another serious practical reason for this debate was concerned with the prevention of abuse. If episcopal consecration was sacramental, did that mean that a lay person could be ordained directly to the episcopacy, receiving the full powers of deacon, priest and bishop in the one ceremony? There had been examples of this both in the very early Church before the distinction between priest and bishop was clear and under some of the more corrupt bishops and popes. If a candidate to the episcopal office had to work through all the previous orders before he could be validly ordained, then there was less risk of an unsuitable appointment.

> (the candidate for ordination) must also have received confirmation and the lower orders preceding the one to which he is raised. This last requirement does not affect the validity of the order conferred, as every order gives a distinct and independent power. One exception is made by the majority of theologians and canonists, who are of the opinion that episcopal consecration requires the previous reception of priest's orders for its validity. Others, however, maintain that episcopal power includes full priestly power, which is thus conferred by episcopal consecration. They appeal to history and bring forward cases of bishops who were consecrated without having previously received priest's orders, and though most of the cases are somewhat doubtful and can be explained on other grounds, it seems impossible to reject them all. It is further to be remembered that scholastic theologians mostly required the previous reception of priest's orders for valid episcopal consecration,

because they did not consider episcopacy an order, a view
which is now generally abandoned.[58]

This rather lengthy quote summarises the two positions—the
majority of theologians argue that bishops must have received the
sacrament of priestly ordination for the consecration to be valid,
but this ignores history and the false grounds on which this
argument is based. The minority position is that, as bishops have
all the powers of a priest, even when they have never been priests,
episcopal ordination must include all the powers of both priest
and bishop. The article on bishops from the same encyclopaedia
gives us more details:

> (the title Bishop is) the title of an ecclesiastical dignitary who
> possesses the fullness of the priesthood to rule a diocese as
> its chief pastor, in due submission to the primacy of the pope.

> It is a controverted question whether the bishops hold their
> jurisdiction directly from God or from the sovereign pontiff.
> The latter opinion, however, is almost generally admitted at
> the present day, for it is more in conformity with the
> monarchical constitution of the Church, which seems to
> demand that there should be no power in the Church not
> emanating immediately from the sovereign pontiff. Authors
> who hold the contrary opinion say that it is during the
> episcopal consecration that bishops receive from God their
> power of jurisdiction. But habitually before their consecra-
> tion the bishops have already all powers of jurisdiction over
> their dioceses (Bargilliat, I, 442–445).[59]

This article, written some four years before the first, is interesting
in that it uses the phrase 'the fullness of the priesthood', suggesting
that episcopal consecration confers the powers of both bishop and
priest. However it says that the bishop receives his jurisdiction
from the pope. While it does not spell out the distinction between
spiritual and juridical powers, it seems to imply that there *is* a
distinction and that the first is conferred by the grace of the
sacrament and the second by the authority of the pope. In the
language of canon law, there is a distinction between something
being valid and being licit. The author of the article seems to be
suggesting that episcopal consecration confers the power, received

directly from God, to validly act as both priest and bishop but that these actions will be illicit unless also authorised by the pope.

This brings us to the teaching of Vatican II that the bishop receives the 'fullness of the sacrament of orders'.[60] At last the debate was ended: episcopal consecration was part of the sacrament of ordination but conferred a distinct order, not simply a higher dignity within the one order of the priesthood. This consecration conferring the *munera* of teaching, sanctifying and ruling. However the bishops only receive these powers if they meet the canonical requirements in force at the time and are in communion with the pope.[61]

So is it correct to say that, if the bishop receives the fullness of the sacrament, then priests and deacons only receive part of it? Can we think of the grace of the sacrament being 'topped up' from the level needed for the diaconate to that for the priesthood and then reaching the 'full' mark for the episcopate? While this does not seem consonant with the dignity of the sacrament at all levels, it does correspond to popular perceptions of both grace and the sacrament. There has been surprisingly little written about the distinction between priests and bishops. There seems to be a general acceptance that the sacrament of ordination has a built-in hierarchy and one progresses from deacon to priest to bishop, receiving greater powers with each step. The Council of Trent as quoted above, lends itself to this interpretation by listing those powers held by bishops but not priests; primarily, the powers of confirmation and ordination. However a closer reading of Vatican II shows that this is not the sense in which they are using the phrase 'fullness of the sacrament':

> But episcopal consecration is not something added to one who has previously been ordained a priest. When conferred on one simply baptised, it at once bestows the fullness of priestly power, enrolling him in the ranks of the supreme pastors of the Church.[62]

Thus, Rahner supports the minority opinion discussed in the lengthy quote above. The practice of conferring episcopal ordination only on those who have already been ordained as priests belongs to canon law and has evolved for practical reasons, it is not essential for theological reasons. Current practice is that a bishop must have first received the orders of deacon and priest but this was not always so. The apostolic and Patristic Church ordained men directly to the episcopate. In the Middle Ages, there were several examples of men being ordained deacon, priest and bishop in one ceremony, or within days of each other. This was even the case where they were then consecrated as pope. The debates of the nineteenth and early twentieth centuries on the nature of the episcopal consecration and the relationship between the pope and bishops were addressed by Vatican II and we have already discussed the doctrine of collegiality and quoted the teaching of *Lumen Gentium* on the fullness of the sacrament. Cardinal Avery Dulles defends this teaching as part of the continuity of development of doctrine, not part of the 'hermeneutic of discontinuity', a phrase used by those who try to portray Vatican II as causing a rupture with the earlier Church.

> The council here exercises its doctrinal authority to settle a question previously disputed among theologians in the West ... The advance follows the normal lines of dogmatic development.[63]

Unfortunately, Dulles does not take the next step of explaining why he feels that this clarification is so important that it is 'The most important doctrinal pronouncement of the entire council'.[64] To a senior theologian of the modern Church, the importance of the pronouncement may have seemed too obvious to need elaboration. To the ordinary layman, it simply confirms what he or she knew already, that the bishop has more powers than the priest. To others, it raises more questions than it answers. Some of these questions, though not all, are addressed by Galot, who agrees with Dulles that

> The most significant advance in the doctrinal teaching of Vatican II lies in the statement that the episcopate is a sacrament ... It intended to put an end to the debate concerning the sacramentality of the episcopate as an order distinct from the presbyterate.[65]

Galot explains that the episcopate is sacramental because of the liturgical rite of consecration used and the functions that the bishop is then empowered to perform:

> These functions are conferred through a sacramental rite,
> the laying-on of hands, and words of consecration. This rite
> produces a twofold result: grace and character. These enable
> the bishop to act in the name of Christ by exercising in
> eminent fashion the three priestly functions.[66]

Galot also says that, by episcopal consecration, the bishop becomes
a member of the College of Bishops. He exercises his authority only
while a member of this college and cannot act independently of it:

> Thus, we come to a better understanding of the fullness of
> the priesthood of bishops. What is involved is a fullness
> which, in the exercise of power over the universal Church,
> is collegial by its very nature and subject to the authority of
> the pope.[67]

According to the Catechism of the Catholic Church, the College of
Bishops was instituted by Christ as a permanent assembly with
Peter at its head. It represents both the universality and unity of
the Church. It has supreme and full authority over the whole
Church, but only when acting as one body with the Pope at its
head.[68]

Some of the evidence quoted above suggests that we can
differentiate between the sacramental and the juridical powers
received through episcopal consecration, concluding that the
sacramental powers come from God, the juridical from the pope.[69]
However the evidence of, for example, Matthew 16:19; 'I will give
you the keys of the kingdom of heaven, whatever you bind on
earth will be bound in heaven; whatever you loose on earth will
be loosed in heaven' does not support such a separation of functions.

This difference in understanding suggests that the full significance of the teaching has yet to be clarified. Perhaps this will only
happen when another ecumenical council clarifies the distinction
between bishops and priests. It is time to turn our attention to the
sacrament of ordination as it applies to priests.

Priest

> The office of this ministry has been handed down, in a lesser
> degree indeed, to the priests. Established in the order of the
> priesthood they can be co-workers of the episcopal order for

the proper fulfilment of the apostolic mission entrusted to
priests by Christ.[70]

The above quote suggests a simple, practical relationship between
bishops and priests in that priests are given a share in the mission
of bishops in order to help the bishops fulfil their duties as the
successors of the apostles. This is indeed the modern understanding. However its roots in Scripture are not as clear as we tend to
assume: 'The oldest passages which refer to presbyters as leaders
of Gentile Christian congregations are Acts 14:23; 20:17–38.'[71] In
both passages, the NJB and the RSV uses 'elders', not 'presbyters'
as the above quote would lead one to expect. As we have seen from
the discussion on bishops, the offices and titles of the early Church
leaders took some time to become standardised.

Any discussion of priesthood in the New Testament and the life
of the Church must include an examination of the Letter to the
Hebrews.[72] Here Jesus is presented as the eternal high priest,
superior to both Moses and Melchizedek. By his perfect sacrifice,
he is forever the source of salvation and no further sacrifice is
necessary.

> The emphasis is on the eternity of Jesus' one and only
> sacrifice ... Jesus' self offering is a heavenly, not an earthly
> reality ... a sharing in Jesus' sacrificial worship, through
> which Christians have access to God ... Jesus' sacrifice is the
> basis on which he is mediator of the new covenant. Through
> it he has brought deliverance ... from the sins committed
> under the old covenant.[73]

It was mainly the Letter to the Hebrews that convinced the
Reformers that there was no need for an ordained priesthood. So,
much of the counter-Reformation debate on the priesthood
focussed on the nature of the sacrificial priesthood. In more recent
times the emphasis has been on understanding and interpreting
the historical details of the bishops as successors of the apostles
and the priests as receiving their authority from the bishops. While
the Church has never denied the teaching on the priesthood of the
laity, she has always insisted on a sacramental priesthood as
instituted by Christ. There are two participations in the priesthood
of Christ, the priesthood of all the baptised (discussed in chapters
three and fifteen) and the ministerial priesthood.

> While the common priesthood of the faithful is exercised by
> the unfolding of baptismal grace ... the ministerial priest-
> hood is a means by which Christ unceasingly builds up and
> leads his Church ... Through the ordained ministry, espe-
> cially that of bishops and priests, the presence of Christ as
> head of the Church is made visible in the midst of the
> community of believers.[74]

We have already seen in chapter eight that the very early Church
appointed successors to the apostles and these successors delegated some of their tasks to both deacons and priests. There is
considerable debate and uncertainty over the exact evolution of
the roles of deacon and priest, starting as early as the first recorded
example of the apostles delegating powers.

Acts 6:1–6 and beyond

This story of the election of seven men to assist the apostles has
traditionally been seen as the institution of the office of deacon.
However the passage does not actually use this word and some
modern exegetes argue that it is describing the institution of the
presbyters/priests, as what little we hear of their activities has more
in common with a priestly than a diaconal role. In addition to the
task for which they were elected, the daily distribution of bread
(Ac 6:1), Stephen works miracles and debates with visiting Jewish
leaders. Philip preached the good news in Samaria and worked
miracles among them, including casting out demons (Ac 8:5–13),
and baptising them (Ac 8:12). He also explains Scripture to, and
baptises, the Ethiopian eunuch (Ac 8:26–38).

> Luke does not call the chosen seven 'deacons', and this term
> may have been given to the Seven as a title or rank because
> he twice uses the word *diakonia* ('service' v4; translated
> 'distribution' in v1) see Ph 1:1a; Tt 1:5c. All seven have Greek
> names, the last is a proselyte, see 2:11f. ... the functions of
> the seven overlap those of the Twelve; for they both preach
> and baptise.[75]

The document of the International Theological Commission '*From
the Diakonia of Christ to the Diakonia of the Apostles*' is clear in its
teaching on this, even if its logic loses something in the translation:

Pagan authorities are also in the service of God (Rom 13:4): the deacons are the servants of the Church (Col 1:25; 1 Cor 3:5). In the case where the deacon belongs to one of the churches, the Vulgate does not use the word *minister*; but retains the Greek word *diaconus*. This fact shows clearly that in Acts 6:1–6 it is not the institution of the diaconate which is being referred to.[76]

This document's explanation, given below, for its interpretation of Ac 6:1–6. is widely accepted:

It is possible that the Apostles appointed the Seven to be at the head of the 'Hellenists' (baptised Greek-speaking Jews) to fulfil the same task as the presbyters among the 'Hebrew' Christians. The reason given for the designation of the chosen Seven (complaints by the Hellenists) is in contradiction with their actual activities as later described by Luke. We hear nothing about serving at tables. Out of the seven, Luke only speaks of the activities of Stephen and Philip; or more precisely, Stephen's discourse in the synagogue at Jerusalem, and his martyrdom, and the apostolate carried out in Samaria by Philip, who also baptised people.[77]

The first mention of deacons as a title for people holding a specific office is in St Paul's letter to the Philippians (Ph 1:1);

Already in this phrase there emerges a decisive point for our understanding of the office, namely, that the deacons are linked with the bishops and mentioned after them. That the diaconate stands in closest relationship to the episcopate is confirmed by Tm.3:1ff.[78]

Whatever the specific functions of the various positions mentioned in Scripture, it is clear that the Church fairly quickly developed a hierarchical structure to allow it to pass on the good news and to protect it from heresy. By the time of the letter of Clement of Rome to the Corinthians, there are bishops and deacons and the bishop of Rome has some degree of authority over the others. Approximately ten years later, the letters of Ignatius of Antioch describe a reasonably clear distinction between bishops, priests and deacons, although he used the word 'clergy' rather than 'priest'. Ignatius's main concern was with the theology of the episcopate. He seems to regard the presbyters as a college advising the bishop while deacons gave practical support.

By the time of the *Apostolic Tradition* of Hippolytus, there is a clearer division of authority and a change in the relationship between bishops and priests.

> By the middle of the third century can be seen the beginnings of the episcopate as an absolute monarchy with the presbyters as no more than assistants to the episcopal office ... The collegiality of bishop and presbyters was replaced by a greater emphasis on the collegiality of bishops with one another.[79]

The development of the collegiality of bishops, combined with the support of the emperor Constantine, allowed for the calling of the first general council of the Church at Nicaea in AD 325. The main purpose of the council was to combat Arianism, (a widespread heresy teaching that God the Son was created in time by God the Father and therefore 'there was a time when he was not') by confirming the full divinity of God the Son and his equal status with the Father. The council also passed several decrees concerning bishops, priests and deacons. These give us some idea of the development of these roles by this time in Church history. So we find that, for example, each province had several bishops, of whom one was recognised as metropolitan. Within the group of metropolitans, some were more senior than others, as established by ancient custom. The bishop of Jerusalem had special honour but was not a metropolitan. All the bishops of a province voted on, and gave written consent to, the ordination of a new bishop. At least three of them had to take part in the ordination and the metropolitan was in charge of proceedings. They were to meet twice a year to discuss matters of common interest, especially excommunications. An episcopal ordination without the consent of the metropolitan is invalid but, where there is personal rivalry preventing unanimity, a majority vote is sufficient. Deacons must remember that they are ministers of the bishop and subordinate to the presbyters. They must not distribute Holy Communion to their superiors nor sit with them. [80]

We can see from the decrees of this council that the Church had a well-organised hierarchy with an established governance. Many canons were simply confirmed by Nicaea and must therefore have pre-existed the council. The emphasis is on bishops, priests and deacons but other clerical ranks existed, including deaconesses. These deaconesses, mentioned in canon 19, are among those followers of Paul of Samosata who have come over to the Catholic Church. All of the group must be rebaptised and their clergy, if worthy, must be reordained. 'The same thing must be done with respect to deaconesses.'[81] They seem to have been listed on the roll of the Paulinist clergy but not to have received the same ordination rites as the male clergy. Nicaea says that they are to be numbered among the laity but it is not clear whether or not they can be rebaptised and ordained with their male colleagues.[82] Celibacy was expected of all clergy. It seems from the last item on the list that there was already the sense that ranks were determined by one's relationship to the Eucharist. This was an important concept throughout the history of the Church:[83]

> If we look at the history of the birth and establishment of the various orders and ministries we shall see how quickly the Church concentrated ordination almost exclusively on her ministries *ad intra* ... For the main theological implication of this is connected with the fact that ordination is related to the eucharistic community, and for this reason the ministries or 'orders' that are suggested by the structure of this community become the *decisive* ones for all ministries. By reserving ordination to these ministries, the Church has at least preserved the correct visible point of reference for its ministry.[84]

Zizioulas then returns to his main theme of the priest as a relational link between Christ and the members of the Church:

> Thus the ordained person becomes a 'mediator' between man and God not by presupposing or establishing a distance between these two but by relating himself to both in the context of the community of which he himself is part. It is in this way that the gradual application of the term priest was extended from the person of Christ, for whom alone it is used in the New Testament, to the bishop, for whom again alone it was used until about the fourth century ... The true and historically original meaning of the term is this: as Christ (the only priest) becomes in the Holy Spirit a community

(His body, the Church), His priesthood is realised and portrayed in historical existence here and now as a eucharistic community in which His 'image' is the head of this community offering with and on behalf of the community the eucharistic gifts.[85]

The ideas expressed in these two quotes from a member of the Greek Orthodox Church are also expressed in recent documents of the Roman Catholic Church: 'The other sacraments, as well as with every ministry of the Church and every work of the apostolate, are tied together with the Eucharist and are directed towards it.'[86] Also, 'From this (the participation of the priest in the life of the Trinity) one perceives the essentially 'relational' characteristic (John 17:11.21) of the priest's identity.'[87]

However we have got slightly ahead of ourselves! To return to the Council of Nicaea, it is worth noting that the translations still use the word 'presbyter' rather than 'priest': 'Presbyters were understood to share in the priesthood of the bishop through their association with his ministry, but were not themselves called "priests" unequivocally until the fifth century.'[88] The usual reason given for this is that this word was widely used in Judaism and the various pagan religions: 'Probably the title "priest" (*hiereus*) was not given to the apostles, bishops and presbyters in the New Testament lest they be confused with the priests of the Old Law or those of the pagan religions.'[89] Ashley adds a footnote, saying: 'Instead the term *presbyteros* or elder, common for synagogue leaders, was used.'[90]

The Council of Nicaea was a watershed event in Church history, not just for its theological teachings but also because it marked the beginning of a new style of Church governance, general councils, where the bishops could get together and formulate teachings that then became binding on the universal Church. It can be difficult to differentiate between teachings that belong to the Tradition of the Church and those that belong to the Magisterium. Aidan Nichols limits magisterial teaching to the preaching and teaching of bishops and pope in their everyday activities: 'Sunday by Sunday and day by day, bishops and pope are teaching Christian doctrine ... Such everyday teaching is referred to in current parlance as the "activity of the ordinary Magisterium"'.[91] He classes the teachings of councils as Tradition: 'Tradition includes such monuments as councils and conciliar creeds and definitions ... Such creeds and definitions are not simply aids in the discernment of Tradition. They are Tradition, for they are monuments, that is, embodiments of Tradition.'[92] The content of the Council deliberations are only to be thought of as Tradition when they have been formalised in creeds and definitions. Much, if not all, of the Vatican II teachings are non-definitive. This does not mean that they can be ignored! Nichols goes on to say that the teaching of the ordinary Magisterium can be sub-divided into definitive and non-definitive categories. Church teaching on the nature of the priesthood, while ultimately based on Scripture, is a mixture of Tradition (those teachings which are to be regarded as beyond dispute) and Magisterial (those teachings which could be changed from time to time, unless they were promulgated with the intention of being definitive). So we need to concentrate on the official teachings of the Church regarding priesthood rather than examining the purely historical developments. We have already discussed the Lateran Councils of the eleventh and twelfth centuries under the heading of Tradition. It might have been more logical to discuss them here but we can now at least fill in the gap between the Council of Nicaea and the Lateran councils.[93]

The pre-Nicene Church was centred very much on the individual bishops as successors of the apostles and shepherds of their flock: 'The role of the priest emerges only marginally in history, since he remained in the shadow of the bishop as a member of his council.'[94] The support of Constantine allowed the clergy many privileges, especially exemption from municipal duties and military service.[95] This allowed them to develop their role as community leaders. It also facilitated the development of monasteries.

We have already seen that the Council of Nicaea declared that priests must not be recent converts, must be of good character, be celibate, remain in the church to which they were ordained and not practise usury. They were subordinate to their bishop but superior to the deacons.

The early councils were concerned almost exclusively with combating heresies and clarifying Church teaching on such issues as the Trinity and Christology. Surprisingly little is said about the roles of bishop, priest and deacon. The literature on the subject tends to concentrate on the practicalities of the relationship between Church and state and the complex power struggles both between Church and state and within the Church itself: 'A historical study of the development of Christian ministry would probably show that the Church in every age has adjusted its structures and offices so as to operate more effectively in the social environment in which it finds itself.'[96]

So the office of priest has varied from providing an advisory body for the bishop, to being a helper of the bishop, to being overshadowed by deacons, to being regarded as sacramentally equal to bishops and finally to the dual role of being *in persona Christi capitis*, with the necessary grace received directly from Christ, and co-worker of the bishop, through whom they have the authority to practise their ministry. Throughout these adjustments, there are four consistent features: priestly ordination is a sacrament; the priest has three functions: to sanctify; to preach; and to govern. The Eucharistic sacrifice and the sacrament of confession are at the centre of the priests ministry and the priest receives his authority from the bishop.

Rather than trace each of these points through each stage of its history, we can go to the documents of Vatican II and the Catechism of the Catholic Church for a modern synthesis of this development. We have already looked at the sacrament of ordination, both in this chapter and in chapter eight. The other points can be covered fairly briefly. Vatican II produced several documents that included teachings concerning the priesthood: *Lumen Gentium*; *Christus Dominus*; *Presbyterorum Ordinis* and *Optatam Totius*.

Lumen Gentium is concerned with the nature of the Church as a hierarchy. It gives a summary of the priesthood that includes all the elements that I am suggesting have always been regarded as essential to the nature of priesthood. The quote is long but difficult to abbreviate. It provides footnote references to official documents of the Church from many different centuries, from Gregory Nazianzus (330–380 apr.) and Innocent I (401–17) through the Council of Trent (1545–1563) to the modern day:

> Priests, although they do not possess the highest degree of the priesthood, and although they are dependent on the

Bishops in the exercise of their power, nevertheless they are united with the bishops in sacerdotal dignity. By the power of the sacrament of Orders, in the image of Christ, the eternal high Priest, they are consecrated to preach the Gospel and shepherd the faithful and to celebrate divine worship, so that they are true priests of the New Testament. Partakers of the function of Christ the sole Mediator, on their level of ministry, they announce the divine word to all. They exercise their sacred function especially in the Eucharistic worship or the celebration of the Mass by which acting in the person of Christ and proclaiming His Mystery they unite the prayers of the faithful with the sacrifice of their head and renew and apply in the sacrifice of the Mass until the coming of the Lord the only sacrifice of the New Testament namely that of Christ offering Himself once for all a spotless Victim to the Father. For the sick and the sinners among the faithful, they exercise the ministry of alleviation and reconciliation and they present the needs and the prayers of the faithful to God the Father.[97]

Christus Dominus is concerned with the College of Bishops and the individual bishops' responsibilities to the priests and laity of his diocese. He should regard the priests as 'sons and friends'.[98]

Presbyterorum Ordinis is a detailed study of the life of priests, whose function it describes as follows:

Priests by sacred ordination and mission which they receive from the bishops are promoted to the service of Christ the Teacher, Priest and King. They share in his ministry, a ministry whereby the Church here on earth is unceasingly built up into the People of God, the Body of Christ and the Temple of the Holy Spirit.[99]

The decree discusses the functions of priests under the headings of 'ministers of God's Word', 'ministers of the Sacraments and the Eucharist' and 'rulers of God's people'.

Optatam Totius summarises the aims of seminaries as: 'Here the entire training of the students should be oriented to the formation of true shepherds of souls after the model of our Lord Jesus Christ, teacher, priest, and shepherd.'[100]

We can see from these quotes that the four characteristics of the priesthood listed in chapter three in the section on the priesthood of Christ (its centre is Jesus Christ; it is universal; it is dynamic and it is based on love, not fear) are clearly still regarded as foundational elements of the priesthood.

Summary

The priesthood is defined as a relationship between the priest and the one high priest, Jesus Christ, and as a relationship between the priest and the laity, who have a share in this priesthood. The essentials of the priesthood have remained constant throughout the history of the Church. Priesthood is conferred by the bishop through the sacrament of ordination. Priests exercise their power under obedience to their bishop but receive the power directly from God. The ordained share Christ's roles as priest, prophet and king. Of these, the Eucharistic sacrifice and the sacrament of confession have always been central.

Bishops are the successors of the apostles, priests are not. Bishops have the fullness of the sacrament of ordination in that the grace of the sacrament does not so much build up through the ranks of deacon, priest, bishop as flow down from God onto the bishop. The bishop can then delegate certain aspects of his ministry to priests and to deacons, conferring the grace of the sacrament of ordination on them in the degree appropriate to their mission. Not only is the episcopal ordination a true sacrament in its own right, it is only through the grace of this sacrament that the bishop has the power to ordain priests and deacons. Bishops form a college with the pope as its head and have a responsibility both to their own diocese and to the wider Church. They can only exercise this responsibility in communion with their fellow bishops.

Deacons

We have already mentioned that the selection of the seven in Acts 6:1–6, traditionally taken to be the institution of the diaconate, is now thought to be the institution of the episcopate/presbyterate.[101]

> P. Gaechter has taken the position that this institution represents the first episcopal consecration ... But it is anachronistic to speak here of the institution of bishops, since the episcopal function had not yet been differentiated

from the function of presbyters, as would be the case later
... It seems, then, that the ordination of the Seven should be
regarded as a 'presbyteral' ordination.[102]

If the above argument is correct, the term 'deacon' is later than the
institution of the seven. It is first used by Paul: 'The term deacon
can be applied to ministries of different ranks. Paul calls himself
by this term (2 Co 3:6, 11:23; Ep 3:7), but he uses the same term to
designate other ministries inferior to the apostles in rank.'[103]

It is important to understand that the term 'deacon' or 'servant'
had quite different connotations in the Jewish and the Greek
communities. To the Jews, service was a noble activity as Abraham
had waited at table. Serving a master was serving God (Lv 19:18).
If one's master was a great person, then the servant shared in that
glory. To the Greeks, a servant was a humble and lowly person.
Paul and the other early Church writings use the word in its Jewish
sense.

As with the orders of bishop and priest, that of deacon took
some time to develop and its early history is unclear.[104] At the time
that the Didache was written (before AD 130) deacons were to be
'Mild men, fair minded, truthful and reliable, for they too fulfil
towards you the offices of prophets and teachers'.[105] They were
responsible for the works of charity, particularly towards widows
and orphans. By the time of St Justin (AD 165), deacons were
involved in the Eucharistic services, presenting the offerings,
helping to distribute communion and taking communion to those
who could not be present. The *Didascalia* (third century) adds the
duties of ushering in new-comers and pilgrims, taking care of the
offerings, supervising orderliness and silence and ensuring that
people are suitably dressed. There seems to be some tension
between priests and deacons in that priests have a higher rank than
deacons but, in practice, deacons have greater power and prestige:
'The deacons are called the "third ones", which probably suggests
that they come after the bishop and the priests. However, the status
and activity of deacons undoubtedly seem to have surpassed those
of priests.'[106]

By the time of the *Traditio Apostolica* of Hippolytus of Rome (AD
235), there was a distinction between 'institution' and 'ordination'
into the Church hierarchy. Ordination was distinguished by the

imposition of hands and was conferred by the bishop. Bishops, priests and deacons were ordained: 'Thus, in the course of the third century, the imposition of hands already constituted the distinctive sign of the rite of ordination to major orders. In the fourth century it was extended to minor orders as well.'[107]

By the end of the fourth century, the diaconate is being seen as a transitory grade towards the presbyterate. The difference between the two was not always clear and deacons regularly needed to be reminded that they came after priests in the hierarchy:

> This tendency to invade the field of competencies of priests, which was also manifested in the claim to preside at the Eucharist (albeit as an exception) was put a stop to by the synod of Arles (314) and particularly by the Council of Nicaea (325, can 18).[108]

From the end of the fifth century, as the priestly 'career path' became fixed, it absorbed the various functions that had been autonomous, permanent positions. Functions which had been seen as the specific field of activity of deacons were either taken over by monasteries (mainly the charitable works), performed by the transitory deacons (mainly the liturgical rites) or now seen as so important that they needed to be under the authority of priests or bishops (the administration). By the ninth century, the ordination rites of deacons suggest that their main function was reading the gospel in the liturgy, a task just as readily performed by transitory deacons. The role of the permanent deacon was no longer essential to either the administration or the liturgy of the Church.

While the documents of the Church of the first millennium consistently refer to deacons as being ordained and being part of the same hierarchy as priests and bishops, there was no consistent teaching on the sacramentality of their position. This was partly because the Church had not yet formalised its teaching on the sacraments. It was not until the writings of Peter Lombard in the twelfth century that the number of sacraments was fixed at seven, with Holy Orders having several grades (these varied from seven to nine). From the time of St Thomas Aquinas, these grades were decided by the relation of the function to the Eucharist. So deacons were below priests as they were ordained to assist in the administration of the sacraments whereas the priest was ordained to consecrate the elements. Priests could touch the sacred host but deacons could only administer the precious blood because it was contained in a vessel and therefore did not need to be handled.[109] The next major source of teaching on the sacrament of Holy Orders is the Council of Trent. We have already looked at its teaching on the hierarchy.[110] Trent confirmed that there were seven sacraments, including Holy Orders. While it included deacons in the hierarchy, it was not very precise. Is it referring to the transitory diaconate or the permanent, or both? Is the diaconate a sacrament? Does diaconal ordination confer character? The debate on these questions continued. Vatican II reintroduced permanent deacons but did not definitively end the debate on their status.

> Concerning deacons or the diaconate in the texts of Vatican II ... the sacramentality of both modes (permanent and transitory) was taken for granted ... Taken all together, the texts of Vatican II repeated what had been the majority opinion in theology up to that time, but went no further.[111]

The key text of Vatican II regarding deacons is contained in *Lumen Gentium* where it reintroduced permanent deacons. The chapter starts with the following:

> At a lower level of the hierarchy are deacons, upon whom hands are imposed 'not unto the priesthood, but unto a ministry of service'. For strengthened by sacramental grace in communion with the Bishop and his group of priests they serve in the diaconate of the liturgy, of the word and of charity to the people of God.[112]

Debate over the sacramentality and character of the diaconate continued even after the publication of the Motu Proprio, *Sacrum Diaconatus Ordinem,* putting the Council's decisions into effect.[113]

> In spite of the fact that some doctrinal questions could not be sufficiently clarified, the restoration of the permanent diaconate evinces the Church's effort to unfold all the possibilities immanent in the sacrament of order. The Church paves the way for a sacramental ministry which is not priestly and yet is called to collaborate in the discharge of the priestly functions.[114]

Appendix II, section E) contains excerpts from the *Summa Theolog-ica* and summaries of journal articles. These give a picture of the current thinking on the position of deacons. While some argue that Vatican II abandoned the Scholastic definition of the sacrament of ordination and redefined it in terms of the three *munera*,[115] most authors work on the premise that both viewpoints are necessary to an understanding of the sacrament, and therefore the place of deacons within the hierarchy. It seems clear from the Catechism of the Catholic Church that the Magisterium intended the diaco-nate to be part of the sacrament of ordination, and therefore to include a permanent character: 'Deacons share in Christ's mission and grace in a special way. The sacrament of Holy Orders marks them with an imprint (character) which cannot be removed and which configures them to Christ.'[116] The council renewed the permanent diaconate in order to both ease the burden on priests and to expand the Church's work of evangelisation and charity.

Vatican II and further documents, especially *Pastores dabo vobis*, refer to the priest and bishop as acting *in persona Christi*. This phrase is never used for deacons. Instead the phrase *in nomine Christi* is used. Diaconal ordination fits the person for an office in the Church by conferring a sacred power not shared by the laity.

There is much debate over the role of permanent deacons. Some of their liturgical duties seem to blur the distinction between them and priests, others could equally well be done by lay people. Parish priest, deacons and the parishioners are left wondering just what position the deacon has in the parish. Many trees have been sacrificed on the altar of historical research into the role of deacons in the early Church and the linguistic nuances of the various titles used. An alternative approach would be to accept that historical evidence is seldom absolute, that the efforts of the Reformation churches to 'return to our roots' was not entirely successful and that the Holy Spirit is still guiding the Church. If this Holy Spirit has prompted the fathers of the Council to reintroduce permanent deacons, then there must be a reason for this. A greater sense of obedience and humility among all concerned might help us to work out what this reason is. Combine this with a spirit of 'onwards and upwards' and we could begin to harvest the fruits of the Council's deliberations.

We can see from these quotes that the permanent deacon is not a priest but is asked to cooperate in the priestly tasks of sanctifying, teaching and governing. He is not a lay person but is asked to share in the life of the community through work, family life and charitable activity. Instead of looking on this as a problem, we can see it as a way of bringing the fullness of the sacrament of ministry/diakonia into effect. The deacon represents Christ, who came 'not to be served but to serve' (Mk 10:45) and is a reminder to us that we are all, laity and ordained, meant to share in this ministry. His life-long commitment is a witness for all to copy. The power of the sacrament means that he is acting in an official capacity as servant and representative of the bishop.

Judging by the rulings of the Council of Arles and of Nicaea on the role of deacons, the problem of deacons misjudging just where their duties end and those of priests begins has always been a problem. It seems to me that one possible solution is, not to look to the example of the early Church, or even to the pressing pastoral needs of the modern Church, but to Scripture. All aspects of sacramental ordination are founded on two events, the life of Christ and his instructions to the apostles. The above quote from Mark 10:45 is often used as a 'proof text' for the theology of Christ-the-servant, but we need to remember the second half of the sentence 'and to give his life as a ransom for many'. So the office of *diakonia* is one of total self-giving, just as is the office of priest and bishop. All three offices result from Jesus choosing twelve apostles (Mk 3:13), giving them the task of spreading the good news (Mt 28:18–20) and the authority to organise the community in such a way as to facilitate this task (Mt 16:19). Quite how the apostles went about this and how their successors then adapted things to suit the changing needs of the Church is of importance but not fundamental to the nature of the sacrament. We have already seen that the hierarchy of Bishop, Priest, Deacon was established early in the life of the Church. Tradition and the Magisterium teach that the bishop is the successor of the apostles, with their authority to govern, as established in Matthew 16:19. The bishops use this authority to delegate their tasks and have done so in two ways; the priest exercises the same *tri munera* as the bishop and acts *in persona Christi capitis;* the deacon exercises those parts of the *tri munera* that the bishop deems appropriate and acts *in nomine Christi*. Some magisterial documents also speak of the deacon as *in persona Christi*, particularly when they are referring to the sacrament of ordination as a whole. However there has been a trend towards reserving *in persona Christi* for those presiding at the Eucharist. The recent changes to canon law mentioned in chapter twelve also clarify this point.

While bishops and priests act as members of a college, reminiscent of 'the twelve', deacons do not. While bishops and priests have the priestly duty of mediation between the people and God, the deacon does not. While all, laity and clergy, have a duty of service to others, this is particularly the role of the deacon. The common meaning of the word 'service' suggests practical, lowly tasks and acts of charity and there has been an emphasis on this aspect in the modern definition of the role of the permanent deacon, using John 13:1–16 as the proof-text. However the original Scriptural context was not so narrow and included all forms of service to others, either as individuals or as communities.[117] So permanent deacons are allowed to stand for public office and to hold influential teaching, administrative or advisory posts. The only occupation for which they need specific episcopal permission is that of military service. The important point is that they are acting in a spirit of service, humility and obedience to their bishop, just as Christ the king obeyed his father by becoming the slave of all (Ph 2:7).

This return to Scripture shows that all of the clergy are called to total self-giving and that the bishops have the authority to organise the duties of those to whom they have delegated some of their tasks, the priests and deacons. Priests share in the apostolic, collegial power of the apostles, deacons do not. Deacons are particularly called to a ministry of service but this does not limit their activity to menial tasks. As this delegation occurred in the post-apostolic Church, we have to turn to Tradition and the Magisterium for further clarification of the difference between priests and deacons. The simplest explanation that I have read so far is that presented by Gaillardetz:

> In the midst of the diverse ministerial activity that has characterised the work of deacons, it must be said that deacons did not ever, as an ordinary dimension of their

ministry, exercise pastoral oversight of a local eucharistic community (any examples are exceptional). This then is the crucial distinction between the ministry of the deacon and that of the bishop and presbyter.[118]

So the deacons act either *in persona Christi* or *in nomine Christi*. Only bishops and priests can be described as acting *in persona Christi capitis*.[119] The deacon does not share in the duty of the bishop to exercise authority over his local churches or of the College of Bishops to exercise authority over the universal Church. The priest, on the other hand, does have a share of this pastoral oversight within his own parish.

Summary

The beginnings of the order of deacons is unclear but it is very early in the life of the Church, being used in several letters by Paul. By the time of Ignatius of Antioch, priests and deacons were seen as assistants to the bishops. As their duties increased, bishops instituted a system of delegating their duties of overseeing the community and their duties as priest, prophet and king in their entirety to priests[120] but selectively to deacons.

Deacons have always been associated with the liturgy and the charitable work of the Church. With the growth of monastic orders and the development of a transitory diaconate, the need for permanent deacons gradually decreased. By the eleventh century, they had disappeared and the diaconate only existed as a preparatory stage of the priesthood.

The Second Vatican Council in the 1960s reintroduced the permanent diaconate, partly in response to the shortage of priests and partly to contribute to the Church's work of evangelising and contributing to charitable efforts among the world's poor. The teaching of the Magisterium on the diaconate makes it clear that it is part of the sacrament of Holy Orders. However there are no clear pronouncements on the character conferred by the sacrament. Studies of Conciliar and post-Conciliar documents show that diaconal ordination is sacramental and confers a permanent character, allowing the deacon to act *in nomine Christi*. The deacon has both liturgical and pastoral duties, of which the pastoral are the more normative as the deacon is conformed to Christ-the-servant. While the deacon shares in the *tri munera* of sanctifying, preaching and leading, he does not share in the overseeing of a community. The difference between leadership and oversight may seem to be slight but leadership is in terms of example and exhortation rather than power and authority; authority includes disciplinary and administrative measures. As mentioned earlier when discussing the role of women in Scripture, Jesus led by example in washing the feet of the apostles. This diaconal act of service inaugurated a new form of leadership, to be practised by deacon, priest and bishop. The bishop and priest also have to exercise disciplinary and administrative powers in order to maintain the structures necessary to allow this new form of leadership to flourish.

Deaconesses

If the history of the origins and development of deacons is unclear, that of deaconesses is even more so. The last paragraph of the dictionary article on deacons, quoted above, is as follows:

> Alongside the deacons there were also deaconesses. Their history begins with Rm 16:1 where Paul describes Phoebe as 'a deaconess of the Church at Cenchreae'. It is, of course, an open question whether he is referring to a fixed office or simply to her service on behalf of the community. Similarly, there is no agreement whether 1 Tm 3:11 refers to the wives of deacons or to deaconesses. It is indisputable, however, that an order of deaconesses did quickly arise in the Church. A particular part was played here by widows who, on the strength of their chaste conduct on the one side and their loving service on the other, already received official recognition in 1 Tm 5:3ff.[121]

There is some debate over whether or not Phoebe was the equivalent of a male deacon. Whatever her role, she was highly respected by Paul and was regarded as a leader of the community: 'What seems clear is that Phoebe exercised a recognised service in the community of Cenchreae, subordinate to the ministry of the apostle.'[122]

We have looked at the history of deaconesses fairly briefly in chapter ten. We will look at it again in part four. Here, we will limit ourselves to three sources: a 'Notification' from the Congregation for the Doctrine of the Faith on women as ordained deacons, the International Theological Commission's study *'From the Diakonia of Christ to the Diakonia of the Apostles'* and an essay 'The Character-istics and Nature of the Order of the Deaconess' by Kyriaki Karidoyanes Fitzgerald. [123]

Notification

The Notification from the Congregation for the Doctrine of the Faith is on women as ordained deacons. As it is quoted on web sites as an authoritative and binding statement on women deacons, it is worth looking at in detail.[124] The key paragraphs read:

> Our offices have received from several countries signs of courses that are being planned or underway, directly or indirectly aimed at the diaconal ordination of women. Thus are born hopes which are lacking a solid doctrinal founda-tion and which can generate pastoral disorientation.

> Since [the Church] does not foresee such ordination, it is not licit to enact initiatives which, in some way, aim to prepare women candidates for diaconal ordination.[125]

The note reminds the reader that the teachings of John Paul II included many examples of ways in which women could serve the Church. It concludes by asking the bishops of the world to apply this teaching and to explain it to their congregations.

It is difficult to argue with this note. There is indeed little point in providing courses to prepare people for a task which they cannot carry out. Women cannot be ordained as deacons until such time as canon law is changed. As I discuss in my introduction, trying to force the Church's hand or presenting it with a *fait accompli* does more harm than good. In this example, the relevant Vatican Congregations had to bear in mind that many groups were both campaigning for and illicitly practising the ordination of women. There are many groups purporting to be the voice of the Church who show scant understanding of her teachings. Sadly, and inexplicably, this includes both priests and theologians.[126] The Congregation could not produce a conciliatory note as it would be misread to be more supportive of these groups than is the case. As at the time of the Reformation, demands for change are actually having the opposite effect. At the other end of the debate, groups opposed to the diaconal ordination of women have seized on the phrase 'lacking a solid doctrinal foundation' as teaching that women can never be ordained as deacons. However this was not necessarily the meaning intended by the authors. There is a fine but important distinction between 'doctrinal' and 'Scriptural' foundations which they would have been well aware of. Their purpose was to end inappropriate practices, not to give a final and definitive teaching on the underlying theology. This is clear from the next document that we will look at. The International Theological Commission was instructed to give an account of the history and theology of the diaconate, with a specific remit to examine the possibility of having ordained female deacons, both in the past and in the future. This work would have been unnecessary if the Notification of September 2001 had been a definitive statement banning the ordination of women to the diaconate. The Commission published their findings, 'From the Diakonia of Christ to the Diakonia of the Apostles' in 2002.

From the Diakonia of Christ to the Diakonia of the Apostles

This document looks at the ministry of deaconesses within the larger picture of the development of the diaconate in the early Church. Having acknowledged Pheobe as having a recognised service, it goes on to look at the first letter to Timothy, which mentions women who may have been either deaconesses or the wives of deacons. They were not to teach or rule over men (but neither were deacons at this stage in Church history). The first clear mention of deaconesses in an ecclesiastical document is in the *Didascalia Apostolorum* around AD 240. 'From the Diakonia of Christ' then gives a brief outline of the history of deaconesses, referring the reader to Gryson, Martimort and Hauke for further details.[127] It stresses the differences between deacons and deaconesses but does admit that, by the fourth century, deaconesses were treated as part of the clergy. It confirms that deaconesses faded from history for very much the same reasons as had deacons. Their roles in the liturgy and charitable works were taken over by religious orders; in effect, they became nuns. 'From the Diakonia of Christ' ends with two points to be considered in the debate over the ordination of deaconesses; the deaconesses of the early Church 'were not purely and simply equivalent to the deacons' and the unity of the sacrament of Holy Orders, with the episcopal and priestly ministry on one hand and the diaconal ministry on the other, has always been taught by the Magisterium.[128]

When I first read this study, I was struck, not by its negative tone and obvious reluctance to support the reintroduction of deaconesses, but by its very careful use of language so that it does not actually deny this possibility. A careful reading of the document shows that it is not as biased as is sometimes claimed. Much of it is taken up with tracing the development, disappearance and reintroduction of permanent deacons. When discussing the reintroduction of permanent deacons at Vatican II, the Commission suggests that the Church had three reasons for taking this step: restoring this degree returns the hierarchy to the form willed by God; it helps the Church to meet the pastoral needs of communities; it gives a more complete incorporation into the ministry of the Church of those who are already *de facto* exercising the ministry of deacon. None of these reasons are incompatible with ordaining deaconesses. Indeed the second and third reasons are regularly quoted in support of having deaconesses.

The Commission also recognised that Vatican II had indirectly clarified the role of the priest by allowing ordained deacons to share in the duties of a parish priest. This is relevant to the debate on ordaining women as deacons as it shows that there is more to the sacrament of ordination than setting men aside for specifically priestly duties.

> In consequence, the Church would be able to experience the riches of different degrees of Holy Orders. At the same time Vatican II enabled the Church to go beyond a narrowly sacerdotal understanding of the ordained ministry. Since deacons were ordained 'non ad sacerdotium, sed ad ministerium', it was possible to conceive of clerical life, the sacred hierarchy and ministry in the Church beyond the category of the priesthood.[129]

This acknowledgement that deacons are of a different order to priests is fundamental to the argument for female deacons as it answers the question 'If women became deacons, would they then not also be able to become priests?' As I discuss elsewhere, the two orders are quite separate 'career paths' and admission to one does not bring any rights of access to the other. Another point made by the Commission struck me as worth more comment than it seems to have received.

> It is however interesting to note that nowhere did the Council claim that the form of the permanent diaconate which it was proposing was a restoration of a previous form ... What it re-established was the principle of the permanent exercise of the diaconate, and not one particular form which the diaconate had taken in the past.[130]

This point is of great importance for the development of the diaconate, male or female. It is saying that we do not need to have detailed linguistic analysis of ordination rites to ascertain the roles of the early deacons. We do not need to get bogged down in obscure Vatican documents giving or rescinding permission for deacons and deaconesses to perform specific tasks. We do not need to scratch moss from ancient gravestones in order to check whether or not women had been given the title of deaconess. We can ignore those who insist that deaconesses were only needed for adult baptisms. It is not what they did centuries ago that matters. What matters is the present and future need for permanent deacons and deaconesses. What matters is the relationship between bishop, priest and deacon. What matters is the nature of the sacrament of ordination and whether or not women can be ordained to the permanent diaconate.

This document, generally recognised as at the very least not encouraging the idea of deaconesses, has in fact clarified that permanent deacons are of a different order from priests, thus protecting the all-male priesthood, and that the historical evidence for the duties of deacons and deaconesses is of historical interest only—it is for the modern Church to discern how the modern diaconate can best serve the community.

Fitzgerald

This essay became the basis for the book *'Women Deacons in the Orthodox Church'*, summarised in Appendix V. It concentrates on the documents the *Syriac Didascalia* (third century) and the *Apostolic Constitutions* (fourth century). Both documents rank deaconesses with the clergy. They agree that the deaconesses chief task was to assist the bishop with baptisms. However they include many other tasks—

> She exchanged the kiss of peace with the women in the assembly during the eucharist. Moreover, she was the keeper of the doors, responsible for the female part of the congregation. It was her responsibility to keep the women in order and to receive female visitors into the worshipping community ... the deaconess was the leader of the female segment of the congregation ... no woman was permitted to speak to the bishop, or even the deacon, without first speaking to the deaconess. The deaconess had important catechetical and charitable responsibilities as well.[131]

However there was a distinct difference between the deaconess and the deacon and the deaconess did not take part in any priestly duties. The liturgical rites for the ordination of deaconesses have never been rescinded and there are several examples of nuns being ordained as deaconesses.

So the debate over women deacons continues without any obvious way forward. In the early Church, deaconesses were more numerous in the East than in the West. However they disappeared at about the same time. A study of the Greek Orthodox understanding of the diaconate concluded that they ended the practice of ordaining women to the diaconate when they adopted the medieval Western position of viewing the diaconate as the first step towards priesthood. As the diaconate is part of the fullness of the priesthood shared by the three orders of bishop, priest and deacon and women cannot become priests, so they cannot become deacons.[132] However Orthodoxy never rescinded its ordination rites for deaconesses and there were occasional examples of its use in the twentieth century. The Holy Synod of the Greek Orthodox Church of October 2004 voted to formally restore the female diaconate. However, so far, its use has been limited to remote monasteries.

> The Armenian Apostolic Church has always had female deacons, including those working in the community.

There are two recent declarations of unity—agreements of mutual recognition of the validity of sacraments and of orders—between Rome and the Armenian Church, one signed by Pope Paul VI and Catholicos Vasken I in 1970, another between John Paul II and Catholicos Karekin I in 1996.[133]

Summary

Deaconesses existed in the early Church and were included in the clerical hierarchy. They were gradually replaced by nuns. The current debate over whether or not they could be reintroduced is connected to the role of the diaconate as a stage in the preparation for the priesthood; if the priesthood is reserved to men, does the diaconate have to be also? Orthodox and Armenian Churches, whose sacraments we accept, do ordain women deacons.

Notes

[1]   CCC, §774.

[2]   The following is taken from E. Cutrone 'Sacraments' in A. Fitzgerald (ed.), *Augustine Through the Ages: An Encyclopedia* (Cambridge: Eerdmans, 1999), pp. 744–746.

[3]   ST, Q 3:60.2. He uses 'men' in the sense of 'people'—he is not denying the sacraments to women!

[4]   ST, Q 3a.60.3.

[5]   ST, Q 3:60.7.

[6]   ST, Q 3a.60:5.

[7]   ST, Q 3a.60:8.

[8]   ST, Q 3a.64:8.

[9]   M. Luther, 'The Pagan Servitude of the Church' in J. Dillenberger (ed.), *Martin Luther: Selections From His Writings* (New York: Anchor Books, 1961), p. 256.

[10] P. Jackson, 'Theology of the Liturgy' in Lamb & Levering, (ed.), *Vatican II Renewal Within Tradition* (Oxford: OUP, 2008), p. 113.

[11] *Ibid.*, p. 115. I wonder if the author has made a mistake here by crediting Pope Benedict XIV with the authorship of *Summi Pontificatus*? Pope Pius XII wrote an encyclical of that name in October 1939. Pope Benedict XIV wrote an encyclical, *Allatae Sunt*, in 1755 which said that the Latin rite should be

preferred over all other rites, a sentiment which does not correspond to the author's statement that 'The rationale for openness to adapting the liturgy to other cultures' could be traced to Pope Benedict XIV (*Ibid*, p. 345).

12 CCC, published in 1993.

13 The relevant sections of the CCC are §1076–1130.

14 CCC, §1103.

15 CCC, §1105, 1108.

16 CCC, §1103.

17 CCC, §1131.

18 Examples of other changes are mentioned in Benedict Ashley *Justice in the Church: Gender and Participation* (Washington: The Catholic University of America Press, 1996), p. 78 f. 22. They include the reception of the Eucharist under both kinds, then under one only, then back to both; alcoholics are allowed to use lightly fermented grape juice instead of wine; baptism by immersion, then pouring, then optional.

19 P. Bradshaw, 'Recent Developments' in Jones, Wainwright et al, *The Study of Liturgy* (London: SPCK, 1992), p. 397.

20 CCC, §1538.

21 J. Zizioulas, *Being as Communion* (New York: St Vladimir's Seminary Press, 1997), defining 'ordination' as 'assignment to a particular "ordo" in the community', p. 216.

22 CCC, §1273.

23 CCC, §1305, quoting St Thomas Aquinas, *S Th III, 72. 5 ad 2*.

24 See CIC 1983 canon 1010, 1016, 1019, 1025 §3, 1034.

25 J. Zizioulas, *Being as Communion*, p. 219.

26 For example, R. Bunnik, in J. Galot, *Theology of the Priesthood* (San Francisco: Ignatius Press, 1985), p. 195.

27 For example, Congregation for the Clergy, *Directory on the Ministry and Life of Priests* §5 (1994), 'The grace and the indelible character conferred with the sacramental unction of the Holy Spirit' quoting Trent *De Sacramento Ordinis*.

28 J. Galot, *Theology of the Priesthood*, p. 220.

29 See also the comments on name changes in chapter three 'The Apostles as Successors of Christ'.

30 J. Zizioulas, *Being as Communion*, p. 226. See also K. FitzGerald, *Women Deacons in the Greek Orthodox Church: Called to Holiness and Ministry* (Massachusetts, Holy Cross Orthodox Press, 1999), p. 99, 128.

31 J. Zizioulas, *Being as Communion*, p. 233.

32 B. Ashley, *Justice in the Church: Gender and Participation* (Washington: The Catholic University of America Press, 1996), p. 88.

33 DMLP, §2–5.

34 J. Bannerman, *The Church of Christ* (Edmonton: Still Waters Revival Books, reprinted 1991, first edition 1869), p. 469. This is a standard textbook (now perhaps dated) of the Presbyterian Church of Scotland. Interestingly, it gives a description of ordination which only lacks the word 'sacrament' to be

acceptable to 'popish' readers.

35   F. Hawkins, 'Ordination' in Jones, Wainwright et. al. *The Study of Liturgy* (London: SPCK, 1992), p. 342.

36   *Ibid.*, p. 340.

37   J. Galot, *Theology of the Priesthood*, p. 177.

38   F. Hawkins, 'Ordination' in Jones, Wainwright et. al. *The Study of the Liturgy*, p. 354. Hawkins is quoting from The Apostolic Tradition, 9.2.

39   *Ibid.*, p. 356.

40   See above in chapter fourteen 'Magisterium: Ordination; Sacrament'.

41   PO, §12.

42   The General Council of Trent twenty third session, *Doctrine on the Sacrament of Order* (1563) canon 6, as quoted in ND §1719.

43   H. Beyer, 'Bishop' in G. Kittel, TDNT vol II p. 606.

44   *Ibid.*, p. 608.

45   See the footnote to the verse in the NJB.

46   H. Beyer, 'Bishop' in G. Kittel, TDNT vol. II p. 614.

47   *Ibid.*, p. 616.

48   With the footnote 'The word *episkopos* (overseer) has not yet acquired the meaning "bishop", see Tt 1:5seq. The deacons are their assistants, Ac 6:1–6; 1 Tm 3:8–13'.

49   J. Galot, *Theology of the Priesthood*, p. 156.

50   W. Beinert, 'Bishop', in K. Rahner (ed.), *Encyclopaedia of Theology* (London: Burns and Oates, 1975), p. 146.

51   See especially Sess. XXIII, c. iv, can. 6.

52   The General Council of Trent twenty third session 'Doctrine on the Sacrament of Order' in ND §1711, p. 545.

53   For details, see chapter two 'Scripture: Interpreting Scripture; Church Teaching.'

54   W. Beinert, 'Bishop', in K. Rahner (ed.), *Encyclopaedia of Theology*, p. 146.

55   The word 'power' here is not being used in its normal sense of 'being able to wield authority over others' but refers to the power of the priest to administer the sacraments and of the bishop to administer confirmation and Holy Orders and to exercise teaching and administrative authority.

56   *The Catholic Encyclopedia* Classic 1914 edition on CD; article on Holy Orders, written in 1911.

57   F. Hawkins, 'Orders and Ordination in the New Testament' in Jones, Wainright et. al. *The Study of Liturgy*, p. 378.

58   The Catholic Encyclopedia Classic 1914 edition on CD article on Bishops, written in 1907.

59   *Ibid.*

60   See chapter twelve 'Magisterium: General Notes; Authoritative Teaching'.

61   LG § 24.

62   J. Lecuyer, 'Bishop' in K. Rahner (ed.), *Encyclopaedia of Theology*, p. 148.

63   A. Dulles, 'Nature, Mission, and Structure of the Church' in M. Lamb and M.

Levering (ed.), *Vatican II Renewal Within Tradition* (Oxford: OUP, 2008), p. 32.
64 *Ibid.*, p. 32.
65 J. Galot, *Theology of the Priesthood,* p. 183.
66 *Ibid.*, p. 184.
67 *Ibid.*, p. 185.
68 CCC, §880 – 887.
69 'Juridical' can be defined as 'The practical step of defining the immediate extent of a duty'.
70 PO, §2, quoting LG §28, *Acta Apostolicae Sedis* 56 and the Roman pontifical preface.
71 G. Bornkhamm, 'Elder' in G. Kittel, TDNT vol. VI, p. 665.
72 See also chapter three 'Scripture: Guarding the Truth; The Priesthood of Christ.'
73 NJBC, §60:53–54.
74 CCC, §1547 and §1549.
75 NJB, footnote to Acts 6:5.
76 DCDA, p. 9. P. Fransen, 'Orders and Ordination' in the *Encyclopaedia of Theology* concurs that Acts 6:1–6 may be describing the first presbyters or elders rather than deacons. Kittel's influential *Theological Dictionary of the New Testament* also feels that the description of the duties of the seven suggests that they were not deacons. (See H. Beyer 'deacons' in TDNT vol. II p. 90: 'The seven are set alongside the Twelve as representatives of the Hellenists, and that they take their place with the evangelists and apostles in disputing, preaching and baptising. This fact shows that the origin of the diaconate is not to be found in Ac. 6'.)
77 DCDA, p. 10. There is a footnote reference to Acts 8:12, 26–40 and 21:8, where Philip is called 'the evangelist'.
78 H. Beyer, 'Deacon' in G. Kittel, TDNT, vol. II, p. 89.
79 P. Bradshaw 'Recent Developments' in Jones, Wainwright et al *The Study of Liturgy*, p. 356.
80 N. Tanner, lecture 'The Early Church Councils' at Maryvale Institute, Birmingham, June 2004.
81 First General Council of Nicaea.
82 See A. Martimort, *Deaconesses: An Historical Study* (San Francisco: Ignatius Press, 1982), p. 101.
83 See also part II on Tradition and Ignatius' letter to the Smyrnaeans teaching that only the bishop, or someone delegated by him, had the power to celebrate the Eucharist.
84 J. Zizioulas, *Being as Communion*, p. 221.
85 *Ibid.*, p. 231.
86 PO, §5.
87 DMLP, §5.
88 F. Hawkins, 'Ordination' in Jones, Wainwright et al, *The Study of the Liturgy*, p. 356.

89   B. Ashley, *Justice in the Church*, p. 79.
90   *Ibid.*, p. 79 f. 25.
91   A. Nichols, *The Shape of Catholic Theology* (Collegeville: The Liturgical Press, 1991), p. 248, quoting F. A. Sullivan, *Magisterium: Teaching Authority in the Catholic Church*.
92   A. Nichols, *The Shape of Catholic Theology*, p. 248.
93   The reasons for not discussing them here are explained towards the end of chapter ten 'Tradition: Women'.
94   P. Fransen, 'Orders and Ordination' in K. Rahner (ed.), *Encyclopaedia of Theology*, p. 1131.
95   It has been suggested that the inclusion of the 'lesser orders' in the sacrament of ordination was more to do with protecting them from military service than any theological considerations.
96   A. Dulles, *Models of the Church: A Critical Assessment of the Church in all its Aspects* (Dublin: Gill and MacMillan, 1976), p. 152.
97   LG, §28.
98   CD, §16.
99   PO, §1.
100 Second Vatican Council, Decree on the Training of Priests *Optatam Totius* §4.
101 See chapter eight 'Tradition: The Church; Apostolic Succession'.
102 J. Galot, *Theology of the Priesthood*, p. 169.
103 *Ibid.*, p. 169.
104 Much of the following is simply a summary of DCDA.
105 As quoted in DCDA, p. 12.
106 DCDA, p. 14.
107 *Ibid.*, p. 15.
108 *Ibid.*, p. 17.
109 See ST part III.
110 See chapter fourteen 'The Magisterium: Ordination; Bishop.'
111 DCDA, p. 43.
112 LG, §29.1 with a quote from the Constitutions of the Egyptian Church and the *Didascalia*. The original quotes included the phrase 'of the bishop' after the word 'ministry'.
113 Pope Paul VI, Motu Proprio *Sacrum Diaconatus Ordinem* 1967. The text can be found in AAS 59 (1967) 697–704.
114 J. Galot, *Theology of the Priesthood*, p. 189.
115 For example, K. Osborne, *The Permanent Diaconate* (New York: Paulist Press, 2007).
116 CCC, §1570, referring to LG §41 and AG §16.
117 See especially the work of John Collins.
118 R. Gaillardetz, 'On the Theological Integrity of the Diaconate' in Cummings et al, *Theology of the Diaconate: The State of the Question* (New York: Paulist Press, 2005), p. 90.
119 The Code of Canon Law was amended to clarify this point following the Motu Proprio of Pope Benedict XVI, *Omnium in Mentem*, in 2009 (see §1008

and §1009). It repeated the CCC distinction that 'Those who are constituted in the order of the episcopate or the presbyterate receive the mission and capacity to act in the person of Christ the Head, whereas deacons are empowered to serve the People of God in the ministries of the liturgy, the word and charity' (CCC n.29). See also the section above, 'Magisterium: some general notes'.

[120] But normally reserving the powers of confirmation and ordination to themselves.

[121] H. Beyer, 'Deacon' in G. Kittel, TDNT vol. II p. 93.

[122] DCDA, p. 21.

[123] See Appendix III for quotes from DCDA and Appendix IV for comments on FitzGerald's book.

[124] For example, the web page 'Adoremus' says that 'The Holy See issued a Notification on September 17 reaffirming that the ordination of women is not possible ...' There is no named author of the page. See <www.adoremus.org/1001womendeacons.html> [accessed 23 November 2011].

[125] Congregations of the Faith, for Divine Worship and the Discipline of Sacraments and for Clergy, Notification on Women as Ordained Deacons (17 September 2001) at <www.adoremus.org/1001womendeacons.html> [accessed 22 November 2011].

[126] See for example the article by German academics 'The Church 2011: A Necessary Departure' and other articles at <www.we-are-church.org.uk> [accessed 22 November 2011].

[127] All of whom we will look at later in chapter fifteen 'Magisterium: The Laity'.

[128] For more detailed quotes from DCDA, see Appendix III.

[129] DCDA, p. 58.

[130] DCDA, p. 62.

[131] K. FitzGerald, 'The Characteristics and Nature of the Order of the Deaconess' in T. Hopka (ed.), *Women and the Priesthood* (New York: St Vladimir's Seminary Press, 1983), p. 81.

[132] See G. Macy, *The Hidden History of Women's Ordination: Female Clergy in the Medieval West* (Oxford: OUP, 2008), p. 17.

[133] P. Zagano, 'Grant Her Your Spirit' in *America*, vol. 192 no 4, (Feb 7, 2005). Also available at <www.americamagazine.org/content/article.cfm?article_id =3997>.

15 THE LAITY

W E HAVE ALREADY explored this topic in the previous parts on Scripture and Tradition. Also, in the section of chapter eight, 'The Church in History', especially the letters of Clement and Ignatius, we saw that by the end of the first century there was a clear differentiation between those who had specific tasks and authority, the bishops, priests and deacons, and the ordinary community members. All were united by baptism but some received the laying on of hands for specific tasks within the community. The word 'laity' for those Church members who did not have a special function was first used by Clement in his letter to the Corinthians:[1]

> It follows, then, that there ought to be strict order and method in our performance of such acts as the Master has prescribed for certain times and seasons ... The High Priest, for example, has his own proper services assigned to him, the priesthood has its own station, there are particular ministries laid down for the Levites, and the layman is bound by regulations affecting the laity.[2]

As the Church grew, the gap between the clergy and the laity became wider and wider. Monasteries and convents were established where people could cut themselves off from everyday life in order to study the Scriptures and grow in holiness. Priests and bishops in the community wore distinctive clothing and had their hair cut in a distinctive way. They developed formal links with the forces of secular power. The services were said in Latin, which began as the common vernacular language but was a foreign language in non-Italian countries. As the Mass became more stylised, much of it was said by the priest inaudibly. Then a physical barrier in the form of a rood-screen was used to further emphasise the divide between the ordained clergy and the laity.

One of the main aims of the Reformers of the sixteenth century was to return Church worship to the more egalitarian pattern of the early Church. Different denominations adopted varying

degrees of this, so that today we have some with the full comple-
ment of bishops, priests and deacons, and others with no ministers
or sacraments at all. The Catholic Church's reaction to the Reformation was to reaffirm the authority of the hierarchy. However
this does not necessarily require a view of the laity as totally
subordinate to priests and bishops in all respects. The Platonic
scheme of a linear progression, with each order purifying and
containing all the qualities of the previous order, was not the one
in vogue at the time of Trent. The Council was greatly influenced
by the teachings of Aquinas, who followed the Aristotelian model
of a non-linear hierarchy.

> Any entity in the chain of being is generically subordinated
> to its superiors but not totally so, since it also has unique
> specific or individual characteristics not contained in any of
> its superiors except the Creator ... the hierarchy of offices in
> the Church does, of course, constitute its members as
> functionally unequal, yet because each member functions to
> make a unique contribution to the common good, all
> members equally have a right to participate in the common
> good.[3]

Luther (1483–1546) denied the validity of the sacrament of ordination, indeed he accepted only baptism and the Eucharist as valid
sacraments.[4] Instead, he laid great emphasis on the priesthood of
all believers. As all the baptised were priests, they had no need of
a priestly caste acting as mediators for them; all had equal access
to the mercy of God. Initially, he taught that all believers could
baptise, forgive sins and distribute communion. He soon realised
that this was a recipe for anarchy and modified it by teaching that,
while all believers had the potential to perform these tasks, only a
selected few should actually do so. As his ideas developed, he
moved from trying to reform the priesthood to removing it
altogether to realised that believers still needed pastors to guide
them. He taught that ministers of word and sacrament were
instituted by Christ and appointed by the people, under the
guidance of the Holy Spirit, to fulfil a function in the church. Their
appointment did not have a lasting effect on them and, if deposed
or retired, they resumed their place in the community as ordinary
citizens. Thus, he abandoned the theology of sacramental character

or seal. Ontological change and relationality as concepts are foreign to the post-Reformation churches, which does simplify their theology of ministry. However it also makes it very difficult for them to understand us.

Calvin (1509–1564) represents the 'second wave' of the Reformation movement. His main contribution was to give a systematic presentation of the theology of the new movement. Calvin taught that the church was established by divine will and that Scripture provided instructions on how it was to be governed.[5] The Church can be recognised by the two marks of preaching the Word of God and correctly administering the sacraments.[6] According to Calvin, the Roman Catholic Church failed on both counts! Calvin used Cyprian of Carthage's image of the Church as mother as his explanation of the need for an institutional Church. It is through the Church that God gathers his children to himself and provides that means by which they can mature in faith. Calvin shared Luther's rejection of the Mass as a sacrifice (though differing in his Eucharistic theology, which need not concern us here) and so rejected the role of the priest and ordination as a sacrament. All that was needed was a minister to explain the Scriptures to the people.

Even before Luther's rejection of the Church, there had been calls from within the hierarchy for reforms. However these did not come until the Council of Trent, which sat for the first time in the year of Luther's death, 1546. It continued over three periods until 1552. The purpose of the Council was not to review all aspects of Church theology and practice but to address those issues that had been raised by the Reformers. Here we will look only at those points pertaining to the priesthood.

The fifth session reminded the bishops of their duty to preach or to delegate this task to suitable persons if they have legitimate reasons for not doing it themselves:

> And indeed preaching is the main (*praecipuum*) office of the bishops—the Holy Synod has ordained and decreed that all bishops, archbishops, primates and all other prelates of the Church are bound to preach the Holy Gospel of Jesus Christ by themselves, unless a legitimate reason prevents them.[7]

The decree refers back to similar teaching from the Fourth Lateran Council of 1215.

The seventh session concentrated on the sacraments in general. It confirmed that there were seven sacraments, all instituted by Jesus Christ. They are sources of grace. The sacraments of baptism, confirmation and Order confer a permanent character and cannot be repeated. The minister must have the intention of doing what the Church intends. The sacrament is valid even if the minister is in a state of mortal sin. The minister cannot change the sacramental rituals by himself.

The twenty-third session of the Council discussed the sacrament of Order. They taught that ordination is a true sacrament 'performed by words and outward signs' and quoting 2 Tm 1.6 cf. 1 Tm 4:14 which confers a permanent character (1 Co 12:39; Ep 4:11). The bishops are the successors of the apostles and have the power to govern the Church (Ac 20:28). A priesthood with the power to consecrate the true body and blood of the Lord and to remit or retain sins is present in the New Testament. The Church hierarchy of bishops, priests and ministers exists by divine ordinance.

The Council did not intend a comprehensive description of the theology of the priesthood but concentrated on those aspects that had been challenged by the Reformers:

> The Church upheld strongly against the Reformers the existence of the sacrament of Order. Due to the historical circumstances of the times, she did so with special stress on the ministerial power to offer the eucharistic sacrifice and to remit sins. This emphasis on the cultic aspects of the ministry led, in post-Tridentine times, to a certain impoverishment of its theology.[8]

One of the areas that was rather neglected was that of the role of the laity. For a long time after Trent, the laity themselves felt that their role was to 'pay and pray'. An isolated example of acknowledging the place of the laity is found in 1854, when Pope Pius IX asked all the bishops to consult their laity on the proposed dogma of the Immaculate Conception. (This had been a matter of debate in the Church from at least the fourth century. Pope Pius IX issued a Papal Bull in 1854, *Ineffabilis Deus*, confirming the dogma.) Another lone voice supporting the right of the laity to be consulted was that of Cardinal Newman (1801–1890). The issue did not really attract significant attention until the post-war Europe of the 1940s and 1950s, when the shortage of priests stimulated debate on possible alternative forms of parish ministry. An important contribution to this debate was Pope Pius XII's letter on the liturgy, *Mediator Dei*, published in 1947. This included teaching on the priesthood of Christ, the priesthood of the laity and the ministerial priesthood.

This change of emphasis was reflected in the work of the Second Vatican Council:

> In the RC Church the emphasis has been modified by the Second Vatican Council: this Council stressed the role of the laity as part of 'the people of God' in the Constitution on the Church (1964); in the Constitution on the Liturgy (1963) the laity were said to have a share in the 'priestly, prophetic and royal office of Christ' and were assigned various duties in public worship; while the 'Decree on the Apostolate of the Laity' (1965) recognised their special gifts (*charismata*) for building up the body of Christ and stressed their vocation to ameliorate the social order as well as their part in preaching the gospel.[9]

One of the great ironies of the campaign by Luther to reform the Church is that several of the changes that he fought for were introduced comparatively peacefully by Vatican II; the use of the vernacular in the Mass, distributing Holy Communion under both kinds and greater participation by the laity. This now includes helping in the local administration of the parish through parish councils; teaching in seminaries and universities; providing expert advice to tribunals; leading services (but not Mass!) in the absence of a priest; running prayer groups, bible study classes and so on. In emergency they can even officiate at baptisms and weddings. (I wonder what Luther would have thought of women as readers and helping to distribute Holy Communion?)

Summary

The history of the early and mediaeval Church is one of increasing differentiation between clergy and laity. The Reformed churches tried to return to the simpler structures of the early Church. The

Council of Trent reaffirmed the existence of seven sacraments. The sacrament of ordination was hierarchical, conferred a permanent character and could be traced back to Holy Scripture. The role of the laity was not discussed in any detail until the post-World War II years. It was discussed in detail at Vatican II.

Notes

1. The word comes from the Greek 'laos'. It is defined in LG §31 as 'all of the faithful except those in holy orders and those in the state of religious life specially approved by the Church'.
2. Pope Clement I, *The First Epistle to the Corinthians*, in ECW, p. 39, §40.
3. B. Ashley, *Justice in the Church: Gender and Participation* (Washington: The Catholic University of America Press, 1996), pp. 11–12.
4. The following summary is taken from several sources—mainly James Bannerman, *The Church of Christ*, McGrath, *Christian Theology* and two unpublished papers—an essay on ordination by a monk of Pluscarden Abbey and a Master's dissertation by Margaret Coll, Aberdeen.
5. J. Calvin, *Institutes of the Christian Religion book IV* (London: James Clark and Co., 1962), 'We must now speak of the order by which the Lord wishes his Church to be directed' chapter III.1.
6. J. Calvin '(guarding against) the corruptions of the papacy, by which Satan has adulterated all that God had appointed for our salvation.' (*Institutes*, book IV, chapter 1.1) and 'wherever we see the word of God sincerely preached and heard, wherever we see the sacraments administered according to the institution of Christ, there we cannot have any doubt that the Church of God has some existence.' (*Institutes*, book IV, chapter 1.9) and 'Besides these two (baptism and the Lord's Supper) no other has been instituted by God.' (*Institutes*, book IV, chapter XVIII.19).
7. The General Council of Trent fifth session. 'Decree on Teaching and Preaching the Word of God' in ND §1203.
8. Introduction to the chapter on the sacrament of Order, ND, p. 537.
9. F. Cross and E. Livingstone (ed.), 'Laity' in *The Oxford Dictionary of the Christian Church 2nd ed.* (Oxford: OUP, 1983).

16 OUR LADY

A REGULAR CRITICISM OF Roman Catholicism is that we give Our Lady honour and titles that cannot be supported by Scripture. This criticism can be answered using what must be the best-known passage of Scripture—the conversation between the angel Gabriel and Mary at the Annunciation, which gives us some of the most fundamental articles of faith on Mary. They can be summarised as follows: she was a virgin for all of her life; she was free from the effects of original sin; she made a free choice to cooperate in God's plan; she was the totally human mother of God and she set a perfect example of obedience to the divine will.

Other passages in Scripture lead to the teaching that Mary was assumed body and soul into Heaven, is the mother of the Church and acts as a mediator between us and her son. While popular piety does indeed contain a wealth of devotions to Our Lady whose link with Scripture may not be obvious, much Marian devotion also exists within the official teaching and liturgy of the Church. Mention of Mary in the Mass may be as old as the papacy of Leo the Great (440–461) and specific feast days of Mary are recorded from the fourth century.

In an attempt to become more obviously in line with biblical exegesis and true to Scripture, we are perhaps in danger or losing this great treasure of the Church, whose roots go back to the earliest Christian communities. Marian devotions and Marian liturgical prayers are not simply a reaction to the Reformation condemnations of Marian feast days and asking for Mary's intercession.

> Research into the early Egyptian Liturgy has been summarised thus: 'According to available documents, the divine motherhood is being thought of in the second century; in the third, it is invoked liturgically with the *Sub tuum praesidium*: and certainly by the fourth century it is honoured, in the Lord's Nativity as the subject of a feast.'[1]

Despite this rich heritage, the Church has only four formal dogmas regarding Our Lady: she was conceived without sin, she remained a virgin for all of her life, she was the mother of God and she was assumed into heaven, body and soul.

The Immaculate Conception of Our Lady is celebrated on the eighth of December. The dogma was declared by Pope Pius IX in the papal bull *Ineffabilis Deus* on the eighth of December 1854, after hundreds of years of debate. It declares that Mary, by the power of God and in preparation for her role as mother of God, was created free from original sin. Many Protestants follow the argument of Thomas Aquinas that Mary could not have been born without sin as that would have meant that she had no need of redemption. The Catholic Church follows the teaching of Duns Scotus that 'prevention is better than cure' and to have been preserved from the effects of original sin is a greater grace than to be set free from sin. So Mary benefited from the redemptive work of Jesus in an even more powerful way than the rest of us.

The significance if this teaching for humanity is that the Immaculate Conception marked the victory of good over evil. The ultimate purpose of the incarnation has already been achieved in one person and can therefore be achieved in all of us:

> The symbol of the immaculate conception shows that even the accumulated sinfulness of the world cannot overcome God's desire to save. It is therefore an eschatological symbol, a strong foundation for Christian hope, and a powerful impetus to a Christian commitment to justice in a world of global violence and exploitation.[2]

Mary was conceived free of original sin in preparation for her role as the mother of God and the title 'Mother of God' is one of the oldest in the Church. Nestorius of Constantinople preferred the title *Christotokos* to *Theotokos* for Mary as he was concerned that the latter title did not reflect Christ's manhood. There was much heated debate on the subject, resulting in the Church's first official statement on Mary at the Council of Ephesus in 431. In reply to the teachings of Nestorius, Cyril of Alexandria and his supporters declared that Mary was '*Theotokos*', the mother of God. Despite the decidedly undemocratic workings of the Council, the teaching has been universally accepted. Its purpose was Christological as it emphasised that Jesus was both divine and human from the time of his conception.

The third dogma regarding Our Lady is that she remained a virgin. Augustine summarised the teachings of the Early Fathers when he said that she was a virgin before, during and after Jesus's birth.[3] Despite, or perhaps because of, the universal acceptance of this belief, it was not included in official documents of the Church until the Lateran Council of 649 and only became solemn teaching in the Constitution *Cum Quorumdam Hominum* of Pope Paul IV in 1555.

The fourth dogma, on the assumption of Our Lady body and soul into heaven, was only officially declared in 1950 by Pope Pius XII.[4] Again, this has been a persistent belief of the Church, both East and West from the earliest days. There was debate over whether or not she died and was buried or was assumed into heaven at the point of death. The dogma of Pius XII left the matter open by using the phrase 'when the course of her earthly life was finished'. While the teaching is not directly related to a 'proof text' in Scripture, the Old Testament tells us that Elijah was carried up to heaven without having died and there is some evidence that Moses also was not buried.[5] As Mary was greater than them, it is fitting that she also would have been assumed into heaven.

At Vatican II, there was much debate over how to include teachings on Our Lady. Many participants wanted a separate constitution devoted to her. However there was also concern that Marian devotions had become excessive and were hindering ecumenical relations. In the end, the topic was limited to the last chapter of *Lumen Gentium*, the document on the Church. It was felt to be important to stress that Mary was not above the Church but part of it. The chapter speaks of Mary as the mother of the members of the Church.[6] *Lumen Gentium* teaches that Mary is mother of God and mother of men. She is the greatest of all created beings. Foretold in the Old Testament, she was created free of all sin. She freely cooperated in God's plan of salvation, thus overcoming Eve's disobedience. Mary was instrumental in the beginning of Jesus's public ministry and followed him in faith right up to the foot of the cross. She also shared in the outpouring of the Spirit at Pentecost. At the end of her life, her perpetual virginity and state of sinlessness was honoured by her assumption into heaven. There, she demonstrates her love for her son's brethren by interceding for us. Therefore titles such as Advocate, Auxiliatrix, Adjutrix, Mediatrix are suitable for her, while not taking away from the position of Christ as the one mediator. Mary is an encouragement and example to men to draw nearer to her son.

Mary is a type of the Church in the order of faith, charity and perfect union with Christ. Just as she brought forth the firstborn son, so the Church brings forth the faithful. Just as Mary fulfilled the will of God, so the Church loyally receives the word of God. Both Mary and the Church maintain their virginal integrity and purity of faith, hope and love. The Church rightfully honours Mary but must ensure that its teachings are based on Scripture, the Fathers, Doctors and Liturgy of the Church and are neither exaggerated nor too narrow.

Ten years after the end of Vatican II, Pope Paul VI issued his letter on Marian devotions, *Marialis Cultus*. He repeated the warnings of *Lumen Gentium* on excessive and non-Scriptural devotions. However he also encouraged attempts to present a picture of Mary that was more meaningful to modern women. Paul VI rejects the image of Mary as timid and submissive and points out that she is a good role model for both men and women who are fighting for social justice, independence and dignity.

Redemptoris Mater was written in 1987 in anticipation of the millennium. Celebrating the birth of Jesus Christ must include a meditation on the mother who brought forth the baby. A major theme was that of Mary as mediator. With ecumenical relations in mind, the document stresses that Mary mediates for us in Christ, as his mother and from within the Church, not above it. It also stresses the motherhood of Mary as being poured out on the whole Church. The title of *Theotokos*, shared by the Churches of East and West, acts as a source of unity. The sentiments of the Magnificat can also be shared by all those who have a concern for the poor.

There are many aspects of Marian theology and devotion that we have not covered here; Mary as the new Eve, as the bride of Christ, as the fulfilment of Old Testament prophecies, Marian apparitions, Mary's place in the liturgy of the Church. A lifetime would not be enough to exhaust the possibilities! Here we had to focus on our aim of examining the role of Mary as a model for women within the official teaching of the Church.

Summary

Despite the vast literature on Mary, the official teaching of the Church at its highest level is limited to four dogmas regarding Mary; she was conceived free of original sin, she was a virgin, she was the mother of God and she was assumed into heaven. Everything else is deduced from these facts. Modern statements encourage us to see Mary as a champion of the poor and oppressed and a role model both for those who wish to grow in faith and those who wish to fight for social justice. Indeed, Mary can help us to do both by helping us to approach closer to her Son.

Notes

1   M. O'Carroll, 'Liturgy' in *Theotokos: A Theological Encyclopedia of the Blessed Virgin Mary* (Eugene: Wipf and Stock Publishers, 1982), p. 220.

2   K. Coyle, *Mary in the Christian Tradition: from a Contemporary Perspective* (Leominster: Gracewing, 1996), p. 42.

3   See chapter nine 'Tradition: Our Lady' for more details.

4   Pope Pius XII, Apostolic Constitution *Munificentissimus Deus* 1 November 1950, in ND §713.

5   Is it coincidence that these two, representing the Law and the Prophets, appear with Jesus at His Transfiguration?

6   At the end of the Council, Pope Paul VI, in his closing speech, proclaimed Mary as 'Mother of the Church' in response to those many bishops who had wanted this to be made clearer in the document.

17 WOMEN

T HERE IS VERY little in the magisterial documents of the Church specifically on women. What there is, is mainly in regard to those in religious orders. The most important statements for our purposes here are those regarding the sacraments. On ordination, the Catechism of the Catholic Church states clearly that only men can receive this sacrament:

> 'Only a baptized man (vir) validly receives sacred ordination'. The Lord Jesus chose men (viri) to form the college of the twelve apostles, and the apostles did the same when they chose collaborators to succeed them in their ministry. The College of Bishops, with whom the priests are united in the priesthood, makes the college of the twelve an ever-present and ever-active reality until Christ's return. The Church recognises herself to be bound by this choice made by the Lord himself. For this reason the ordination of women is not possible.[1]

So the Catechism of the Catholic Church argues that, as the College of Bishops is the continuation of the college of apostles and they were selected by Jesus specifically as an all-male group, then the Church must continue this practice. We will look at this in more detail in chapter twenty.

The Code of Canon Law says that a married candidate for the permanent diaconate must have the consent of his wife.[2] The only other mentions of women state that men who have attempted marriage while bound by a civil bond or religious vow are irregular for the reception of orders,[3] and that a man who has a wife is simply impeded from receiving orders unless he is destined for the permanent diaconate.[4]

There are, however, several mentions of tasks that may be performed by 'people', that is, by either men or women. In the section on the obligations and rights of the laity, only one canon specifically uses the word 'men' (can 230§1 states that men can be given the stable ministry of lector and of acolyte). The other canons use the word 'people'. So both men and women have the right and duty to teach the gospel and give witness to it in their lives. Where they have the requisite knowledge and experience, they can hold ecclesiastical offices and act as advisors to councils. They have the duty to be familiar with Church teaching and to live it, teach it and defend it to whatever level they are capable. All lay people can be temporary lectors or commentators, cantors and similar roles. Where ministers are not available, they 'can supply certain of their functions, that is, exercise the ministry of the word, preside over liturgical prayers, confer baptism and distribute Holy Communion, in accordance with the provisions of the law'.[5] Can 339 §2 states that an ecumenical council may call others to help it in its deliberations. Can 861 §2 states that the bishop can delegate a catechist or other suitable person to confer baptism and, in emergency, anyone can baptise. Can 1112 §1 allows for bishops to delegate 'lay persons' to assist at marriages, including preparation of the couple, where there are no priests or deacons available. Can 830.§1 allows the Bishop to appoint 'persons whom he considers competent' as his *censor* to judge whether or not a manuscript is free from doctrinal and moral error and can be granted an *imprimatur*.

We can see from this list that women can hold many positions in the Church. Indeed, the only posts that they cannot hold are those reserved for the clergy—the reasons for the reservation of the position of permanent lector to men is not stated but is presumably because this is seen as one of the steps leading to priestly ordination. These rights and duties of the laity are not restricted to any one age group or affected by the lay person's marital status.

Modern works on the role of women in the Church emphasise her place as champion of the poor and oppressed, the rock on which the family unit is built, the backbone of parish life. John Paul II marked the Marian year of 1987–1988 with an encyclical letter on the role and dignity of women in the Church, *Mulieris Dignitatem*. He returns to the theme of his Theology of the Body lectures, which spoke of the essential differences between men and women, balanced by their equal dignity in the sight of God.

> For every individual is made in the image of God, insofar as he or she is a rational and free creature capable of knowing God and loving him ... Being a person in the image

and likeness of God thus also involves existing in a relationship, in relation to the other 'I'.[6]

This relationship was damaged by Original Sin. While women
have the right to try to return the balance to what was originally
intended, they must be careful to do this in a way that is compatible
with their distinct nature: 'In the name of liberation from male
"domination", women must not appropriate to themselves male
characteristics contrary to their own feminine "originality"'.[7] John
Paul II summarises the place of women in the gospels, emphasising
Jesus's inclusive attitude to women, even to having Mary
Magdalen as the apostle to the apostles. He reminds us that St Paul
taught that 'You are all one in Christ Jesus' (Ga 3:28) and that both
Paul and Acts tell us of both male and female prophets, fulfilling
the prophecy 'I shall pour out my spirit on all humanity. Your sons
and daughters shall prophecy' (Jl 3:1). John Paul II defines 'prophecy' as follows: '"To prophecy" means to express by one's words
and one's life "the mighty works of God" (Ac 2:11), preserving the
truth and originality of each person, whether man or woman.'[8]
Women can act as prophets only within the limits of their femininity, which expresses itself in love for others: 'The dignity of woman
is measured by the order of love, which is essentially the order of
justice and charity.'[9] Indeed, there is a hint of a return to the Old
Testament stereotype of the salvific female figures of, for example,
Judith and Esther: 'It is significant that the woman always figures
in Israel's thought and belief, not as a priestess, but as a prophetess
and judge-saviour. What is specifically hers, the place assigned to
her, emerges from this.'[10] According to John Paul II, Mary is the
highest expression of the prophetic character of women because
of her intimate link with the Holy Spirit. We can examine her role
more closely by looking at the biblical 'woman' who appears in
Genesis 3:20, Nazareth and Revelation 12:4 as the source of all
humanity and of eternal life. The lesson to be learned is that
woman's vocation is to love others as though they have been
entrusted to her by God, which in a sense they have been.

The problem for the Magisterium today is that there is disagreement as to how this love should be expressed. There is a growing
body of opinion arguing for the admission of women to the
diaconate.

Summary

The laws on what women can and cannot do in the Church are often determined as much by sociological factors as by theology. However, the ruling that they are specifically excluded from the sacrament of priestly ordination is based on the example of Jesus's choice of an all-male apostolate, not on socio-cultural grounds. (We will look at the possibility of female diaconal ordination in chapter twenty three.) In the modern Church, they can take part in all other aspects of Church life. It is important to maintain the essential differences between masculine and feminine roles in both Church and society, while acknowledging that both are equally loved by, and made in the image of, God.

Notes

[1]   CCC, §1577, quoting CIC 1983 can1024 and referring to Mk 3:14–19; Lk 6:12–16; 1 Tm 3:1–13; 2 Tm 1:6; Tt 1:5–9; St Clement *Ad Cor*.42, 4;44,3: PG 1,292–293; 300 Pope John Paul II *Mulieris Dignitatem* 26–27; CDF, Declaration *Inter Insigniores*: *Acta Apostolicae Sedis* 69 (1977) 98–116.

[2]   CIC 1983, can 1031.2.

[3]   CIC 1983, can 1042.1.

[4]   CIC 1983, can 1042.1.

[5]   CIC 1983, can 230.3.

[6]   Pope John Paul II, Apostolic letter On the Dignity of Women *(Mulieris Dignitatem)* §7 (1988).

[7]   *Mulieris Dignitatem*, §10.4.

[8]   *Mulieris Dignitatem*, §16.4.

[9]   *Mulieris Dignitatem*, §29.3.

[10]   J. Ratzinger, *Daughter Zion: Meditations on the Church's Marian Belief* (San Francisco: Ignatius Press, 1977), p. 20.

18 CONCLUSIONS FROM THE MAGISTERIUM

T HE MAGISTERIUM OF the Church is its teaching authority, based on Scripture and Tradition. Throughout the centuries, this teaching has been clarified by general councils. Vatican I defined papal infallibility and Vatican II confirmed that bishops had the fullness of the sacrament of ordination but only had authority as part of the College of Bishops, with the pope at their head.

The essential matter in the ordination rites of bishops, priests and deacons is the laying on of hands. The form is the words of ordination, as laid down in the appropriate liturgical books. We can see from the ordination rites that deacons are servants and in a different relationship to the bishop from the priest, who is a co-worker with the bishop. Both deacon and priest depend on the bishop for the authority to exercise their vocation. The bishop inherits apostolic authority, some of which he delegates to the priest but not to the deacon. These relationships are clearly expressed in canon law.

The Church's definition of a sacrament has not changed in any essentials in its history:

> The sacraments are efficacious signs of grace, instituted by Christ and entrusted to the Church, by which divine life is dispensed to us. The visible rites by which the sacraments are celebrated signify and make present the graces proper to each sacrament. They bear fruit in those who receive them with the proper dispositions.[1]

The Council of Trent fixed the number of sacraments at seven and confirmed that the sacrament of ordination had an inbuilt hierarchy of bishop, priest and minister.

The priesthood is defined as a relationship between the priest and the one high priest, Jesus Christ, and as a relationship between the priest and the laity, who have a share in this priesthood. The essentials of the priesthood have remained constant throughout the history of the Church.

Bishops are the successors of the apostles, priests are not. Bishops have the fullness of the sacrament of ordination in that the grace of the sacrament does not so much build up through the ranks of deacon, priest, bishop as flow down from God through the bishop to his co-workers. Not only is the episcopal ordination a true sacrament in its own right, it is only through the grace of this sacrament that the bishop has the power to ordain priests and deacons. Bishops form a college with the pope as its head and have a responsibility both to their own diocese and to the wider Church. They can only exercise this responsibility in communion with their fellow bishops.

Deacons are mentioned in the letters of St Paul. They have always been associated with the liturgy and charitable works. The permanent diaconate died out by the eleventh century but was reintroduced by Vatican II. Deacons share in the priestly duties of sanctifying, preaching and leading but not of oversight.

Deaconesses are also mentioned in the letters of St Paul, or at least one of them is, Phoebe. They were included in the clerical hierarchy. They were gradually replaced by nuns. The current debate over whether or not they could be reintroduced is connected to the role of the diaconate as a stage in the preparation for the priesthood. If the priesthood is reserved to men, does the diaconate have to be also? We will return to this question later in chapter twenty three.

The history of the early and mediaeval Church is one of increasing differentiation between clergy and laity. The Reformed churches tried to return to the simpler structures of the early Church. The role of the laity was not discussed in any detail until the post-World War II years. It was discussed in detail at Vatican II.

The Church teaches four dogmas regarding Mary: she was conceived free of original sin, she was a virgin, she was the mother of God and she was assumed into heaven. She can be seen as a champion of the poor and oppressed and a role model both for those who wish to grow in faith and those who wish to fight for social justice.

The role of women in the Church has been influenced as much by sociological factors as by theology. In the modern Church, women are specifically excluded from the sacrament of priestly

ordination but can take part in all other aspects of Church life. Pope
John Paul II emphasised the need to maintain the natural differences between men and women while maintaining the equality of
each before God.

Notes

1   CCC, §1131.

Part Four
THE ANALOGY OF FAITH

The title for this part is taken from Romans 12:4–8. Just as different parts of the body are inter-dependent, so are different parts of the Church. In order to grow, they have to work together, each using what gifts they have been given. The Catechism of the Catholic Church defines 'analogy of faith' as 'the coherence of the truths of faith among themselves and within the whole plan of Revelation' (§114).

19 VALID PROGRESSION OR SCHISMATIC DIGRESSION?

NOTHING IN CREATION stays the same. Mountains rise up as the result of geological changes and get worn down by wind and rain. Deserts and forests come and go. Even man has evolved over the ages. Within the comparatively short time-span of recorded history, human nature has not changed but cultures and languages have. Anthropological and archaeological evidence suggests that man has always had a sense of the divine but the actual beliefs and ways of expressing them have varied both over time and between cultures. So we have to expect change within any system and Christian theology is no exception. The early Church took over three hundred years to formalise its teaching on topics such as the Trinity and the human and divine nature of Christ. These topics are still being explored and explained in new ways to each new generation. We only need to compare a chapter from the King James Bible with the same chapter in a modern bible such as the New Jerusalem Bible to realise how rapidly language can change. So this continuing search for a deeper understanding and more accurate translations is a necessary process. However the Church also needs procedures for ensuring that this process stays within the bounds of acceptable teaching. We learn from Acts that the apostles had the final say in any disputes over what was or was not acceptable. While there were still leaders who could remember listening to the apostles, direct appeal could still be made to their teachings. As the Church spread and time passed, many disputes arose. Some were honest differences of interpretation, some were heretical and schismatic groups who split from the Church. Gradually, the Church formalised a three-branched tool for deciding what was acceptable debate and what was unacceptable heresy: any new teachings had to be true to Scripture, part of the unchanging Tradition of the Church and in agreement with the Magisterium. The Vatican II document *Dei*

Verbum summarises the relationship between Scripture, Tradition and the Magisterium:

> Sacred Tradition and Sacred Scripture form one sacred deposit of the word of God, committed to the Church ... But the task of authentically interpreting the word of God, whether written or handed on, has been entrusted exclusively to the living teaching office of the Church, whose authority is exercised in the name of Jesus Christ ... It is clear, therefore, that sacred Tradition, Sacred Scripture and the teaching authority of the Church, in accord with God's most wise design, are so linked and joined together that one cannot stand without the others, and that all together and each in its own way, under the action of the one Holy Spirit, contribute effectively to the salvation of souls.[1]

Even with this system for interpreting both the Scriptures themselves and the teachings of theologians, there can be disagreement or misunderstanding. It is then the role of theologians to set out the arguments and for the Magisterium to make a judgement as to what is authentic teaching. The *'Instruction on the Ecclesial Vocation of the Theologian'* identified four levels of magisterial statements.[2] The most authoritative are infallible statements from the pope or the universal episcopate. These are contained at least implicitly in Scripture and apostolic Tradition and therefore the faithful are obliged to accept them. The next most authoritative are definitive declarations of non-revealed truths which are closely connected with revelation and the Christian life; this category includes teaching on faith and morals essential to the safeguarding and implementation of the revealed truths of Scripture. Then there are non-definitive but obligatory teaching of doctrine that contributes to the right understanding of revelation. Most teachings of ecumenical councils would fall into this category. Reverence for the authority of the Magisterium leads the faithful to accept the teaching, although there may be individual cases where a theologian may be unable to offer interior assent. Lastly, there are prudential admonitions or applications of Christian doctrine in a particular time or place. These are instructions and statements that are binding at the time but may be changed as and when the Magisterium decides that the time is right. An example would be

Divino Afflante Spiritu (1943) which allowed theologians to use modern techniques of biblical hermeneutics that had previously been banned.

In practice, statements belonging to the first two groups are rare and are usually only issued when there is universal acceptance of their truth, the most obvious example being the declaration on the Immaculate Conception of 1854. Anyone who publicly and consistently refused to accept such statements would be excluding themselves from the Church and could be declared excommunicated. Statements in the next two groups are more likely to lead to dissent and the '*Instruction on the Ecclesial Vocation of the Theologian*' gives guidance for theologians who find that they cannot give full assent.

> In such cases the critical response of theologians may provide the Magisterium with 'a stimulus to propose the teaching of the Church in greater depth and with a clearer presentation of the arguments' (30) For this reason theologians who feel unable to give intellectual assent may have a positive duty to inform the hierarchical teachers of the problems they find ... Through dialogue of this kind, tensions between theologians and the Magisterium can contribute to doctrinal progress.[3]

The document goes on to list forms of dissent that are harmful to the Church and should therefore be avoided. These can be summarised as assuming that one's views are correct and using the mass media to stir up support for these views against the Magisterium. There is not a ban on scholarly debate and sharing of views as long as it is done in a spirit of humility.

> In the last analysis, however, popes and bishops cannot be infinitely permissive. They have the painful duty of setting limits to what may be held and taught in the Church. There is no guarantee that true doctrine will always be pleasing to the general public. Jesus uttered hard sayings, with full awareness that in doing so he was alienating some of his followers. Peter spoke for the believing minority when he exclaimed 'Lord, to whom should we go? You have the words of eternal life' (John 6:68).[4]

Cardinal Ratzinger

One theologian who has had to examine this area from both sides is Cardinal Ratzinger in his role as prefect of the Congregation for the Doctrine of the Faith. He was much criticised for his condemnation of various theologians but particularly the Liberation Theologians of the 1970s and 1980s in South America, such as Leonardo Boff and Gustavo Gutierrez. He sought to clarify the role of the modern theologian in a collection of essays published in 1993. He argues that theology is different from the philosophy of religion in that it is only meaningful when it is practised within the boundaries set by the Church. Theologians must believe in the existence of truth and therefore need an organisation outwith themselves to arbitrate in disputes over what teachings do or do not bring us closer to that truth.

> There can be no office of teaching theology if there is no ecclesiastical Magisterium, for in its absence theology would enjoy no greater certainty than the liberal arts, that is, the certainty of hypothesis, which may be the subject of debate but which no one can stake his life on.[5]

Rather than restrict our freedom, obedience to the Magisterium of the Church prevents us from being trapped by any one political or social system. History teaches that political mono-cultures, no matter how altruistic the motives of their founders, quickly degenerate into totalitarian regimes where freedom of belief and practice is severely limited. The search for truth, inspired by faith, gives us norms by which to live that are not tied to any one political system. The Church herself is also a pluralistic society in that, while it has a defining, unifying content, which has to be accepted by its members, this unity is expressed in many ways. The Early Fathers identified four forms of unity: the unity of the Old and New Testaments; the unity of Christians among themselves; the unity of men with God; the unity of man with himself, body and soul. Ratzinger goes on to discuss the unity of the universal Church with the particular churches. The hierarchy of the Church avoids the opposing dangers of despotic regimes and those governed by collegial bodies where no one has to take personal responsibility for decisions. The parish priest is responsible both to his congregation and to his bishop. The bishop is responsible both to his presbytery and to the College of Bishops. The pope is responsible both to the College of Bishops and to the universal Church: 'The Church becomes tangible and answerable in persons; these persons cannot make decisions arbitrarily but only insofar as they are bound in conscience to the faith of the universal Church.'[6]

Finally, Ratzinger looks at the unity of theology and the theologian. He refers to the 'Hinduisation' of faith whereby belief is reduced to a state of spiritual experience which cannot be defined in words. Dogmas no longer matter and theologians no longer have a job to do. He argues that the Catholic Church is the opposite of this and has a duty to express the faith anew for each generation in dogmas and formulae that can be readily understood by all. In order to do this, the Church must have the authority to identify the truth:

> In consequence, the Church herself must have a voice; she must be capable of expressing herself as Church and of distinguishing false belief from the true faith. This implies that faith and theology are not identical and that each has its own characteristic voice but that the voice of theology is dependent upon that of faith and oriented towards it. Theology is interpretation and must remain such.[7]

The work of the theologian is not to cut away the outdated dogmas of the past and create a 'clean slate' for his personal theories but to make connections between existing statements of belief, new ways of expressing them and ways of incorporating genuinely new experiences.

> It is thus evident that two things are essential for the theologian. First, the methodological rigor which is part and parcel of the business of scholarship ... But he also has need of inner participation in the organic structure of the Church; he needs that faith which is prayer, contemplation and life. Only in this symphony does theology come into being.[8]

We can see from the above that Cardinal Ratzinger was arguing for a sense of theology as the process of clarifying an already existing truth and theologians who were willing to accept the judgement of the Magisterium regarding the acceptability or otherwise of their work. He had experienced at first hand the damage that could be done to the Church by theologians who came to believe that their personal opinions were more important than the wisdom of the universal Church. He had a particular aversion to theologians who, doubtful of winning the argument by debate alone, enlisted the help of the media in support of their cause:

> Today it is very easy to mobilise the influence of the media against the Magisterium of the Church. I find it inconceivable that anyone can entertain the notion that truth and unity in the Church are to be served by these expedients.[9]

Summary

The Church is a living, growing organisation and as such is always changing. It has to interpret its teachings for each generation. This is the work of theologians, with the help of Tradition and the Magisterium. We can judge the work of an individual theologian by looking at its place in the living Tradition of the Church. Is it true to Scripture, the teachings of the Early Fathers and the Magisterium? We can also look at the lives of the theologians themselves. Are they obedient to the Church or do they place themselves above it?

Cardinal Newman

Another theologian who had to examine what was and was not acceptable in the area of the boundaries between academic freedom and assent to Church teaching was John Cardinal Newman. Writing in a very different environment and on the verge of converting from Anglicanism to Roman Catholicism, he examined in detail the process of the development of an idea and listed seven criteria, or 'notes', that could be used to differentiate between genuine development and corruption.[10] These are preservation of idea; continuity of principles; power of assimilation; early anticipation; logical sequence; preservative additions; chronic continuance. (Quite what is meant by these notes is discussed in chapter nineteen.) While it might not be possible to examine any one idea under all of the seven criteria and arrive at a positive conclusion for each one, it can be seen that there is a similarity and pattern to the criteria. An idea which clearly had a negative relationship with one of the criteria would probably fail to match others also. However an idea which matched some criteria and at least did not contradict others could be considered as a development rather than a corruption.

Newman gives several examples of questions that are not answered in Scripture and therefore demand a development of doctrine, for example, the canon of Scripture, infant baptism and the intermediate state between death and resurrection.[11] He further argues for the need for the doctrine of infallibility to allow the Church to arbitrate over the inevitable differences of interpretation that will develop.

> It is abundantly evident to any one … that, if things are left to themselves, every individual will have his own view of things, and take his own course; that two or three agree together today to part tomorrow; that Scripture will be read in contrary ways … There can be no combination on the basis of truth without an organ of truth … the only general persuasive in matters of conduct is authority; that is, when truth is in question, a judgement which we consider superior to our own.[12]

Newman also suggests, a suggestion that one feels Cardinal Ratzinger would approve of and St Benedict advised,[13] that obedience is of benefit to the individual's spiritual development regardless of the rights or wrongs of the academic argument: 'so obedience to our ecclesial superior may subserve our growth in illumination and sanctity, even though he should command what is extreme or inexpedient, or teach what is external to his legitimate province.'[14]

Summary

Newman presents a case for the necessity of the development of doctrine, tools to assess the various ideas produced and a defence of papal infallibility as the only way of preserving unity of both form and doctrine. The individual theologian can grow in sanctity by obeying his superiors, even while believing them to be wrong.

Notes

1   DV, §10.
2   The following is taken from A. Dulles, *The Craft of Theology: From Symbol to System* (New York: Crossroads, 1995), pp. 108–118.
3   *Ibid.,* p. 114.
4   *Ibid.,* p. 118.
5   J. Ratzinger, *The Nature and Mission of Theology* (San Francisco: Ignatius Press, 1993), p. 46.
6   *Ibid.,* p. 87.
7   *Ibid.,* p. 93.
8   *Ibid.,* p. 105. See chapter two 'Scripture: Interpreting Scripture' for related comments on the hermeneutic of continuity.
9   *Ibid.,* p. 117.
10 J. Newman, *An Essay on the Development of Christian Doctrine* (Harmondsworth: Penguin Books, 1974, first published 1845), p. 116.
11 *Ibid.,* p. 153.
12 *Ibid.,* p. 177.
13 St Benedict, *A Rule for Monasteries* translated by L. Doyle, (Collegeville: The Liturgical Press, 1948), chapter 5.
14 J. Newman, *An Essay on the Development of Christian Doctrine,* p. 174.

20 THE THEOLOGICAL ARGUMENT

W E ARE NOW in a position to gather together our information on Church authority, the sacrament of ordination and the role of women in the Church, apply the criteria supplied by Ratzinger and Newman and find out what we are left with. Our first task is to look in greater detail than in previous chapters at the arguments for and against women priests and deacons. We will rely on four main texts; those by Martimort, Hauke, Müller and Butler, as they are the standard sources for arguments for retaining the status quo.

Martimort

Fr Aime Georges Martimort was a leading French expert on the liturgy. He completed his study of the history of deaconesses in 1980. His book is a detailed study of the existing literature on the subject through the centuries. While he took every opportunity to praise the similar study by his colleague Roger Gryson, his book was clearly meant to be an answer to the perceived flaws in that work, which had concluded that women had been ordained as deaconesses in the past and could be so again.

While Martimort is often referred to as the definitive guide for those arguing against the reintroduction of deaconesses, his position was not as clear-cut as is often suggested. He acknowledged the ambiguities of terminology and linguistics and throughout his book he tried to be even-handed in his presentation of the evidence for and against the existence of women who were ordained as deaconesses. In his first chapter, he discussed in detail various possible interpretations of Paul's description of Phoebe as a deaconess. He pointed out that the word 'diakonos' itself had several meanings, even when applied to men:

> St Paul employs the word often but qualifies it in various ways ... All of these Pauline senses of the word certainly go beyond the simple profane notion of 'servant'; they suggest in each case some sort of mission, some sort of effective

action that transcends the person who is acting. None of these correspond to the diaconate as such, however.[1]

While accepting that opinions have varied over the centuries, Martimort concluded this section with the suggestion that the most plausible interpretation is that Pheobe was simply a helper or protector:

> This term suggests activities pertaining to the established and accepted practices, recognised by all, of providing hospitality and assistance. This interpretation is especially plausible when we remember that Cenchreae was the port of Corinth facing east; it was there that the Christian brethren from Syria or Asia Minor would normally have debarked in Greece.[2]

However Martimort did not deny that deaconesses existed. He gave examples from both East and West over many centuries, including Rome itself:

> In Rome, the existence of deaconesses is attested to incidentally from about the end of the eighth century and the beginning of the ninth. On November 29, 799, as Leo III was returning to Rome (he was met by various groups, including deaconesses). Again in 826, a council warned the Roman people against illegitimate unions (mentioning deaconesses). In both of these texts, there can be no question that the wives of deacons could have been the ones being referred to. No: here deaconesses were clearly considered as forming a category similar to but distinct from those of virgins and women religious.[3]

When Martimort was talking about the deaconesses of the early Church, he freely referred to them as being ordained. However when he came to discuss the liturgical rituals used from the tenth century onwards, he referred to 'blessings' even when the rites themselves used the word 'ordination'.

> At the end of the thirteenth century, the bishop of Mende, Gulielmus Durandus, compiled a new pontifical ... Did he bring back the ritual for blessing a deaconess? Yes, he did, but purely as a documentary and historical exercise. Following the *De benedictione abbatissae* but before the *De*

> *benedictione et consecratione virginum* was his presentation of
> the *De ordinatione diaconissae*.[4]

Martimort did not explain this usage and clearly supported the
'deaconesses received a blessing, not ordination' argument. While
deaconesses did exist, we cannot assume that they were simply
the female equivalent of the male deacons. He emphasised that the
ordination rites of deaconesses differed in several important
respects from that of deacons, that deaconesses played a more
limited role in the public life of the Church than deacons and they
had no liturgical role at all. He also emphasised that the position
of deaconess overlapped with that of abbesses for several centuries
and disappeared completely at some point during the twelfth
century. He concluded that:

> If the restoration of the institution of deaconesses were
> indeed to be sought after so many centuries, such a restora-
> tion itself could only be fraught with ambiguity. The real
> importance and efficaciousness of the role of women in the
> Church has always been vividly perceived in the conscious-
> ness of the hierarchy and of the faithful as much more broad
> than the historical role that deaconesses in fact played. And
> perhaps a proposal based on an 'archaeological' institution
> might even obscure the fact that the call to serve the Church
> is urgently addressed today to all women, especially in the
> area of the transmission of Faith and works of charity.[5]

Hauke

Fr Manfred Hauke's work *Women in the Priesthood* began as a
doctoral thesis and was published in its present form in 1988. It is
a comprehensive attempt to examine the topic using the various
tools of the modern social sciences in conjunction with theology.
As the book contains 482 pages of text, it is impossible to do it
justice here and the following is merely an attempt to pick out what
is relevant to our own purposes. Hauke has made this slightly
easier by concentrating on the priesthood.

> The question of admitting women to the diaconate can only
> be touched on in an excursus, since it would require a
> detailed study of its own. As the office of priest (and bishop)

is essentially different from that of deacon, however, treating
it separately can be justified.[6]

Hauke also helps the reader by providing summary chapters. His
summary of the arguments from anthropology/sociology states:
'One thing alone is undeniably clear: *if* God, in and through his
historical actions, reserves the public priesthood for one of the two
sexes only, *then* it is not just arbitrary to choose the male sex.'[7] He
suggests that 'The sociological findings are strengthened, in the
religious sphere, by the symbolic references, which clearly align
men with the officeholder's eccentric self-surrender to God as
represented in public worship'.[8] The study of religions gives an
explanation of why the image of God has more masculine than
feminine traits and therefore why men are chosen as his priestly
representatives.

We need to expand on these conclusions slightly. Hauke starts
with a brief biology lesson. There are clear differences between the
sexes. These are part of the natural order of creation as humans
were created as relational beings in order to reflect the relationality
of the Trinitarian God. Our sexuality is not some superficial factor
of our humanity, a necessary evil for procreation. It is an essential
part of every cell of our body, as every cell contains the XX or XY
chromosomes, and impacts on all aspects of our being. Masculinity
is exemplified by 'eccentricity' or an abstract, outward looking
approach; femininity is exemplified by 'centrality' or an approach
that tends towards following the rhythms of nature and concentrating on the here and now. Man has a greater ability to distance
himself from his immediate surroundings and to concentrate on a
clear goal despite varying moods and feelings. Woman has a
greater ability to respond to spiritual, intuitive experiences and
feelings. Men tend to want to organise their lives by controlling,
categorising, segregating whereas women tend to want to organise
their lives by sharing, including, linking/relating. Women tend to
recede behind their children and husbands, men tend to dominate.
These female and male traits can be attributed to God and are
clearly seen in pagan belief systems. Because God is transcendent
and masculinity is more transcendent than femininity, which is
more immanent, masculine symbolism is more appropriate for

depicting God. It is no coincidence that the Christian God is depicted as masculine.

> God contains in himself, in an analogical way, all creaturely perfections, which he thereby transcends: *Deus semper major.* Occasionally, as we will see with respect to the Old and New Testaments, feminine traits, too, are ascribed to God. But masculine traits outweigh these.[9]

If God is best depicted using masculine symbolism, this dictates a masculine priesthood, especially in the liturgy, which depends on symbolism for its meaning. To impose a feminine symbolism would disturb our image of God and therefore our relationship with him. As our sense of the masculine and feminine lies much deeper than mere sociological influences, this change could seriously damage our sense of connectedness with God.

This concludes the first half of Hauke's study; male and female as part of the created order. He then goes on to look at the order of redemption. Here, he covers the standard areas of the place of women in the Old Testament: the language of Scripture and the early fathers describing God as Father; Christ as male, convenience or revelation?; the Holy Spirit as feminine; Mary as type of both the Church and mankind; Christ's actions; St Paul; the Early Fathers; the Middle Ages; a summary of the arguments. These follow standard lines of argumentation and it is only necessary to look at the sections on Christ's actions and the writings of St Paul. On the chapter on Christ's actions, Hauke ends with a useful section of 'objections and replies' to the traditional position.

One of the most common objections to the status quo is that, while Jesus did not call any women to be apostles, he also did not call any gentiles and we did not stick to that. Hauke reminds the reader that Jesus instructed the apostles to go out to all nations, so the call to gentiles was never in doubt. Another common argument is that the Church has over-stated the position of the apostles as the first bishops. However, while the apostles were in a unique position, their office has to continue until the second coming and they therefore had to hand on their authority, which they did by prayer and the laying on of hands.

An argument that we will meet elsewhere is that the emphasis on Jesus's masculinity is foreign to the New Testament, it is his humanity that counts (quoting Ph 2:7 and Jn 1:14).[10] However, as we also discuss elsewhere, to be human means to be either male or female. Jesus's masculinity is an essential part of his humanity and of his relationality with God the Father. A similar argument is that, as Jesus brings grace to both men and women equally, both need to be equally involved in this priestly task. The laity do indeed have a share in the priesthood of Christ but the sacramental priesthood is a service of its own sort, distinct from the common priesthood. The priest represents Christ both with the community and set apart from the community. From his many followers, Jesus chose a very small number for this task. It is worth noting that they were chosen by Christ, not by the Church (Jn 15:16), so the grace of the sacrament comes from God, not the Church.

The last two arguments are based on the ideas of representation and symbolism. Just as the male priest represents both Christ and his bride, the Church, so a female can represent the bridegroom. Hauke points out that the priest only represents the Church because it is the body of Christ; he primarily represents Christ, the head of the Church. The priest can exercise the authority of Christ through the sacraments, which nourish the body of Christ. The symbolism of Christ as the bridegroom and head of the Church is strengthened when the priest is male. The last argument in Hauke's list states that, as women can represent men in secular positions, they should be able to do so in religious ones also. Hauke replies that the relationship between Christ and his representatives is not merely legalistic; the sacrament of ordination effects an ontological change in the priest, in other words, his whole being is involved. The apostles were redemptive symbols and this symbolism has to retain its integrity if the sacraments are to remain effective.

In his writing on Paul, Hauke devotes most of the chapter to the prohibition on women speaking in church (1 Co 14:34–38). He examines many arguments for and against the authenticity of the verses and their meaning, including comparisons with other, seemingly contradictory, verses. He rejects claims that verses 34–35 are interpolations. He differentiates between glossolalia, prophecy and teaching. Prophecy is acting as a mouthpiece for God and simply passes on God's messages to the community. It is the result of inspiration and is not associated with an official office. Glossolalia, similarly, is inspired by the Holy Spirit and is not limited to official office bearers. Women can practise both of these forms of communicating God's message to the community, even in the assemblies. The assemblies themselves are not quite what we expect at our Sunday services:

> Before (and possibly after) the 'breaking of bread' in the celebration of the Eucharist, there was a process of actualizing the gospel in which not just one person took part. Along with one element in the style of an address, there were also questions and answers. The officially appointed teachers were surely represented in a prominent position within this educative conversation.[11]

So, in keeping with the practice of the day, there would be discussion and debate rather than a monologue or sermon as we know them today. Hauke is sure that 1 Corinthians 14:34 does refer to such assemblies, not to smaller house meetings. He decides that Paul is referring to different types of speaking in 1 Corinthians 14:34 and in 1 Corinthians 11:5. In the first, he is talking of formal, public teaching and in the second of prophesying and praying. While women can prophecy and pray (which is what glossolalia amounts to), they cannot teach. He suggests that the questioning and discussion of the prophecies could have become a source of disorder:

> The ban on speaking thus ultimately means a ban on teaching. Through questions, women could easily be drawn into the instructive conversation and may occasionally have felt inclined to act as teachers themselves ... The self-appointed 'pneumatics' are now confronted by Paul, in verse 37, with the 'command of the Lord'.[12]

This passage does not explain what is so wrong with women becoming involved in teaching. However if we refer back to the previous quote, we can find the answer; there would be too great a risk of the women taking on the role of leader of the assembly. This is the role that was handed on by the apostles and developed into that of bishop and priest. It included presiding at the 'breaking of bread'. As such, it was not open to women, for reasons that are more wide ranging than simply the weekly assemblies. This interpretation also applies to 1 Tm 2:11–15:

> In the given context, teaching means official instruction, especially during the divine service ... Consequently, 1 Timothy 2 forms an authentic interpretation of 1 Corinthians 14 by the New Testament itself ... Conclusion: the ban on speaking in 1 Corinthians 14 is a ban on teaching that is directed against the participation of women in official teaching activities during the divine service.[13]

Hauke places great emphasis on the phrase 'what I am writing to you is a commandment from the Lord' (1 Co 14:37). This phrase only applies to the teaching of verses 34–35 if they are in their original position and not an interpolation. He gives a detailed analysis of the various arguments for and against the verses being an interpolation, including the suggestion that the confusion was caused by Marcion, who produced 'revised' versions of Paul's letters. He concludes that in fact they match Paul's normal pattern of presenting an argument when they are in their traditional position, they are not an interpolation. Therefore the prohibition on women having a teaching role during the assemblies is a command of the Lord.[14]

Hauke examines the situation in the early Church and concludes that women priests were never tolerated. This was not because of the inferior social or educational position of women but because of the teaching of Paul in 1 Corinthians 14 and 1 Timothy 2 and the example of Jesus, who called only men to be apostles. The early Church in fact, unlike the Jewish communities, encouraged women to study theology and to devote themselves to building up the Church and the official positions of widows and virgins was unique to Christianity. So the rule banning them from the priesthood was not based on any sense of their inferiority as persons but on the will of Christ. This teaching is part of the Tradition of the Church and is repeated in varying forms throughout its history. St Thomas Aquinas explains that women cannot receive ordination because, as a sacrament, it is a sign of what the sacrament signifies. The priest signifies Christ, the head of the Church and therefore must be male. Thomas allows that women can be secular rulers but not spiritual ones. Women can be prophets because prophecy is not a sacrament.

Hauke looks briefly at the position of deaconesses and concludes that they were of a different order to male deacons. He suggests that the ordination rite for a deaconess was more akin to a sacramental than a sacrament. He concludes:

> To reinstate the diaconate of the early Church would be an anachronism (visits to female living quarters and assistance at baptism ...). On the other hand, to establish a female diaconate equivalent to the male diaconate would be a step in the direction of priesthood for women. If a female diaconate should be created, then these two fundamental difficulties would require consideration.[15]

Hauke concludes his study by highlighting three criteria for refusing priesthood to women: the 'command of the Lord' in 1 Corinthians 14; the constant Tradition of the Church and the theological and canonical assumption that sacramental ordination of a woman is invalid in principle. He also adds a fourth point, which summarises the first part of his work:

> Official priesthood for women would obscure the spiritual nature of the relationship Christ—Church and endanger the Christian image of God. The polarity of the sexes, in its symbolic effectiveness, is so deeply anchored in man's being that disavowing it in connection with our question would be likely to lead, in the longer term, to devastating consequences.[16]

Müller

Gerhard Müller's *Priesthood and Diaconate* was published in English in 2002 and therefore has the advantage of being written after Pope John Paul II's 1994 statement on the inadmissibility of women to the priesthood, *Ordinatio Sacerdotalis*. Unlike the other two, it looks at both the priesthood and the diaconate. However it treats them quite separately. It is more argumentative in tone than the other two, perhaps out of frustration at having to repeat what the author sees as indisputable truths.

Müller bases his argument on the non admissibility of women to the priesthood on the teachings of Paul on marriage: 'The standard for the ethical conduct of spouses is mutual subordination, whereby they both take as their spiritual model the obedience of Christ, who in his fidelity to the Father subordinated himself to the logic of his mission.'[17] Just as the man is the head of his wife, so Christ is the head of the Church. Priests are 'A sign through which Christ, the High Priest, accomplishes the life-giving actions of his Church.' Priesthood is not an occupation or role, it denotes a personal relationship or representation of Christ by the priest. The priest therefore has to be male. Women represent the Church, the bride of Christ. So, just as man and woman become one flesh, so Christ and the Church become one spiritual unity.

Müller deals with the diaconate in two parts. Before the section on the priesthood, he examines the work of Dorothea Reininger on whether or not women could be validly and licitly ordained to the diaconate. Müller makes no attempt at impartiality but describes her proposal as 'a change of strategy' in response to *Ordinatio Sacerdotalis* and her interpretation of that document as 'problematic'. He goes on to state that

> Although there are records of the liturgical installation of deaconesses dating back to the fourth century, one must not overlook the fact that the selfsame authors who testify to this practice also make it clear that the consecration of deaconesses was not the ordination of women to the diaconal ministry; on the contrary, it was a question of a different ecclesiastical office.[18]

As we have seen in other chapters, this statement is contradicted by most other writers that we have looked at. Müller states that bishops, priests and male deacons were instituted by the apostles and the Holy Spirit and all other variations were non-sacramental consecrations introduced by ecclesial authorities. From the early third century, the priest and deacon were distinguished by their relationship to the bishop. The priest shares in the *sacerdotium* or apostolic, spiritual authority of the bishop, the deacon is at the service of the bishop (*ministerium episcopi*). Together, they receive the one sacrament of Holy Orders. Müller accuses Reininger and others of trying to separate the sacrament into three, which would go against firm magisterial teaching. He denies her assertion that the deaconesses of the early Church were ordained and therefore could be reintroduced. He concludes that the author needs to do far more work on the strictly theological aspects of her research.

> It is not, after all, a matter of modifying the office of deaconess found in the early Church so as to arrive at some form of ecclesiastical office with a brand-new set of functions; rather it is a question of whether or not the consecration of deaconesses was an independent sacramental degree within the one Sacrament of Holy Orders and whether it was also received by the Church as binding in faith.[19]

Müller's strong belief that the sacrament of ordination is fixed as consisting of bishop, priest and male deacon only, does not mean that he is unsympathetic to the feelings of women in the Church today. He realises that the presentation of Church teaching has a very negative tone: 'Many still feel deeply hurt by the statement that their status as women is considered the reason for their non-admission to Holy Orders in principle.'[20] He feels that all Catholics have a right to a clear explanation of the Church's teaching on this. It cannot be based on a lack of trust in women's ability to cope with the academic, psychological, physical or spiritual demands of the job as women are already exercising these qualities in many areas of Church life. The basis of the teaching can be summarised as either 'theological necessity or sociological conditioning'. The answer must be decided on the strength of theological reasoning, based on the understanding of the nature of the sacrament of Holy Orders. Here Müller goes on to compare the sacrament of Orders with that of matrimony. Love can only be fruitful if the partners are of a different sex, in other words, marriage can only exist between a man and a woman. Similarly, the priest represents the personal relationship of Christ the head to his Church, the Logos, who by his surrender of himself, has become one with the Church.

We have now come back to the point in Müller's arguments where we started, that the male priesthood is essentially a relationship with Christ on the same level as the relationship between husband and wife.

Sarah Butler

Sister Sarah Butler is a respected theologian in the Church today, having held senior positions in the Vatican, American universities and on international commissions. When she first took an interest in the subject of women and the priesthood, she supported the movement for the priestly ordination of women. However more mature thought convinced her that this was not in line with Church teaching, and never could be. Her book *The Catholic Priesthood and Women* was published in 2006. It is exclusively about the priesthood and ignores the question of deacons, which is a pity as this is the most readable of the four books examined.[21]

Butler starts by examining *Ordinatio Sacerdotalis* in detail and reminds us that it teaches that the debate must be founded on the Church's belief that ordination is a sacrament instituted by Jesus Christ and passed on by the apostles. The Church does not have the authority to change what Christ has fixed. The debate was taking place in a spirit of expectation of change, fuelled by both theological and sociological studies. One of the more influential of these was the work of Haye van der Meer. He made a detailed study of the history of the Church's attitude to women and concluded that misogynist views had influenced Church teaching. As this teaching was based on sociocultural arguments rather than theology, it could be changed. This became a very popular argument. Pope Paul VI and Pope John Paul II both based their statements on the will of Christ and the nature of ordination as a sacrament perpetuating the position of the apostles as representatives of Christ. The honour given to Mary and the female saints through the centuries demonstrate that this decision is not based on any disregard for the dignity of women.

Butler traces the teaching on women in the pre-Vatican II Church and shows that, while the language could be interpreted as 'trying to keep women in their place in the home' in fact the popes were trying to safeguard the family unit against the threats of communism, divorce and the sort of feminism that denied women their natural role as wives and mothers. At the same time, they were promoting the involvement of women in cultural and political movements aimed at improving the dignity of all. The

Vatican II documents, especially *Gaudium et Spes*, stressed the equal dignity of women and their rights to the same cultural, educational and civic opportunities as men. In more recent times, John Paul II has spoken of the need for 'a culture of equality'. There has been a gradual shift of emphasis from women as wives and mothers to women as persons. However the Church is careful to retain a distinction between men and women, who are equal in dignity but different in their sexuality. This demands that account be taken of women's role as wife and mother, otherwise injustices could be perpetrated in the name of a false equality. Women must have the right, and financial support, to choose to raise their children at home. Society should honour this work as being of equal value to their work outside the home.

The Church then faced accusations of not practising what it was preaching. An examination of the Code of Canon Law of 1917 shows that there was a certain justification for this criticism. However the revised Code of 1983 deliberately removed any inequalities so that non-ordained men and women now have equal status under Church law. There are only three situations where this is not the case: if there is doubt about a child's place of origin, it is settled as that of the mother; if there is doubt about a child's rite, it is settles as that of the father; the lay ministries of lector and acolyte may be permanently conferred on a man but only temporarily on a woman. This latter is due to the long tradition of these offices being part of the preparation for the priesthood. For many centuries they were treated as part of the sacrament of ordination.

The Church has paid particular attention to its teaching on marriage. The new Canon Law describes it as a 'partnership'. John Paul II spelt out how this can be reconciled with the statements in the letters of St Paul. He argues that Christ has freed us from the curse of Genesis 3:16. Jesus set an example of treating women with dignity and Paul is teaching that men and women are mutually subject to each other out of reverence for Christ. This applies in all walks of life, not just within marriage. Butler concludes this section with a warning:

> We should note, however, that the equality of the baptised
> has to do with access to salvation, not access to particular
> offices or vocations. The Church teaches that different

> vocations and gifts are bestowed by the Holy Spirit ... The
> Lord himself has entrusted certain offices to some and not
> to others. These gifts and offices are not the subject of a
> 'right', but are free gifts given to build up the body of Christ
> so that all may reach salvation and attain the holiness of the
> saints.[22]

Butler addresses three objections to Church teaching. The most
common of these is that excluding women from leadership roles
is based on stereotyped attitudes to women and is unjust. She
replies that the Church is not a democratic, voluntary society, it is
the Kingdom of God. Being denied priestly ordination in no way
hinders women from achieving their place in this Kingdom.
Priesthood is not a career and no man has a right to be ordained;
it is a position of service to others, to which some men are called
by God. She points out that women in fact do have access to
leadership roles in the Church. They can take up positions as
professionals, advisers and leaders at all levels from their local
parish council to international commissions and Vatican congregations. Women religious have been serving the Church in a public
role as educators, missionaries, health and social workers for
generations.

The next objection is from feminist theologians who argue that
the Magisterium's appeal to the maleness of Christ and the nuptial
symbolism that it favours relies on a flawed theory of sexual
complementarity, a flawed anthropology. Butler gives three replies
to this argument. Firstly, the Church accepts that women are
capable of leadership roles. They are not barred from the priesthood because it is a leadership role, which it is not, but because
that is the will of Christ. Secondly, while there have been periods
in the past when the Church did have a 'faulty anthropology', this
is not part of the modern Church's reasons for a male priesthood.
Certainly, the Church does believe in the complementarity of the
sexes, but does not base its teaching on ordination on this. Thirdly,
there is a difference between fundamental reasons and the theological arguments supporting them. Fundamental reasons include
the facts and the unbroken Tradition of the Church. It is a fact that
Jesus chose only men to be apostles and that they and their
successors continued this practice. This is what the Church bases

her teaching on. The theological arguments explaining why this is the case may come and go, the teaching remains. As *Inter Insigniores* says, we cannot prove one way or the other that Jesus's attitude was socioculturally defined. We therefore have to just accept that that is how he behaved.

The third objection is that if women can be baptised, they can be ordained. Butler suggests that this argument depends on a Protestant definition of ordination, where the minister is an office-bearer appointed by the church to represent the priesthood of the baptised. Certainly, baptism pertains to salvation and gives all equal status before Christ. However Christ is free to give spiritual gifts and vocations to whom he chooses. These are intended to build up the Church and are to be used in the service of others. The ministerial priesthood differs in kind, not only in degree, from the common priesthood. All the baptised share in the common priesthood but only a few are called to the ministerial priesthood. They exercise this ministry on the strength of the sacrament of ordination, not baptism.

The teaching of the Church on ordination is rooted in its sacramental nature. Butler lists three characteristics of a sacrament. Firstly, sacraments are instituted by Christ, who determined their matter, form and subject. The matter of ordination is the laying on of hands, the form is the prayer over the subject and the subject is an adult male. Just as the Eucharistic bread and wine cannot be changed to some other significant food and drink, so the elements of ordination cannot be changed. Secondly, sacraments differ from other liturgical rites in that they can be traced back to Christ. So the sacrament of ordination is based on Christ's call of the twelve. Traditionally, this is identified with the Last Supper but modern theologians have widened the institution to include several other events; the original call, the missionary mandate and Pentecost. Thirdly, sacraments are efficacious signs as they impart grace specific to that sacrament. So only someone who has been ordained can act *in persona Christi*.

Lumen Gentium taught that bishops were successors of the apostles and that this office was conferred by Christ, not the pope. The bishop becomes a member of the episcopal college, which makes present the ever active reality of the college of apostles. As this college was male, only males can participate. As the priest shares in the office of the bishop, he also must be male. In a sense, the priest becomes a sacrament when acting *in persona Christi* as he is a visible sign of Christ and a source of the grace of the sacrament. As a sign of Christ, he has to be of the same sex.

Butler continues to look at some more standard objections to Church teaching. The first of these is that Jesus's choice of 12 men is irrelevant as they were appointed to symbolise the 'ingathering' of the twelve tribes and were not replaced. Instead, the development of office bearers in the early Church was guided by the Holy Spirit. This argument ignores the Scriptural evidence that the apostles were sent out to act in Jesus's name and the Tradition of the Church is that they were representative of Christ.

The next objection is that Paul refers to several people, other than the twelve, as apostles, including Junia (Rm 16:7). Butler replies that only men received the apostolic charge by the laying on of hands; we do not know whether or not Junia was a woman; it is unlikely that the Church departed from the example of Jesus so early in its history and it would mean that the pastoral letters represented a schism in the Church. This in turn would undermine the authority of Scripture.

A familiar argument is that all the baptised act *in persona Christi*, in other words, we all put on Christ at baptism and can all be Christ-like.[23] Butler points out that there is a difference between acting in the person of Christ and acting in imitation of Christ. The minister is sacramentally configured to represent Christ and act as his minister with respect to the rest of the baptised, helping them to imitate the example of Christ. A related argument is that the priest acts *in persona Christi* only because he first acts *in persona Ecclesiae*. It is actually the other way round. The priest is primarily representing Christ as he makes present the sacrifice on the cross. Because he represents Christ, who is the head of the Church, he then also represents the Church.

Another argument mentioned elsewhere states that the importance of the incarnation is that Jesus became human, his maleness is irrelevant.[24] Butler repeats the teaching that to be genuinely human means to be either male or female. To deny Jesus's masculinity is to diminish his humanity. Our sexuality affects our biology, psychology, spirituality as well as our roles as spouses and parents. A more sophisticated version of this argument is that the risen Christ transcends maleness because all the baptised are part of his body. This ignores the teaching that the historical Jesus did not cease to exist after the resurrection. Christ is not identical with the Church but is united in love with it in the way that a husband and wife become one flesh.

The last argument is that, if Jesus's choice of 12 men was significant, then they would also have to be Jewish. Butler replies that the early Church always condemned women exercising priestly functions, they never condemned gentile priests. Once the conditions for admitting gentiles to baptism and participation in the community had been agreed, there was never any further suggestions of them being treated differently. So the Tradition of the Church is consistently in favour of male gentile priests and against any women exercising a priestly function.

The Council of Trent identified three marks of a divinely instituted Tradition: it must have the gospels as its source; it must have been the practice of the apostolic Church; it must have been the constant practice of the Catholic Church. The practice of ordaining only men meets all of these three conditions.

Butler also uses one of Newman's 'notes', that of 'conservative action on the past', to examine the issue of women's ordination. This shows that the greater emphasis on the equality of women is an authentic development which has been assimilated into Church teaching without damaging any other teachings. The question of women's priestly ordination fails the test as it would call into question the doctrine of priesthood, marriage, the hierarchical structure of the Church and even its apostolic foundation: 'It appears to lead to the disintegration and dismantling of the received Tradition, not its consolidation and confirmation.'[25] The Magisterium, on the other hand, has benefited from the debate, which has helped it to a new synthesis of its teaching on the common and ministerial priesthood in an ecclesiology of communion.

The document *Ordinatio Sacerdotalis* has affected the whole Christian community as it has ended any realistic hopes of a change in Church practice. While the debate goes on, it is for theologians to further explain the Church's position and to explore other ways in which women can serve the Church.

Summary

We have looked at four quite different presentations of the arguments for and against women as priests and deacons. They were chosen specifically because they are regarded as the definitive authorities in the argument against women as deacons or priests.

Martimort looked at the diaconate only. He gave a historical study of the subject which in fact is not as negative as is sometimes suggested. He accepted that deaconesses did exist in the Church up to the end of the eleventh century and that they were ordained. However he pointed out that the ordination rites were different from those for deacons and the 'job description' also differed. He felt that reintroducing deaconesses might actually restrict the role of women in the Church as this is currently far broader than the historical role of deaconesses. It could also 'be fraught with ambiguity'.

Hauke gives a brief excursus on deaconesses and concludes that they were not ordained but received a blessing and had a different role from that of deacons. The tasks that they existed to perform no longer exist. To create a female diaconate equivalent to the male diaconate would be a step towards a female priesthood. The bulk of Hauke's work is devoted to explaining why we cannot have a female priesthood. His arguments fall into two groups—those based on creation theology and those based on revelation. In the first section, Hauke uses the tools of sociology and psychology to build up an argument for the essential symbolism of masculinity in our understanding of God. Just as we relate to each other as masculine or feminine, so we relate to God and the Church as symbolised by masculine and feminine characteristics. Because the priest represents Christ, the symbolism of masculinity is essential, especially in the liturgy, which depends on symbolism for much of its meaning.

In the second part of his work, Hauke looks at the Scriptural evidence and concludes that women cannot be priests because they cannot teach in an official capacity at the formal assemblies, there is no tradition of women priests in the Church and the consistent teaching, theological and canonical, is against it.

As with Martimort, Hauke is not as negative as he is often portrayed. He limits the teaching of Paul in 1 Corinthians 14 and 1 Timothy 2 to formal, official teaching which might blur the boundaries between women and the episcopal role of the community leaders. In other settings, women can teach and have a leadership role. While he has reservations about reintroducing deaconesses, he does not rule it out altogether, simply warning of the dangers of not actually having a role for them and of endangering the teaching on a male-only priesthood.

Müller is the most negative of the four. He denies that women were ever ordained as deaconesses, basing his argument mainly on the unity of the sacrament. He uses Paul's teaching on marriage and the symbolism of Christ as bridegroom and the Church as bride to rule out women priests. He insists that any debate must be conducted in terms of theology.

Hauke and Müller both convincingly dismiss the social/cultural conditioning arguments as reasons for the early Church not having women priests. They both base their arguments on the necessity of a male priesthood on theological grounds. They both argue, although from slightly different angles, that the symbolism of the male priest as representative of Christ is essential to our understanding of both God and the Church.

Butler focuses on the recent teachings of the Church, particularly *Ordinatio Sacerdotalis*. She shows that its teachings are consistent with the constant teaching of the Magisterium. She shows that the various popular arguments for women priests do not stand up to detailed theological examination. She places particular emphasis on the constant Tradition of the Church, also on the difference between fundamental and theological reasons for doctrine. She demonstrates the use of Newman's 'notes' for deciding whether or not a proposal was a valid development or a corruption. Unfortunately, Butler does not examine the argument for women deacons.

All four sources emphasise that Jesus did not choose any women as apostles, that the apostles continued this practice and that therefore the Church cannot change this. They point out that Mary was the perfect disciple but was not chosen as an apostle.

Notes

1   A. Martimort, *Deaconesses: An Historical Study* (San Francisco: Ignatius Press, 1982), p. 18.

2   *Ibid.*, p. 20.

3   *Ibid.*, pp. 204–5. The quote included two sections in Latin which I have had to paraphrase.

4   *Ibid.*, p. 585.

5   *Ibid.*, p. 250.

6   M. Hauke, *Women in the Priesthood?: A Systematic Analysis in the Light of the Order of Creation and Redemption* (San Francisco: Ignatius Press, 1988), p. 25. The reader might be interested to know that Hauke has published an article *Observations on the Ordination of Women to the Diaconate* in *The Church and Women: A Compendium* in preparation by Ignatius Press when he was writing *Women in the Priesthood*.

7   *Ibid.*, p. 195.

8   *Ibid.*, p. 195.

9   *Ibid.*, p. 183.

10   See chapters 22 and 23.

11   *Ibid.*, p. 363.

12   *Ibid.*, p. 377.

13   *Ibid.*, p. 380.

14   It is interesting to compare these views with those of E. Clowney. See chapter five 'Scripture: Women; St Paul'.

15   M. Hauke, *Women in the Priesthood*, p. 444.

16   *Ibid.*, p. 479.

17   G. Müller, *Priesthood and Diaconate* (San Francisco: Ignatius Press, 2002), p. 103.

18   *Ibid.*, p. 48, with a footnote referring to another work by himself for supporting references.

19   *Ibid.*, p. 58.

20   *Ibid.*, p. 64.

21   Butler explains in footnote no 3 that she uses the word 'priesthood' rather than 'Holy Orders' as she does not intend to consider the position of deacons. However see Appendix IV for a summary of an article that she wrote on deaconesses.

22   S. Butler, *The Catholic Priesthood and Women: A guide to the Teaching of the Church* (Chicago: Hillenbrand Books, 2007), p. 38.

23   See chapter three, 'The priesthood of the laity'.

24   See chapter 22, 'Anglican arguments'.

25   *Ibid.*, p. 111.

21 GATHERING TOGETHER

W<small>E HAVE NOW</small> examined our various areas of interest under the headings of Scripture, Tradition, the Magisterium and the most relevant theologians. It is time to start consolidating our various conclusions.

Conclusions from Scripture

The Church is bound by the words of Scripture. She can translate and re-interpret them for every generation but she cannot add to, delete or ignore any part of them. Any re-interpretation that depends more on wishful thinking than good scholarship will not bear good fruit. The Church was established by Jesus (see especially Mt 16:18–19) as a hierarchical structure whose function was to spread the good news of the Kingdom of God. The apostles were the founder members and had the authority to make whatever decisions were necessary for the good of the Church.

The place of women in this Church is not clear. Equality is something to be worked towards. We can look to Mary for ideas on just how this equality is to operate, yet she was not given an apostolic role by Jesus. The reasons for this cannot be found in Scripture alone. This is where Tradition and the Magisterium need to be consulted. Perhaps Jesus did give Mary a leading role as the mother of the Church. We have seen that the Gospel of Luke hints at this and the gospel of John makes it explicit. The Church has given her this title but perhaps it needs to be pondered on more than it has been. How does this affect her role as a model for all other women in the Church?

Scripture tells us that women are of equal value to men. They can be both disciples and apostles, active and contemplative but they do not have a share in the apostolic powers to confect the Eucharist, forgive sins or govern the Church. They can be prominent workers in Church communities. They fulfil the message of Scripture best when they concentrate on providing the conditions necessary for others to do the will of God and grow in faith.

Conclusions from Tradition

Tradition and Scripture together form the deposit of faith, entrusted to the Magisterium of the Church. The Church is the kingdom of God on earth. It has a hierarchical structure, established by Jesus Christ and passed on through the College of Bishops, with the pope at their head. The transmission of authority is effected by the sacrament of ordination and has both a historical and collegial element. Ordination to the priesthood is reserved for men only. There is much debate over this. A modern school of theology, popularised by John Paul II's work on the theology of the body, suggests that Jesus's masculinity was an essential part of his identity. He was the Son of God, not simply the child of God. This has implications for the debate on women priests.

Church Tradition on Our Lady goes back to Ignatius of Antioch and has consistently taught that she was the mother of God, remained a virgin all her life, was free from sin, gives us an example of faith and is both the mother of and a type of the Church.

The role of women in the Church has varied considerably. There is no historical evidence for the official existence of female priests but there is evidence for deaconesses, from Paul's companion, Phoebe, until some time in the eleventh century. Neither Scripture not Tradition can end the argument over their status and whether or not they could legitimately be reintroduced into the Church.

Conclusions from the Magisterium

The bishop has the fullness of the sacrament of ordination but exercises authority only as part of the College of Bishops, with the pope at its head. The bishop receives the same grace and authority as the apostles. The priest is a co-worker with the bishop and has a delegated share in his apostolic authority but is not a successor of the apostles. The deacon is a servant of the community, with powers delegated from the bishop but does not share in his apostolic authority. He has a share in the priestly duties of sanctifying, preaching and leading but not of oversight. Deaconesses existed in the early Church and were included in the clerical hierarchy. They were gradually replaced by nuns. The current debate over whether or not they could be reintroduced centres on the unity of the sacrament of ordination. How would such a step affect the all-male priesthood?

The laity are also part of the Church, with their own rights and duties. The Magisterium did not consider them in any detail until Vatican II.

There are four official teachings on Our Lady: her Immaculate Conception; her perpetual virginity; her role as the mother of God; and her assumption into heaven. Women are specifically excluded from the sacrament of priestly ordination but can take part in all other aspects of Church life.

Conclusions from the Theologians

All four theologians categorically rule out women priests, but that is why they were selected, so this does not come as a surprise! While they give various reasons, the 'bottom line' is that Jesus chose only male apostles and they in turn chose only male successors. These successors are our bishops and their co-workers, the priests. As the episcopacy and priesthood are sacramental and sacraments are founded on the actions of Jesus, the Church cannot change this practice. While it is just possible that Jesus was acting in accord with the local sociocultural traditions, the Scriptural evidence for this is lacking. Indeed, the opposite argument, that Jesus ignored such restrictions, would be easier to defend from Scripture. This is the argument used by the Church in the statements by Paul VI and John Paul II on the inadmissibility of women to priestly ordination. Our four theologians have not blindly repeated Church teaching but have tried to give the underlying reasons for it. Butler in particular has methodically answered the more common arguments for women priests.

On the topic of deaconesses, Butler is totally silent, Muller is against on the grounds of Tradition and the unity of the sacrament and Martimort and Hauke are both unenthusiastic but not totally against. Martimort felt that the deaconessses of the early Church had different ordination rites and different roles from deacons and were more restricted than modern women in the Church. Any reintroduction would be 'fraught with ambiguity'. Hauke is concerned that there is no obvious role for deaconesses in the modern Church and their reintroduction would threaten the all-male priesthood.

These conclusions can themselves be reduced to a few statements. From Scripture, we learn that the Church is hierarchical, with Mary as its mother, and that women exercised diaconal but not priestly powers. From Tradition, we learn that authority in the Church rests with the bishops and that there have been women deacons in the past. From the Magisterium, we learn that the bishop has the fullness of the sacrament of ordination while priests are co-workers of the bishop and deacons are servants; the role of deaconesses could only be reintroduced if it was clear that this did not contradict the unity of the sacrament of ordination. From theologians, we learn that Jesus's choice of men only as apostles must be honoured, regardless of speculation as to his motives.

So the reintroduction of deaconesses is theologically possible but several questions need to be answered before this could be implemented. The most pressing questions are whether or not they could receive the sacrament of diaconal ordination, what their relationship to the all-male priesthood would be and what they would actually do. We need to look at our evidence in more detail.

22 A MORE DETAILED ARGUMENT

THE INTRODUCTION TOUCHED on the problem of women with skills that the Church needs struggling to remain loyal to the Church because of its teaching on the role of women or wasting their talents on a debate that is leading nowhere. Despite being one of the standard references arguing for the status quo, Hauke was well aware of this:

> (Church teaching needs to be most clearly stressed); otherwise, all too many theologically educated women of goodwill are in danger of expending themselves on false goals and, like Don Quixote, jousting with windmills ... The need of the hour is not an 'emancipatory war' between the sexes in the Church but rather a *cooperation* between men and women.[1]

Theologians cannot simply sit back and repeat the teachings of *Ordinatio Sacerdotalis* or *Inter Insigniores*. They have to explain, far more effectively than they have done up to now, just why the Magisterium teaches what it does. In doing so, they have to reach out to the general public, many of whom would be struggling to read and understand the Catechism of the Catholic Church, let alone documents from the Vatican congregations.[2] Priests have to understand and accept the teaching at a more sophisticated level so that they can explain it to their parishioners and defend the Church's teaching at ecumenical meetings.[3] Lay theologians have to be prepared to sound politically incorrect by teaching that in fact there is a difference between men and women and that we can classify human characteristics as, on average, masculine or feminine and that therefore some tasks are more suited to one sex than the other. An interesting point was made by Cardinal Scola:

> In the Christian tradition all of this (humans as sexual beings) necessarily leads us back to creation (footnote to CCC §279). One can thus argue that the human being's ontological, creaturely dependence on God is inscribed even in his sexual nature. There is an important consequence of

> this truth: in a world which seeks to eliminate God, it
> becomes impossible to consider sexual difference.[4]

I wonder if the reverse is also true; in a world that seeks to
eliminate sexual difference, does it become impossible to consider
God? As Jesus was the son of God and the Trinity consists of
Father, Son and Holy Spirit, it is difficult to discuss the nature of
God in asexual terms.

The point that our sexuality is part of our God-given identity is
one that needs more examination. Pope John Paul II clearly
believed passionately in the need for societies to grant women
equal rights. He also believed passionately in the God-given
differences between men and women: 'Perfection for women does
not mean being like men, masculinizing themselves until they lose
their specifically womanly qualities. Their perfection ... is to be
women, equal to men but different.'[5] He then went on to destroy
any good-will among his female readers by stating: 'Women have
understanding, sensitive, compassionate hearts, giving them a
tactful and practical approach to charity.'[6] As a woman, I fail to
see myself in this description. I could think of a few women who
might answer to such a description but I can think of many more
who do not. I can also think of some men who could be described
in these terms. It is of course possible that the original was more
subtle and the translator has been insensitive. However this style
of stating that 'All women are ...' and 'All men are ...' is common
to many Church documents and causes much irritation. Even a
phrase such as 'On average' or 'We typically find that' would have
improved the sentence. As it stands, it commits the fault of treating
women as an amorphous group rather than as individuals. If it is
valid to say that 'All women are kind and sensitive' then it is
equally valid to say that 'All women are moody and unpredictable'.

Much more work needs to be done to popularise the work of
Jung, Edith Stein, Balthasar and John Paul II on humanity as
masculine and feminine. Among 'ordinary' people there is an
instinctive understanding of this, it is after all part of the human
nature shared by all of us. We can see this in simple things such as
popular catch-phrases: 'I am a woman, so I can multi-task'; 'He
has flu, she has a cold'. Jokes about mothers-in-law or men's
inability to read instructions are funny because we recognise the

underlying truth in them. Where it has gone wrong in modern society is that it has become politically incorrect to admit to these differences and make allowances for them. The feminist movement has harmed the cause of women by demanding that women be treated as though they were men instead of being treated with dignity as women. There is something terribly sad about a society that places no value on women as mothers and organises itself so that it is very difficult for women to put their child-rearing duties at the top of the list. While women who do not feel called to stay at home with their children should not be made to do so, the opposite is also true, women who do want to stay at home and spend their time bringing up their children should not be forced to go out to work. The Church teaches that women have equal dignity with men but different ways of being. Unfortunately, it struggles to get this message across without sounding simply sexist.

Another area where Church teaching needs to improve is in explaining why Jesus's choice of male apostles was not influenced by sociocultural factors. Several of the books mentioned above examine this in great detail. They explain the differences between Jewish, Greek and Roman attitudes to women and the various sects that existed at the time of Jesus. They thus demonstrate that women actually had more freedom than is commonly thought and could have exercised leadership roles similar to that of the apostles. There are, however, several holes in their arguments, the most basic and practical being that very few members of any average parish will have access to these books, let alone the desire and time to read them. So their arguments, no matter how plausible, are not reaching the people who need to be familiar with them.

These sources also forget that Jesus lived and taught in a strictly Jewish environment, not a Greek or Roman one. He certainly set an example of treating women with respect and ignored the conventions of the day but he became very unpopular as a result. If his followers had all had a similar working life span to himself, the turnover rate would have been very high! While women could perhaps have functioned as apostles in the early Church in the Roman and Greek areas,[7] could they really have done so in Judea and Galilee during Jesus's lifetime? I think that most people's response to the suggestion that sociocultural considerations are not important is one of scepticism. History tells us that men are perfectly capable of treating women in a barbaric fashion if they feel that the women are stepping out of line. Jewish law allowed the stoning of women and Roman law allowed their crucifixion. It also allowed men to kill their female babies regardless of the mother's feelings. In our own country in far more 'civilised' times Quaker women of the seventeenth century were literally whipped at the post for preaching in public and 'witches' were burned at the stake. So because Jesus lived an unconventional life does not necessarily mean that his female followers could get away with doing so too or would be accepted as apostles. This argument needs far more careful exploration than it has so far received. Specifically, it needs to be looked at from the point of view of the lives of women, not simply Jesus's own actions.

The standard sources of Church teaching often include the role of Mary in the argument and point out that Jesus had the perfect disciple to hand but did not include her in the twelve. He therefore did not want any women in the group, a decision that was nothing to do with their personal qualities but simply their sex. There are at least two counter-arguments to this. Firstly, as I mentioned in chapter four, Mary was to be the mother of the Church, so she could not also be an apostle. (I am assuming that the two roles are mutually exclusive but this may not be the case. This is a separate argument which I do not have space to include here.) Secondly, if the sociocultural conditions in fact meant that women could not act in an apostolic role, then that includes Mary.

I am not suggesting that in fact Jesus was influenced by sociocultural factors which are now obsolete and therefore we can now appoint female successors to the apostles. I am simply suggesting that the counter-argument is not as straightforward as is often suggested. One counter argument that I have not seen in the standard literature is that in fact modern women are not as liberated as those of us in the affluent West might think. We forget that the Church has to operate throughout the world. There are still large areas of the world where a female religious leader would be simply unacceptable. Perhaps this will always be the case; perhaps sociocultural factors were a consideration in Jesus's time and always will be.

Anglican Arguments

Another way of looking at how to explain the Church's position on women priests is to look at the arguments that other Christian churches used as the basis for their decision to have women priests or ministers. This is complicated by the difference in attitude to the sacramental nature of the minister. In theory, the Anglican communion shares our position on this. So their arguments are the most relevant. The following points came from a conversation with a female priest from an Anglican background.

The priest's first point was that, when Saul was on the way to Damascus and was struck down, he heard Jesus say to him 'Why are you persecuting me?' As Saul was persecuting both men and women, Jesus is identifying both men and women as representing him. I would suggest two possible responses: the persecuted men are representative of Jesus and the women are 'optional extras'; far more likely is that Jesus is the head of the Church and Saul is persecuting the Church, not just individuals. The sex of these individuals is irrelevant and Jesus's question would have been the same if Saul had only persecuted men.

The next point was the fairly common argument that, if the Last Supper was a Passover meal, then women must have been present. In fact there is debate over whether or not the Last Supper was actually a Passover meal as John does not present it as such.[8] The synoptics do present it as a Passover meal but make it clear that only Jesus and the twelve are there 'When evening came he was at table with the Twelve' (Mt 26:20); 'When evening came he arrived with the Twelve' (Mk 14:17); and 'When the time came he took his place at table, and the apostles with him' (Lk 22:14). Indeed, Jesus had carefully planned it to be so 'They set off and found everything as he had told them and prepared the Passover' (Lk 22:13).

The priest whom I was speaking to is a linguist and was able to say that the Greek creed uses '*anthropos*' where the Latin creed uses '*homo factus est*' and both translate as 'human' rather than 'male'; in other words, it was Jesus's humanity that was important, not his masculinity. We have already discussed the point that we can only express our humanity as either male or female and there is significance attached to which of these Jesus was.

Then there was the sociological argument, which states that the position of women in society has changed as a result of Christianity and this needs to be continued. It is certainly true that the early Church introduced a more positive attitude towards women and that this is something that needs to be constantly reinforced. However ordination to the priesthood is a sacrament; it is not a civic right or a matter of equal treatment. As already discussed in chapter twenty, priests are chosen by God, they do not select themselves and most men are not chosen. 'You did not chose me, no, I chose you' (Jn 15:16).

Another common argument is that Jesus called Mary Magdalen as an apostle. We looked at this in chapter five and concluded that several women could meet the definition of apostle. However none of them were part of the twelve and therefore, as discussed above, were not present at the Last Supper.[9] So they did not receive the authority to confect the Eucharist.

The last point was that women are made in the image of God and therefore can represent him. Certainly, we are all made in the image of God but quite *how* has not been settled. Also, the priest is *in persona Christi* not *in persona Deus*.

These brief replies to the Anglican points show that they are far from conclusive. When the Anglican communion was debating the introduction of women priests, the Pope wrote to the Archbishop of Canterbury warning him that this move would mean an irreconcilable doctrinal difference between them and the Roman Catholic Church. He explained the Catholic Church's position using the argument of Jesus's choice of male apostles only; what Jesus did, the Church must copy regardless of his reasons for so doing. Despite this, the Anglican communion did decide to introduce women priests.

So there is still much work to be done on the subject of women priests. At the same time, we need to turn our attention to what role Jesus did intend women to have.

> The ultimate goal of any debate about priesthood for women should be to bring out the greatness and beauty of the respective callings of men and women in the Church ...

> General theological reflection must, of course, be carried
> over into pastoral practice. Determinate for both, in my
> opinion, are the figures of Jesus and Mary, in which,
> respectively, the basic structures of masculine and feminine
> activity are predelineated.[10]

Jesus is the one High Priest, from whom all priests receive their
authority. The relationship between Mary and the other women
of Scripture to the Church is not so clear. Perhaps it will become
clearer if we gather together the various conclusions from the
previous three parts.

Scripture and Our Lady

The Old Testament tells us that Mary will be the enemy of the devil.
Paul tells us that she was a Jewish mother who brought her son
up within the law. Luke tells us that Mary is a contemplative who
obeys the will of God as soon as it is made known to her and works
out the whys and wherefores afterwards; she is law-abiding, a loyal
wife and devoted mother but also a founder-member of the
Church. John tells us that she is the new Eve, the mother of the
Church, the perfect example of faith.

Scripture and Women

Women were created by God as equal to men but different. Both
are created in the image of God. Because of the sin of Eve, women
have to constantly struggle to have this equality accepted by men.
Jesus demonstrated that the various taboos of the Old Testament
no longer applied. There are many possible explanations of the
teachings of Paul on the role of women, both at home and in
church. Of the examples that we have looked at, the one that seems
to give the best 'fit' is that of Edmund Clowney. He argues that
women can exercise an official diaconal ministry but not one that
includes a ruling function. This agrees with the work of Hauke,
who writes that this teaching goes back to the earliest days of the
Church when women as active participants in the church meetings
could have blurred the distinction between them and those leaders
presiding at the Eucharist, which is a priestly, apostolic function
reserved to men.

The message from Matthew's genealogy is speculative but could be that the role of women is to be examples of faith, of keeping the law and being 'helpmates' to their male relatives, encouraging them to do the right thing. His gospel shows that several women met the definition of 'apostle'.

The message from John's gospel is similar to that of Matthew. Women are to be treated as worthy of receiving the gospel message and of acting as apostles and disciples. They played an active role in furthering the aims of Jesus's mission.

Tradition and Our Lady

A brief look at the teachings of the Early Fathers shows that the core beliefs of the Church regarding Mary can be traced back to its earliest writings which talk of her as the mother of God, her perpetual virginity, her sinlessness, her faith as an example for us to follow, her role as mother of the Church and as a type of the Church.

Tradition and Women

I have concentrated on the work of two scholars who both provide evidence for the existence of deaconesses and abbesses who were ordained with the approval of the Church. They both acknowledge that there is insufficient evidence for the existence of women priests. Both Morris and Macy identify changes in the eleventh and twelfth centuries as responsible for the loss of status by women. These changes are principally the reintroduction of Aristotelian philosophy, the adoption of Roman law as a basis for canon law and an emphasis on ordination as empowering the recipient to confect the Eucharist. These changes were detrimental to the position of women.

The Magisterium and Our Lady

Despite the vast literature on Mary, the official teaching of the Church at its highest level is limited to four dogmas regarding Mary: she was conceived free of original sin, she was a virgin, she was the mother of God and she was assumed into heaven.

Everything else is deduced from these facts. Modern statements encourage us to see Mary as a champion of the poor and oppressed and a role model both for those who wish to grow in faith and those who wish to fight for social justice. Indeed, Mary can help us to do both by helping us to approach closer to her son.

The Magisterium and Women

The role of women in the Church is determined as much by sociological factors as by theology. They have always been specifically excluded from the sacrament of priestly ordination. Their role as ordained deacons is still debated but they can take part in all other aspects of Church life.

Summary

We have found that Scripture tells us that Mary is the enemy of the devil; obeyed the law; contemplated on the word of God; showed immediate obedience; is both a founder member and the mother of the Church; is the new Eve and is the perfect example of faith. Tradition tells us that she is Theotokos; a perpetual virgin; sinless; a perfect example of faith; mother of the Church and a type of the Church. The Magisterium tells us that she was assumed into heaven and is a role model for those who wish to grow in faith and who wish to fight for social justice.

Similarly, Scripture tell us that women are equal to, but different from, men; created in the image of God; struggling to overcome domination by men—a result of original sin; able to be apostles and able to exercise a diaconal ministry but not a ruling one. Tradition tells us that women have been ordained as deaconesses and abbesses but not priests; suffer from changes in social and Church practices of the eleventh and twelfth centuries and suffer from changes in the definition of the word 'ordination' and the perception of what it means to be a priest. The Magisterium tells us that women can take part in all aspects of Church life except that of the ordained priest or, at the moment, ordained deacon.

The quote from Hauke, above, suggested that we need to look to Mary to work out what role Jesus intended for women. However Mary is the mother of the Church and as such has a unique role.

From the summary, above, we can only select some behaviours and qualities of Mary's that ordinary women could aspire to or use as a model. We can obey the law; contemplate the word of God; show obedience; have faith; fight for social justice. Following the example of the other women of Scripture, we can struggle against the effects of original sin; be apostles (in the sense of having been sent by Christ to proclaim the gospel); exercise all non-priestly ministries in the Church including a diaconal ministry.

This 'narrowing down' of the previous summaries has left us with various qualities that women should practise: obedience to both God and the law of the land; contemplation of God's word; faith; concern for our neighbour; struggling against the effects of original sin. We saw in chapter fourteen that the earliest deacons had a dual duty of assisting in the liturgy and works of charity, so this ministry would seem to be compatible with the list of qualities that women should practise.[11] Is it compatible with a wider view of the Church? There are two ways of judging this. We can have a general discussion of the role of the deacon and of women in the Church, using the material gathered here. This will allow us to have a less restricted approach than the one just employed of taking a narrower and narrower focus on our initial material. However it will be rather subjective. A more objective approach would be to use the seven 'notes' of Cardinal Newman, as demonstrated by Sarah Butler. These notes have already been listed in this chapter. In order to have a balanced and impartial view, we will use both methods. By happy coincidence, this means that we will examine our material using both a feminine and a masculine approach.

Notes

[1] M. Hauke, *Women in the Priesthood?: A Systematic Analysis in the Light of the Order of creation and Redemption* (San Francisco: Ignatius Press, 1988), p. 481.

[2] I remember being at a training day for people producing information for the general public. One statistic was that the average reading age of the British public is 9 years. The popular daily papers know this and adopt an appropriate writing style—how much of the Church's literature is at the same level?

[3] In a recent conversation with a German nun, she told me that 'everyone' in Germany, including the clergy, assume that the introduction of women priests is just a matter of time—if not under this pope, then certainly under

the next one.

4   Cardinal A. Scola, *The Nuptial Mystery* (Michigan: Eerdmans, 2005), p. 23.

5   Pope John Paul II *Agenda for the Third Millennium* (London: Fount Paperbacks, 1996), p. 49.

6   Pope John Paul II, *Agenda for the Third Millennium*, p. 49.

7   Although we have to remember that the Greeks accepted the teaching of Socrates that 'A man's fortitude is shown in ruling, a woman's in obeying' and of Aristotle that males naturally ruled females, whose souls have imperfect deliberative faculties (see *Politics*, p. 24).

8   See also page 1 of the introduction.

9   See the introduction and chapter five.

10 M. Hauke, *Women in the Priesthood?*, p. 481.

11 I am not implying that this list contains all the qualities that women should practise—it is simply those that are most relevant to the topic in hand!

23 APPLYING OUR DIAGNOSTIC TOOLS

A General Discussion

As ALWAYS, a good starting point is the official teaching documents of the Church. We have already seen that *Inter Insigniores* and *Ordinatio Sacerdotalis* rule out ordaining women to the priesthood. However they carefully use the phrase 'priestly ordination', leaving the question of diaconal ordination unanswered. The Catechism of the Catholic Church §1577 states clearly that 'only a baptized man (*vir*) validly receives sacred ordination'. However the following sentences refer to the College of Bishops 'with whom the priests are united in the priesthood' and Jesus's choice of the twelve. The paragraph does not mention deacons. As they are not part of the College of Bishops, it is quite possible to read the paragraph as applying only to the priesthood. The Code of Canon Law is more specific. Canon 1024 is clearly referring to men as opposed to women and the next canon talks of both the priesthood and the diaconate. So it is clear that the Code of Canon Law is including both orders in the phrase 'sacred ordination'. Therefore the introduction of women deacons would need a change in canon law. As the current set of canon laws dates from 1983 and includes several changes in the law regarding women from the previous set of 1917, another change is not impossible.[1] Indeed, the 1983 edition gave women the right, either as a matter of routine or in an emergency, to perform most of the tasks undertaken by deacons. So a revision allowing them to be ordained as deacons would have great theological significance but would not add greatly to the tasks that they could undertake. It would be a logical progression from the previous changes, thus being a simple doctrinal development rather than a potentially disruptive innovation.

The International Theological Commission examined the historical development of the diaconate in order to provide a sound basis for the debate on women deacons. It concluded that Church documents differentiate between priestly and diaconal ministries.

The Council statement that the deacon is not ordained for priesthood but for ministry was taken up by various documents of the post-Conciliar Magisterium ... The diaconate, by the very nature if its way of participating in the one mission of Christ, carries out this mission in the manner of an auxiliary service.[2]

A footnote points out that the phrase *in persona Christi Capitis*, used in the Code of Canon Law for all three degrees of Holy Orders, is now being restricted to bishops and priests.[3] On the subject of women deacons, the Commission makes two points:[4]

(1) The deaconesses mentioned in the tradition of the ancient Church, as evidenced by the rite of institution and the functions they exercised, were not purely and simply equivalent to the deacons;

(2) The unity of the sacrament of Holy Orders, in the clear distinction between the ministries of the Bishop and the Priests on the one hand and the Diaconal ministry on the other, is strongly underlined by ecclesial tradition, especially in the teaching of the Magisterium.[5]

Because of the negative tone of these two points, some readers have concluded that the document teaches that women were never, and cannot be in the future, ordained as deacons. This is not the case, as the following quote from the conclusion of the document shows.

It pertains to the ministry of discernment which the Lord established in his Church to pronounce authoritatively on this question.[6]

So the Commission is saying that the Church has still to decide whether or not it can reintroduce deaconesses but, if it did, it would need to clarify their position vis-à-vis male deacons and within the sacrament of ordination. These warnings remind me of the conclusions of Martimort, Hauke and Müller. So it would probably be worth looking at them all together. Martimort had three main concerns. He felt that a restoration would be fraught with ambiguity; that women currently have a much broader range of activities in the Church than was practised by deaconesses and that, as the Church urgently needs the service of all women, not just those who might be called to be deaconesses, there was a danger of the existence of deaconesses dissuading other women from coming forward. Hauke, while not looking at deaconesses in detail, adds further concerns. He felt that, historically, deaconesses were of a different order to deacons, the ordination rites were more akin to sacramentals than sacraments and there is no longer a role for deaconesses.[7] Müller declares firmly that deaconesses received non-sacramental consecrations and that, as the unity of the sacrament is an official doctrine of the Church, as is the male priesthood, women cannot receive the sacrament.

Historical evidence of various groups of women (widows, hermits etc) co-existing with deaconesses in the early Church suggests that Martimort's last concern is groundless. Hauke's last point is also contradicted by the current demand for a diaconal role for women.

If we assume that Martimort's 'ambiguities' correspond to the *From the Diakonia of Christ*'s worries about the position of deaconesses vis-à-vis male deacons and within the sacrament of ordination, we can reduce these various concerns to a few areas. The most complex from a theological point of view concerns the unity of the sacrament of ordination and whether or not this would be compromised by having both male and female deacons but only male priests. Then there is the historical question of whether or not the deaconesses of the early Church were really ordained or simply received a blessing. If they were not ordained then, would it be valid to ordain them now? There is also the more practical issues of how deaconesses would relate to deacons with regard to their place in the hierarchy and their role in parish life and what they would actually do that women do not already do.

The question of the unity of the sacrament is often raised. The Council of Trent fixed the sacraments at seven, with ordination as a unity. There is no possibility of adding in another sacrament to give women an official place in the hierarchy. However it seems to me that this is not such a great problem. Sacraments are occasions of communion with God and 'outward signs of inward grace' as the old penny catechism said or 'actions of the Holy Spirit at work in his body, the Church' as the Catechism of the Catholic Church puts it. They are therefore interconnected with each other and with the whole life of the Church. The sacraments of baptism, confirmation and the Eucharist are linked together as the 'sacraments of initiation' and we are not considered full members of the Church until we have received all three. Baptism is in a sense incomplete without confirmation, hence the Orthodox practice of administering them both at the same time, even to newborn babies. Baptism, confirmation and ordination cause an ontological change in the person. Marriage has two stages in canon law, the liturgical ceremony and the consummation. The absolution of the sacrament of reconciliation is normally given on a 'one-to-one' basis but can be given to a group in an emergency. Ordination already has three degrees, with the bishop receiving the 'fullness' of the sacrament and delegating it in different ways to priests and deacons. The last rites can be given under various conditions. Some sacraments can be administered by either bishop, priest or deacon, some only by the bishop or priest and others only by the bishop. The sacrament of baptism can be administered by an atheist or member of another faith in an emergency.

Given this wonderful provision for the communication of a life of grace to the body of Christ, it does not seem beyond the bounds of possibility to make some arrangement for changing the sacrament of ordination from having three degrees to having four or for deciding that the third degree is open to women but the other two are not, bearing in mind that it used to have seven degrees! The various offices of the Church that come within the sacrament of ordination has varied over the centuries, with sub-deacons, readers, lectors and acolytes sometimes being included and sometimes not. Women can now be temporary lectors and acolytes, posts which were part of the sacrament of ordination for centuries.

My preferred option would be for maintaining the three degrees and constructing a sound theological argument for admitting women to the diaconate but not the priesthood or episcopate. Why? Because we have argued elsewhere that men and women are 'equal but different'.[8] To place female deacons below male ones in the hierarchy (or above them, for that matter!) would be to contradict this principle and would be a cause of permanent friction.

This leaves us the task of identifying a suitable theological argument. In fact this too is not as difficult as opponents of change imply. We have already quoted 'From the Diakonia of Christ' on the essential difference between deacons and priests; one is ordained for service, the other for sacerdotal duties. These are two quite distinct ministries and it is not difficult to demonstrate that being appointed to one does not automatically give the right to progress to the other. The key factor is the nature of the authority of the bishop. What does having the fullness of the sacrament of ordination mean in practice? It means that the bishop has received the same apostolic authority or duty of oversight that Christ passed on to the twelve. As the priest cooperates in the episcopal office in a delegated way, he has a certain share in this authority. The deacon is the servant of the community and does not have a share in this apostolic authority (hence the realisation that the phrase *in persona Christi capitis* is inappropriate for deacons).[9] So, while the priest and deacon are both under the authority of the bishop, they stand in quite different relationships to him. The deacon assists the bishop in the discharge of his ministry of service to the community, the priest assists the bishop in his ministry of oversight of the community and in providing the sacraments.

One of the problems is that the diaconate is most commonly thought of as being the final stage in the training for the priesthood. There is insufficient distinction being made between the transitional and the permanent diaconate, so there is a perception that the permanent deacon is only a step away from being a priest. Indeed, it is possible that many permanent deacons see themselves in this light. There are several possible answers to this problem. We could simply wait and hope that the problem will go away once people become more used to permanent deacons. A more proactive solution would be to provide more education on the difference between the transitional and permanent diaconate and between deacons and priests. Another possibility is that, as the requirement for candidates to the priesthood to be ordained as deacons and to spend at least six months as deacons is laid down in canon law, not divine law, it could be changed. However this might cause as many problems as it would solve.

As the deacon is not representing Christ (or at least no more so than the laity), the arguments presented earlier regarding the necessity for masculine symbolism in the priest do not apply. Similarly, the arguments about masculine qualities and feminine qualities are simplified. As the deacon is a servant, not a ruler or leader in any authoritarian sense, the strictures of St Paul on the place of women are not a problem. Indeed, the role of deacon seems to be eminently suitable for people with the feminine qualities listed by John Paul II. If we turn back to the section 'St Paul' in chapter five and the work of Edmund Clowney, we will find that his conclusion that women could be deacons without contradicting the teachings of St Paul fit very well with this argument.

So we have shown that, as deacons serve rather than rule, there is no reason why they could not be female. As the bishop has the fullness of the sacrament of ordination, the unity of the sacrament resides in the bishop; he delegates certain powers associated with it but retains others for himself. The number of different offices to which he delegates does not affect the essential unity of the sacrament. The Tradition of the Church allows for varying offices within the sacrament and the number of delegated positions has varied from one to seven through the history of the Church. So admitting women to the diaconate would not threaten the unity of the sacrament.

This brings us to the second concern: were deaconesses of the early Church ordained? We have already suggested that this is one area where people will believe what they want to believe, almost irrespective of the evidence. The relevant evidence is the use of the word 'ordained', the liturgies used and the continuing practice of the Church. We have seen that the word originally simply denoted a change in status, civic or religious. It gradually developed a specifically religious meaning. If we compare ordination rites from the same era, we can see that the word had the same meaning in the rites for ordaining priests and deacons as it had in the rites for deaconesses. This suggests that everyone concerned regarded the deaconesses as just as ordained as the deacons. What are the criteria for a valid ordination? Again, we have seen that there has been considerable debate over this for many centuries. Indeed it was not until the laying on of hands was decreed by Pope Pius XII as the essential matter and the central petition as the form.[10] In chapter fourteen, we showed that ordination rites have always included at least three elements: the laying on of hands; a central petition; and conferring a sign of office. The surviving ordination rites for deaconesses include these three elements, with the sign of office usually being a stole, as it was for a deacon. The deacon usually also received a sign relating to his liturgical duties of reading the gospel and assisting with distributing Holy Communion. The deaconess did not receive these signs as she could not enter the sanctuary and therefore could not assist with the liturgy.

At this point, the 'anti-deaconess' group will argue that this difference in function is so fundamental that it means that the woman was not ordained at all but merely received a blessing for a specific function. The 'pro-deaconesses' group will argue that, as the three essential elements were there, any additional signs are irrelevant to the point, the rite was an ordination and it is clear from the liturgical texts that that is what the Church of the day intended. The practice of the Church varied for both men and women but deaconesses were included in lists of clergy. Ordination rites (and that is what they were called!) for deaconesses were in use for centuries. They could not enter the sanctuary but they participated in the liturgy by reciting the daily office, passing the sign of peace to the female section of the congregation and taking Communion to the sick. As women can now enter the sanctuary and participate more directly in the liturgy, even helping to distribute Holy Communion, it seems that, from a liturgical point of view, the early rites of ordination could be reintroduced and modified to be even closer to those for deacons than they were originally. The major point of difference between the two groups has already been removed.

People often point out that the deaconesses of the early Church had quite different roles from the deacons, implying, or simply stating, that this meant that they were not 'really' ordained in the way that deacons were. There are several counter arguments to this. Why does no one argue that, as deacons could not baptise females or visit women and children at home, they were limited in their functions and were not 'really' ordained? We only need to look around to see examples of men and women exercising the same office in different ways and most professional groups show a male/female bias: female lawyers are more likely to specialise in family law than male lawyers; female doctors are more likely to specialise in paediatrics than male doctors. This does not mean that female lawyers or doctors are any less members of their profession than their male colleagues. The priestly vocation also shows various ways of expressing itself. Priests can be parish priests, full-time academics, enclosed monks, army chaplains or various other possibilities—they are all equally ordained priests. It is not what they do that makes them priests but what they are. It is the same for deacons.

The idea of judging people by their nature and relationships rather than their job description is alien to our culture, where one's position in the social hierarchy is very much determined by one's occupation. We instinctively wonder what deaconesses actually did as compared to their male colleagues. This is perhaps to miss the point that their chief function was to bear witness to the gospel by devoting their whole lives to service of their communities through the Church. Looked at from this angle, deaconesses were just as ordained as deacons according to the meaning of the term at the time. For a valid diaconal ordination today, it would need to be possible to do so according to the meaning of the term as it is used today. With the restrictions on women entering the sanctuary already lifted, there is no reason why a rite of ordination could not be in place that would only need the occasional modification of replacing 'he' with 'she' to allow it to be used for either deacons or deaconesses.

We now need to turn to more speculative matters. How would deaconesses relate to deacons with regard to their place in the hierarchy and their role in parish life? The point about the hierarchy cannot be ignored. The Council of Trent confirmed that the Church was a hierarchical organisation and that this hierarchy existed even within the sacrament of ordination. The Council of Nicaea had confirmed that deacons came below priests in this hierarchy. However the superiority/inferiority of male and female deacons would have to be decided. First, a warning:

> Both sexes each in its own way, aspire to 'power', and use the most varied methods to gain it. Power is connected subterraneously with humanities' original sin and concupiscence and, naturally, also makes itself felt as a motive within the Church. It is by no means a prerogative of men.[11]

The most obvious solution is to maintain the constant practice of the Church and list deaconesses immediately after deacons. This, after all, conforms to the social norms of today, for example, we refer to 'Mr and Mrs' and telephone directories are listed according to the husband's initial. To maintain the nuptial imagery, it would be important to stress St Paul's teaching on the husband loving the wife as his own body. If the deacon and deaconess both have a truly Christian attitude to each other, then neither should mind what the official order is; indeed, they should be anxious to promote the other and not themselves.

Another possible system is to give each priority according to their date of ordination, regardless of their sex. The Rule of St Benedict uses this system for deciding the priority of the monks (although he did not have to worry about their sex!)

> Let all keep their place in the monastery established by the time of their entrance, the merit of their lives and the decision of the Abbot ... Except for those already mentioned, therefore, whom the Abbot has promoted by a special decision or demoted for definite reasons, all the rest shall take their order according to the time of their entrance.[12]

This does not seem to me to be a very attractive option, mainly because it falls into the trap of ignoring the masculine and feminine aspects of our nature instead of embracing them. It would also not solve the problem of impersonal lists. It could be used within individual parishes if there were several deacons and deaconesses.

It is within the individual parish that our Christianity is lived out and tested. The everyday roles of deacons and deaconesses would, normally, be lived out in the parish. Would we end up with unseemly manoeuvrings to be the one to 'do' the weddings or the baptisms or whatever? Would the deaconess always end up in the kitchen helping with the washing up while the deacon chatted to the important guests? It might be useful to find out what other churches that already have both male and female deacons do. It is also important to remember that both deacons and deaconesses are servants of the community and at the end of the day it is up to the bishop to decide who does what. Hopefully, he would allocate people according to their individual talents and they would accept his instructions in a spirit of obedience. All parties would have to work at getting the 'equal but different' balance right. I feel that it would be a mistake to try too hard to allocate the various tasks on a totally 'unisex' pattern: 'Because of her unique structures, the Catholic Church is perhaps humanity's last bulwark of genuine appreciation of the difference between the sexes'.[13] While it would be wrong to assume that all deaconesses would be able and willing to run the child-care facilities and all deacons would be happy to drive the mini-bus, it would be equally wrong to insist on each taking turns at both. Which brings us to the last consideration; what would deaconesses do that women do not already do?

Women can now exercise all ministries in the Church except that of ordained priests and bishops. For some ministries, this is for emergency use only; for others they can do so on a temporary basis only (although there is no limit on how long 'temporary' is!). While women can give a talk to groups and even when leading a Communion service, baptism or wedding, they cannot give the sermon during Mass. Canon Law distinguishes between preaching in general and the homily.

Can 766

> The laity may be allowed to preach in a church or oratory if in certain circumstances it is necessary, or in particular cases it would be advantageous, according to the provisions of the Episcopal Conference and without prejudice to Can 767§1. The most important form of preaching is the homily, which is part of the liturgy, and is reserved to a priest or deacon.[14]

The guidance for deacons is that they may give the homily but should only do so if there is a specific reason for the parish priest not doing so; it should not be the standard practice.

So those that argue that there is no practical need for deaconesses do have a valid point. However the same point could be made for deacons as they have very few functions that cannot be performed by the laity. Despite this, the Church decided that there was a need for a permanent diaconate. I think that the answer lies in the point made earlier about priests, it is not what they do that defines them but what they are.

> The testimony of our tradition does appear to affirm that what distinguished the ancient diaconate was not what the deacon did or did not do, it was his commitment to be sent in service of the needs of the Church as discerned by the one charged with apostolic oversight (the bishop).[15]

The argument that women do not need to have an official title, let alone be ordained, is no more valid than it is for men. Those sacraments that cause an ontological change in the recipient—baptism, confirmation, ordination, do so because they affect the person's relationship to the Church. Ordination marks a commitment to service, not just to the universal Church but also to the local bishop. This is perhaps even more marked in the deacon that in the priest and can be seen in the liturgy where the deacon stands at the side of the bishop, receives his blessing before reading the gospel and exercises his other functions in the name of the bishop. The symbolism of the deacon as a member of the clergy is important.

> One can recognise many different ministries in the Church today, but not all of them are participations in an 'apostolic office'. It is the deacon's explicit service to the pastoral oversight of the bishop and presbyter that justifies his share in the apostolic office.[16]

If women are to exercise a similar service to the bishop, they need a similar sign of their new ecclesial relationship.

There is also the point that some people find that they can function in an official role in a way that they would hesitate to do in a private capacity. We are all called to be good neighbours and to support our local church. There are many ways of doing this. The deacon is expected to set an example and to be a visible sign of God's love for all. There are some people who are happy to be the visible face of the Church but for the wrong reasons. There are others who would be much better representatives of Christian charity but who will not put themselves forward out of a sense of modesty and humility. This second group can be persuaded to take on official tasks if they are given a title, and perhaps even a uniform, to hide behind. They can put on the desired persona with the uniform and present themselves to the public as an office-holder, not a private individual. Many people in the uniformed services can witness to the psychological effect of putting on the uniform. Even school children have been shown to behave better if they are wearing a school uniform. For deacons, the uniform may be no more than a dog-collar and a name badge but this could be enough to allow people to come forward who would otherwise not consider doing so. For many, it is easier to knock on a door and introduce yourself as the representative of the local church than to knock on the same door and introduce yourself as the neighbour down the road (interfering? nosy? critical?).

Being an official representative also has the advantage that it tells the other parties that you have been approved, and perhaps trained, for your role. They are more likely to accept that you have the right and ability to do whatever the task in hand is, not to mention the duty to act in a professional manner. This can overcome many barriers.

So, having deaconesses would bring a new type of person into active service for the Church. It would provide a balance between male and female that does not exist at the moment. People will argue that women do have a powerful position in the Church. They will claim that the average parish is really run by women: attendance at Mass, especially midweek Mass, is dominated by women; the parish council will probably have a majority of women; catechesis of the children is almost always done by women; not to mention church cleaning and flower arranging! However this work, no matter how valuable, is different to that of an ordained servant who has made a public, permanent commitment. Much of it is also invisible, with the result that the Church is seen as a male-dominated organisation.

One novel idea for giving women a more powerful voice in the Church is to allow them to be cardinals.[17] There would actually be fewer theological problems with this than with ordaining them as deaconesses. The position of cardinal was created to meet the need for the pope to have easy access to reliable advice on a variety of topics. These advisers were originally laymen. In order to cut out corruption and nepotism, it became the rule that they had to be ordained. For similar reasons, the various Vatican councils and commissions have to have an ordained cardinal at their head. The unforeseen effect of this is that it prevents women from taking up positions that they would otherwise be well qualified for. I believe that the most senior woman at the Vatican at the moment is Sister Enrico Rosanna, the under-secretary (no. 3 in the hierarchy) for the Congregation for Institutes of Consecrated Life and Societies of Apostolic Life. She was appointed in 2004 and was (and still is) the only woman to reach this level in the Curia.[18] The only reason that she is not number one in the Congregation is that that post must be held by a cardinal. Simply removing the rule that such posts must be held by an ordained cardinal would solve the problem and would mean that the current rules on electing a pope would not have to be changed. Even the most ardent feminist would presumably not expect the pope to be elected by anyone other than his fellow bishops. On the other hand, having a senior body of laymen and women advising the pope would improve the public image of the Church (is this important?) and would strengthen the 'equal but different' argument.

A note of caution: we need to remember Edmund Clowney's argument, based on St Paul, that women can take part in numerous activities as long as these do not include ruling over men. Any posts that involve exercising apostolic authority are not open to women, but where do you draw the line? Perhaps the system does need a bishop with the 'casting vote' in each Congregation so that it is clear that the teachings of the Church are determined by those with apostolic authority. However, if we accept the idea of Hauke that the restrictions on the roles of women in the early Church was to prevent them encroaching on the functions of the 'presiding elder', we can perhaps be a bit more relaxed about their functions in the modern Church. The early Church did not have the clearly defined hierarchy of bishop, priest and deacon that exists in the modern Church. So it is easier for the modern Church to define those functions that are reserved to men and those that could be exercised by either men or women. What is lacking is clear teaching on why some functions are reserved to men and then acceptance of this teaching by both men and women.

Summary

We have wandered rather far from our original four areas of concern. To return to them, I feel that it is reasonable to conclude that, while those who are instinctively against the idea of deaconesses may not be convinced, it is possible to answer all four concerns. The threat to the unity of the sacrament of ordination is lifted if we remember that the fullness of the sacrament is found in the bishop and that the deacon does not have a share in the episcopal duty of oversight. It seems that the deaconesses of the early Church were just as ordained as their male counterparts and 'what the Church has done before, she can do again'.[19] While the relationship between male and female deacons would need to be considered, this exercise would provide a wonderful opportunity for both groups to practise their duty of obedience to the bishop and Christian charity towards each other, just as priests and deacons have to do now. The point that women can already take part in all activities that we think of as diaconal is answered in the same way as it is for deacons, it is not so much what they do that is important as what they are.

We certainly have not come up against an argument for which there is no reply. However, much of this section is subjective. We need to turn to our second analytical tool, Newman's notes, and see where that takes us.

Newman's Notes

We have already listed Cardinal Newman's seven criteria for determining whether or not a change in doctrine was acceptable. In order to apply them, we need a one-sentence hypothesis to test. 'Women could be ordained to the diaconate without contradicting Scripture, Tradition or the Magisterium' is not exactly imaginative but it is clear and unambiguous, so that is what we shall test.

Preservation of Idea

This note concerns the essential elements of a doctrine. These have to be constant, although the superficial details surrounding them can change. So we need to identify the essential elements of Scripture, Tradition and the Magisterium regarding our hypothesis and then analyse whether or not our proposed change would contradict any of them. Even one contradiction would be enough to disprove our hypothesis.

The essential elements of Scripture are the practice of Jesus in only appointing male apostles and the teachings of St Paul on the role of women. We have shown that the apostles are the foundation of the episcopal college. As the deacons are not part of this college, their composition is not determined by Jesus's appointment of the twelve. We have also shown that the teachings of St Paul prohibit women from taking up a position of apostolic authority in the Church. As deacons do not have a share in this authority, they are not limited by this teaching.

The essential element of Tradition is the historical evidence for the existence of deaconesses in the early Church. As St Paul gives Phoebe the title of deaconess and even people in the 'anti-deaconess' camp such as Martimort admit that they did exist, we can allow this essential element to exist.

The essential element of the Magisterium is the existence of official documents of the Church confirming the ordination of women as deaconesses in the past and the acknowledgement that reintroducing them would not be in breach of current teaching. We have shown that, while one can argue backwards and forwards over the status of the rites used, liturgies were in use for centuries that were named as ordination rites for deaconesses. The most important Church document of recent times on the role of women in the Church is *Inter Insigniores*.[20] This document gives a more detailed analyses of Church teaching than the letter by Pope Paul VI to the Archbishop of Canterbury reminding him that the Catholic Church 'holds that it is not admissible to ordain women to the priesthood, for very fundamental reasons'.[21] Both documents, and the confirmation of their teaching by Pope John Paul II, *Ordinatio Sacerdotalis*, carefully use the phrase 'priestly ordination'. They do not address the question of diaconal ordination. The main document addressing the diaconate specifically is 'From the Diakonia of Christ', which leaves the question of women deacons open for debate: 'In the light of these elements which have been set out in the present historico-theological research document, it pertains to the ministry of discernment which the Lord established in his Church to pronounce authoritatively on this question.'[22]

So our hypothesis passes the first note by not contradicting the essential elements of Scripture, Tradition and the Magisterium on the subject.

Continuity of Principles

This note is met if the basic principles of Christianity, as summarised in the Beatitudes, are retained. The Beatitudes (shortened) are as follows:

> Blessed are the poor in spirit; blessed are the gentle; blessed are those who mourn; blessed are those who hunger and thirst for uprightness; blessed are the merciful; blessed are the pure in heart; blessed are the peacemakers; blessed are those who are persecuted in the cause of uprightness. (Taken from Mt 5:3–10.)

The theme of Matthew's beatitudes is entry into the kingdom.[23] Luke lists four blessings based on life on earth and four maledictions based on future punishment:

> blessed are the poor, the hungry, the sad and the persecuted; alas for the rich, those who have plenty to eat, those who are laughing and those who are praised. (Taken from Lk 6:20–26.)

As a fundamental aspect of the diaconate, masculine or feminine, is service to others and being the visible face of the Church's charitable works, it is difficult to think of a way in which they could threaten either the letter or the principle of the Beatitudes. Scripture, Tradition and the Magisterium have always given a consistently uniform message on the meaning of the Beatitudes. Men and women are equally called to live out the Beatitudes, whether lay, religious or ordained. So our hypothesis passes the second note by retaining the principles summarised in the Beatitudes.

Power of Assimilation

This note is met if the principle is strong enough to retain its identity despite absorbing some new ideas, rejecting others and even making the occasional mistake.

The general principle of the ordination of women deacons has a sufficiently strong identity to have survived several upheavals.

New ideas that have been absorbed could include the religious orders, who took over many of the diaconal functions of the early Church; while they are no longer so dominant, they have shown many ways in which women can contribute to society. Just as they replaced deaconesses, the reverse could now happen. The post-Vatican II lifting of restrictions on women entering the sanctuary and distributing Holy Communion is an innovation that could ease the reintroduction of female deacons. The main idea that has been rejected whenever it appeared through history is extending the role to include the priesthood. The most obvious item under 'occasional mistakes' is the negative attitude to women of the eleventh and twelfth centuries, as discussed in chapter ten. The Church has admitted that some of the views expressed during this period were wrong. The long period without women deacons is due as much to societal attitudes to women as to the teaching of the Magisterium.

So our hypothesis passes this test as the role of deaconess, as practised in the early Church, can be envisioned as fitting in to today's Church, with suitable modifications.

Early Anticipation

This note is met if the mature idea is anticipated in the early stages of its development.

As the idea of deaconesses is still developing, it is difficult to define the mature idea. Even the role of permanent deacons is still evolving. However, if we assume that deaconesses would work in similar areas to deacons, we can see that this is very similar to what we know of the life of deaconesses in the early Church. While they are no longer needed to assist at baptisms of total immersion, they would still be involved in baptisms; indeed they could now have a greater role as they would then be the chief celebrant. In some cultures, they would no longer be needed to bring the good news to women who were not allowed to mix with men. However this could well be a role in other cultures and, with Islam spreading into Europe, could become an important role here also. They could also teach in schools, universities and seminaries, represent the Church on ecumenical committees and be part of the decision-making process,[24] all functions not available in the early Church.

They could now play a much greater role in the liturgy than they did in the early Church.

We can see that a modern deaconess would in fact be involved in the same general areas as in the past but could now perform these functions at a deeper level. So our hypothesis passes this note.

Logical Sequence

This note is met if there is continuity in development and a natural progression from the original idea to its fruits.

It would be difficult to present a case for continuity of development for a position in the Church that died out in the eleventh century and has only been considered for reintroduction in the last fifty years or so! However there is a consistent pattern of the Church encouraging the involvement of women. As mentioned in chapters four and five, the early Church was seen as a liberating force for women. Even in the middle ages, when it was sidetracked by the teachings of Aristotle and Aquinas, women could have considerable influence, just think of Hildegard of Bingen, Catherine of Siena, Teresa of Avila. During this time, abbesses wielded considerable power and influence. In the previous note, we showed that there was a natural progression in the duties performed by women in the Church, which would be enhanced if they could be ordained as deaconesses. Indeed, it can be argued that the 'blip' in the position of women in the Church was not caused by the Magisterium but by the Reformation. The Reformed churches placed far more restrictions on the activities of women than the Roman Catholic Church has ever done and this was reflected in the laws of the states of Europe, for example, not allowing female university students. Until surprisingly recently, the only way in which a woman could receive a university-level education was by becoming a nun.

So, while the history of women's involvement in the official life of the Church has had its 'stops and starts', it has always moved in the same direction and followed a logical sequence of stages. Our hypothesis has therefore passed this note.

Preservative Additions

This note is met if new ideas are assimilated in such a way that they enhance the original concept, not distort or limit it.

Again, we can see from what has been said under the previous notes that, with the exception of the Aristotelian developments, which the Church has admitted were mistaken, the concept of women's service in the Church has been enriched by modern approaches to the role of women in the life of the Church. In the early Church, women could prophecy during services and deaconesses could assist at baptisms and take Holy Communion to the sick. Today, they can enter the sanctuary during services, allowing then to be readers and distribute Holy Communion at Mass, conduct Communion services, preach (outside Mass), and generally do whatever is necessary without threatening the male priestly role. In the early Church women passed on the faith to their own families (see 2 Tm 1:5) and the order of widows provided charitable help. These roles have gradually expanded. Today female catechists and teachers, lay and religious, pass on the faith to many and varied groups of children and adults worldwide. They can take on a wide variety of public roles, paid and voluntary, at home and abroad, that provide charitable help. These developments would be further enhanced if they were given the formal recognition of belonging to the role of deaconess. This might also encourage more women to serve the Church.

The original idea of what a deaconess could do has been broadened by modern attitudes towards women in the sanctuary and participating in public life in general. The overall role could be reintroduced without any new limits but with many extensions of the original duties. So the hypothesis passes this note.

Chronic Continuance

This note is met if we can show that faithful developments have endured through time, corruptions have tended towards violence and dissolution.

As so often, it is easier to look at the negatives than the positives! So it is easier to look at the corruptions than the faithful developments. The most obvious corruption is the introduction of women priests. In the pre-Reformation Church, the few examples on record were quickly suppressed and, in the long term, did little damage. However, in modern times, we are seeing some post-Reformation churches being torn apart by disputes about female priests and bishops. Others are avoiding damaging disputes by simply avoiding formal definitions of their teaching. Others again are breaking up into smaller and smaller sects as more and more differences surface. Even from within the Catholic Church, there are breakaway groups who practise 'ordinations' of women. Other groups, while remaining members of the Church, campaign for women priests. Both groups cause considerable damage to the Church. The other main corruption is the Aristotelian view of women, already covered. We must not forget that the most persistent corruption is that caused by Original Sin. As modern feminists have pointed out, throughout history, women have had to battle against the male instinct to 'keep them in their place'.

What faithful developments could we mention? Perhaps one would be the advances in biblical hermeneutics. This has allowed a greater understanding of Scripture, particularly in the understanding of the sociocultural influences on the authors. It has given us reliable translations which are acceptable to most denominations, thus encouraging ecumenical movements. This in turn has aided the debate on what women can and cannot do in the Church and allowed the Magisterium to present a more nuanced approach to the role of women. In this work, we have made use of the work of Edmund Clowney's interpretation of the teachings of St Paul despite his being from a different tradition. We have already discussed the faithful development in the official duties that women can perform. If we allow for the Aristotelian and Reformation corruptions, we can see a logical development from Phoebe and Lydia to modern women running parishes, training priests and advising Vatican commissions. Another possible faithful development is in the theology of ontological change. We demonstrated in chapter three that this principle goes back to the New Testament and Jesus giving Simon a new name. The whole debate, including the idea of relationality, has enriched our perception of what a priest is and therefore in what ways he differs from a deacon. This in turn has allowed us to present an argument for allowing female deacons without jeopardising the teaching on male priests.

The official role of women in the Church has developed from that of Phoebe to the early deaconesses, to modern parishes where women can take on all duties except those reserved to the clergy. Developments in the theology of the priesthood, stimulated by the debate on the role of women in the Church, have allowed a clearer understanding of the relationship between bishop, priest and deacon and have shown that it is possible to have deaconesses without threatening the male priesthood. Corruptions, principally women priests, have led to schism.

So we can say that corruptions of our hypothesis have led to dissension and division, developments have enriched our understanding and therefore our hypothesis has passed the seventh of Newman's notes.

A modern system of evaluating ideas, designed for examining models of the Church, gives us another set of criteria to measure our hypothesis against.

> In any effort at evaluation we must beware of the tendency of each contestant to polemicize from a standpoint within his own preferred position. To make any real progress we must seek criteria that are acceptable to adherents of a number of different models.[25]

Dulles lists seven criteria:

1. Basis in Scripture.

2. Basis in Christian tradition.

3. Capacity to give Church members a sense of their corporate identity and mission.

4. Tendency to foster the virtues and values generally admired by Christians.

5. Correspondence with the religious experience of people today.

6. Theological fruitfulness.

7. Fruitfulness in enabling Church members to relate successfully to those outside their own group.

I will leave it up to the reader to decide whether or not our hypothesis passes this test also!

Summary

We have now examined all of Newman's notes in relation to our hypothesis that 'Women could be ordained to the diaconate without contradicting Scripture, Tradition or the Magisterium'. We have found that, at the very least, our hypothesis does not contradict any of the notes. While it fits some of them better than others, it passes the test in each case. Unless I have become too biased to present a balanced argument, the hypothesis has been proved as a valid progression of doctrine.

We have listed, but not analysed, the criteria suggested by Avery Dulles as useful for giving an unbiased conclusion.

The only other test that we have mentioned which we could apply to this work is that mentioned in our summary of Cardinal Ratzinger's work *The Nature and Mission of Theology*. I repeat it here for convenience:

> We can judge the work of an individual theologian by looking at its place in the living Tradition of the Church—is it true to Scripture, the teachings of the Early Fathers and the Magisterium? We can also look at the lives of the theologians themselves—are they obedient to the Church or do they place themselves above it?

This test has guided my choice of source materials in that I have avoided those theologians who have refused to remain obedient to the Church's teachings.

Notes

1   For example, being 'partners' in marriage rather than subject to their husbands; acting as advisors on commissions and juridical panels, acting as Extraordinary Ministers of the Eucharist.
2   DCDA, p. 99.
3   *Ibid.*, p. 99 f. 334. This restriction has now been formalised in canon law following the Motu Proprio *Omnium in Mentem*. See note 119 of the chapter 'The Magisterium: The Sacrament of Ordination'.
4   See Appendix III for more quotes from DCDA and comments on it.
5   DCDA, p. 100.

6   *Ibid.*, p. 100.

7   Sacramentals are sacred signs that render various occasions in life holy and predispose us to receive the grace of the sacraments (see CCC §1667–1673).

8   See the sections on Edith Stein and Pope John Paul II in chapter eight 'Tradition: The Church; Reserved to Men Alone'.

9   See notes on the Motu Proprio *Omnium in Mentem* in chapter twelve 'Magisterium: General Notes; Authoritative Teaching'.

10 See chapter fourteen 'Magisterium: Ordination; Sacrament'.

11 H. U. von Balthasar, 'Women Priests?' in *New Elucidations,* translated by M. Skerry (San Francisco: Ignatius Press, 1979), p. 197.

12 St Benedict, *A Rule for Monasteries* translated by L. Doyle (Collegeville: The Liturgical Press, 1948), chapter 63.

13 H. U. von Balthasar, 'Women Priests?' in *New Elucidations,* p. 195.

14 CIC 1983, can 767.1.

15 R. Gaillardetz, 'On the Theological Integrity of the Diaconate' in Cummings et al *Theology of the Diaconate: The State of the Question* (New York: Paulist Press, 2005), p. 89.

16 *Ibid.*, p. 89.

17 The person who proposed this to me would probably prefer to remain anonymous!

18 Another senior post is held by Sister Mary Ann Gleson, the president of the Pontifical Council for Social Policy. Also, the previous US ambassador to the Holy See was a woman. Outwith the Vatican, the posts of secretary general of the bishop's conference in New Zealand and South Africa are held by women (from an article 'Nun is Named Secretary General' in the Catholic Herald of 23 December 2011, p.4 col 7).

19 It can be argued that this is not a valid argument, after all the Church used to do many things that it no longer does. It certainly does not mean that past practices can be reintroduced without any new authorisation. However it does mean that the practice is not against Scripture, Tradition or any fundamental teaching of the Church.

20 Sacred Congregation for the Doctrine if the Faith, Declaration on the Admission of Women to the Ministerial Priesthood *Inter Insigniores* (1976).

21 Pope Paul VI, 'Response to the Letter of His Grace the Most Reverend Dr F.D. Coggan, Archbishop of Canterbury, concerning the ordination of Women to the Priesthood', as quoted in S. Butler, *The Catholic Priesthood and Women: A Guide to the Teaching of the Church,* p. 5.

22 DCDA, p. 100.

23 See NJB, Mt 5:1–10 footnote 5d.

24 Roles already undertaken by lay women.

25 A. Dulles, *Models of the Church: A Critical Assessment of the Church in all its Aspects* (Dublin: Gill and MacMillan, 1976), p. 180.

24 CONCLUSION

WE STARTED THIS part by summarising the views of Cardinal Ratzinger and Cardinal Newman on how to identify valid progression of doctrine. We then looked at the opinions of four theologians who are regarded as the leading opponents of the ordination of women (Martimort, Hauke, Muller and Butler). From their work and the previous parts on Scripture, Tradition and the Magisterium, we concluded that a case for women priests could not be made but a case for women deacons could be presented without contradicting any fundamental principles of the Church.

Women cannot be priests because ordination is a sacrament and sacraments are based on the actions of Jesus Christ. Jesus chose only male apostles and they chose only male successors. As we do not know the reasons for Jesus's choice, we must simply accept that this is what he decided; we cannot assume that it was governed by sociocultural considerations or any other possible reason without a Scriptural base for this. The conclusion that women cannot be priests is part of the constant practice and teaching of the Church.

We further distilled out four areas of concern regarding deaconesses mentioned by these four theologians and by the International Theological Commission in its document 'From the Diakonia of Christ'. Basing our remarks almost entirely on information and opinions gathered during the course of this work, we concluded that all four areas could be satisfactorily answered. Firstly, the unity of the sacrament is not threatened as it resides in the bishop; Scripture gives him the authority to delegate as necessary and Tradition allows for several grades within the sacrament. Secondly, the deacon does not share in the episcopal duty of governance, the priest does. So the diaconate and the presbyterate are quite separate roles. The deacon does not act *in persona Christi capitis* and therefore does not have to be male. Thirdly, the deaconesses of the early Church were ordained according to the meaning of the word at the time and therefore can be so again. Finally, the relationship between male and female deacons can be worked out in a spirit of obedience to the bishop. Their specific duties are not important; as with priests, it is what they are, not what they do that is significant for the life of the Church.

We then examined the hypothesis that 'Women could be ordained to the diaconate without contradicting Scripture, Tradition or the Magisterium' using Cardinal Newman's seven 'notes' as described in his essay on the development of doctrine. We concluded that the hypothesis did not contradict any of the notes and was therefore a valid progression of doctrine.

We conclude that women could be deacons because deacons do not have a share in the apostolic task of governance and therefore exercise a different ministry from bishops and priests. Taking this step would not contradict Scripture, Tradition or the Magisterium or threaten the unity of the sacrament of ordination. It would not even be an innovation as it has been the practice of the Church in the past.

For anyone wanting to investigate the background to my conclusions, the key arguments are to be found in five works. Sarah Butler in *The Catholic Priesthood and Women* gives a clear statement of the Church's teaching against women priests and for the use of Newman's notes. An article by Richard R. Gaillardetz, 'On the Theological Integrity of the Diaconate', in *Theology of the Diaconate: The State of the Question* gives a useful exposition of the difference between priests and deacons with reference to apostolic authority. A rather surprising, but very useful, source was the book by Edmund Clowney, *The Church*, which demonstrated that the case can be made for women deacons without going through any literary hoops with the writings of St Paul. Then the analysis of the role of women in the Church of the middle ages depended on the work of Joan Morris in *Against Nature and God* and Gary Macy in *The Hidden History of Women's Ordination: Female Clergy in the Medieval West*.

Another key text is the phrase 'fullness of the sacrament', given magisterial approval in the Vatican II document *Lumen Gentium*, with regard to episcopal ordination. The principle behind this phrase allowed us to conclude that the unity of the sacrament of ordination would not be threatened by having women deacons.

Scripture must always be our primary source. In the previous chapters, we have shown that there are some surprising links on the topic of the role of women: Matthew and John emphasise the role of women as 'facilitators' for the men in their lives; Luke and John portray women as apostles whose theological understanding is equal to, if not greater than, the male apostles. They all exclude women from the Last Supper and from the bestowal of the power to loose and to bind. Paul, whose teaching on women has been much misunderstood over the centuries, is happy for women to exercise a diaconal role, including prophesying and teaching, as long as they do not encroach on the duties of the 'presiding elder'.

We began this work by looking at the practical reasons for reintroducing deaconesses. We argued that deaconesses would help the Church to fulfil her dual role of spreading the gospel and growing in holiness. We have now demonstrated that this step would not contradict the teachings of Scripture, Tradition or the Magisterium. There is therefore no theological reason why the College of Bishops, with the pope at its head, could not authorise this development.

It only remains for me to remind my readers of the message of the Reformation that revolution does not hasten reform but more often delays it. Change cannot be forced on the Church from outside and strident protests are almost always counter-productive. If this step is needed for the welfare of the Church, then the Holy Spirit is perfectly capable of ensuring that it will happen. He may work through us but we need to leave Him to do so in His own time!

It seems fitting to end with a warning from St Paul 'I urge you, brothers, be on your guard against the people who are out to stir up disagreements and bring up difficulties against the teaching which you learnt. Avoid them' (Rm 16:17).

BISHOPS' CONFERENCE OF SCOTLAND

Briefing paper no 9, 'Women Priests'

☩ Christ did not call any women as his apostles—the first Bishops of the Church. Yet Jesus was no respecter of social convention. He associated with tax collectors and prostitutes. He ate on the Sabbath. He publicly disagreed with the Pharisees. Is it therefore credible to believe that Christ didn't call women to be his apostles only because of the social conventions of the time, especially when most of the other religions of that time had priestesses themselves?

☩ From earliest times the Church has held this to be true. All the early Fathers of the Church confirm this. Writing in AD 215 Hippolytus wrote; 'When a widow is to be appointed, she is not to be ordained, but is designated by being named a widow ... Hands are not to be imposed on her, because she does not offer the oblation and she does not conduct the liturgy.' Similarly the Council of Laodicaea in AD 360 clearly stated that 'The so called 'presbyteresses' or 'presidentesses' are not to be ordained'.

☩ For 2000 years the Church has consistently taught that women are equal to men but simply have a different role to perform. The founder of the Catholic Church, Jesus Christ, had many female disciples such as Mary Magdalen. It was women like her who stayed close to him at the foot of the cross while most of the apostles fled.

☩ Throughout its history women have found the Church to be a constant defender and promoter of their dignity. The highest place of honour in the Church belongs to a woman, Our Lady—the Mother of the Church.

☩ In 1994 Pope John Paul II in *Ordinatio Sacerdotalis* restated that this teaching is not just a matter of discipline, neither is it a matter open to debate, when he stated 'I declare that the

Church has no authority whatsoever to confer priestly ordination on women and that this judgement is to be definitively held by all the Church's faithful.' This has been the teaching of the Church for 2000 years.

The first point is the 'sociocultural' one discussed in the introduction and in the section on the work of Sarah Butler. The point about priestesses has not been mentioned elsewhere but is of doubtful value as some of these priestesses were in fact little more than temple prostitutes.

The second point about widows fails to point out that widows and deaconesses were two separate groups, in existence from the time of the first letter to Timothy (for deaconesses, see 1 Tm 3:11 and for widows, 1 Tm 5:9). Widows were not ordained but deaconesses were, as discussed in detail in chapter fourteen.

The third point ignores several centuries of statements from senior figures in the Church on the inferiority of women, not to mention canon law which was not entirely 'equal but different' until the 1983 revision.

The fourth point is almost true but ignores some very dubious statements on the rights of a husband over his wife and on the position of pregnant or menstruating women or those in the few weeks after childbirth. However modern statements on issues of justice and peace do promote the dignity of women.

The last point is undoubtedly true and has been discussed elsewhere.[1]

Notes

[1]   See the introduction and chapter 20.

APPENDIX II

Section A) referring to Part I Chapter 3

Scriptural References to the Priesthood of the Laity

Matthew 10:17
Be prepared for people to hand you over to sanhedrins and scourge you in their synagogues.

Matthew 16:24
If anyone wants to be a follower of mine, let him renounce himself and take up his cross and follow me.

Romans 12:1
I urge you, then, brothers, remembering the mercies of God, to offer your bodies as a living sacrifice, dedicated and acceptable to God; that is the kind of worship for you.

1 Corinthians 3:16–17
Do you not realise that you are a temple of God with the Spirit of God living in you? If anyone should destroy the temple of God, God will destroy that person, because God's temple is holy, and you are that temple.

1 Corinthians 6:19–20
Do you not realise that your body is the temple of the Holy Spirit, who is in you and whom you received from God? You are not your own property, then; you have been bought at a price. So use your body for the glory of God.

2 Corinthians 1:21–22
It is God who gives us, with you, a sure place in Christ and has both anointed us and marked us with his seal, giving us as pledge the Spirit in our hearts.

Ephesians 1:13–14
Now you too, in him, have heard the message of the truth and the gospel of your salvation, and have put your trust in it. You have been stamped with the seal of the Holy Spirit of the Promise.

Ephesians 4:30
Do not grieve the Holy Spirit of God who has marked you with his seal, ready for the day when we shall be set free.

Philippians 2:17
Indeed, even if my blood has to be poured as a libation over your sacrifice and the offering of your faith, then I shall be glad and join in your rejoicing.

Philippians 4:18
I am fully provided, now that I have received from Epaphroditus the offering that you sent, a pleasing smell, the sacrifice which is acceptable and pleasing to God.

Hebrews 13:15
Through him, let us offer God an unending sacrifice of praise, the fruit of the lips of those who acknowledge his name. Keep doing good works and sharing your resources, for these are the kinds of sacrifice that please God.

James 1:26–27
Nobody who fails to keep a tight rein on the tongue can claim to be religious; this is mere self-deception; that person's religion is worthless. Pure, unspoilt religion in the eyes of God our Father, is this: coming to the help of orphans and widows in their hardships, and keeping oneself uncontaminated by the world.

1 Peter 2: 5, 9
So that you, too, may be living stones making a spiritual house as a holy priesthood to offer the spiritual sacrifices made acceptable to God through Jesus Christ ... But you are a chosen race, a kingdom of priests, a holy nation, a people to be a personal possession to sing the praises of God.

Revelation 1:5–6
He loves us and has washed away our sins with his blood, and made us a Kingdom of Priests to serve his God and Father.

Revelation 5:9–10
And with your blood, you bought people for God of every race, language, people and nation and made them a line of kings and priests for God, to rule the world.

Revelation 20:6

Blessed and holy are those who share in the first resurrection; the second death has no power over them but they will be priests of God and of Christ and reign with him for a thousand years.

Section B) referring to Part I Chapter 5

St Paul and the Role of Women

Romans 16:1
I commend you to our sister Phoebe, a deaconess of the Church at Cenchreae; give her, in the Lord, a welcome worthy of God's holy people and help her with whatever she needs from you—she herself has come to the help of many people, including myself.

1 Corinthians 7:16
As a wife, how can you tell whether you are to be the salvation of your husband?

1 Corinthians 11:3–16
But I should like you to understand that the head of every man is Christ, the head of woman is man, and the head of Christ is God. For any man to pray or to prophecy with his head covered shows disrespect for his head. And for a woman to pray or prophecy with her head uncovered shows disrespect for her head; it is exactly the same as if she had her hair shaved off. Indeed, if a woman does go without a veil, she should have her hair cut off too; but if it is a shameful thing for a woman to have her hair cut off or shaved off, then she should wear a veil.

But for a man it is not right to have his head covered, since he is the image of God and reflects God's glory; but woman is the reflection of man's glory. For man did not come from woman; no, woman came from man; nor was man created for the sake of woman, but woman for the sake of man: and this is why it is right for a woman to wear on her head a sign of the authority over her, because of the angels. However, in the Lord, though woman is nothing without man, man is nothing without woman; and though woman came from man, so does every man come from a woman, and everything comes from God.

Decide for yourselves: does it seem fitting that a woman should pray to God without a veil? Does not nature itself teach you that if a man has long hair, it is a disgrace to him, but when a woman has long hair, it is her glory? After all, her hair was given to her to be a covering.

If anyone wants to be contentious, I say that we have no such custom, nor do any of the churches of God.

1 Corinthians 11:5

And for a woman to pray or prophecy with her head uncovered shows disrespect for her head; it is exactly the same as if she had her hair shaved off.

1 Corinthians 11: 11–12

However, in the Lord, though woman is nothing without man, man is nothing without woman; and though woman came from man, so does every man come from a woman, and everything from God.

1 Corinthians 14: 26, 31–33

Then what should it be like, brothers? When you come together each of you brings a psalm or some instruction or a revelation, or speaks in a tongue or gives an interpretation ... You can all prophecy, but one at a time, then all will learn something and all receive encouragement. The prophetic spirit is to be under the prophets' control, for God is a God not of disorder but of peace.

1 Corinthians 14: 34–35

As in all the churches of God's holy people, women are to remain quiet in the assemblies, since they have no permission to speak: theirs is a subordinate part, as the Law itself says. If there is anything that they want to know, they should ask their husbands at home: it is shameful for a woman to speak in the assembly.

2 Corinthians 11:3

But I am afraid that, just as the snake with his cunning seduced Eve, your minds may be led astray from single-minded devotion to Christ.

Galatians 3:25–29

For all of you are the children of God, through faith, in Christ Jesus, since every one of you that has been baptised has been clothed in Christ. There can be neither Jew nor Greek, there can be neither slave not freeman, there can be neither male nor female—for you are all one in Christ Jesus.

Ephesians 5:21–29, 33 (cf. Gn 2:23–24)

Be subject to one another out of reverence for Christ. Wives should be subject to their husbands as to the Lord, since, as Christ is head of the Church and saves the whole body, so is a husband the head of his wife; and as the Church is subject to Christ, so should wives be to their husbands, in everything. Husbands should love their wives, just as Christ loved the Church and sacrificed himself for her to make her holy by washing her in cleansing water with a form of words, so that when he took the Church to himself she would be glorious, with no speck or wrinkle or anything like that, but holy and faultless. In the same way, husbands must love their wives as they love their own bodies; for a man to love his wife is for him to love himself. A man never hates his own body, but he feeds it and looks after it; and that is the way Christ treats the Church ... To sum up: you also, each one of you, must love his wife as he loves himself; and let every wife respect her husband.

Philippians 4:2–3

I urge Euodia, and I urge Syntyche to come to agreement with each other in the Lord; and I ask you, Syzgus, really to be a 'partner' and help them. These women have struggled hard for the gospel with me, along with Clement and all my other fellow-workers, whose names are written in the book of life.

Colossians 3:18–20

Wives, be subject to your husbands, as you should in the Lord. Husbands, love your wives and do not be sharp with them. Children be obedient to your parents always, because that is what will please the Lord.

1 Timothy 2: 9–15

Similarly, women are to wear suitable clothes and to be dressed quietly and modestly, without braided hair or gold and jewellery or expensive clothes; their adornment is to do the good works that are proper for women who claim to be religious. During instruction, a woman should be quiet and respectful. I give no permission for a woman to teach or to have authority over a man. A woman ought to be quiet, because Adam was formed first and Eve afterwards, and it was not Adam who was led astray but the woman who was led astray and fell into sin. Nevertheless, she will be saved by child-bearing, provided she lives a sensible life and is constant in faith and love and holiness.

2 Timothy 1:5
I also remember your sincere faith, a faith which first dwelt in your grandmother Lois, and your mother Eunice, and I am sure dwells also in you.

Section C) referring to Part II Chapter 8

Comparing the First Family with the Holy Family

Adam and Eve
Adam welcomes his helpmate with joy,
He does not try to protect her from the devil, instead he follows her lead,
He tries to blame her for their sin,
Eve speaks with the devil and accepts his statement without question,
She disobeys the one commandment,
She encourages Adam to do the same.

Joseph and Mary
Joseph and Mary seem to be planning a virginal marriage,
He is not willing to accept her as his wife if she has sinned but avoids making this sin public,
He obeys the angel in silence,
He protects her from her scandalous position at home and from Herod,
Mary questions the angel and tries to understand his words,
She obeys the will of God,
She lives under Joseph's protection (see Mt 2:11–15; 19–23),
She gives Joseph his place as Jesus's father (see Lk 2:48),

Adam and Eve ignore God's will; Joseph and Mary do God's will,
Adam and Eve do wrong and bring death into the world; Joseph and Mary do right and bring life into the world,
Adam and Eve damage each other; Joseph and Mary respect each other.

Summary

Without stretching the analogy further than the text warrants, we can see that Adam is all bluster. He fails in his duty to protect Eve from harm and then tries to lay the blame on her when things go wrong. Joseph is the strong, silent type. We do not hear of any words of Joseph's. He behaves throughout with honour and dignity. He accepts responsibility for his wife and her child, even including exile in Egypt. When danger threatens, he acts immediately and decisively.

Lesson?

That the traditional pattern of the male as leader, protector, provider is the one intended by God? That things go wrong when the woman takes the lead?

On an ecumenical note, it is interesting that Karl Barth (1886–1968) defended Mary's virginity but had no time for any other Catholic teaching on Mary. He felt that Joseph was a better model of the Church; just as he took care of the Child, so he takes care of the Church.[1]

The general conclusion that the traditional roles work best fits with female deacons and male priests (but what about male deacons?).

Section D) referring to Part III Chapter 13

Prayers of Consecration

PRAYER OF CONSECRATION OF A DEACON

Almighty God, be present with us by your power. You are the source of all honour, you assign to each his rank, you give to each his ministry.

You remain unchanged, but you watch over all creation and make it new through your son, Jesus Christ, Our Lord. He is your word, your power and your wisdom. You foresee all things in your eternal providence and make due provision for every age. You make the Church, Christ's body, grow to its full stature as a new and greater temple. You enrich it with every kind of grace and perfect it with a diversity of

members to serve the whole body in a wonderful pattern of
unity.

You established a threefold ministry of worship and service
for the glory of your Name. As ministers of your tabernacle
you chose the sons of Levi and gave them your blessing as
their everlasting inheritance. In the first days of your Church
under the inspiration of the Holy Spirit the apostles of your
son appointed seven men of good repute to assist them in
their daily ministry, so that they themselves might be more
free for prayer and preaching. By prayer and the laying on
of hands the apostles entrusted to those chosen men the
ministry of serving at tables.

Lord, look with favor on this servant of yours, whom we
now dedicate to the office of deacon, to minister at your holy
altar.

Lord, send forth upon him the Holy Spirit, that he may be
strengthened by the gift of your sevenfold grace to carry out
faithfully the work of the ministry.

May he excel in every virtue: in love that is sincere, in
concern for the sick and the poor, in unassuming authority,
in self-discipline, and in holiness of life.

May his conduct exemplify your commandments and lead
your people to imitate his purity of life.

May he remain strong and steadfast in Christ, giving to the
world the witness of a pure conscience.

May he in this life imitate your son, who came not to be
served but to serve, and one day reign with him in heaven.
We ask you this through Our Lord Jesus Christ your Son,
who lives and reigns with you and the Holy Spirit, one God
for ever and ever.

The new deacon is invested with the stole and dalmatic and
presented with the book of the gospels. His hands are anointed
and he is presented with the ciborium and chalice being used at
the Mass.

PRAYER OF CONSECRATION OF A PRIEST

Come to our help, Lord holy Father, almighty and eternal
God; you are the source of every honour and dignity, of all
progress and stability. You watch over the growing family
of man by your gift of wisdom and your pattern of order.
When you had appointed high priests to rule your people,

you chose other men next to them in rank and dignity to be with them and to help them in their task; and so there grew up the ranks of priests and the offices of Levites, established by sacred rites.

In the desert you extended the spirit of Moses to seventy wise men who helped him to rule the great company of his people. You shared among the sons of Aaron the fullness of their father's power, to provide worthy priests in sufficient number for the increasing rites of sacrifice and worship. With the same loving care you gave companions to your son's apostles to help in teaching the faith: they preached the gospel to the whole world.

Lord, grant also to us such fellow workers, for we are weak and our need is greater.

Almighty Father, grant to this servant of yours the dignity of the priesthood. Renew within him the Spirit of holiness. As a co-worker with the order of bishops may he be faithful to the ministry that he receives from you, Lord God, and be to others a model of right conduct.

May he be faithful in working with the order of bishops, so that the words of the gospel may reach to the ends of the earth, and the family of nations, made one in Christ, may become God's one, holy people.

We ask this through our Lord Jesus Christ, your son who lives and reigns with you and the Holy Spirit, one God, for ever and ever.

The new priest is invested with the stole and chasuble.

PRAYER OF CONSECRATION OF A BISHOP

God the Father of our Lord Jesus Christ, Father of mercies and God of all consolation, you dwell in heaven, yet look with compassion on all that is humble. You know all things before they come to be; by your gracious word you have established the plan of your Church.

From the beginning you chose the descendants of Abraham to be your holy nation. You established rulers and priests, and did not leave your sanctuary without ministers to serve you. From the creation of the world you have been pleased to be glorified by those whom you have chosen.

So now pour out upon this chosen one that power which is from you, the governing Spirit whom you gave to your beloved Son, Jesus Christ, the Spirit given by Him to the holy apostles, who founded the Church in every place to be your temple for the unceasing glory and praise of your name.

Father, you know all hearts. You have chosen your servant for the office of bishop. May he be a shepherd to your holy flock, and a high priest blameless in your sight, ministering to you night and day; may he always gain the blessing of your favor and offer the gifts of your Church. Through the Spirit who gives the grace of high priesthood grant him the power to forgive sins as you have commanded, to assign ministries as you have decreed, and to loose every bond by the authority which you gave to your apostles.

May he be pleasing to you by his gentleness and purity of heart, presenting a fragrant offering to you, through Jesus Christ, your Son, through whom glory and power and honor are yours with the Holy Spirit in your holy Church, now and for ever.

The bishop is already wearing the pectoral cross. He is presented with a ring, pastoral staff and mitre.

BLESSING OF AN ABBOT

This rite is not an ordination, as the abbot-elect will already be an ordained priest. While abbots have many of the responsibilities of a bishop, they do not have the fullness of the sacrament of ordination. The rite varies slightly depending on whether or not the abbot-elect will have jurisdiction over a territory. There are four possible prayers of blessing. The following is the shortest.

Almighty God and Father, you sent your son into the world to minister to your flock and to lay down your life for them. Bless your servant N., chosen to be abbot of this monastery, and make him holy. Strengthen him by your grace for his heavy burden of guiding souls and of adapting himself to the various needs of those he serves. Give him a heart full of compassion for the brothers entrusted to his care, so that he may not lose even one. And may the Lord, when he comes in glory on the last day, give him the reward of his stewardship.

We ask this through Christ our Lord.

The abbot is already wearing a pectoral cross. He is presented with a copy of the rule of the community and with a ring and pastoral staff. He may be presented with a mitre.

BLESSING OF AN ABBESS
The abbess-elect, assisted by two religious from her monastery, is given a place in the sanctuary. There are four possible prayers of blessing. The following is the shortest.

> Lord, hear our prayer for your servant N., who has been chosen to guide this monastic community. Look on her with love, and strengthen her with every blessing. Guide her in the way of grace and peace, in the footsteps of your Son, and reward her at last with the joy of everlasting life.
> We ask this through Christ our Lord.

The abbess is presented with a copy of the rule of the community and with a ring.[2]

Section E) referring to Part III, Chapter 14

On the Nature of the Permanent Diaconate
ST III q60a2

> Signs are given to men, to whom it is proper to discover the unknown by means of the known. Consequently a sacrament properly so called is that which is the sign of some sacred thing pertaining to man; so that properly speaking a sacrament, as considered by us now, is defined as being the 'sign of a holy thing so far as it makes men holy.

ST III q63a3

> A character is properly a kind of seal, whereby something is marked, as being ordained to some particular end: thus a coin is marked for use in exchange of goods, and soldiers are marked with a character as being deputed to military service. Now the faithful are deputed to a twofold end. First and principally to the enjoyment of glory … Secondly, each of the faithful is deputed to receive, or to bestow on others, things pertaining to the worship of God. And this, properly speaking, is the purpose of the sacramental character. Now the whole rite of the Christian religion is derived from Christ's

priesthood. Consequently, it is clear that the sacramental character is specially the character of Christ, to Whose character the faithful are likened by reason of the sacramental characters, which are nothing else than certain participations of Christ's Priesthood, flowing from Christ Himself.

ST III: q63a6

But it is the sacrament of order that pertains to the sacramental agents: for it is by this sacrament that men are deputed to confer sacraments on others: while the sacrament of baptism pertains to the recipients, since it confers on man the power to receive the other sacraments of the Church; whence it is called the 'door of the sacraments.' In a way confirmation also is ordained for the same purpose ... Consequently, these three sacraments imprint a character, namely, baptism, confirmation, and Order.

From an article by Didier Gonneaud:[3]

1. The sacrament of Order has both unity and diversity.
If we emphasise the unity, we face the problem of diaconal formation—if we try to make this a copy of priestly formation, it will be impossible for the deacons to achieve. We also make it difficult to consider women deacons as this would open a gulf between them and priests and bishops.
If we emphasise the diversity, we can devise a training programme more suited to the diaconal ministry, including taking greater cognisance of their wives. By emphasising the diversity, originality and value of the diaconate as distinct from the other two ministries, we could seriously consider women deacons.
The sacramentality of the diaconate is a participation in the sacramentality of the bishop, yet the deacon is not the deacon of the bishop but of Christ.
2. The episcopate, and in a less well defined way, the presbyterate, has a collegial structure; the diaconate does not. So deacons are not responsible for the three munera together but can put them in an order of priority, as decided by the bishop in consideration of the needs of the local church. Remembering that there is an almost universal pattern of priestly ordination being preceded by diaconal ordination and that the minor orders are attached to the diaconate rather than the presbyterate, we can look on the

diaconate as the fullness of the sacramental order of ministry in the same way that the episcopate is the fullness of the sacrament of ordination.

From an article by Fr Alphonse Borras:[4]

Vatican II debated the restoration of the permanent diaconate. The preliminary discussions highlighted two main concerns, the shortage of priests and the need for more workers in the field of evangelisation. Some felt that the Church needed a twofold clergy, others saw this as a threat to priestly celibacy. Eventually, the motion in favour of introducing the permanent diaconate was passed by a large majority. The list of duties of the deacon found in *Lumen Gentium* differs in emphasis from that in *Ad Gentes*, reflecting a certain tension in the Church regarding the role of the deacon. The overall impression is that deacons were to take over some of the tasks of the priest (LG) and of the catechist (AG). Forty years after Vatican II, the ITC identified two models of the diaconate—assistant to the priest and pastoral care. It decided that pastoral care was the decisive element in reintroducing the permanent diaconate.

The phrase "ordained not with a view to priesthood but to ministry" is more likely to have been used to encourage cooperation and involvement in a shared ministry of service than to be an attempt to explain their different roles. All share in the diaconate of Christ. As servants of the bishop, the deacons assist him by their threefold ministry of the liturgy, the Word and charitable works (not the *tri munera* of prophecy, priesthood and kingship shared by bishops and priests.) The diaconal tasks can be summed up as those of charity and administration. Deacons receive the sacrament of orders and therefore participate, in their own way, in the mission of the apostles. They are a sign of the diaconal vocation of the whole Church.

From an article by Fr Alphonse Borras:[5]

The theology of sacramental character is based on the teachings of St Thomas Aquinas. (see ST III, q63.3.) So the diaconal ordination must confer character. Current teaching can be found in the CCC §1570/1121. JPII in *Insegnamenti* §649 says 'In its own degree the deacon personifies Christ-the-servant of the Father, in participation of the threefold function of the Sacrament, through the occurrence of the Sacrament of Orders.' The Congregation for the Clergy's *Directory for the Ministry and Life of Permanent Deacons* §21.28 says that 'The seal of the sacrament brings configuration to Christ-the-deacon which corroborates the fidelity of God to his gift, implies non-repeatability of the sacrament and stability in ecclesial service.'

Notes

[1]   See M. O'Carroll, 'Theotokos', p. 70.

[2]   She may also be presented with a crozier, if this is the custom of the place.

[3]   D. Gonneaud, 'The Sacramentality of the Diaconal Ministry' in *New Diaconal Review* Issue 1 (November 2008).

[4]   A. Borras, 'Where are We? Part I' in *New Diaconal Review*, Issue 2 (May 2009), pp. 31–40.

[5]   *Ibid.*, pp. 18–28.

APPENDIX III

Quotes from From the Diakonia of Christ to the Diakonia of the Apostles

I discuss *From the Diakonia of Christ* in chapters fourteen and twenty three of this work. It is often quoted as finding that the Church has never ordained women as deacons and therefore cannot introduce this practice. Even such reliable sources as leaflets published by the Catholic Truth Society take this line:

> In 2002, the International Theological Commission, which advises the Pope, reported that there was no evidence of ordained female deacons in the early Church ... Many Catholics will find it unlikely that a tradition of over 2,000 years of practice could ever be reversed.[1]

In fact, while I suspect that the Commission would have been happy to draw the conclusion attributed to it by CTS, they did not do so, honest scholarship preventing such a firm conclusion. Indeed, they include several passages that support the idea that the deaconesses of the early Church were in fact ordained. I include them here.

> The concept of *klèros* was broadened to all those who exercised a liturgical ministry, who were maintained by the Church and who benefited from the privileges in civil law allowed by the Empire to clerics, so that the deaconesses were counted as belonging to the clergy, while the widows were excluded.[2]

> Deaconesses took up their functions through an *epithesis cheirôn* or imposition of hands that conferred the Holy Spirit, as did the lectors ... The deaconesses were named before the sub-deacons.[3]

> At Constantinople, the best known of the fourth-century deaconesses was Olympias ... She was "ordained" (*cheiro-tonein*) deaconess with three of her companions by the patriarch. Can. 15 of the Council of Chalcedon (451) seems

to confirm the fact that deaconesses really were "ordained" by the imposition of hands (*cheirotonia*). Their ministry was called *leitourgia* and after ordination they were not allowed to marry.[4]

Was this ministry conferred by an imposition of hands [of the female deacons] comparable to that by which the episcopate, the priesthood and the masculine diaconate were conferred? The text of the *Constitutiones Apostolorum* would seem to suggest this.[5]

Despite these quotes, the Commission did not give a definitive ruling on whether or not the Church had ordained women as deacons in the past. I quote their conclusion in full.

With regard to the ordination of women to the diaconate, it should be noted that two important indications emerge from what has been said up to this point:

(1) The deaconesses mentioned in the tradition of the ancient Church—as evidenced by the rite of institution and the functions they exercised—were not purely and simply equivalent to the deacons;

(2) The unity of the sacrament of Holy Orders, in the clear distinction between the ministries of the Bishop and the Priests on the one hand and the Diaconal ministry on the other, is strongly underlined by ecclesial tradition, especially in the teaching of the Magisterium.

In the light of these elements which have been set out in the present historico-theological research document, it pertains to the ministry of discernment which the Lord established in his Church to pronounce authoritatively on this question.

Point (1) has been addressed in the section 'The Analogy of Faith: Diagnosis' where I point out that people can exercise their calling in typically male or female ways without being any the less members of their profession. It should not surprise us that male and female deacons in the early Church had different roles. We cannot deduce from this that either group was superior or inferior to the other or that one group was ordained while the other simply received a blessing.

Point (2) is addressed in the section on the Vatican II teaching that bishops have the fullness of the sacrament of ordination (chapter fourteen, 'Bishop'). This teaching protects the unity of the sacrament by clarifying that this unity resides in the bishop. The bishop can delegate some of his powers to a priest and some to a deacon but the apostolic authority conferred by the sacrament exists in its unity only with the bishop.

Phyllis Zagano, whose book 'Holy Saturday' I review in Appendix IV, wrote an interesting article on 'From the Diakonia of Christ' when it was first published. She points out the inconsistencies in the arguments, the gaps in the evidence presented and the internal politics affecting the Commission's conclusions.[6]

Notes

[1] Catholic Truth Society, 'Why Not Women Priests' (2005), in the CTS Essentials series, LF 25 (London: CTS, 2005).
[2] International Theological Commission, From the Diakonia of Christ to the Diakonia of the Apostles (London: CTS, 2008), p. 23.
[3] *Ibid.*, p. 24.
[4] *Ibid.*, p. 25.
[5] *Ibid.*, p. 27.
[6] P. Zagano, 'Catholic Women Deacons' in *America Magazine* (17 February 2003), available at <www.americamagazine.org/content/article_id=2778> [accessed 23 November 2011].

APPENDIX IV

Additional Material

Since completing the draft of this manuscript, I have read several books and articles that would have been useful sources for my writing. I have used the technique of having appendixes to add some of this material. In this appendix, I give a brief summary of the work of two American female theologians, Sara Butler and Phyllis Zagano. The reader has already met Sara Butler, whose book on the priesthood is discussed in chapter twenty. She has since turned her attention to the question of female deacons in an article 'Women Deacons and Sacramental Symbolism' published in the *New Diaconal Review* of May 2011. In this article, Butler gives an overview of the arguments used in the document *From the Diakonia of Christ to the Diakonia of the Apostles* and concentrates on that document's two 'important indicators' that suggest that deaconesses were not ordained. She emphasises the importance of the subject of a sacrament—while the matter and form of the sacrament of ordination for the diaconate may (or may not) be the same for men and women, the subject cannot be. So the two rites cannot be identical. She points out that the other sacraments use the same rites for males and females. So why the difference with diaconal ordination? Butler points out that the rites for deaconesses were clearly designed for women undertaking a specifically feminine ministry:

> The candidates are women, and they are clearly being chosen for a 'women's' ministry. And in this respect, despite their many similarities, the rites themselves differ significantly. This appears to be compelling evidence that women were admitted not to a gender-neutral diaconate but to a women's order in the Church with its own *gestalt*.[1]

One of the differences in the rites that Butler finds significant is the use of female 'icons' of ministry—Miriam, Huldah, Deborah, Anna, Pheobe. She concludes that:

> There seems to be no obstacle, in principle, to the
> creation of a female diaconate, distinct from the sacra-
> ment of Holy Orders. The pastoral service of women
> might well be incorporated into the structure of the
> Church as a 'fourth order' through formal installation
> by the bishop.[2]

When I first read Butler's article, I got the impression that she was
trying to keep her options open while not saying anything too
controversial. On re-reading it, I decided that she was firmly in the
'deaconesses only received a sacramental' camp. Yet again, people
will believe what they want to believe and no argument, however
scholarly, will convince someone who is firmly in one camp or the
other. Being in the other camp, I found several weak points to
Butler's arguments. In the past, the sacrament of marriage used
different words for the vows made by the bride and groom (he
endowed her with his worldly wealth, she promised to obey) — did
only the groom receive the sacrament? Men also were not being
admitted to a gender-neutral diaconate. Indeed, this difference fits
very well with the diaconal ministry of service. As discussed
elsewhere, men and women typically have different skills to offer
and different ways of serving, so it is perfectly logical and fitting
that the rites used in their admission into the diaconate should
reflect this. It is also fitting that the rite for male deacons should
suggest male role models and the rite for deaconesses should
suggest female role models. None of these differences are incompatible with the belief that both rites conferred sacramental grace.
Butler's final suggestion of a 'fourth order' has already been tried,
as I discuss in chapter one, where I suggest that it causes as many
problems as it solves. (The lay pastoral assistant that I mention had
been formally installed by the bishop, as Butler recommends.)

I read *Holy Saturday: An Argument for the Restoration of the Female
Diaconate in the Catholic Church* by Phyllis Zagano after completing
the draft of this book. Rather than try to incorporate her findings
into my own work, I have included some of her arguments here.[3]
I had two reasons for this,

✢ While the book meets my criteria of being within Church
    teaching, it only just manages this and one gets the impression

that the author's private views would include the possibility
of female priests.

✟   I do not agree with the author's portrayal of the iconic argument as the fundamental reason for the Church refusing to
consider female priests. I also find some of her descriptions of
the sacrament of ordination and the differences between priests
and deacons dubious.

Having said that, we do come to the same conclusion and she does
give some answers to my academic critic's comment about not
providing reasons why the Church might want to reintroduce
female deacons. So I have summarised her reasons here.

Reasons for Reintroducing Female Deacons

1.   All the reasons given for reintroducing male deacons at the
time of Vatican II apply equally to female deacons. The
National Conference of Catholic Bishops of the U.S.A.
requested permanent deacons in 1968, giving five areas of
need:

✟   strengthen current diaconal ministry,

✟   enlist new workers to ministry,

✟   expand liturgical and charitable services to the People of God,

✟   provide official and sacramental presence, especially where
priests are not available,

✟   provide impetus for creative adaptation of diaconal ministries
to the needs of the society.

All of these areas could be served by either men or women.

2.   By restoring the female diaconate, the Church would be
proclaiming the Gospel of Jesus Christ in supporting the equal
dignity of all persons. The work of the Church is there to be
done by all. Women need a structure within which to do this
work.

3.   Bringing women who are already involved in diaconal ministry within the permanent diaconate would also bring them
within the legal framework of the Church. It would thus give
them a clearly defined function and add to the stability of the
Church. Currently, there are various all-female groups and

communities, reflecting women's desire to serve the Church. However non-sacramental gatherings weaken the Church rather than unite it. They can become political rather than religious. Following the principle of subsidiarity, such groups need leaders who are recognised as Church leaders.

4. There would still be a need for the service of non-ordained women such as nuns, teachers, catechists and professionals. The distinction between vows and orders would still be important. Those who have taken vows in a religious order can often take a wider view of things and react more quickly and flexibly than those with a responsibility to a specific geographical area.

5. Canon Law gives the laity only the right to 'cooperate with' the Church's exercise of its juridical powers, whereas the clergy have the right to participate in this power. Thus all women are officially excluded from many juridical positions even when they are exercising this ministry in practice. Women are thus exercising a parallel ministry rather than one that is integrated into the hierarchy of the Church.

6. The increasing need to give women extraordinary[4] faculties to perform baptisms, weddings suggests the need for them to have a position that would give them these faculties on an ordinary, permanent basis.

7. There is some confusion among deacons as to their priorities— are they ordained primarily to liturgical or to pastoral service? Just how do they differ from priests and bishops? Having female deacons, who are permanently barred from the priest-hood, would give a strong symbolic message that, not only are women worthy to approach holy things, but the diaconate is an order in its own right and not some form of incomplete priesthood.

8. The Church recognises that she has the power to ordain women to the diaconate—hence the many requests from the American bishops for the Vatican to take this step and the various Vatican responses, all on the lines of 'we need to

consider this in more detail', not 'this is not compatible with Church teaching'.

9. The Orthodox Churches, whose sacraments we recognise, never abandoned the order of deaconesses, although it fell into disuse. It has been in continuous use in the Armenian Apostolic Church to this day. This creates an ecumenical anomaly, which could be solved by reintroducing deaconesses into the Western Church.

Notes

[1]   S. Butler, 'Women Deacons and Sacramental Symbolism' in *New Diaconal Review* Issue 6 (May 2011), p.49, col 2.

[2]   *Ibid.*, p. 49, col 2.

[3]   For an introduction to the ideas of Phyllis Zagano, see her extended essay in *Women Deacons: Past, Present, Future* (New York: Paulist Press, 2011). I have the same reservations about this essay as I had about her book! (see Appendix IV). However there are some interesting points, particularly on the effect of having ordained female religious in a community setting.

[4]   Permission has to be given from the bishop for that specific situation, the person does not have any automatic authority to perform the task. Similarly, the bishop is the 'ordinary' minister of confirmation and the parish priest is the 'extraordinary' minister and has to apply to the bishop for permission whenever he wishes to exercise this ministry.

APPENDIX V

The Orthodox Church

As with the book by Phyllis Zagano, Kyriaki Karidoyanes FitzGerald's text *Women Deacons in the Orthodox Church* came to my attention after completing the draft of this work. I found it extremely interesting and relevant to my argument. Unlike Zagano, I had no sense of the author wishing to change Church teaching, she simply wants it to go back to a practice that has fallen into disuse for historical reasons. I have inserted several notes[1] referring the reader to this book and regret that I did not know of it in time to include its findings in the body of the text. One of the most interesting features is the realisation that the Churches of East and West have been following parallel lines over the debate on the role of women within the Church. The arguments put forward by FitzGerald, being based on the teaching and practice of the early, undivided Church, are as relevant to the Western debate as they are to the Eastern.

I give a chapter by chapter summary of *Women Deacons in the Orthodox Church* below.

Chapter One

A look at the evidence of Scripture and the Early Fathers for the role of female deacons. Clement, Origen and John Chrysostom all write of the importance of female deacons in the life of the Church.

Chapter Two

A detailed examination of the Syriac *'Didascalia'* and the 'Apostolic Constitutions', concluding that

1. deaconesses, widows and virgins are separate ranks within the Church;

2. deaconesses were part of the ordained clergy;

3.   deaconesses assisted the bishop, much of their work parallel-
      ing that of the male deacons;

4.   the differences in the work carried out by male and female
      deacons can be explained by cultural expectations.

Chapter Three

Hagiographical testimony to the life and work of those early
deaconesses who are recognised in the Greek Orthodox Church as
saints. This shows them performing a wide variety of ministries,
always under the authority of the bishop.

Chapter Four

A sentence-by-sentence examination of the ordination rite
described in the 'Apostolic Constitutions', concluding that

1.   it is God who calls women to serve him and the Church;

2.   the woman deacon is to be a servant-leader, a teacher, a
      prophet;

3.   sin, not social convention, prevents us from worshipping God.
      Ritual impurity is not part of the new dispensation.

Chapter Five

A sentence-by-sentence examination of the ordination rite used in
Constantinople in the eighth Century, concluding that

1.   it follows the same pattern as rites for male deacons, presby-
      ters and bishops;

2.   the prayers do not specify her liturgical or pastoral responsi-
      bilities;

3.   her actual activities would have been culturally conditioned.

Chapter Six

Did the early deaconesses receive an ordination into the major
orders or did they receive an appointment, installation or blessing?
The author examines the work of Professor Karmiris, who argues
for the equality of all, but the reservation of the charism of

ordination to men. She then examines the work of Professor Theodorou, whose work very much informs her own. He argues that women were ordained to major orders as deacons, but not to any priestly responsibilities involving presiding at the liturgy. The Inter-Orthodox Consultation on Rhodes in 1988 publicly endorsed the work of Professor Theodorou.

Chapter Seven

The author discusses the various reasons for the decline in the order of deaconesses, looking at changing liturgical practices, Western reluctance towards women deacons, reactions against Gnosticism, the spread of Islam and the continuing sense of women being 'unclean' while menstruating.

Chapter Eight

A history of the modern movement to bring back the order of deaconess, which started over a hundred years ago. This movement now has global support and official approval from the most senior leaders of the Orthodox Church.

Notes

1   See chapters ten 'Tradition: Women' and fourteen 'Magisterium: Ordination'.

Errors and the Church's Response[1]

Some heresies

Arianism:
Taking its name from the Alexandrian presbyter, Arius, this belief was so popular that refuting it was the main aim of the Council of Nicaea in 325. Arius taught that God the Son was created by God the Father as an instrument for the redemption of mankind. Thus God the Son was a created being.

Atheism:
A position that asserts that there is no God, a step further than agnosticism, which says that we cannot argue for or against the existence of God.

Deism:
A line of thought that accepts the existence of God but denies man's ability to understand him in any mystical way. Kant and Locke supported this view.

Docetism:
An over-emphasis on the divinity of Jesus, to the point that it denies his humanity.

Fideism:
The view that certain beliefs, particularly religious ones, require the operation of faith and remain inaccessible to reason alone. It is thus an anti-rationalist view, to the extent that it places limits on the powers of reason, but it is also irrationalist in setting aside a group of beliefs as beyond the scope of reason.

Gnosticism:
A diverse group of beliefs, sharing a common thread of matter as evil and the existence of divine knowledge, given only to a chosen few.

Materialism:
Refers to various theories relating mental activity to matter in motion and simply a product of brain activity.

Marcionism:
In a variation on Gnosticism, Marcion tried to separate Christianity
from its Jewish roots and rejected all of the Old Testament and all
but Luke and Paul of the New Testament. He taught that the
created world was a sham and Jesus' flesh an illusion. God was
not the God of judgement of the Old Testament but a God of love.
Modernism:
A general term for a variety of views supporting the influence of
the Holy Spirit on expressed dogma in each generation, as opposed
to Traditional teachings and beliefs. Pius X opposed the more
extreme positions in *Pascendi*.
Pantheism:
A theory that regards God as residing in everything, rather than
being set above or alongside the world. A modern example of this
is Spinoza's equating God with the world as a whole. On such a
view there can be no creation of the world, since that would mean
God creating himself.
Pelagianism:
Derived from the teachings of the English monk Pelagius, who
emphasised the salvific effect of good works and the necessity for
individual moral responsibility. His teachings were opposed by
Augustine as denying the need for grace.
Rationalism:
The philosophical position that sees all knowledge of the world as
based on reason alone.
Traditionalism:
Exemplified by the teaching of L. E. M. Bautain (1786–1867), who
denied the ability of human reason to attain to any truths, espe-
cially those of theology.
Variations on these beliefs resurface in every generation and the
Church needs to regularly defend the truth of her constant
teaching. The most authoritative way of formulating teaching is
through General Councils, a summary of which are set out below.

The General Councils of the Church

Nicaea (325)
Convened by the emperor Constantine in response to the Arian crisis, it is most famous for giving us the Nicene Creed which declares that God the Son is of one being with God the Father.

Constantinople (381)
Condemned Arianism and gave the Nicaean Creed its final form, still used today in both East and West. Important for the doctrine of the divinity of the Holy Spirit.

Ephesus (431)
Settled the debate on the title of Theotokos/God bearer for Our Lady by confirming that Jesus Christ was both God and man from the moment of his conception in Mary's womb. Notorious for the bitter dispute between Nestorius and Cyril of Alexandria.

Chalcedon (451)
Famous for its favourable reception of the papal letter 'The Tome of Leo', it confirmed the two natures of Christ in the one person, he was consubstantial with the Father in his divinity and consubstantial with us in his humanity.

Constantinople II (553)
Stated that teaching is based on the living Tradition of the Church. Condemned three dead theologians for dyophysite views but the whole episode discredited by the pressure exerted by the Emperor Justinian on Pope Vigilius.

Constantinople III (681)
Possibly actually the sixth general council held in Constantinople! It finally ended the debate that Chalcedon had been struggling with and found a form of words acceptable to both East and West.

Nicaea II (787)
Called as a result of the iconoclast movement, which tried to suppress the use of icons and other forms of religious art, it confirmed the propriety of using icons as an aid to devotion by

distinguishing between adoration of God and veneration of God's creation.

Lateran I (1123)
The first council to be held at Rome. It abolished the right claimed by lay princes, of investiture with ring and crosier to ecclesiastical benefices and dealt with Church discipline and the recovery of the Holy Land from the infidels.

Lateran II (1139)
Condemned the errors of Arnold of Brescia. Declared all clerical marriages both illegal and invalid.

Lateran III (1179)
Concerned with Church structure and discipline.

Lateran IV (1215)
Convened to counter the heresies of the Albigensians, Cathars, Amalricians and Waldensians. It also formalised the sacrificial and eucharistic character of the priesthood, based on Christ's priesthood. It introduced the rule of annual confession and reception of Holy Communion at least at Easter time.

Lyons I (1245)
It excommunicated and deposed Emperor Frederick II and directed a new crusade, under the command of St Louis, against the Saracens and Mongols.

Lyons II (1274)
It effected a temporary reunion of the Greek Church with Rome. The word *filioque* was added to the symbol of Constantinople and means were sought for recovering Palestine from the Turks. It also laid down the rules for papal elections. It banned all mendicant friars of orders founded after 1215.

Vienne (1311)
The synod dealt with the crimes and errors imputed to the Knights Templars, the Fraticelli, the Beghards, and the Beguines, with projects of a new crusade, the reformation of the clergy, and the teaching of Oriental languages in the universities.

Constance (1414)

Held during the great Schism of the West, with the object of ending the divisions in the Church. It became legitimate only when Gregory XI had formally convoked it. Owing to this circumstance it succeeded in putting an end to the schism by the election of Pope Martin V, which the Council of Pisa (1403) had failed to accomplish on account of its illegality. The rightful pope confirmed the former decrees of the synod against Wycliffe and Hus.

Florence (1445)

The last attempt to heal the breach between the East and West. The issues being debated were the *filioque* clause; purgatory; the use of unleavened bread; the wording of the prayers of consecration and the power of the papacy. While an agreement was reached at the council, this was never accepted by the Church of Constantinople.

Lateran IV (1517)

It issued an enlarged creed (symbol) against the Albigenses (Firmiter credimus), condemned the Trinitarian errors of Abbot Joachim, and published 70 important reformatory decrees. One of its concerns was the widespread mood of expectation of the end times. It banned preaching on the subject.

Lateran V (1512–1517)

Its decrees are chiefly disciplinary. A new crusade against the Turks was planned, but came to naught, owing to the religious upheaval in Germany caused by Luther.

Trent (1545–1563)

Convened to address the issues raised by the Reformation, it reaffirmed traditional Church teaching on Tradition, the use of the Vulgate version of the Bible, the authority of the Church to interpret Scripture, that there were seven sacraments, the doctrine of transubstantiation, that the Church was hierarchical.

Vatican I (1870)

Interrupted by war, its one achievement was to define papal infallibility.

Vatican II (1965)

Rarely, this council was not called in response to a crisis but simply to give the Church an opportunity to examine itself and its relationship to the modern world. Its most obvious changes were in the liturgy, with the introduction of Mass in the vernacular and the priest facing the people. It reintroduced permanent deacons. It showed ecumenical tendencies lacking in previous councils.

Notes

[1]   These definitions are taken from *The Encyclopaedia of Theology* by Karl Rahner, *Collins Dictionary of Philosophy* by Vesey & Foulkes, and *The Shape of Catholic Theology* by Aidan Nichols.

READING LIST

Ashley, Benedict. *Justice in the Church*: *Gender and Participation*, The Catholic University of America Press, Washington, 1996.

The title is rather confusing and attention has to be paid to the sub-title as the book is not concerned with social justice but the question of the role of women in the Church. Ashley sets out to answer the feminist accusation that it is unjust for the Church to deny positions of influence and power to women purely on the basis of their sex. This he does in a clear and scholarly manner, always in line with official Church teaching. It seems a pity that he felt the need to devote so much effort to refute arguments that frequently do not warrant it. The answer to the feminist argument needs to be, and could be, reduced to one paragraph to be repeated whenever necessary. However the book provides a detailed analysis of the role of women in the Church which is worth reading independently of the feminist position which inspired it.

Bauckham, Richard. *Gospel Women: Studies of the Named Women in the Gospels*, T & T Clark, Edinburgh, 2002.

This is a collection of semi-independent studies, some previously published as articles, on some of the women who played important roles in the Scriptures. The first two chapters of the book are taken up with the women named in Matthew's genealogy. However Bauckham does not conclusively answer his own question 'Why are these women here?' He also examines the information on the prophetess Anna, Joanna, Mary of Clopas, the two Salomes and the women witnesses to the resurrection. While the work is detailed and scholarly, there is also much conjecture. Some conclusions depend on non-canonical sources such as 'The Secret Gospel of Mark'.

Boadt, Lawrence. *Reading the Old Testament: An Introduction,* Paulist Press, New York, 1984.

A standard textbook, this gives a detailed account of both the cultural and religious life of the Old Testament Israelites. It

examines the development of the canon of Scripture and gives
short explanations of the main themes of the Old Testament. It
includes study questions and reading lists. Easy to read, this book
is an excellent starting point for anyone with an interest in the
background to the Old Testament Scriptures.

Brown, Raymond. *The Community of the Beloved Disciple: The life,
    loves and hates of an individual Church in New Testament Times,*
    Paulist Press, New York, 1979.

This comparatively short book acts as a summary of the authors
copious works on the gospel and epistles of John. He suggests that
the Johannine community was a sect within Christianity which
later split, with one group being absorbed into 'mainstream'
Christianity and the other moving through docetism to gnosticism.
This is outwith the scope of this work but the book is of interest as
it contains an appendix 'Roles of Women in the Fourth Gospel'
which originally appeared in *Theological Studies* 36 (1975) pp.
688–99. Brown concludes that the Johannine author wanted to
emphasise the important role of women: Martha gives a profession
of faith similar to that of Peter; Mary Magdalen sees the risen Lord
before Peter does, Jesus loves Mary and Martha. Mary, the Mother
of Jesus, is important as an example of perfect discipleship and as
the Mother of all believers, represented by the beloved disciple.
Brown suggests that the Johannine community had achieved the
Pauline ideal of a truly equal society. Yet John also describes the
disciples' astonishment at Jesus speaking to the Samaritan woman
and their reluctance to ask him what he was speaking to her about.
Brown suggests that it is time for the Church to ask 'What do you
want of a woman?'

Fahey, Michael A. 'Church' in Fiorenza & Galvin (ed.), *Systematic
    Theology,* Fortress Press, Minneapolis, 1991.

The main concern of this article is the lack of unity among the
various Christian denominations. The author argues for greater
flexibility by the Catholic Church in its relations with other
denominations. Much of the article is taken up with images of the
Church as presented in the documents of Vatican II. Fahey
introduces this theme with a useful summary of the development
of the early Church and continues with an examination of the

various roles and tasks within the Church. The article is informative and easy to read but should perhaps only be used in conjunction with more traditional sources.

FitzGerald, Kyriaki Karidoyanes. *Women Deacons in the Orthodox Church: Called to Holiness and Ministry*, Holy Cross Orthodox Press, Massachusetts, 1999.

The author is a well known academic of the Greek Orthodox Church. This book is a scholarly examination of the history of female deacons. It concentrates on the early ordination rites, the teachings of the Early Fathers and the modern debate over whether or not those early deacons were ordained or simply received a blessing. It also touches on the relationship between bishop, priest and deacon. Basing her findings very much on the work of Professor Evangelos Theodorou, she concludes that the early women deacons were indeed ordained and she endorses the decision of the inter-Orthodox symposium of Rhodes in 1988 to encourage the reintroduction of this order. One point of interest is the way in which the debate over the position of women in the Church has followed the same pattern in both East and West. Much of what is said is as applicable to the Western Church as to the Eastern and this book is a valuable addition to the debate.

Galot, Jean. *Theology of the Priesthood*, Ignatius Press, San Francisco, 1985.

A classic definition of the priesthood, written with the intention of differentiating it from the priesthood of the laity. It emphasises the ontological change effected by the sacrament of ordination. Thorough and scholarly, so needs careful reading.

Lamb, Matthew & Levering, Matthew (ed.), *Vatican II: Renewal Within Tradition*, Oxford University Press, 2008.

A collection of essays on the main documents of Vatican II. Each contributor gives a commentary on one document, with the emphasis on the elements of continuity rather than innovation. The general thrust of the book is that Vatican II was not a revolutionary break with Tradition but an attempt to work out how the Church could best operate in the modern world.

Moloney, Francis. *Mary: Woman and Mother*, The Liturgical Press, Collegeville, 1988.

This slim book takes us through the Marian passages of the New Testament in a simple and logical manner. While itself fairly basic, it gives copious notes to more technical studies. It makes a good starting point for any work on Mary.

McGrath, Alister. *Christian Theology* 3rd edn., Blackwell Publishing, Oxford, 2001.

A standard textbook designed with the first year theology student in mind. Written by a non-Catholic, it nevertheless gives clear teaching on Catholic theology and almost achieves its aim of 'avoiding any form of denominational or theological bias'. Written in a clear style, it covers the main historical and theological developments in the Church.

Nixon, Rosemary. *The Priority of Perfection*, Movement for Whole Ministry in the Episcopal Church, Edinburgh, 1994.

This pamphlet is number six in a series concerned with the debate within the Scottish Episcopal church on the ordination of women priests. The author examines the creation accounts in Genesis 1 and 2 in very similar terms to those used by John Paul II. Not until the very last few sentences does her interpretation deviate from Roman Catholic teaching:

> Human kind is the priest-mediator of the image of God in creation. Man cannot be man without woman: nor can the male be in the image of God without the female. Thus the completeness, wholeness or *shalom* of priesthood in this created order is dependent upon the full inclusion of women.

The assumptions behind this summary are not part of the RC Tradition and highlight the different concepts of priesthood that have evolved over the centuries since the Reformation—another example of inter-church dialogue being hampered by each side using the same word but meaning different things by it.

Osborne, Kenan. *The Permanent Diaconate*, Paulist Press, New Jersey, 2007.

The author is an American priest who is involved in the training of deacons. He suggests that Vatican II introduced five major changes in the leadership and ministry of the Church: the ministry of all Christians, the sacramentality of episcopal ordination, the redefinition of the priesthood, the renewal of the permanent diaconate and a more inclusive ministry for the laity. The author clearly belongs to the 'Vatican II as a break with Tradition' school and approves of these changes. To my mind, he overstates the changes wrought by Vatican II. For example, he talks of the reintroduction of the episcopate into the sacrament of ordination but it had never left it; there had been centuries of debate on the question which Vatican II attempted to end. Similarly with the priesthood, Vatican II did not so much redefine the priesthood itself as broaden the discussion on the ministry of the priest. Overall, this book is a bit too aggressive in tone for me. The author's genuine concern for the pastoral problems that he faces threatens to override his scholarship and the result is a rather biased presentation.

Ratzinger, Cardinal Joseph. *The Nature and Mission of Theology: Approaches to Understanding its Role in the Light of Present Controversy*, Ignatius Press, San Francisco, 1995.

This is more a collection of essays than a full-blown text book. It has its origins in the battles between the Congregation for the Doctrine of the Faith and the liberation theologians of the 1970s and 1980s, especially those working in Latin America. Cardinal Ratzinger puts forward a detailed but readable and thoughtful argument for the necessity of theologians to work within the limits set by the Magisterium of the Church. Theology is not philosophy, as it is based on faith and is searching for truth. Theologians need to have their conclusions tested by an independent body which has the authority to declare their work compatible with the established teaching of the Church, or not. A theologian who is genuinely searching for the truth will accept the authority of the Church and put him or herself under obedience to it.

Ulanov, Ann Belford. *The Female Ancestors of Christ*, Diamon Verlag, Enfield, 1993.

A study of the four Old Testament women of Matthew's genealogy from the point of view of Jungian psychiatry. Well written and with interesting ideas but slightly over-psychoanalytical. It ignores the other women in the Old Testament who also exhibit the features that she identifies in the named four, so why these four rather than the others?

Zagano, Phyllis. *Holy Saturday: An Argument for the Restoration of the Female Diaconate in the Catholic Church*, Crossroads, New York, 2000.

The author is an American academic who accepts the authority of the Church, although one gets the impression that she is doing so through gritted teeth and would much rather be arguing for women priests. The book is at its weakest when discussing the priesthood and at its strongest when discussing the contribution that women deacons could make to the Church. (See Appendix IV for a more detailed summary.)

BIBLIOGRAPHY

Scripture and the Magisterium

The Holy Bible, Revised Standard Version.

New Jerusalem Bible, Study Edition, 1994.

Catechism of the Catholic Church, 1994.

Code of Canon Law, 1983.

Standard References

Flannery, A. (ed.), *Vatican Council II: The Conciliar and Post Conciliar Documents*. Dublin: Dominican Publications, 1975.

Flannery, A. (ed.), *Vatican Council II: More Post Conciliar Documents*. Leominster: Fowler Wright Books Ltd., 1982.

Neuner, J. and Dupuis, J. (ed.), *The Christian Faith: Doctrinal Documents of the Catholic Church 5th edn*. London: HarperCollins, 1992.

Dictionaries and Encyclopaedias

Alexander, T. and Rosner, B. (ed.), *New Dictionary of Biblical Theology*. Leicester: Inter-Varsity Press, 2000.

Brown, R. Fitzmyer, J. and Murphy, R. (ed.), *The New Jerome Biblical Commentary*. London: Geoffrey Chapman, 1990.

Cross, F. *The Oxford Dictionary of the Christian Church*, 2nd edn. Oxford: O.U.P., 1983.

Friedrich, G. and Kittel, G. (ed.), (tr. Bromiley, G.), *Theological Dictionary of the New Testament*, vol. VI. Michigan: Eerdman's, 1968.

Kittel, G. (ed.), (tr. Bromiley, G.). *Theological Dictionary of the New Testament*, vol. II. Michigan: Eerdman's, 1964.

Leon-Dufour, X. *Dictionary of Biblical Theology*, 2nd edn. London: Burns & Oates, 1988.

McKenzie, J. *Dictionary of the Bible.* London: Geoffrey Chapman, 1965.

O'Carroll, M. *Theotokos: A Theological Encyclopedia of the Blessed Virgin Mary.* Eugene: Wipf and Stock Publishers, 1982.

Rahner, K. (ed.), *Encyclopedia of Theology.* London: Burns & Oates, 1975.

The Catholic Encyclopedia Classic 1914 edition on CD by New Advent, 2003.

Pius XII

Encyclical Letter on the Unity of Human Society *Summi Pontificatus* (1939).

Encyclical Letter on Biblical Studies *Divino Afflante Spiritu* (1943) in Neuner, J. & Dupuis, J. (ed.), *The Christian Faith* 5th edn. London: HarperCollins, 1991.

Apostolic Constitution on the Dogma of the Assumption *Munificentissimus Deus* (1950).

Encyclical Letter on the Marian Year *Fulgens Corona* (1953).

Encyclical Letter on Mary, Queen of all creation *Ad Caeli Reginam* (1954).

Paul VI

Motu Proprio *Sacrum Diaconatus Ordinem* 1967. The text can be found in AAS 59 (1967) pp. 697–704.

Apostolic Exhortation *Marialis Cultus* (1974), in Neuner, J. & Dupuis, J. (ed.), *The Christian Faith* 5th edn. London: HarperCollins, 1991.

Apostolic Exhortation on Evangelisation in the Modern World *Evangelii Nuntiandi* (1975).

John Paul II

Encyclical Letter on the Mother of the Redeemer *Redemptoris Mater* (1987), London: CTS, 1987.

Apostolic Exhortation on the Vocation and Mission of the Lay Faithful *Christifideles Laici* (1988).

Apostolic Letter on Reserving Priestly Ordination to Men Alone *Ordinatio Sacerdotalis* in *Origins*, 24 (1994), p. 49.

Encyclical Letter on the Commitment to Ecumenism *Ut Unum Sint* (1995).

Audiences *The Theology of the Body: Human Love in the Divine Plan*. Boston: Paulist Books, 1997.

Encyclical Letter on Faith and Reason *Fides et Ratio* (1998).

Apostolic Letter on the Dignity and Vocation of Women *Mulieris Dignitatem* (1998).

Encyclical Letter on the Eucharist and the Church *Ecclesia de Eucharistia* (2003).

Apostolic Letter on the Agenda for the Third Millennium *Tertio Millennio Adveniente* (1994) .

Pope Benedict XVI

Address at the General Audience, Wednesday 14 February 2007, 'Women of the Early Church' in *Position Paper* 425, (May 2009), pp. 163–167.

Message for the 47th World Day of Prayer for Vocations (25 April 2010).

The Holy See

Second Vatican Council, Dogmatic Constitution on the Church *Lumen Gentium* (1964).

Second Vatican Council, Dogmatic Constitution on Divine Revelation *Dei Verbum* (1965).

Second Vatican Council, Decree on the Church's Missionary Activity *Ad Gentes Divinitus* (1965).

Second Vatican Council, Decree on the Training of Priests *Optatam Totius* (1965).

Second Vatican Council, Decree on the Pastoral Office of Bishops in the Church *Christus Dominus* (1965).

Second Vatican Council, Decree on the Life and Ministry of Priests *Presbyterorum Ordinis* (1965).

Second Vatican Council, Pastoral Constitution on the Church in the World Today *Gaudium et Spes* (1965).

Sacred Congregation for the Doctrine of the Faith, Declaration on the Admission of Women to the Ministerial Priesthood *Inter Insigniores* (1976).

Congregation for the Clergy *Directory on the Ministry and Life of Priests* (1994).

Congregation for Catholic Education *Permanent Diaconate*. London: CTS, 2006.

Congregation for the Doctrine of the Faith *Aspects of Evangelisation* (2007).

The Pastoral Commission of the S.C.E.P. *The Role of Women in Evangelization* (1976), in International Theological Commission *From the Diakonia of Christ to the Diakonia of the Apostles*. London: CTS, 2003.

Congregations of the Faith, for Divine Worship and the Discipline of Sacraments and for Clergy, 'Notification on Women as Ordained Deacons' (17 September 2001), in *Adoremus Online Edition vol. VII no 7* October 2001, available at <www.adoremus.org/1001womendeacons.html> [accessed 22 November 2011].

Sources Cited

Books

Ashley, B. *Justice in the Church: Gender and Participation*. Washington: The Catholic University of America Press, 1996.

Aquinas, St T. (tr. Hill, E.), *Summa Theologiæ vol. XIII*. London: Blackfriers, 1964.

Aristotle (tr. Warrington, J.), *Politics: The Athenian Constitution.* London: Heron Books by arrangement with J. M. Dent and Sons Ltd. 1959.

Augustine, St T. (tr. Bettenson, H.), *Concerning the City of God against the Pagans.* London: Penguin Books, 1972.

Balthasar, H. (tr. Skerry, Sister M. T.), *New Elucidations.* San Francisco: Ignatius Press, 1979.

Balthasar, H. *Theo-Drama: Theological Dramatic Theory III Dramatis Personae: Person in Christ.* San Francisco: Ignatius Press, 1978.

Bannerman, J. *The Church of Christ.* Edmonton: Still Waters Revival Books, reprint edition 1991, First Edition 1869.

Barclay, W. *The Daily Study Bible* vol.1. Edinburgh: St Andrew's Press, 1975.

Bauckham, R., *Gospel Women: Studies of the Named Women in the Gospels.* Edinburgh: T and T Clark, 2002.

Beattie, T. *Rediscovering Mary: Insights From The Gospels.* Liguori: Triumph Books, 1995.

Benedict, St (tr Doyle, L.), *St Benedict's Rule for Monasteries.* Collegeville: The Liturgical Press, 1947.

Boadt, L. *Reading the Old Testament: An Introduction.* New York: Paulist Press,1984.

Brown, R. *An Introduction to the New Testament.* New York: Doubleday, 1997.

Brown, R. *The Birth of the Messiah.* London: G. Chapman, 1977.

Brown, R. *The Community of the Beloved Disciple.* New York: Paulist Press, 1979.

Butler, S. *The Catholic Priesthood and Women: A Guide to the Teaching of the Church.* Chicago: Hillenbrand Books, 2007.

Calvin, J. (tr. Owen, J.), *Commentaries on the Epistle of Paul the Apostle to the Hebrews.* Grand Rapids: Baker Book House, 1979.

Calvin, J. (tr. Beveridge, H.), *Institutes of the Christian Religion, vol. II.* London: James Clark & Co., 1962.

Cavallini, G. *Catherine of Siena*. London: Geoffrey Chapman, 1998.

Clowney, E. *The Church*. Leicester: Inter-Varsity Press, 1995.

Comby, J. and McCulloch, D. *How to Read Church History, vol. II*. London: SCM Press, 1989.

Congar, Y. *The Meaning of Tradition*. San Francisco: Ignatius Press, 2004.

Coyle, K. *Mary in the Christian Tradition: From a Contemporary Perspective*. Leominster: Gracewing, 1996.

Cummings, O. F., Ditewig, W., Gaillardetz, R. *Theology of the Diaconate: The State of the Question*. New York: Paulist Press, 2005.

Danielou, J. *The Infancy Narratives*. London: Burns and Oates Ltd, 1968.

Dillenberger, J.(ed.), *Martin Luther: Selections from His Writings*. New York: Anchor Books, 1961.

Dulles, A. *The Craft of Theology: From Symbol to System*. New York: Crossroads, 1995.

Dulles, A. *Models of the Church: A Critical Assessment of the Church in all its Aspects*. Dublin: Gill and MacMillan, 1976.

Dulles, A. *Models of Revelation*. Dublin: Gill and MacMillan, 1983.

Dunn, J. (ed.), *The Cambridge Companion to St Paul*. Cambridge: CUP, 2003.

Edwards, R. *The Case for Women's Ministry*. London: SPCK, 1989.

Ellis, P. *The Genius of John: A Composition Critical Commentary on the 4th Gospel*. Collegeville: The Liturgical Press, 1984.

Fiorenza, F. and Galvin, J. (ed.), *Systematic Theology vol. I and II*. Minneapolis: Fortress Press, 1991.

Fitzgerald, A. (ed.), *Augustine Through the Ages: An Encyclopedia*. Cambridge: Eerdmans, 1999.

FitzGerald, K. 'The Characteristics and Nature of the Order of the Deaconess' in Hopka, T. (ed.), *Women and the Priesthood*. New York: St Vladimir's Seminary Press, 1983.

FitzGerald, K. *Women Deacons in the Orthodox Church: Called to Holiness and Ministry.* Massachusetts: Holy Cross Orthodox Press, 1999.

Galot, J. *Theology of the Priesthood.* San Francisco: Ignatius Press, 1985.

Graffy, A. *Trustworthy and True: The Gospels Beyond 2000.* Dublin: The Columba Press, 2001.

Hauke, M. *Women in the Priesthood?: A Systematic Analysis in the Light of the Order of Creation and Redemption.* San Francisco: Ignatius Press, 1988.

Hooker, M. *From Adam to Christ: Essays on Paul.* Cambridge: Cambridge University Press, 1990.

Hughes, P. *The Church in Crisis: A History of the General Councils, 325–1870.* London: Burns and Oates, 1960.

Jones, C. Wainwright, G. Yarnold, E and Bradshaw, P. (ed.), *The Study of Liturgy.* London: SPCK, 1992.

Keenan, Fr J. *In God's Image: John Paul II's Theology of the Body.* Pluscarden Abbey: Pentecost Lectures, 2006.

Kelly, C. (ed.), *Feminism v Mankind.* Scarborough Ontario: Canisius Books, 1990.

Lamb, M. and Levering, M. (ed.), *Vatican II: Renewal within Tradition.* Oxford: OUP, 2008.

Latourelle, R. *Theology of Revelation.* Cork: Mercier Press Ltd, 1968.

Laurentin, R. *The Truth of Christmas.* Massechusetts: St Bede's Publications, 1986.

Macy, G. *The Hidden History of Women's Ordination: Female Clergy in the Medieval West.* Oxford: Oxford University Press, 2008.

Macy, G. Ditewig, W. and Zagano, P. *Women Deacons: Past, Present, Future.* New York: Paulist Press, 2011.

Madigan, K. and Osiek, C. *Ordained Women in the Early Church: A Documentary History.* Baltimore: The John Hopkins University Press, 2005.

Martimort, A. G. *Deaconesses: An Historical Study*. San Francisco: Ignatius Press, 1982.

Moloney, F. *Mary: Woman and Mother*. Collegeville: The Liturgical Press, 1989.

Morris, J. *Against Nature and God: The History of Women with Clerical Ordination and the Jurisdiction of Bishops*. London: Mowbrays, 1973.

Muller, G. *Priesthood and Diaconate*. San Francisco: Ignatius Press, 2002.

McGrath, A. *Christian Theology: An Introduction*. 3rd edn. Oxford: Blackwell Publishing Ltd, 2001.

McGrath, A. *Reformation Thought*. 3rd edn. Oxford: Blackwell Publishing Ltd, 1999.

Neame, A. *Agenda for the Third Millennium*. London: HarperCollins, 1996.

Newsom, C. and Ringe, H. *The Women's Bible Commentary*. London: SPCK, 1992.

Newman, J. H. *An Essay on the Development of Christian Doctrine.* Harmondsworth: Penguin Books, 1974, (first pub. 1845).

Nichols, A. *The Shape of Catholic Theology*. Collegeville: The Liturgical Press, 1991.

Nixon, R. *The Priority of Perfection*. Edinburgh: Movement for Whole Ministry in the Scottish Episcopal Church, 1994.

Oakes, E. and Moss, D. *The Cambridge Companion to Hans Urs von Balthasar*. Cambridge: CUP, 2004.

Oben, F. M. (tr.), *The Collected Works of Edith Stein, vol. II*, Washington: ICS Publishers, 1996.

Ormond, M. *Building Bridges: Dominicans Doing Theology Together*. Dublin: Dominican Publications, 2005.

Osborne, K. *The Permanent Diaconate*. New York: Paulist Press, 2007.

Payne, S. *Saint Theresa of Lisieux: Doctor of the Universal Church*. New York: St Paul's, 2002.

Ratzinger, Cardinal J. *Daughter Zion: Meditations on the Church's Marian Belief.* San Francisco: Ignatius Press, 1977.

Ratzinger, Cardinal J. *The Nature and Mission of Theology.* San Francisco: Ignatius Press, 1993.

Ratzinger, Cardinal J. and Messori, V. *The Ratzinger Report.* San Francisco: Ignatius Press, 1985.

Rousseau, A. et Doutreleau, l. (ed.). *Irénée de Lyon. Contre les Hérésies. Livre III, tome 2.* Paris: Cerf, 2002.

Schmidt, P. *How To Read The Gospels: Historicity and Truth in the Gospels and Acts.* Slough: St Pauls, 1993.

Scola, Cardinal A. *The Nuptial Mystery.* Michigan: Eerdmans, 2005.

Schweizer, E. *Church Order in the New Testament.* London, SCM Press Ltd, 1961.

Staniford, M. (tr.), *Early Christian Writings.* Harmondsworth: Penguin Books, 1968.

Stanton, G. N. (ed.), *The Gospels and Jesus.* Oxford: Oxford University Press, 1989.

Stein, E. (tr. Oben, F. M.), *The Collected Works of Edith Stein 2: Essays on Woman.* Washington: ICS Publications, 1996.

Sullivan, F. *The Church We Believe In.* Dublin: Gill and MacMillan Ltd, 1988.

Till, B. *The Churches Search for Unity.* Harmondsworth: Penguin Books, 1972.

Ulanov, A. *The Female Ancestors of Christ.* Enfield: Daimon Verlag, 1993.

Ward, Sister B. (tr.), *The Prayers and Meditations of St Anselm.* Harmondsworth: Penguin Books, 1973.

Warrington, J. (tr.), *Aristotle's Politics: The Athenian Constitution.* London: Heron Books, 1959.

Warner, M. *Alone of All Her Sex.* London: Picador, 1985.

Zagano, P. *Holy Saturday: An Argument for the Restoration of the Female Diaconate in the Catholic Church.* New York: Crossroad, 2000.

Zeisler, J. *Pauline Christianity.* Oxford: Oxford University Press, 1990.

Zizioulas, J. *Being as Communion.* New York: St Vladimir's Seminary Press, 1997.

Periodicals and Journals

Beattie, T. 'A Man and Three Women—Hans, Adrienne, Mary and Luce' in *New Blackfriers vol. 79*; no 924 (February 1998), pp. 97–105.

Butler, S. 'Women Deacons and Sacramental Symbolism' in *New Diaconal Review issue 6* (May 2011), pp.38-49.

Crawford, D. 'Natural Law and the Body' in *Communio vol. XXXV no 3*, (Fall 2008), p. 332.

Jeremiah, Sister M. 'The Theological Anthropology of Catherine of Siena' in *Communio vol. XX no 2*, (Summer 1993), pp. 457–462.

Loone, S. 'The Forgotten Annunciation', in *The Pastoral Review vol. 5 issue 6*, (November/December 2009), pp. 40–44.

Schindler, D.' Catholic Theology, Gender and the Future of Western Civilisation' in *Communio vol. XX no. 2*, (Summer 1993), pp. 200–239.

Zagano, P. 'Catholic Women Deacons' in *America*, (17 February 2003) available at <www.americamagazine.org/content/article.cfm?article_id=2778> [accessed 23 November 2011].

Zagano, P. 'Grant Her Your Spirit' in *America*, (7 February 2005) or from <www.americamagazine.org/content/article.cfm?article_id=3997> [accessed 11 January 2010].

CDs

Aquinas, St, *Summa Theologica.* translated by Fathers of the English Dominican Province (Benziger Bros. Edition). Npl:, n.pub., 1947.

Kevin Knight (ed.), *The Catholic Encyclopedia 1914 edition* in 'New Advent edition 2.1', 2009.

Sources Consulted

Standard References

Vorgrimler, H. (ed.), *Commentary on the Documents of Vatican II.* London: Burns and Oates, 1967.

The Holy See

The Pontifical Biblical Commission. *The Interpretation of the Bible in the Church.* Rome: Libreria Editrice Vaticana, 1993.

Congregation for the Clergy, Congregation for Catholic Education. *Permanent Diaconate.* London: CTS, 1998.

Congregation for the Doctrine of the Faith. *On the Collaboration of Men and Women in the Church and the World.* London: CTS, 2004.

Books

Brown, R. *The Gospel according to John I–XII.* Newhaven: Doubleday, 1966.

Cross, F. L. *The Early Christian Fathers.* London: Duckworth and Co, 1960.

Goergen, D. and Garrido, A.(ed.), *The Theology of Priesthood.* Collegeville: Michael Glazier/The Liturgical Press, 2000.

Grant, R., *Irenaeus of Lyons.* London: Routledge, 1997.

Graves, R. and Patai, R. *Hebrew Myths: The Book of Genesis.* London: Cassell, 1964.

Hamer, J. *The Church as a Communion.* London: Geoffrey Chapman, 1964.

Herbstrith, W. *Edith Stein: A Biography.* San Francisco: Ignatius Press, 1985.

Kehland, M. and Loser, W. (ed.), *The Balthasar Reader.* Edinburgh: T and T Clark, 1982.

McGrath, A. *In The Beginning: The Story of the King James Bible.* London: Hodder and Stoughton, 2001.

Nichols, A. *Holy Order.* Dublin: Veritas, 1990.

Ramsay, B. *Beginning to Read the Fathers.* London: SCM Press, 1993.

Periodicals and Journals

Gonneaud, D. 'The Sacramentality of the Diaconate'. In *New Diaconal Review, issue 1,* November. 2008, pp. 4–17.

Collins, J. 'A German Catholic View of Diaconate and Diakonia'. In *New Diaconal Review, issue 2.* May 2009, pp. 41–46.

Gooder, P. 'Women in the Pauline Churches'. In *The Pastoral Review, vol. 5, issue 3,* May/June 2009, pp. 10–15.

Lauchlin, G. 'Sexing the Trinity'. In *New Blackfriars, vol. 79,* pp. 18–25.

INDEX OF SCRIPTURAL REFERENCES

Colossians

1

18	35
25	223

3

18-20	351

1 Thessalonians

4

1-2	110

5

1-2	110
12	44
12-13	209

2 Thessalonians

2

5	110
15	110

1 Timothy

2

288, 299

9-15	351
11	94
11-13	93
11-15	70, 288
14	165

3

45

1	213
1-13	266
2	47, 70
5	47

8-13	46, 246
11	238, 346
16	202

4

14	45, 46, 129, 254

5

9	346
17	47
18	98
19	46
20	46
22	47, 129

2 Timothy

1

5	335
6	46, 55, 122, 129, 254, 266

2

14	96

3

16	19

Titus

1

5	46, 47, 55, 209, 222, 246
5-7	213
5-9	93, 266
7	47
7-9	45

Hebrews

1

1-2	41

GENERAL INDEX

A

Aaron 75, 124, 147, 355
Abbesses 134, 159f, 170, 283, 312f, 334, 357
Abel 76
Abigail 70
Abihu 124
Abraham 25, 58, 75, 84, 124, 231, 356
Ackerman, S. 99
Adam 69, 70, 75, 97, 101, 122, 131, 136, 143f, 151, 152, 153, 351, **352**, 353
Ad Caeli Reginam 68, 388
Ad Gentes Divinitus 389
Alexander of Alexandria 153
Alexander, T. 55
Ambrose 154
Amiot, F. 55
Amos 18, 65
Anna 61, 366, 382
Anacletus 117
Ananias 44
Anselm, St 23, 28, 183, 185
Apostles xix, xx, 15f, 18, 19, 21, 23, 27, **31–48**, 49, 51, 62, 64, 71, 74, 80f, 91, 103f, 109f, 113f, **126–135**, 152, 158, 162f, 177f, 195f, 207, 213f, 221f, 226–240, 254, 263f, 284f, 292, 295f, 312f, 331, 342f, 345, **354–356**, 359, **361–363**, 365

Aquinas, St Thomas xx, 23, 83, 91, 165, 175, **200–204**, 232, 252, 258, 297, 334, 359, 390
Archbishop of Canterbury xx, 310, 331, 339
Aristotle 161, 163, 165, 166, 174, 315, 334
Arles, Council of 232, 235
Arnold of Brescia 378
Athenagoras 20
Ashley, B. 226
Augustine, St 17, 27, 120, 244, 259, 376

B

Barclay, W. 99
Barth, K. 353
Basil the Great 153
Bathsheba **76f**, **85–101**,
Balthasar, H. 135–138, 146, 149, 306, 339
Barnabas 44, 128, 147
Bauckham, R. 81, 84, 86, 98, 100, 382
Bautain, L. 376
Bannerman, J. 245, 256
Beattie, T. 137, 149
Beaumont, B. 194
Beinert, W. 246
Beleth, J. 175
Beneden, P. 167, 174
Benedict, St 279, 280, 325, 339
Benedict VIII, Pope 170
Benedict XIV, Pope 204, 244f

Lamb, M. 88, 194, 244, 246, 384
Lamsa, G. 55
Lateran Council 165, 167f, 171, 172, 227, 254, 259
Latourelle, R. 28, 29
Lazarus 72f,
Lecuyer, J. 197, 246
Leo IX, Pope 170
Leon Dufour, X. 55, 100, 148, 387
Levering, M. 194, 244, 247, 383
Levine, A. 100
Linus 117
Livingston, E. 256
Locke, J. 375
Lombard, P. 200, 232
Loone, S. 65
Louis, St 378
Louth, A. 147
Luke 17, 44, 60, 61f, 71, 72, 74, 76, 81f, 86, 91, 92, 99, 104, 105, 109, 126, 128, 133, 207, 222, 223, 301, 311, 332, 343, 376
Lumen Gentium xix, 5, 10, 31, 52, 53, 68, 95, 120f, 152, 186, 187f, 196, 197, 219, 228, 233, 259, 260, 295, 242, 359
Luther, M. 55, 78, 111, 113, 202, 244, 252, 253, 255, 379

M

Macy, G. 54, 158, 159, 163, 166–175, 194, 197, 249, 312, 342
Martin V, Pope 379
Matthias 103, 127
Madigan, K. 159, 170, 175, 393,
Magnificat 61, 153, 260
Marcion 17, 27, 287, **376**
Margaret of Scotland, St 161, 174

Marialis Cultus 260
Mark 17, 28, 58f, 67, 71, 72, 81, 82, 100, 104, 109, 126, 133, 235, 381
Martha 71f, 91, 101, 174, 382
Marthana 162
Martimort, A. 158, 170, 171, 175, 194, 240, 247, **281f**, 298, 299, 300, 303, 318, 319, 331, 341
Mary (see also Our Lady) xxiii, xxiv, 53, **57–68, 73**, 74, 76, 78f, 84, 85 , 86, 89, 99, 100, 104, 105, 141, 144, 145, **151–155**, **257–261**, 177, 268, 285, 292, 299, 301f, 304, 308, 309, 311f, 345, 352, 353, 377, 382, 384
Mary (of Bethany) 71, 72, 73, 74, 91, 382
Mary of Clopas 381
Mary Magdalen xx, 71, 72, 73, 82, 83, 91, 101, 174, 265, 310, 345, 382
Mary,Mother of Joset 82
Matthew 17, 32f, 36, 38, 59, 60, 65, 67, 71, **74–82, 84–90**, 99, 100, 104, 109, 120, 126, 133, 144, 220, 235, 312, 332, 343, 347, 381, 386
McGrath, A. xxv, 28, 113, 256, 384, 394, 398
McKenzie, J. 54, 148, 149, 388
Mediator Dei 203, 255
Melchizedek 40, 124, 221
Messori, V. 29
Metz, R. 175
Ministerial priesthood 37, 39, 51, 52, 221, 222, 255, 295, 297, 339

Titus 18, 45, 213

Tome of Leo, the Great, Pope 116, 377

Trent, Council of 17, 18, 21, 23f, 55, 151, 155, 161, 162, 186, 200, 203, 204, 207, 211, 214, 215, 218, 228, 233, 245, 246, 252, 253, 255, 256, 267, 297, 320, 324, 379,

U

Ulanov, A. 100, 386

Universal priesthood 49f

Urban VI, Pope 139

Uriah the Hittite 76, 80, 84, 87, 88

Ut Unum Sint 53, 121

V

Vatican Council I 21, 24, 25, 27, 33

Vatican Council II 27, 32, 53, 120, 151, 237, 248, 255

Vessey, M. 27

Vigilius, Pope 377

Viviano, B. 99

W

Wainwright, G. 245, 246, 247

Walsh, L. 185, 194

Warner, M. 68

Weber, L. 174

Williams, R. 194

Wives of deacons (see: deacons, wives of)

Wycliffe 21, 379

Z

Zagano, P. 11, 173, 249, 363, 366, 369, 371, 386

Zebedee 35

Zerah 76, 88

Zeisler, J. 55

Zizioulas, J. 148, 206, 225, 245, 247

CPSIA information can be obtained at www.ICGtesting.com
Printed in the USA
LVOW11s2151130214

373680LV00001B/145/P